Modern Accounting 2

John Margers Limited
London

John Margers Limited
126-148 Madeira Avenue, Bromley, Kent BR1 4AS
Telephone 081-460 4920   Fax 081-313 0075

First Edition Published 1993

British Library Cataloguing-in-Publication Data.
Kerrigan, John
Modern Accounting. Book 2
I. Title
657

ISBN 1-872810-02-0

All rights reserved. No part of this publication may be reproduced, stored in a retrieval system, or transmitted, in any form or by any means, electronic, mechanical, photocopying, recording or otherwise without the prior written permission of the publishers.

Copyright © John Kerrigan 1993

Cover Design by Andrew Rogers

ISBN 1 872810 02 0

Printed by Longdunn Press Limited, Bristol

Contents

Chapter		Page
	Modern Accounting 1	iv
	List of Questions and Answers	v
	Acknowledgements	vi
1	Effect of Inflation on Accounting Statements	1
2	Current (or Constant) Purchasing Power Accounting	11
3	Current Cost Accounting	51
4	The Uses and Shortcomings of CCA and CPP	103
5	CCA in CPP	133
6	Discounted Cash Flow	169
	Table of Discount Factors	220
7	Definitions of Economic Income	231
8	Consolidations	243
9	Foreign Currencies	305
10	Interdivisional Pricing	367
11	Computer Accounting	387
12	Monthly Management Information Packs	395
13	Budgeting	399
	INDEX	408

Modern Accounting 1
ISBN 1 872810 01 2

Modern Accounting 1 is also published by John Margers at the same price and contains the following chapters :

Why do Businesses Produce Accounts?

Balance Sheets

Profit and Loss Accounts

Debits and Credits

T Accounts and Double Entry

Stock and Work-in-Progress

Depreciation

The Disposal of Fixed Assets

Bad and Doubtful Debts

Accruals and Prepayments

Accounting for Limited Companies

Accounting for Partnerships

U K Business Taxation

The Advantages and Disadvantages of Limited Companies, PLCs and Partnerships

Classification of Costs for Decision Making

The Interpretation of Accounts

Book-keeping

Incomplete Records

Cash Flow Statements

Questions and Answers

Question Number	Question Page	Answer Page
Chapter 2 : CPP Accounting		
2.1	12	41
2.2	12	41
2.3	23	41
2.4	29	41
2.5	33	41
2.6	34	42
2.7	36	46
2.8	39	-
Chapter 3 : Current Cost Accounts		
3.1	58	92
3.2	68	93
3.3	81	94
3.4	82	95
3.5	84	98
3.6	86	-
3.7	88	101
Chapter 5 : CCA in CPP		
5.1	154	160
5.2	156	163
5.3	158	-
Chapter 6 : DCF		
6.1	173	221
6.2	173	221
6.3	173	221
6.4	173	222
6.5	179	222
6.6	180	-
6.7	184	223
6.8	185	223
6.9	188	225
6.10	188	225
6.11	188	225
6.12	191	226
6.13	198	226
6.14	203	227
6.15	203	227

Question Number	Question Page	Answer Page
6.16	204	227
6.17	210	227
6.18	210	228
6.19	214	228
Chapter 7 : Economic Income		
7.1	238	242
Chapter 8 : Consolidations		
8.1	249	292
8.2	250	-
8.3	254	292
8.4	255	-
8.5	273	293
8.6	274	-
8.7	275	294
8.8	276	295
8.9	284	298
8.10	286	300
8.11	287	-
8.12	288	301
8.13	290	-
Chapter 9 : Foreign Currencies		
9.1	318	346
9.2	319	352
9.3	332	353
9.4	334	355
9.5	335	357
9.6	336	-
9.7	337	-
9.8	342	364
9.9	344	-
Chapter 10 : Interdivisional Pricing		
10.1	381	383
10.2	382	385
Chapter 13 : Budgeting		
13.1	404	-

Acknowledgements

I must thank Peter Blowes, Jane Hayward, Jean Marshall and Robert Liston for reading the drafts of this book. They and my colleagues at Sundridge Park made many helpful suggestions. Of course the responsibility for errors and omissions remains with me.

John Kerrigan

London
April 1993

Chapter One

Effect of Inflation on Accounting Statements

It has been claimed that traditional Historic Cost Accounts are misleading in periods of high price inflation. These accounts are groups of statistics of costs and sales measured in the currency of the time each transaction took place. But they are recorded in Balance Sheets and Profit and Loss Accounts that are presented at a later date.

Traditional Historic Cost Accounts may be misleading because they are inaccurate or because the statistics they contain have not been adequately defined. Some would go further. For example G A Lee (in Modern Financial Accounting[1]) refers to "the inadequacy of historical-cost accounting as an intellectual concept and as a practical methodology of economic measurement".

The main concerns about using Traditional Historic Costs in times of inflation are

In the Balance Sheet :

1   Fixed Assets shown in the Balance Sheet can appear 'too low' especially if they were purchased a long time before the Balance Sheet Date.

2   Liabilities shown in the Balance Sheet can appear 'too high' especially if they do not bear interest, are fixed in money terms and do not have to be settled for a long time after the Balance Sheet Date.

3   Balance Sheet figures comparing one year with another are designed to show the progress and health of the firm but it may be that a comparison of last year with this year is not comparing like with like.

1

Modern Accounting 2

In the Profit and Loss Account :

4   The Depreciation Charge for the year appears 'too low' in comparison with the other figures on the Profit and Loss Account. Frequently it also appears too low in comparison with the sums that need to be spent on Fixed Assets if the business is to maintain the same capacity to produce the same number of units of product.

5   The Cost of Sales appears 'too low' in comparison to the sums that need to be spent in order to maintain stocks. This means that the Gross Profit appears 'too high' in comparison with the sums that are available to spend on expenses and to retain as profit.

6   No account is taken in normal historic Profit and Loss Accounts of the loss in value over the year of any loans or borrowings that are legally or contractually expressed in terms of currency. If £1,000 is left in a bank account for a year, it may lose some of its 'value' - if that value is defined in terms of its ability to purchase goods and services - because prices have risen over the year. The same is true of £1,000 lent to a customer of the business and of £1,000 borrowed from a supplier. Businesses make a loss 'in real terms' holding cash, bank balances and debtors and a profit 'in real terms' owing money to creditors.

7   Just as with comparative figures on the Balance Sheet, it can be argued that comparing last year's historic cost profits with this year's is not comparing like with like. Both profit figures are expressed in terms of currency and the value of units of that currency will have changed if the prices of goods and services have changed.

In this list the phrases *too low* and *too high* have been shown in inverted commas. One might ask : Too low or high for what purpose? Traditional Historic Cost Accounts are groups of statistics prepared according to certain definitions. Sometimes some of those definitions have not been tightly defined. These Traditional Historic Accounts are distributed to different users who may use them to take different decisions. No promise is made on the face of accounts that the information they contain will be sufficient (or even useful) in the taking of any individual decision.

Shareholders may want information to enable them to forecast future dividends and share prices while managers may want information so that they can decide which trading policies they should abandon and which they should expand. Suppliers, employees and customers want information so that they can judge the stability of the business. Different Government departments use accounting information to collect taxation and to formulate future tax, economic and social policies.

Any discussion of Inflation Accounting has to consider these different requirements. The two main methods of Inflation Accounting are Current Purchasing Power Accounting (CPP) and Current Cost Accounting (CCA). Most of the proponents of CPP would retain historic cost concepts but re-express them in new units of measurement. Most of the proponents of CCA want to produce completely different statistics. To come to this conclusion, they must hold views as to the main purposes and uses of financial accounts. The arguments for and against these different statistics are discussed in Chapter Four. Chapter Two explains Current Purchasing Power Accounting (CPP) and Chapter Three explains Current Cost Accounting (CCA).

1. Fixed Assets on the Balance Sheet

In the year 2000 a property company may own two identical freehold shops. One was bought in 1990 for £100,000 and one was bought in 1995 for £200,000. A historic cost Balance Sheet would show *Freeholds at cost £300,000*. Does it make sense to add the two figures together. They were units of currency (in this case £s) spent at different times. A unit of currency is a man-made device to facilitate economic exchange; it has no value other than its command over goods and services and that command changes over time. Presumably if the earlier purchase was for US$100,000 (and the later was for £200,000), it would never be sensible to add the 100,000 to the 200,000 and say that it totalled 300,000 (mixed £ and $). We may use the same word : *Pound* to describe monies spent at different dates but £s of the year 1990 may be as dissimilar from £s of the 2000 as £s are to $s. It may be no more sensible to add the £100,000 spent in 1990 to the £200,000 spent in 1995 than it would be to add 100,000 apples to 200,000 pears.

If a unit of currency has no value other than its command over goods and services, then we might translate units of currency spent in different years into units of 'constant value'. For example, suppose that the prices of all goods had doubled from 1990 to 2000, then we could say that the value of money had halved and that £1 in 1990 equals £2 in 2000. We could use a price index to restate the cost of the freehold shops in units of constant purchasing power. The shop that cost £100,000 in 1990 could be stated to have cost the equivalent of 200,000 in the £s of 2000. Because all prices have moved in the same way, this restatement of cost would also be a valuation at 2000. If we paid the market price for the property in 1990, the equivalent market price of the same property in 2000 should be £200,000.

It is rarely as simple as that because there is rarely a perfect Price Index. One reason is that the type and quality of goods changes over the years and another reason is that all prices do not change by the same percentage. If the price of beer has risen by 25% and the price of travel has fallen by 30%, what has happened to the value of money? From the point of view of a consumer, it depends on your lifestyle. A teetotal commuter would reckon that money had become more valuable whereas a beer-swilling stay-at-home would cry about savage inflation.

The best known price indexes, such as the Consumer Price Index and the Index of Retail Prices, give different weights to the different goods and services included in the index. The weights are determined by surveys of the expenditure patterns of average households and they do not remain constant because we change our consumption of different goods over time. Indeed that consumption pattern will respond itself to changing relative prices.

If we use a consumer price index to re-state the original historic cost, this may not give us a current 'valuation'. Note that 'valuation', 'revaluation' and 'value' normally involve estimating the current replacement cost or realisable value of an asset. Restating historic costs with a consumer price index may give a useful opportunity cost - the consumption foregone when the asset was acquired - but this may not be the same as either the cost of buying an equivalent asset today or the proceeds that we could gain by selling the item.

2. Liabilities on the Balance Sheet

Insurance companies have to provide for claims that may be paid many years after the period for which they received premium income. Some of those claims are fixed in money terms. For example typical travel policies provide for a fixed sum of £100,000 to be payable in the event that the insured loses a limb. Other claims may not be for fixed sums but are intended to compensate the claimant for loss of earnings.

In company accounts it is usual to estimate the money sums that will have to be paid in the future and to treat those future money sums as liabilities at the Balance Sheet date. With liabilities fixed in money terms that do not attract interest, it can be argued that this overstates the liability. An insurance company issuing travel policies will estimate the proportion of policy holders who will make a valid claim for the £100,000. Let us assume that they have issued 200,000 such policies in 1995 and they estimate that they will pay £400,000 in five years time in 2000. (It takes time for the outcome of an accident to be known and for sufficient documentary evidence to be assembled so that the insurance company cannot claim that it needs more proof.)

The insurance company will normally show a liability of £400,000 on its balance sheet on 31st December 1995. However a reinsurer would be prepared to take that risk from the primary insurer for considerably less than £400,000 because a liability to pay a fixed sum in the future has a lower *present value* than its future value. Present values are discussed further in Chapter Six. The difference between the present value of those liabilities and the gross sums will depend on rates of interest. Rates of interest have a relationship with inflation.

Liabilities that are not fixed in money terms can be difficult to estimate in economies with high inflation. Employers' Liability insurance contracts make the insurer responsible for unlimited damages for illnesses which were caused during the insurance period but may not become apparent for many years afterwards. Such unlimited damage claims will be affected by prices at the date the claim is settled and not by prices during the insurance period.

3. Balance Sheet Comparative Figures

A chocolate manufacturer's stock of finished bars of chocolate on 31st December 1995 cost £30,000 and the stock on 31st December 1996 cost £32,000. Those figures are shown side by side in published accounts; presumably the intention is to enable the reader to make comparisons between the years. What conclusions can the reader reach? Has the stock increased over the year? What do we mean by the term : 'increased'?

You cannot assume that there are more bars of chocolate in stock without knowing what has happened to the cost of manufacture over the year. If costs have increased by 10%, then the physical quantity of stock has presumably fallen. However we might not be thinking of increases in physical terms; we might be thinking in terms of the 'value' of stock. But then we are back to the problem we encountered with Fixed Assets of how to measure 'value' when the value of money is changing.

4. Profit and Loss Depreciation

Most of the figures on a Profit and Loss Account relate to transactions that took place during (or close to) the same year. Depreciation is the odd one out because it can be a proportion of costs that were incurred several years ago. After a period of high inflation this means that the sales and the other expenses appear high in comparison with a low figure for depreciation. An old-established business may find that the depreciation charge in the Profit and Loss Account is far lower than the sums needed to be spent each year on replacing Fixed Assets.

Talk of 'an old-established business' and 'replacing' Fixed Assets implies a stable state where the business neither expands nor contracts and no changes take place in the sorts of Fixed Assets needed to produce the goods (or services) sold. It will depend on the business and the economy in which it operates whether this is a helpful model. In some circumstances very little Fixed Asset spend is truly *replacement*. The details of the goods and services produced and the ways in which they are produced is in a constant state of change.

5. Gross Profit and Stock

This problem is not usually as serious as the Depreciation problem because depreciation can relate to costs incurred 10 years or more ago whereas Opening Stock was normally purchased close to the start of the year. Nonetheless for a business holding two months worth of stock with inflation of around 12.5% pa, there can be a significant difference between the historic cost and the 'replacement cost of sales'. The replacement cost of sales is the cost of replacing the goods sold at the moment of sale.

Let us assume that this business purchases and sells 10,000 units of stock every month. In November 1994 the cost of each unit of stock was £1 and the selling price was £1.5. If all prices rise by 1% every month, then the prices, purchases and sales will be as follows:

Month	Cost Price £	Purchases £	Selling Price £	Sales £
1994				
November	1	10,000	1.5	
December	1.01	10,100	1.515	
		20,100		
1995				
January	1.0201	10,201	1.53015	15,302
February	1.030301	10,303	1.545451	15,455
March	1.040604	10,406	1.560906	15,609
April	1.051010	10,510	1.576515	15,765
May	1.061520	10,615	1.592280	15,923
June	1.072135	10,721	1.608203	16,082
July	1.082856	10,829	1.624285	16,243
August	1.093685	10,937	1.640527	16,405
September	1.104622	11,046	1.656933	16,569
October	1.115668	11,157	1.673502	16,735
November	1.126825	11,268	1.690237	16,902
December	1.138093	11,381	1.707139	17,071
		129,374		194,061

Modern Accounting 2

In this example, the Replacement Cost of Sales will be the same as Purchases of the Year (£129,374) because the pattern of Purchasing and Selling is constant and the physical number of units in stock never changes. However the Cost of Sales charged in the Trading Account will be less than this because of the stock adjustment. The stock adjustment means that early low-priced opening stock bought last year is added and the most recent high-priced closing stock bought at the end of this year is deducted.
The Trading Account for 1995 would appear as follows :

Historic Cost £s	£	£
Sales		194,061
Opening Stock	20,100	
Purchases	129,374	
	149,474	
less Closing Stock	22,649	
Cost of Sales		126,825
Gross Profit		67,236

The Replacement Cost of Sales is £2,549 greater than the Cost of Sales shown above. If no credit was given by suppliers or granted to customers - in other words, if both purchases and sales are cash transactions - then the Gross Profit figure of £67,236 is £2,549 greater than the cash that was generated by trading.

6. Monetary Gains and Losses

During periods of inflation Monetary Gains are made on Monetary Liabilities and Monetary Losses are made on Monetary Assets. In practice most liabilities are Monetary Liabilities; a Monetary Liability is fixed in terms of currency. In other words, a Monetary Liability is a liability to pay a fixed sum of money (whereas a liability to provide goods or perform a service would not be a monetary liability).

Monetary Assets are assets that are legally or contractually expressed in terms of currency. Coins, ten pound notes, bank balances and debtors are all monetary assets (whereas Plant and Machinery and Freeholds are examples of non-monetary assets).

The idea that a loss is made on holding money notes during a period of inflation is generally acceptable. Inflation means that units of currency are losing some of their command over goods and services and this must imply a loss. If we receive interest on sums deposited in the bank (or lent elsewhere), then this interest may reduce or eliminate the monetary loss but most people would accept that it would be wrong to treat the gross interest received as pure profit.

The idea that a gain is made on monetary liabilities during periods of inflation is more contentious. Many people are unwilling to look at loans separately from how it has been used. Let us assume that a business borrows a million pounds to buy some freehold property and the value of that freehold property goes up in direct proportion to the rise in all other prices. If you accept the idea of monetary gains, you would say that no *real* gain has been made on the property (because that has only maintained its value - in real terms) but a monetary gain has been made on the loan.

The business probably has had to pay interest on the loan and this monetary gain can be set against the interest loss. Interest rates vary between economies. Economies with strong currencies and low rates of inflation tend to have lower interest rates than economies with weak currencies and high rates of inflation.

7. Comparative Figures on the Profit and Loss Account

Comparing Sales from one year to the next on the Income Statement has similar problems to comparing Stock and Debtors between successive Balance Sheets when price levels are changing. However, on Profit and Loss Accounts, there is the additional problem that the single figure of Profit is the figure that is most often compared from one year to the next by many users - shareholders, politicians, trade unions, voters, stockbrokers and managers. Has it gone up or down compared to last year?

Unfortunately, as should be clear from the above points, the Profit figure is an amalgamation of different figures many of which become suspect during periods of high price inflation.

[1] G A Lee; Modern Financial Accounting; published by Nelson UK; 1973

Modern Accounting 2

Chapter Two

Current (or Constant) Purchasing Power Accounting

Current Purchasing Power (CPP) Accounting re-expresses the statistics of business accounts in units of constant real purchasing power. CPP changes the units of measurement but it does not change the nature of the statistics being measured. Most statements that are labelled : *CPP Accounts* are still Historic Cost Accounts. It can be argued that CPP handles all the problem areas identified in Chapter One but this would still not satisfy those whose fundamental objection is to the nature of the statistics shown in Historic Cost Accounts. Most of those objecting would prefer Current Cost Accounting (CCA) which is explained in the next Chapter.

When commentators use the term 'Inflation Accounting', they are likely to mean CPP and, when they refer to 'Accounting for Rising Prices', they almost certainly mean CCA. 'Constant' Purchasing Power Accounting means the same as 'Current' Purchasing Power Accounting but both terms are used less than their initials. CPP uses a Consumer Price Index (CPI) and applies that to business assets. This may produce figures that are very different from either the current replacement cost of those assets or the current realisable value. The CPP figures indicate the number of pounds that you would currently need to replace the consumption foregone when the asset was purchased. CPP adjustments should not be thought of as 'revaluations'. The result is still a collection of historic cost figures but re-expressed in today's money.

CPP Balance Sheets : Non-Depreciating Fixed Assets

To express a cost incurred in year 1 in Current Purchasing Power of year n (CPP_n), take the original number of pounds spent in year 1 and multiply by the ratio by which the Consumer Price Index has

Modern Accounting 2

increased between year 1 and year n. In other words, index it by the factor CPI_n/CPI_1 or multiply by the consumer price index at year n and divide by the consumer price index at year 1.

Example
We bought land for £400,000 on 1st January 1990 when the index was 125. The date today is 1st January 2000 when the index is 200. The cost in $CPP_{1.1.2000}$ is

$$400,000 \times \frac{200}{125} = 640,000 \text{ in } £CPP_{1.1.2000}$$

All CPP figures have to have a note of the current date attached to the heading denoting the units of measurement. Next year on 1st January 2001 the price index is expected to rise to 220. If we still hold the same land on 1.1.2001, its CPP cost will become 704,000 in $£CPP_{1.1.2001}$.

Try to answer the following questions before looking at the answers (which are at the end of this chapter).

Question 2.1 (Answer 2.1 is on page 41)
Alpha plc purchased land for £32,000 on 1.1.85 when the index of retail prices was 134. The same index was 156 on 1.1.2001.
REQUIRED : Express the cost of this land in $CPP_{1.1.01}$

Question 2.2 (Answer 2.2 is on page 41)
Beta Ltd made the following purchases of land :

Date of Purchase	Cost in £	Price Index at Date of Purchase
1.7.80	21,000	102
1.7.85	45,000	191
1.7.90	99,000	245

The price index at 1.7.99 was 300.
REQUIRED : Express the total cost of this land in $CPP_{1.7.99}$

CPP - Current Purchasing Power

CPP Balance Sheets : Depreciating Fixed Assets

Assets, such as Plant and Machinery, are shown on Balance Sheets less Accumulated Depreciation. The Accumulated Depreciation is indexed in the same way as cost. Take the present accumulated depreciation of the original historic cost of the asset and multiply by the index at the Balance Sheet date and divide by the index at the date the cost was incurred.

Note that the date on which the depreciation was charged to the P & L is irrelevant. All the accumulated depreciation for an individual asset will be indexed by the same factor and it does not matter that some was charged to one year's Profit & Loss and some to another year. The same proportion of each asset will be written off in CPP terms as was written off in normal historic cost terms.

Example

We bought a fork lift truck for £10,000 on 1st January 1991. We charge depreciation on a straight line basis assuming a life of 10 years with no residual value. The consumer price index was 105 on 1.1.91 and 189 on 31.12.96 when we have to prepare a Balance Sheet.

On an unadjusted historic cost Balance Sheet at 31.12.96 the truck would be shown as :

	£
Cost	10,000
less Accumulated Depreciation	6,000
Net Book Value	4,000

The factor for indexing into CPP is 189 divided by 105 which is 1.8. Thus the cost rises to 18,000 and the Accumulated Depreciation will be £6,000 multiplied by 1.8 which is 10,800. The equivalent CPP figures will appear as follows :

	£CPP$_{31.12.96}$
Cost	18,000
less Accumulated Depreciation	10,800
Net Book Value	7,200

CPP Balance Sheets : The Split Between Monetary and Non-Monetary Assets

Monetary Assets are those which are legally or contractually fixed in units of currency whereas Non-monetary Assets are not fixed in terms of units of currency and many Non-monetary Assets are tangible.

Paper Currency and Coins are Monetary Assets because they are legally fixed in terms of units of currency. The Balances on Bank Accounts and Debtors are Monetary Assets because they are contractually fixed. Customers contract to pay a sum of money fixed in terms of units of currency rather than in terms of what those units can buy. Banks may agree to pay interest on deposits but any such agreement will fix both the interest and the original capital sum in terms of units of currency. However most Fixed Assets and Stocks are Non-Monetary Assets.

CPP Balance Sheets : Non-Monetary Current Assets

Non-Monetary Current Assets are translated into CPP in the same way as Fixed Assets. Multiply by the index at the date of the Balance Sheet and divide by the index at the date the cost was incurred. In practice this means that most Non-Monetary Current Assets will need hardly any adjustment because they will have been purchased close to the Balance Sheet date. The main Non-Monetary Current Assets are likely to be Stocks which have been purchased item by item over a few months prior to the Balance Sheet date.

CPP Balance Sheets : Monetary Current Assets

Monetary Current Assets held at the Balance Sheet date do not need any adjustment to translate them into £CPP because they are already expressed in the purchasing power of money at the Balance Sheet date. (It could be argued that debtors have not paid you and you should take account of the expected loss of purchasing power before they do, but that is a sophistication which is not part of standard CPP.)

CPP Balance Sheets : Liabilities in CPP

Almost all liabilities are Monetary Liabilities and like Monetary Assets, if they exist at the Balance Sheet date, they will not need adjustment to be translated into £CPP at that date.

CPP - Current Purchasing Power

Example of a Balance Sheet in CPP

The Unadjusted Historic Cost Balance Sheet of Alfreda Wainwright Toggles Ltd on 31st December 1991 appeared as follows :

	£	£
Fixed Assets		
Land, at cost		25,000
Plant and Machinery -		
Cost	56,000	
Accumulated Depreciation	28,000	
		28,000
		53,000
Current Assets		
Stock, at cost	45,000	
Debtors	50,000	
Cash at Bank	3,000	
	98,000	
less Creditors : Amounts Due Within One Year		
Trade Creditors	35,000	
		63,000
		116,000
Share Capital		20,000
Revenue Reserves		96,000
		116,000

The fixed assets were purchased on the following dates :

Date of purchase	Land at cost	Plant at cost	Acc Depn on Plant
	£	£	£
15.1.83	10,000	10,000	9,000
15.1.86	5,000	28,800	17,280
15.1.91	10,000	17,200	1,720
	25,000	56,000	28,000

All plant is fully depreciated over a 10 year life on a straight line basis assuming no residual value, charging a full month's depreciation in the month of purchase. Thus the items bought on 15.1.83 will

Modern Accounting 2

have been depreciated by 90% by 31.12.91; those bought on 15.1.86 by 60% and those bought on 15.1.91 by 10%.

The stock was purchased over the last three months of 1991 and, for the purposes of producing CPP figures, it can be assumed to have all been purchased on 15.11.91. The relevant consumer price index reads as follows :

Date	Index	Date	Index
15.1.83	102	15.6.91	148
15.1.86	123	15.7.91	148
15.11.90	138	15.8.91	148
15.12.90	141	15.9.91	149
15.1.91	143	15.10.91	150
15.2.91	143	15.11.91	152
15.3.91	144	15.12.91	155
15.4.91	145	15.1.92	155
15.5.91	147		

These index numbers (like the UK's Index of Retail Prices) indicate price levels in the middle of each month (rather than at the end). We need an index number for the end of 1991. As it happens, price levels have not changed between December 1991 and January 1992 and so the index number for 31.12.91 must be 155. If price levels were moving between the two months, we would have had to average the December and January numbers to approximate the price index for the end of December.

The table of index numbers can be restated as a table of factors required to restate costs to £CPP$_{31.12.91}$ by dividing 155 (the number for 31.12.91) by the number at each date. This results in the following :

Date	Factor	Date	Factor
15.1.83	1.5196	15.6.91	1.0473
15.1.86	1.2602	15.7.91	1.0473
15.11.90	1.1232	15.8.91	1.0473
15.12.90	1.0993	15.9.91	1.0403
15.1.91	1.0839	15.10.91	1.0333
15.2.91	1.0839	15.11.91	1.0197
15.3.91	1.0764	15.12.91	1.0000
15.4.91	1.0690	15.1.92	1.0000
15.5.91	1.0544		

CPP - Current Purchasing Power

Fixed Assets can be multiplied by the relevant factors to produce the following :

Date	Factors	Land at cost £CPP$_{31.12.91}$	Plant at cost £CPP$_{31.12.91}$	Acc Depn on Plant £CPP$_{31.12.91}$
15.1.83	1.5196	15,196	15,196	13,676
15.1.86	1.2602	6,301	36,293	21,776
15.1.91	1.0839	10,839	18,643	1,864
		32,336	70,132	37,316

The only non-monetary current asset is stock purchased on 15.11.91 and thus the unadjusted historic cost should be multiplied by 1.0197 to show a CPP Historic Cost of £CPP$_{31.12.91}$45,887. The other current assets and the creditors need no adjustment. The CPP Balance Sheet will appear as follows :

Balance Sheet as at 31st December 1991

	£CPP$_{31.12.91}$	£CPP$_{31.12.91}$
Fixed Assets		
Land, at cost		32,336
Plant and Machinery - Cost	70,132	
Accumulated Depreciation	37,316	
		32,816
		65,152
Current Assets		
Stock, at cost	45,887	
Debtors	50,000	
Cash at Bank	3,000	
	98,887	
less Creditors : Amounts Due Within One Year		
Trade Creditors	35,000	
		63,887
		129,039
Shareholders' Equity		129,039

It would be possible to index the Share Capital (if we had details of when it was issued) but here no attempt has been made to analyse Shareholders' Funds.

Comparing Balance Sheets from Different Years

Just as we cannot compare one statement written in francs with one written in dollars without converting them into a single currency by using a rate of exchange; so we cannot compare the CPP Balance Sheet dated 31st December 1990 with the CPP Balance Sheet dated 31st December 1991 without converting them into the same currency - which in this case will be $CPP_{31.12.91}$. We do this by multiplying each figure on the 1990 CPP Balance Sheet by the 'rate of exchange' between the values of money on 31.12.90 and 31.12.91. That is, multiply each item by $CPI_{31.12.91}/CPI_{31.12.90}$. Most people find this idea logical when dealing with Non-Monetary items but it needs more thought when dealing with Monetary items. This year's Monetary items on this year's Balance Sheet have needed no adjustment because they were already expressed in this year's money. However if this year's Monetary items are to be expressed in the purchasing power of some future date, then they will need adjustment.

Let us assume that a company had £1,000 in the bank in 1990 when the index is 100 and it has £1,000 in the bank in the year 1991 when the index is 110. To provide the same spending power in 1991 that the company had with its £1,000 in 1990, the company would need £1,100. Expressed in $£CPP_{1991}$ the company's bank balance has fallen from 1,100 to 1,000 over the year.

Almost all businesses show last year's figures side by side with this year's figures in their main accounts - the 'comparatives'. Companies listed on a stock exchange show an abridged Balance Sheet and Income Statement with the last five year's figures shown side by side - normally towards the back of the published accounts. At the moment those figures are normally raw historic cost but, if they are converted into CPP units, the all the figures on the same statement should be converted into the same units. Otherwise the implied 'comparison' is invalid.

If 1991 was the first year for which the CPP conversion had been done, then the raw historic cost accounts for 1990 would have to be used as the base data to produce the comparatives for 1991. All items would still be multiplied by $CPI_{31.12.91}$ but each item would be divided by the CPI on the date that particular item occurred/was bought/transaction took place. It is easy to forget that the Monetary Items will have to be adjusted with the others.

CPP - Current Purchasing Power

Example

Let us continue the example of Alfreda Wainwright Toggles Ltd and produce comparative figures to be displayed next to the 1991 Balance Sheet. The unadjusted historic cost balance sheet on 31st December *1990* appeared as follows :

	£	£
Fixed Assets		
Land, at cost		15,000
Plant and Machinery - Cost	38,800	
Accumulated Depreciation	22,400	16,400
		31,400
Current Assets		
Stock, at cost	60,000	
Debtors	40,000	
Cash at Bank	10,000	
	110,000	
less Creditors : Amounts Due Within One Year		
Trade Creditors	40,000	70,000
		101,400
Share Capital		20,000
Revenue Reserves		81,400
		101,400

There have been no changes in accounting policy on depreciation and no disposal of Fixed Assets at any time and thus the Fixed Assets at 31.12.90 can be ascertained from the information already given as follows :

Date of Purchase	Land at cost	Plant at cost	Acc Depn on Plant
	£	£	£
15.1.83	10,000	10,000	8,000
15.1.86	5,000	28,800	14,400
	15,000	38,800	22,400

Once again stock at the end of the year can be assumed to have all been purchased in the middle of the previous November. This year there has been some price movement between December 1990 (index 141) and January 1991 (index 143) and so the index at 31st December has to be estimated as 142.

19

Fixed Assets will be indexed up as follows :

Date	Factors	Land at cost £CPP$_{31.12.91}$	Plant at cost £CPP$_{31.12.91}$	Acc Depn on Plant £CPP$_{31.12.91}$
15.1.83	1.5196	15,196	15,196	12,157
15.1.86	1.2602	6,301	36,294	18,147
		21,497	51,490	30,304

Stock will be indexed up as follows :
£60,000 X 1.1232 = 67,392

This time the Monetary items will need indexing by multiplying by 155 (the index at 31.12.91) and dividing by 142 (the estimate of the index at 31.12.90). They will appear as follows :

	£	Factor	£CPP$_{31.12.91}$
Debtors	40,000	1.0915	43,660
Bank	10,000	1.0915	10,915
Creditors	40,000	1.0915	43,660

The full Balance Sheet at 31st December 1991 (with 1990 comparative figures) in £CPP$_{31.12.91}$ will appear as follows :

Balance Sheet as at 31st December 1991   1990   1990
                £CPP$_{31.12.91}$ £CPP$_{31.12.91}$ £CPP$_{31.12.91}$ £CPP$_{31.12.91}$

Fixed Assets
  Land, at cost   32,336   21,497
  Plant and Machinery
    Cost   70,132   51,490
    Depreciation   37,316   30,304
                                32,816   21,186
                                65,152   42,683
Current Assets
  Stock, at cost 45,887   67,392
  Debtors   50,000   43,660
  Cash at Bank   3,000   10,915
                  98,887   121,967
less Creditors : Amounts Due Within One Year
  Trade Creditors 35,000   43,660
                                63,887   78,307
                               129,039   120,990

Shareholders' Equity
At 1.1.90   120,990   *120,990*
CPP HC Profit for the Year   8,049

                                   129,039

CPP Profit and Loss Accounts

Over the year to 31st December 1991 the Unadjusted Historic Cost Shareholders' Equity has risen by £14,600 to £96,000 (from £81,400) and the CPP Shareholders' Equity has risen by £CPP$_{31.12.91}$8,049 (as above). The profits on the CPP Profit and Loss Account have to reconcile this difference.

CPP Profit and Loss Accounts : Revenue and Expenses Other Than Depreciation

In theory, each sale and each expense should be separately indexed up. Multiply by the index at the Balance Sheet date and divide by the index of the date on which the transaction took place or multiply by $CPI_{balancesheet}/CPI_{transaction}$. Note that it is the date on which the transaction took place that is important. The date on which cash was received or paid is irrelevant. If a sale for £1,000 takes place on 4th September, then the 4th September is the date from which the transaction must be indexed and it is irrelevant that the customer did not pay until November. The September transaction gave rise to a debtor (which is a Monetary Asset) and the November receipt just exchanged one Monetary Asset for another.

With expenses, it is the date on which the expense would be charged to the Profit and Loss Account that is important. It may have paid in advance - a pre-payment (Monetary Asset) - or it may be paid in arrears giving rise to a creditor or accrual (Monetary Liability). The Monetary Gains or Losses on these time lags will be calculated separately but the CPP cost of the expense is calculated from the date on which that expense should be charged to the Profit and Loss.

Most businesses will have many individual sales and expenses and it would be a formidable task to index each one on an individual basis. In practice, in the UK, the main price indexes are produced no more frequently than each month and most large businesses produce

Modern Accounting 2

monthly profit statements for management review. Thus it will normally be sensible to group transactions on a monthly basis.

In exam questions (and elsewhere) it is suggested that the whole year's transactions could be treated together on the assumption that all transactions took place evenly over the year. This makes sense to save time in exam questions but it is less sensible with real businesses since they already have the data analysed by month and it can be quickly indexed up on a computer spreadsheet. Almost all businesses are strongly seasonal; very few businesses do have activities which take place evenly throughout the year. People consume different quantities and different products when Summer changes to Winter. Christmas, Easter and August all affect expenditures and activities. If you do need an average or mid-point index for the year, there are two ways of calculating it.

Assumptions (1) for Average Index

If you assume that (a) the cost per unit of the expense approximately followed the index and (b) the physical quantity of the expense consumed each month was approximately equal in each month, then a simple average of the index number is needed. So, if the index behaved as follows :

Jan	103	Jul	119
Feb	105	Aug	123
Mar	107	Sep	125
Apr	110	Oct	129
May	113	Nov	132
Jun	115	Dec	135

Total all twelve index numbers; this comes to 1,416. Divide the total by twelve; this gives 118. Thus, in this case, the average index number is 118.

Assumptions (2) for Average Index

If you assume that approximately the same amount in currency terms of the expense has been consumed in each month, then the reciprocal of the average of the reciprocals of the index numbers is needed. This average is called the 'Harmonic Mean'. (A reciprocal is one divided by the number; most scientific calculators have this function on a single button.)

CPP - Current Purchasing Power

The index numbers as reciprocals read as follows :

Jan	.009708	Jul	.008403
Feb	.009523	Aug	.008130
Mar	.009345	Sep	.008000
Apr	.009090	Oct	.007751
May	.008849	Nov	.007575
Jun	.008695	Dec	.007407

Total all twelve reciprocals; this comes to 0.102482. Divide the total by twelve; this gives 0.008540. Take the reciprocal of this average which is close to 117. Thus, in this case, the average index number is 117.

The differences between the two assumptions are more important the higher the rate of inflation.

Try to answer the following question before looking at the answer (which is at the end of this chapter).

Question 2.3 (Answer 2.3 is on page 41)

Omega Ltd operates in an economy with very high inflation and makes up accounts to 31st December in each year. A consumer price index gave the following readings in the year 2000 :

15.2.2000	110
15.5.2000	180
15.8.2000	250
15.11.2000	330

Assume that price levels in the middle of a quarter can be taken as representative of that period of three months and thus the index on 15th February is representative of the period from 1st January to 31st March.

REQUIRED :

(i) Calculate an average index number for the year to 31st December 2000 for use on expenses where (a) the cost per unit of the expense followed the index and (b) the physical quantity of expense consumed each quarter was equal in each quarter.

(ii) Calculate an average index number for the year to 31st December 2000 for use on expenses where the same currency sums were expended each quarter.

CPP Profit and Loss Accounts : Dividends and Taxation

Dividends are not an expense like the others. If you assume that the dividends of a year relate to the whole of that year, then you would prefer to index them using an average index for the year. However, it is equally logical to assume that they should be indexed on the basis of the date of payment. Whether it is better to relate dividends to the profits of a period of time or to see them as a financial device that should have more to do with Tax advantages and future investment opportunities is discussed further in Chapter Four.

Taxation is normally charged in Profit and Loss Accounts before the date of payment. It should be treated like any other expense. It arises when taxable profits are made. The tax charge could be split in proportion to the profits shown in the monthly management accounts. However, in exam questions, it is probably sufficient to index it on the basis of the average index for the year.

CPP Profit and Loss Accounts : Depreciation

Depreciation charged in a Profit and Loss Account has to be analysed by the date of purchase of the Fixed Assets. Depreciation is a proportion of a cost. Each separate proportion of each separate cost must be indexed from the date on which that cost was incurred. In practice this is less of a problem if Fixed Asset registers are kept on a spreadsheet.

CPP Profit and Loss Accounts : Opening and Closing Stock

Opening Stock on a Profit and Loss Account will follow the figure that is shown on last year's Balance Sheet expressed in this year's £CPP as comparative figures for this year. Closing Stock is the figure shown as stock on this year's Balance Sheet. As on a normal unadjusted historic cost Balance Sheet these stocks are fitted around the Purchases to compute the Cost of Sales.

CPP Profit and Loss Accounts : Monetary Gains and Losses

In periods of inflation Monetary Gains are made on Monetary Liabilities and Monetary Losses are made by holding Monetary Assets. The gain or loss is the difference between the value that it would

CPP - Current Purchasing Power

have risen to if the item had been indexed and the figure that it was fixed at because it was frozen in units of currency.

If we hold £1,000 in a current account between 1.1.2000 and 31.12.2000 while the index rises from 100 to 125, we will make a Monetary Loss of £CPP$_{31.12.00}$250. If the £1,000 had been invested in a non-monetary assets we could have indexed it up by multiplying by 125 and dividing by 100 and it would have become £CPP$_{31.12.00}$1,250. Because it remained a Monetary Asset, it was fixed in units of currency at £1,000. Thus we made a Monetary Loss of the difference.

To calculate the Monetary Gains and Losses for a business over a year, the changes in the net monetary assets must be analysed over the year. Let us take the following example :

Net Monetary Assets (Liabilities) for the Year to 31st December 2000

		£	£	£
1.1.00	Brought forward on 1.1.2000			4,000
1.3.00	Fixed Assets Purchased			7,000
				(3,000)
1.7.00	Sales		33,000	
	Purchases	14,000		
	Other Expenses	9,000	23,000	10,000
				7,000
1.9.00	Dividend Paid			6,000
	Carried forward on 31.12.2000			1,000

Note that this analysis has been made in raw £s and not in £CPP. There have been 3 movements in the Monetary Assets (Liabilities) which took place on 1st March, 1st July and 1st September. The index at the start and end of the year and at the dates on which movements took place reads as follows :

date	index
1.1.00	132
1.3.00	137
1.7.00	143
1.9.00	148
31.12.00	153

Modern Accounting 2

There are two methods of calculating the Monetary Gain or Loss. They must both give the same answer and here they are shown together in order that each reader can choose the one that they find most logical.

Method 1 : Treating Each *Movement* as Giving Rise to a New Asset or a New Liability Held Until the end of the Year

Compute (a) the loss on holding the opening balance as if it were a Monetary Asset held for the whole of the year; (b) the gain on any movement *out* as if it were a Monetary Liability held from the date of the movement until the end of the year and (c) the loss on any movement *in* as if it were a Monetary Asset held from the date of the movement until the end of the year. In this case we have (a) the loss on holding the opening balance to the end of the year, (b) the gain on holding the first movement from 1.3.00 to the end of the year, then (c) the loss on holding the second movement from 1.7.00 to the end of the year and then (d) the gain on holding the third movement from 1.9.00 to the end of the year.

(a) The loss on holding the opening balance for the whole of the year : If it had not been a Monetary Asset it would have risen to

$$4{,}000 \times \frac{153}{132} = 4{,}636 \text{ in } \pounds CPP_{31.12.00}$$

However since it is a Monetary Asset it remains at 4,000 giving a Monetary Loss of $\pounds CPP_{31.12.00} 636$.

(b) The gain on holding a Monetary Liability for the period from 1.3.00 to 31.12.00 : The first movement on Monetary Assets is a movement out and so, if it were the only Monetary item, it would give rise to a Monetary Liability. If that liability had not been a Monetary item it would have risen to

$$7{,}000 \times \frac{153}{137} = 7{,}817 \text{ in } \pounds CPP_{31.12.00}$$

However since it is a Monetary item it remains at 7,000 giving a Monetary Gain of $\pounds CPP_{31.12.00} 817$.

CPP - Current Purchasing Power

(c) The loss on holding a Monetary Asset for the period from 1.7.00 to 31.12.00 : The second movement on Monetary Assets is a movement in and so, if it were the only Monetary item, it would give rise to a Monetary Asset. If that asset had not been a Monetary item it would have risen to

10,000 X $\frac{153}{143}$ = 10,699 in £CPP$_{31.12.00}$

However since it is a Monetary item it remains at 10,000 giving a Monetary Loss of £CPP$_{31.12.00}$699.

(d) The gain on holding a Monetary Liability for the period from 1.9.00 to 31.12.00 : The third movement on Monetary Assets is a movement out and so, if it were the only Monetary item, it would give rise to a Monetary Liability. If that liability had not been a Monetary item it would have risen to

6,000 X $\frac{153}{148}$ = 6,203 in £CPP$_{31.12.00}$

However since it is a Monetary item it remains at 6,000 giving a Monetary Gain of £CPP$_{31.12.00}$203.

The Total Monetary Gain (Loss) for the year will be (a)+(b)+(c)+(d)

- 636 + 817 - 699 + 203 = - 315 or a net Monetary Loss of £CPP$_{31.12.00}$315.

Each Monetary Gain or Loss was calculated as follows :

Sum of money X $\frac{CPI_{year\ end}}{CPI_{movement\ date}}$ - Sum of money

This could be re-expressed as

Sum of money X $\frac{CPI_{year\ end} - CPI_{movement\ date}}{CPI_{movement\ date}}$

Method 2 : Calculating the Gain (or Loss) on Each Separate *Balance*

For method 1 we looked at the *movements* in Monetary Assets as the year progressed but, for method 2, we will look at the *balance* of Monetary Assets as the year progresses. The Balance was (a) £4,000

Modern Accounting 2

from 1.1.00 to 1.3.00, then (b) -£3,000 from 1.3.00 to 1.7.00, then (c) £7,000 from 1.7.00 to 1.9.00 and finally (d) £1,000 from 1.9.00 to 31.12.00.

(a) The loss (in £CPP$_{1.3.00}$) on holding £4,000 in Monetary Assets from 1.1.00 to 1.3.00 (while the index climbed from 132 to 137) will be

Monetary Loss in £CPP$_{period\ end}$ =

Sum of money X $\dfrac{CPI_{period\ end} - CPI_{period\ start}}{CPI_{period\ start}}$

4,000 X $\dfrac{137 - 132}{132}$ = 151.52 in £CPP$_{1.3.00}$

Note that this is in £CPP at the end of the *period* for which this was the balance and *not* at the end of the *year*. To re-express it in £CPP at the end of the year divide by the index at the end of the period and multiply by the index at the end of the year.

£CPP$_{1.3.00}$151.52 is equivalent to 151.52 X $\dfrac{153}{137}$ = £CPP$_{31.12.00}$169

We have calculated this monetary loss in two stages : first calculating the loss in £CPP$_{period\ end}$ and secondly converting that into £CPP$_{year\ end}$. The two stages can be combined as follows :

Monetary Loss in £CPP$_{year\ end}$ =

Sum of money X $\dfrac{CPI_{period\ end} - CPI_{period\ start}}{CPI_{period\ start}}$ X $\dfrac{CPI_{year\ end}}{CPI_{period\ end}}$

4,000 X $\dfrac{137 - 132}{132}$ X $\dfrac{153}{137}$ = 169

(b) The gain (in £CPP$_{31.12.00}$) on holding £3,000 in Monetary Liabilities from 1.3.00 to 1.7.00 (while the index climbed from 137 to 143) will be

3,000 X $\dfrac{143 - 137}{137}$ X $\dfrac{153}{143}$ = £CPP$_{31.12.00}$141

CPP - Current Purchasing Power

(c) The loss (in $£CPP_{31.12.00}$) on holding £7,000 in Monetary Assets from 1.7.00 to 1.9.00 (while the index climbed from 143 to 148) will be

$$7,000 \times \frac{148 - 143}{143} \times \frac{153}{148} = £CPP_{31.12.00} 253$$

(d) The loss (in $£CPP_{31.12.00}$) on holding £1,000 in Monetary Assets from 1.9.00 to 31.12.00 (while the index climbed from 148 to 153) will be

$$1,000 \times \frac{153 - 148}{148} \times \frac{153}{153} = £CPP_{31.12.00} 34$$

Adding the gains and subtracting the losses :
(a) + (b) + (c) + (d) = - 169 + 141 - 253 - 34 = $£CPP_{31.12.00}$-315

As with Method 1 we have made a Monetary Loss of $£CPP_{31.12.00}$315 over the year.

Try to answer the following question before looking at the answer (which is at the end of this chapter).

Question 2.4 (Answer 2.4 is on page 41)

Sigma Ltd had the following movements in Net Monetary Assets (Liabilities) during the year to 30th September 2000 :

Date		£	£	£
1.10.99	Brought forward			21,000
1.11.99	Purchase of Fixed Assets			110,000
				(89,000)
Av Point	Sales		500,000	
	Purchases	450,000		
	Expenses	100,000	550,000	(50,000)
				(139,000)
1.5.00	Proceeds from Sale of Fixed Assets			30,000
				(109,000)
1.7.00	Proceeds - Rights Issue of Ordinary Shares			50,000
30.9.00	Carried forward			(59,000)

A consumer price index gave the following readings :

Date	Index	Date	Index
1.10.99	120	1.5.00	130
1.11.99	122	1.7.00	134
Average for year to 30.9.00	128	30.9.00	138

REQUIRED : Calculate the Monetary Gain of Sigma Ltd for the year to 30th September 2000 in $£CPP_{30.9.00}$.

Modern Accounting 2

CPP Profit and Loss Accounts : An Example

Continuing the example of Alfreda Wainwright Toggles Ltd the Profit and Loss Account for the year to 31st December 1991 reads as follows :

	£	£
Sales		150,000
Opening Stock	60,000	
Purchases	85,000	
	145,000	
less Closing Stock	45,000	
Cost of Sales		100,000
Gross Profit		50,000
less Expenses :		
Sundry Expenses	29,800	
Depreciation of Fixed Assets	5,600	
		35,400
Net Profit		14,600

Depreciation can be analysed from the information already given (on pages 14, 15, 16, 18 and 19) for the Balance Sheets. The assumptions (on pages 15, 16, 18 and 19) as to the dates of purchase for Opening and Closing Stock that were used in computing the CPP Balance Sheets must be used for the Profit and Loss Account. Assume that Sales, Purchases and Expenses occurred evenly over the year (using Assumptions (1) as stated on page 21). The index numbers for every month of the year are stated in the first table on page 15. The average index number for the year is approximately 148.

The transactions that occurred evenly throughout the year can be translated into $CPP_{31.12.91}$ by multiplying each figure by 155 (the index at 31.12.91) and dividing by 148 (the index at the average point) as follows :

	£	£$CPP_{31.12.91}$
Sales	150,000	157,095
Purchases	85,000	89,020
Sundry Expenses	29,800	31,210

CPP - Current Purchasing Power

The Depreciation Charge can be analysed and indexed as follows:

Asset purchased on	Charge in £	Factor	Charge in £CPP$_{31.12.91}$
15.1.83	1,000	1.5196	1,520
15.1.86	2,880	1.2602	3,629
15.1.91	1,720	1.0839	1,864
	5,600		7,013

Since no Fixed Assets were sold, the CPP depreciation charge on the Profit and Loss Account will exactly match the rise in accumulated depreciation on the CPP Balance Sheet.

Movements in Net Monetary Assets can be analysed as follows :

Date			£	£	Index Number
31.12.90	Balance brought forward :				
	Debtors	40,000			
	Cash at bank	10,000			
		50,000			
	less Creditors	40,000			
			10,000	142	
15.1.91	Purchase of Fixed Assets :				
	Land	10,000			
	Plant	17,200			
			27,200	143	
			(17,200)		
Av Point	Sales	150,000			
	Purchases	(85,000)			
	Expenses	(29,800)			
			35,200	148	
31.12.91	Balance carried forward :				
	Debtors	50,000			
	Cash at Bank	3,000			
		53,000			
	less Creditors	35,000			
			18,000	155	

Using method 1 (as described on pages 25, 26 and 27) to calculate the monetary loss :

$$-10{,}000 \times \frac{155 - 142}{142} + 27{,}200 \times \frac{155 - 143}{143} - 35{,}200 \times \frac{155 - 148}{148}$$

$$= -298 \text{ in } CPP_{31.12.91}$$

Thus the CPP Historic Cost Profit and Loss Account appears as follows :

	£CPP$_{31.12.91}$	£CPP$_{31.12.91}$
Sales		157,095
Opening Stock	67,392	
Purchases	89,020	
	156,412	
less Closing Stock	45,887	
Cost of Sales		110,525
Gross Profit		46,570
less Expenses :		
Sundry Expenses	31,210	
Depreciation of Fixed Assets	7,013	
Monetary Loss	298	
		38,521
Net Profit		8,049

This CPP Profit of 8,049 is the same as shown on page 20 as explaining the increase in Net Assets between the Balance Sheets at the start and end of the year. When answering exam questions, expect the figures not to reconcile as perfectly because of rounding errors.

In this case the CPP Gross Profit of 46,570 is lower than the Raw Historic Cost Gross Profit of £50,000. This will not always be the case but (as long as the index continues to rise) the Gross Profit as a percentage of Sales (Gross Profit Percentage) will be consistently lower on CPP statements than on Raw Historic Cost statements. This must be true because Opening Stock will be indexed up by a greater factor than Purchases (or Sales) and Closing Stock will be indexed up by a smaller factor.

CPP - Current Purchasing Power

The other point that stands out when comparing the CPP and the Raw Historic Cost Profit and Loss Accounts is that Depreciation is a much more significant expense on CPP statements. It is normally the figure that has been indexed up by the greatest factor.

Try to answer the following questions before looking at the answers (which are at the end of this chapter).

Question 2.5 (Answer 2.5 is on page 41)

Consider the following events and their effect on a company's Net Monetary Assets :

1. Purchase of Fixed Assets on credit.
2. Payment of the liability incurred in (1) above.
3. Sales to customers on credit.
4. Receipts from customers relating to (3) above.
5. Sale of a Fixed Asset for cash.
6. Issue of loan stock (in exchange for cash).
7. Issue of Ordinary shares (in exchange for cash).
8. Issue of Preference shares (in exchange for cash).
9. Purchases from suppliers on credit.
10. Payment to suppliers resulting from (9) above.
11. The making of a business telephone call (that will increase the bill when that is received from the telephone company).
12. The receipt of a bill from the telephone company.
13. Payment of the bill from the telephone company.
14. Prepayment of cash for a service (expense) that will be provided later.
15. Receipt of the service prepaid in (14) above.

REQUIRED : For each of these events state whether it will
 (a) have no effect on the company's Net Monetary Assets,
 (b) increase the company's Net Monetary Assets or
 (c) decrease the company's Net Monetary Assets.

Modern Accounting 2

Question 2.6 (Answer 2.6 is on page 42)

Gamma Ltd has produced the following Raw Historic Cost statements :

Balance Sheets at 30th June	2000 £	2001 £
Fixed Assets		
Cost	35,000	40,000
less Accumulated Depreciation	18,000	22,000
	17,000	18,000
Current Assets		
Stock	8,000	10,000
Debtors	10,000	9,000
Bank	2,000	1,000
	20,000	20,000
less Creditors Due Within One Year	13,000	14,000
Net Current Assets	7,000	6,000
Total Assets less Current Liabilities	24,000	24,000
less Creditors Due After One Year	8,000	9,000
	16,000	15,000
Provision for Liabilities and Charges	1,000	1,100
	15,000	13,900
Share Capital	1,000	1,000
Revenue Reserves	14,000	12,900
	15,000	13,900

An analysis of Fixed Assets on the above Balance Sheets shows the following :

As At	30.6.2000 Cost £	30.6.2000 Accum'd Depr'n £	30.6.2001 Cost £	30.6.2001 Accum'd Depr'n £
Date of Purchase :				
Oct 1996	14,000	8,000	10,000	7,000
Mar 1998	13,000	7,400	13,000	8,500
May 2000	8,000	2,600	8,000	4,200
Oct 2000			9,000	2,300
	35,000	18,000	40,000	22,000

34

CPP - Current Purchasing Power

Profit and Loss Account for the Year to 30th June 2001

	£	£
Sales		200,000
Opening Stock	8,000	
Purchases	80,000	
	88,000	
less Closing Stock	10,000	
		78,000
Gross Profit		122,000
General Expenses	112,000	
Depreciation of Fixed Assets	6,000	
Loss on Sale of Fixed Asset	600	
		118,600
Net Profit before taxation		3,400
Taxation		1,500
		1,900
Dividends :		
Paid	1,000	
Proposed	2,000	
		3,000
		(1,100)
Balance brought forward		14,000
		12,900

The Fixed Asset disposed of during the year was sold in April 2001. The dividend paid during the year was paid in January 2001 (and this can be taken as the date for CPP indexation). Stocks were purchased over the last three months of each year. Assume that the cost per unit of those items held in stock has followed the index and that the same number of physical units was bought in each of the three months for year-end stock. Assume that the physical units behind Sales, Purchases, General Expenses and Taxation were incurred evenly over the year and that specific price levels have not differed significantly from the consumer price levels measured by the following index :

Modern Accounting 2

Date	Index	Date	Index
15.10.1996	102	15.11.2000	128
15.3.1998	112	15.12.2000	129
15.4.2000	122	15.1.2001	130
15.5.2000	123	15.2.2001	132
15.6.2000	123	15.3.2001	134
15.7.2000	124	15.4.2001	138
15.8.2000	125	15.5.2001	146
15.9.2000	125	15.6.2001	150
15.10.2000	127	15.7.2001	156

REQUIRED : Balance Sheets at 30th June 2000 and 30th June 2001 and a Profit and Loss Account for the year to 30th June 2001 expressed in $£CPP_{30.6.01}$.

Question 2.7 (Answer 2.7 is on page 46)

Epsilon Ltd has produced the following Raw Historic Cost statements :

Balance Sheets at 31st December	2000	2001
	£	£
Fixed Assets		
Cost	111,000	230,000
less Accumulated Depreciation	61,000	82,000
	50,000	148,000
Current Assets		
Stock	10,000	50,000
Debtors	20,000	68,000
Bank	1,000	31,000
	31,000	149,000
less Creditors Due Within One Year	34,000	35,000
Net Current Assets	(3,000)	114,000
Total Assets less Current Liabilities	47,000	262,000
less Creditors : Amounts Due After One Year	7,000	5,000
	40,000	257,000
Share Capital	10,000	20,000
Capital Reserve : Share Premium		5,000
Revenue Reserves	30,000	232,000
	40,000	257,000

CPP - Current Purchasing Power

An analysis of Fixed Assets on the above Balance Sheets shows the following:

As At	31.12.2000		31.12.2001	
	Cost	Accum'd Depr'n	Cost	Accum'd Depr'n
Date of Purchase:	£	£	£	£
Feb 1995	80,000	50,000	30,000	20,000
July 1997	21,000	8,000	18,000	8,000
Aug 1997	10,000	3,000	10,000	6,000
Mar 2001			82,000	20,000
Oct 2001			90,000	28,000
	111,000	61,000	230,000	82,000

Quarterly <u>Profit and Loss Accounts</u>
for the Year to 31st December 2001

Quarter to	31.3.01	30.6.01	31.9.01	31.12.01
	£	£	£	£
Sales	510,000	1,300,000	830,000	250,000
Opening Stock	10,000	40,000	30,000	5,000
Purchases	220,000	430,000	350,000	160,000
(Closing Stock)	(40,000)	(30,000)	(5,000)	(50,000)
	190,000	440,000	375,000	115,000
General Expenses	295,000	546,000	203,000	134,000
Depreciation	14,000	14,000	14,000	20,000
(Profit) Loss on Sale of Fixed Asset	(2,000)		3,000	
	497,000	1,000,000	595,000	269,000
Net Profit before taxation	13,000	300,000	235,000	(19,000)
Taxation	6,000	130,000	110,000	(9,000)
	7,000	170,000	125,000	(10,000)
Dividends:				
Paid		60,000		
Proposed				30,000
	7,000	110,000	125,000	(40,000)
Balance brought forward	30,000	37,000	147,000	272,000
	37,000	147,000	272,000	232,000

The increase in Share Capital and Share Premium arises from a cash rights issue in July 2001. Two Fixed Assets were disposed of during the year; one, purchased in February 1995, was sold in September 2001 when it had a Net Book Value of £10,000 and the other was sold in February 2001. The dividend paid during the year was paid in June 2001 (and this can be taken as the date for CPP indexation). Stocks were purchased over the last two months of each year. Assume that the same number of physical units was bought in each of the three months for year-end stock. Assume that the physical units behind Sales, Purchases, General Expenses and Taxation were incurred evenly over the year and that specific price levels have not differed significantly from the consumer price levels measured by the following index :

Date	Index	Date	Index
15.2.1995	103	15.5.2001	164
15.7.1997	132	15.6.2001	164
15.8.1997	133	15.7.2001	165
15.11.2000	153	15.8.2001	167
15.12.2000	154	15.9.2001	169
15.1.2001	158	15.10.2001	170
15.2.2001	160	15.11.2001	171
15.3.2001	161	15.12.2001	172
15.4.2001	164	15.1.2002	174

REQUIRED :
Balance Sheets at 31st December 2000 and 31st December 2001 and a Profit and Loss Account for the year to 31st December 2001 expressed in $£CPP_{31.12.01}$.

CPP - Current Purchasing Power

Question 2.8 (No answer to this question has been included in this book)

Omicron Ltd has produced the following Raw Historic Cost statements :

Balance Sheets at 30th September

	2000 £	2001 £
Fixed Assets		
Cost	80,000	100,000
less Accumulated Depreciation	45,000	50,000
	35,000	50,000
Current Assets		
Stock	14,000	13,000
Debtors	11,000	12,000
Bank	1,000	3,000
	26,000	28,000
less Creditors Due Within One Year	11,000	12,000
Net Current Assets	15,000	16,000
Total Assets less Current Liabilities	50,000	66,000
less Creditors : Amounts Due After One Year	9,000	4,000
	41,000	62,000
Provision for Liabilities and Charges	2,000	1,000
	39,000	61,000
Share Capital	3,000	4,000
Revenue Reserves	36,000	57,000
	39,000	61,000

An analysis of Fixed Assets on the above Balance Sheets shows the following :

As At	30.9.2000 Cost £	Accum'd Depr'n £	30.9.2001 Cost £	Accum'd Depr'n £
Date of Purchase :				
June 1991	10,000	8,000	10,000	9,000
June 1997	50,000	30,000	50,000	31,000
June 2000	20,000	7,000	20,000	8,000
March 2001			20,000	2,000
	80,000	45,000	100,000	50,000

Modern Accounting 2

Profit and Loss Account for the Year to 30th September 2001

	£	£
Sales		1,500,000
Opening Stock	14,000	
Purchases	944,000	
	958,000	
less Closing Stock	13,000	
		945,000
Gross Profit		555,000
General Expenses	495,000	
Depreciation of Fixed Assets	5,000	
		500,000
Net Profit before taxation		55,000
Taxation		25,000
		30,000
Dividends : Paid	5,000	
Proposed	3,000	
	8,000	
Capitalisation Issue	1,000	
		9,000
		21,000
Balance brought forward		36,000
		57,000

The increase in share capital arises from a capitalisation (bonus) issue of ordinary shares in August 2001. The dividend was paid in March 2001. Stocks were purchased over the last month of each year. Assume that Sales, Purchases, General Expenses and Taxation were incurred at the 'average point' of the year. Use the following consumer price index :

Date	Index	Date	Index	Date	Index
15.6.1991	101	15.9.2000	240	15.9.2001	270
15.6.1997	182	1.10.2000	243	30.9.2001	275
15.6.2000	234	15.3.2001	255		
		average for year to 30.9.2001	260		

REQUIRED : Balance Sheets at 30th September 2000 and 30th September 2001 and a Profit and Loss Account for the year to 30th September 2001 expressed in $£CPP_{30.9.01}$.

CPP - Current Purchasing Power

Answers to Questions 2.1 to 2.7

Answer 2.1

32,000 X 156/134 = £$CPP_{1.1.01}$37,253.73

Answer 2.2

£	Factor		£$CPP_{1.7.99}$
21,000	300/102 =	2.941176	61,765
45,000	300/191 =	1.570680	70,681
99,000	300/245 =	1.224489	121,224
			<u>253,670</u>

Answer 2.3

(i) (110 + 180 + 250 + 330) / 4 = 217.5

(ii) Reciprocals of the 4 index numbers :
0.009090   0.005555   0.004   0.003030

Average of these reciprocals :
0.005419

Reciprocal of this average :
184.5293

Answer 2.4

Method 1
-21,000 X (138 - 120)/120 + 110,000 X (138 - 122)/122 + 50,000 X
(138 - 128)/128 - 30,000 X (138 - 130)/130 - 50,000 X (138 - 134)/134 =
£$CPP_{30.9.00}$11,843.78

Method 2
-21,000 X (122 - 120)/120 X 138/122 + 89,000 X (128 - 122)/122 X 138/128
+ 139,000 X (130 - 128)/128 X 138/130 + 109,000 X (134 - 130)/130 X
138/134 + 59,000 X (138 - 134)/134 = £$CPP_{30.9.00}$11,843.78

Answer 2.5

1   (c) Decreases Net Monetary Assets
2   (a) No effect on Net Monetary Assets
3   (b) Increases Net Monetary Assets
4   (a) No effect on Net Monetary Assets
5   (b) Increases Net Monetary Assets
6   (a) No effect on Net Monetary Assets

7   (b) Increases Net Monetary Assets

8   Either (a) or (b).
The issue of loan stock in 6 above merely raises a monetary asset (cash) in exchange for a monetary liability (the loan stock) and the issue of ordinary shares in 7 above does not create a monetary liability. But the issue of preference shares is part way between the two. Legally preference shareholders are members of the company and are not considered to be a 'liability'. However practically the issue is on fixed 'interest' terms, the holders do not normally have a vote and normally on a liquidation they are entitled to a repayment of just the nominal value - thus they have no interest in profits above those required to satisfy their limited interest.

9   (c) Decreases Net Monetary Assets

10 (a) No effect on Net Monetary Assets

11 In theory - (c) Decreases Net Monetary Assets because the call should be charged against profit immediately it is made - without waiting for the bill to arrive - it should be accrued for.

12 In theory - (a) No effect on Net Monetary Assets because the receipt of the bill simply changes the estimated accrual into a firm creditor.

13 (a) No effect on Net Monetary Assets

14 (a) No effect on Net Monetary Assets. Simple conversion of one monetary asset into another - cash to prepayment.

15 (c) Decreases Net Monetary Assets

Answer 2.6

WORKINGS

The index at 30.6.2001 is estimated at 153 (half way between the index at 15.6.2001 and 15.7.2001).

The analysis of Fixed Assets shows that the cost of those purchased in March 1998 and May 2000 has remained constant. Thus the disposal must relate to the earliest purchase in Oct 1996. The cost of the disposal must be 14,000 - 10,000 = 4,000. Depreciation charged in the Profit and Loss Account was 6,000 but Accumulated Depreciation rose by just 22,000 - 18,000 = 4,000. Thus the accumulated depreciation on the disposal must be 6,000 - 4,000 = 2,000 and the Net Book Value of the disposal must be 4,000 - 2,000 = 2,000. The Profit and Loss Account shows a loss on disposal of 600 and thus the proceeds on sale must have been 1,400.

CPP - Current Purchasing Power

Fixed Assets at cost

30.6.00	30.6.01	Indexation Factor		30.6.00	30.6.01
£	£			£CPP$_{30.6.01}$	£CPP$_{30.6.01}$
14,000	10,000	153/102	1.5	21,000	15,000
13,000	13,000	153/112	1.36607142	17,759	17,759
8,000	8,000	153/123	1.24390243	9,951	9,951
	9,000	153/127	1.20472440	0	10,843
__35,000__	__40,000__			__48,710__	__53,553__

Depreciation on Fixed Assets

30.6.00	30.6.01	Indexation Factor		30.6.00	30.6.01
£	£			£CPP$_{30.6.01}$	£CPP$_{30.6.01}$
8,000	7,000	153/102	1.5	12,000	10,500
7,400	8,500	153/112	1.36607142	10,109	11,612
2,600	4,200	153/123	1.24390243	3,234	5,224
	2,300	153/127	1.20472440	0	2,771
__18,000__	__22,000__			__25,343__	__30,107__

Disposal of Fixed Asset :

	£	Indexation Factor		£CPP$_{30.6.01}$
Proceeds	1,400	153/138	1.10869565	1,552
Cost	4,000	153/102	1.5	6,000
Accumulated Depn	2,000	153/102	1.5	3,000

Thus the CPP loss on Disposal will be -1552 + (6000-3000) = 1448.

Depreciation charged in the year = 30107-25343+3000 = 7764.

The average index for opening stock = (122+123+123)/3 = 122.67
The average index for closing stock = (138+146+150)/3 = 144.67
The average index for sales etc =
(124+125+125+127+128+129+130+132+143+138+146+150)
  12
= 133.083333

	£	Indexation Factor		£CPP$_{30.6.01}$
Opening stock	8,000	153/122.67	1.24724871	9,978
Closing stock	10,000	153/144.67	1.05757931	10,576
Monetary Items on 30.6.2000 :				
Debtors	10,000	153/123	1.24390243	12,439
Bank	2,000	153/123	1.24390243	2,488
Creditors < 1yr	13,000	153/123	1.24390243	16,171
Creditors > 1yr	8,000	153/123	1.24390243	9,951
Provisions	1,000	153/123	1.24390243	1,244

Modern Accounting 2

	£	Indexation Factor		£CPP$_{30.6.01}$
Sales	200,000	153/133.08	1.14968440	229,937
Purchases	80,000	153/133.08	1.14968440	91,975
Gen Exp	112,000	153/133.08	1.14968440	128,764
Taxation	1,500	153/133.08	1.14968440	1,724
Div Paid	1,000	153/130	1.17692307	1,177

The Proposed Dividend needs no indexation because it has not yet been paid.

Movements in Net Monetary Assets (Liabilities)

Date			£	£
1.7.2000	Brought forward :			
	Debtors		10,000	
	Bank		2,000	
	Creditors < 1 yr		(13,000)	
	Creditors > 1 yr		(8,000)	
	Provisions		(1,000)	
				(10,000)
15.10.2000	Purchase of Fixed Asset			(9,000)
				(19,000)
15.1.2001	Dividend Paid			(1,000)
				(20,000)
Av Point	Sales		200,000	
	Purchases		(80,000)	
	General Expenses		(112,000)	
	Taxation		(1,500)	
				6,500
				(13,500)
15.4.2001	Proceeds - Sale of Fixed Asset			1,400
				(12,100)
30.6.2001	Proposed Dividend			(2,000)
30.6.2001	Carried forward :			
	Debtors		9,000	
	Bank		1,000	
	Creditors < 1 yr		(14,000)	
	Creditors > 1 yr		(9,000)	
	Provisions		(1,100)	
				14,100

Monetary Gain (using method 1) :

$10,000 \times (153-123)/123 + 9,000 \times (153-127)/127 + 1,000 \times (153-130)/130 - 6,500 \times (153-133.08)/133.08 - 1400 \times (153-138)/138$
$= £CPP_{30.6.01} 3,333$

CPP - Current Purchasing Power

<u>Balance Sheet</u> as at	30.6.2000	30.6.2001
	£CPP$_{30.6.01}$	£CPP$_{30.6.01}$
Fixed Assets	
Cost	48,710	53,553
Depreciation	<u>25,343</u>	<u>30,107</u>
	<u>23,367</u>	<u>23,446</u>
Current Assets	
Stock	9,978	10,576
Debtors	12,439	9,000
Bank	<u>2,488</u>	<u>1,000</u>
	24,905	20,576
Creditors : Amounts due within one year	<u>16,171</u>	<u>14,000</u>
Net Current Assets	<u>8,734</u>	<u>6,576</u>
Total Assets less Current Liabilities	32,101	30,022
Creditors : Amounts due after one year	<u>9,951</u>	<u>9,000</u>
	22,150	21,022
Provisions	<u>1,244</u>	<u>1,100</u>
	<u>20,906</u>	<u>19,922</u>
Shareholders' Equity 1.7.2000	<u>20,906</u>	20,906
Reduction in reserves over year		<u>984</u>
		<u>19,922</u>

<u>Profit and Loss Account</u> for the year to 30 June 2001

 | £CPP$_{30.6.01}$ | £CPP$_{30.6.01}$
---|---|---
Sales | | 229,937
    Opening Stock | 9,978 |
    Purchases | <u>91,975</u> |
 | 101,953 |
    less Closing Stock | <u>10,576</u> |
 | | <u>91,377</u>
Gross Profit | 138,560 |
    General Expenses | 128,764 |
    Depreciation | 7,764 |
    Loss on Sale of Fixed Asset | 1,448 |
    Monetary (Gain) | <u>(3,333)</u> |
 | | <u>134,643</u>
Profit for the year before taxation | | 3,917
Taxation | | <u>1,724</u>
Profit for the year after taxation | | 2,193
Dividends Paid | 1,177 |
    Proposed | <u>2,000</u> |
 | | <u>3,177</u>
Overdistribution for the year - reduction in reserves | | <u>984</u>

Modern Accounting 2

Answer 2.7

WORKINGS

The index at 31.12.2000 is estimated at 156 (half way between the index at 15.12.2000 and 15.1.2001) and that at 31.12.2001 at 173. The analysis of Fixed Assets shows that the cost of those purchased on Aug 1997 has remained constant. Thus the disposals must relate to the purchases in February 1995 and July 1997. Analysing the cost of those items :

Date of Purchase : On Balance Sheet at	Feb 1995 £	July 1997 £
31.12.2000	80,000	21,000
31.12.2001	30,000	18,000
Cost of Disposals	50,000	3,000

Analysing <u>Accumulated Depreciation</u> :

Date of Purchase	Feb 1995	July 1997	Aug 1997	2001
On Balance Sheet at	£	£	£	£
31.12.2000	50,000	8,000	3,000	0
31.12.2001	20,000	8,000	6,000	48,000
Change over year	(30,000)	0	3,000	48,000
On Disposals	40,000[1]	1,000[4]		
Charged in year	10,000[2]	1,000[3]	3,000	48,000
	30,000	0	3,000	48,000

[1] If the cost of the item purchased in Feb 95 and sold this year is £50,000 and the NBV is £10,000, then the accumulated depreciation on this item must be £40,000.
[2] Balancing figure - to agree the £30,000 change over year.
[3] Balancing figure - to agree a total charge in P & L of 62000.
[4] Balancing figure - to agree the nil change over year.

If the cost of the item purchased in July 1997 and sold this year is £3,000 and the accumulated depreciation on that item is £1,000, then the NBV must be £2,000. If the item with a NBV of £10,000 was sold in Sept at a loss of £3,000, then the proceeds on sale must have been £7,000. If the item with a NBV of £2,000 was sold in June at a profit of £2,000, the proceeds on sale must have been £4,000.

CPP - Current Purchasing Power

Fixed Assets at cost

31.12.00	31.12.01	Indexation	Factor	31.12.00	31.12.01
£	£			£CPP$_{31.12.01}$	£CPP$_{31.12.01}$
80,000	30,000	173/103	1.67961165	134,369	50,388
21,000	18,000	173/132	1.31060606	27,523	23,591
10,000	10,000	173/133	1.30075187	13,008	13,008
	82,000	173/161	1.07453416		88,112
	90,000	173/170	1.01764705		91,588
111,000	230,000			174,899	266,687

Depreciation on Fixed Assets

31.12.00	31.12.01	Indexation	Factor	31.12.00	31.12.01
£	£			£CPP$_{31.12.01}$	£CPP$_{31.12.01}$
50,000	20,000	173/103	1.67961165	83,981	33,592
8,000	8,000	173/132	1.31060606	10,485	10,485
3,000	6,000	173/133	1.30075187	3,902	7,805
	20,000	173/161	1.07453416		21,491
	28,000	173/170	1.01764705		28,494
61,000	82,000			98,368	101,866

Disposal of Fixed Asset purchased on Feb 1995 :

	£	Indexation Factor		£CPP$_{31.12.00}$
Proceeds	7,000	173/169	1.02366863	7,166
Cost	50,000	173/103	1.67961165	83,981
Acc Depn	40,000	173/103	1.67961165	67,184

The CPP loss on Disposal will be -7166+(83981-67184) = 9631.

Disposal of Fixed Asset purchased on July 1997 :

Proceeds	4,000	173/160	1.08125	4,325
Cost	3,000	173/132	1.31060606	3,932
Acc Depn	1,000	173/132	1.31060606	1,311

The CPP profit on Disposal will be 4325 - (3932 - 1311) =1704

The CPP net loss on sale of Fixed Assets will be 9631-1704=7927

Depreciation charged this year =

£CPP$_{31.12.01}$101,866 - 98,368 + 67,184 + 1,311 = 71,993

The average index for opening stock = (153+154)/2=153.5
The average index for closing stock = (171+172)/2=171.5

Modern Accounting 2

The average index for sales etc =
Quarter 1	(158+160+161)/3=	159.666666
Quarter 2	(164+164+164)/3=	164
Quarter 3	(165+167+169)/3=	167
Quarter 4	(170+171+172)/3=	171

	£	Indexation Factor		£CPP$_{31.12.01}$
Opening stock	10,000	173/153.5	1.12703583	11,270
Closing stock	50,000	173/171.5	1.00874635	50,437
Monetary Items on 31.12.2000 :				
Debtors	20,000	173/156	1.10897435	22,179
Bank	1,000	173/156	1.10897435	1,109
Creditors < 1yr	34,000	173/156	1.10897435	37,705
Creditors > 1yr	7,000	173/156	1.10897435	7,763
Div Paid	60,000	173/164	1.05487804	63,293

	Q1	Q2	Q3	Q4	Total
					£CPP$_{31.12.01}$
Indexation Factors :					
	173/159.667	173/164	173/167	173/171	
	1.0835050	1.0548780	1.0359281	1.0116959	
Sales £	510,000	1,300,000	830,000	250,000	
Sales CPP	552,588	1,371,341	859,820	252,924	3,036,673
Purchases					
in £	220,000	430,000	350,000	160,000	
in CPP	238,371	453,598	362,575	161,870	1,216,414
General Expenses					
in £	295,000	546,000	203,000	134,000	
in CPP	319,634	575,963	210,293	135,567	1,241,457
Taxation £	6,000	130,000	110,000	(9,000)	
Taxation CPP	6,501	137,134	113,952	(9,105)	248,482

CPP - Current Purchasing Power

Movements in Net Monetary Assets (Liabilities)	£	£
1.1.2001 Debtors b/f	20,000	
Bank b/f	1,000	
Creditors < 1 yr b/f	(34,000)	
Creditors > 1 yr b/f	(7000)	(20,000)
Q1 Sales	510,000	
Purchases	(220,000)	
General Expenses	(295,000)	
Taxation	(6,000)	(11,000)
Feb 2001 Proceeds - Sale of Fixed Asset		4,000
Mar 2001 Purchase of Fixed Asset		(82,000)
Q2 Sales	1,300,000	
Purchases	(430,000)	
General Expenses	(546,000)	
Taxation	(130,000)	194,000
June 2001 Dividend Paid		(60,000)
July 2001 Proceeds - Issue of Ordinary Shares		15,000
Q3 Sales	830,000	
Purchases	(350,000)	
General Expenses	(203,000)	
Taxation	(110,000)	167,000
Sept 2001 Proceeds - Sale of Fixed Asset		7,000
Oct 2001 Purchase of Fixed Asset		(90,000)
Q4 Sales	250,000	
Purchases	(160,000)	
General Expenses	(134,000)	
Taxation	9,000	35,000
31.12.2001 Proposed Dividend		(30,000)
31.12.2001 Debtors c/f	68,000	
Bank c/f	31,000	
Creditors < 1 yr c/f	(35,000)	
Creditors > 1 yr c/f	(5,000)	<u>59,000</u>

Monetary Gain (using method 1) :
20000X(173-156)/156+11000X(173-159.67)/159.67-4000X(173-160)/160
+82000X(173-161)/161-194000X(173-164)/164+60000X(173-164)/164
-15000X(173-165)/165-167000X(173-167)/167-7000X(173-169)/169
+90000X(173-170)/170+35000X(173-171)/171 = -3364 (a monetary loss)

Modern Accounting 2

Balance Sheet as at	31.12.2000 £CPP$_{31.12.01}$	31.12.2001 £CPP$_{31.12.01}$
Fixed Assets		
Cost	174,899	266,687
Depreciation	98,368	101,866
	76,531	164,821
Current Assets		
Stock	11,270	50,437
Debtors	22,179	68,000
Bank	1,109	31,000
	34,558	149,437
Creditors : Amounts due within one year	37,705	35,000
Net Current Assets	(3,147)	114,437
Total Assets less Current Liabilities	73,384	279,258
Creditors : Amounts due after one year	7,763	5,000
	65,621	274,258
Shareholders' Equity 1.7.2000	65,621	65,621
Rights Issue		15,727
Increase in reserves over year		192,910
		274,258

Profit and Loss Account for the year to 31st December 2001

Sales		3,036,673
Opening Stock	11,270	
Purchases	1,216,414	
	1,227,684	
less Closing Stock	50,437	
		1,177,247
Gross Profit		1,859,426
General Expenses	1,241,457	
Depreciation	71,993	
Loss on Sales of Fixed Assets	7,927	
Monetary Loss	3,364	
		1,324,741
Profit for the year before taxation		534,685
Taxation		248,482
Profit for the year after taxation		286,203
Dividends Paid	63,293	
Proposed	30,000	
		93,293
Undistributed profit - increase in reserves		192,910

Chapter Three

Current Cost Accounting

Current Cost Accounting (CCA) shows assets on Balance Sheets at their current cost, which is normally the cost of replacing them at the Balance Sheet date. And it also requires that expenses charged against revenue should be charged at their replacement cost at the date of consumption - rather than their historic cost. CCA re-defines the statistics contained in business accounts. By itself CCA does not change the units of measurement.

Some proponents of CCA would see it as an alternative to CPP but the two are not in conflict because it is possible to combine the two as 'CCA in CPP'. Several academic authors including W T Baxter[1] have argued in favour of CCA in CPP while most attempts by professional bodies to introduce CCA have not combined it with CPP but have tried to keep the CCA statistics in raw currency. This Chapter considers the professional proposals for CCA in unadjusted currency units, the next Chapter (Chapter Four) looks at the theories behind the systems and Chapter Five considers CCA in CPP.

Strictly, CCA is not a form of 'Inflation Accounting' and its adherents would advocate it even if there was no general price inflation. CCA is best described as 'Accounting for Changing Prices'. 'Changing Prices' sounds like a politician's euphemism for 'Inflation' but the distinction is between (a) the drop in the value of currency (inflation) and (b) specific changes in particular prices (changing prices). If a train fare costs £5 this month and it cost £4 last month, then one could say that value of a pound has gone down or one could say that the cost of that particular item has gone up. If most prices are rising, it is best described as a fall in the value of money (inflation). If most prices are stable but one in particular is rising and another is falling, it is better described as changing prices.

CCA is concerned solely with the prices of the specific assets owned by one business and it ignores general consumer prices or the prices of assets owned by other organisations. Purest CCA would not use any price indexes but would consider the current price of each asset. In practice this information is not available or would cost too much to collect and most businesses that have used CCA have used specific price indexes (SPIs) to estimate the current price of most of their assets. A consumer price index (CPI) looks at many different prices weighting them according to the behaviour of individuals in their private lives whereas an SPI should be based on fewer prices in a tightly defined area covering solely items similar to those held by the business. The more tight the definition, the fewer will be the prices in the index and the more accurate will be the estimate.

Deprival Values

The Deprival Value of an asset is the value that would be lost from the business were that asset to be taken away. Two questions must be asked to determine this value : (a) If the asset were to be taken away, would the business replace the asset? and (b) What would the business have done with the asset if it had not been taken away?

The three values that will help to answer these questions are :

1. Replacement Cost - the current cost of buying another similar asset,
2. Net Realisable Value - the proceeds from sale net of any selling expenses and
3. Economic Value - the present value of the cash flows that will arise from continuing to hold the asset and use it in whatever is the most profitable fashion. 'Present values' are explained in Chapter 6 but the actual mechanics of the calculation are not important at this stage; it can be thought of as what one would pay today for the benefits that will arise from holding the asset.

There are 6 different orders in which 3 values can be arranged:

1. Replacement Cost is highest, Net Realisable Value in the middle and Economic Value is lowest.

Let us assume that Replacement Cost is £6,000, Net Realisable Value is £5,000 and Economic Value is £4,000. (a)If the asset was taken away, it does not make sense to replace it because a cost of

£6,000 cannot be recovered either by reselling or by holding. (b) Even if the asset is *not* taken away, it does not make sense to hold it because it can be sold for more than its Economic Value. If the management of this business are aware of these values, why does the business continue to hold the asset? They may believe that the resale market will improve but, if that is their belief, it should be reflected in the Economic Value. In this case a logical management would sell the asset and not replace it; the Deprival Value is the Net Realisable Value. Most commentators would assume that this is an unusual situation because, if managers know about it, why is the asset still held at the Balance Sheet date?

2. Net Realisable Value is highest, Economic Value in the middle and Replacement Cost is lowest.

Let us assume that Replacement Cost is £4,000, Net Realisable Value is £6,000 and Economic Value is £5,000. (a) If the asset was taken away it now makes excellent sense to replace it because it could be either resold or held at a good profit. (b) If the asset is *not* taken away, it would be resold because this yields a better return than holding it. In this case, Deprival Value is Replacement Cost. One would expect this situation with the trading stock of businesses that sell to other businesses goods which those other businesses use as Fixed Assets.

3. Economic Value is highest, Replacement Cost in the middle and Net Realisable Value is lowest.

This time Replacement Cost is £5,000, Net Realisable Value is £4,000 and Economic Value is £6,000. (a) If the asset was taken away it still makes sense to replace it because it could be held and used at a profit. (b) If the asset is *not* taken away, it would held for use within the business because this yields more than resale. In this case, Deprival Value is Replacement Cost. One would expect this situation with the Fixed Assets of many successful businesses where there is an imperfect second-hand market for those assets. This is at its most extreme where the assets have been produced to the design of their current owners (and hence would have little value to anybody else).

4. Replacement Cost is highest, Economic Value in the middle and Net Realisable Value is lowest.

Let us assume that Replacement Cost is £6,000, Net Realisable Value is £4,000 and Economic Value is £5,000. (a)If the asset was taken away it does not make sense to replace it because a cost of £6,000 cannot be recovered either by reselling or by holding. (b)If the asset is *not* taken away, then it makes sense to hold it and continue to work it because that option yields more than sale. In this case Deprival Value is Economic Value. One would expect this situation with the Fixed Assets of businesses producing a product in decline. It makes sense to continue production until the equipment gives up but it would not make sense to re-equip to produce the same product. This situation does not imply that the management is unsuccessful - the historic cost may be below the values shown above and, when they finish with this product, they may be able to continue with other businesses and other products. In the next chapter we will consider how common this situation is and how it relates to depreciation policy. The advocates of CCA would assume that it is most uncommon.

5. Economic Value is highest, Net Realisable Value in the middle and Replacement Cost is lowest.

Let us assume that Replacement Cost is £4,000, Net Realisable Value is £5,000 and Economic Value is £6,000. (a)If the asset was taken away it makes excellent sense to replace it because it could be either held or resold at a profit. (b)If the asset is *not* taken away, then it makes sense to hold it and continue to work it because that yields more than sale. In this case Deprival Value is Replacement Cost. One would expect this situation with the Fixed Assets of successful businesses where (i) the business has knowledge or buying power greater than that of other businesses which require the same assets or (ii) the assets can be used by consumers.

6. Net Realisable Value is highest, Replacement Cost in the middle and Economic Value is lowest.

Let us assume that Replacement Cost is £5,000, Net Realisable Value is £6,000 and Economic Value is £4,000. (a)If the asset was taken away it makes sense to replace it because it can be resold at a profit. (b)If the asset is *not* taken away, then it makes sense to resell it but not to hold it. In this case Deprival Value is Replacement Cost. One would expect this situation with the trading stock of businesses selling goods either (a) directly to consumers or (b) to other businesses that use them as parts in completed products.

In this analysis four out of the six possibilities gave Replacement Cost as Deprival Value and only possibilities 1 and 4 were exceptions. In the case of possibility 1, Net Realisable Value was Deprival Value, but, if the managers wanted to maximise the firm's wealth and they knew the three values, then this situation would be unstable. It is reasonable to assume that few managers would wish to admit that some assets on their Balance Sheet fell into possibility 1. However possibility 1 must arise more often than anyone knows because most managers do not regularly test the Net Realisable Value of every one of their assets and, even when they do make such tests, they cannot know of all the potential purchasers.

Possibility 4 gives Economic Value as Deprival Value. The professional attempts to introduce CCA have mostly admitted that Economic Value must be the Deprival Value in certain circumstances but have then largely ignored that inconvenient possibility. Estimating Economic Value is very difficult in practice. It would normally have to be estimated for a group of assets because cash flows arising from the working of assets normally come from sales that could be made only if a combination of assets are held. Unfortunately some of the assets in that combination, when viewed separately, will have Deprival Values above Economic Value. Using Economic Values on Balance Sheets for Depreciating Assets has an interesting effect on Income Statements (that is studied in Chapter 7) but this 'interesting effect' is unlikely to appeal to practical men of business. For the moment let us assume that possibility 4 is very rare and can be ignored.

It may not be possible to ascertain certain replacement costs. This is especially likely to be true where there has been technological or fashion change or where the assets - such as fruit or vegetables - are only available on a seasonal basis. Advice in the professional handbooks has been to look for new assets "with equivalent service potential or capacity to produce similar output or service"[2] and to use "an index which corresponds to the long-term trend"[3] of seasonal produce. These sound like imperfect solutions but, to decide how important these imperfections are, one has to consider who would find Deprival Values useful, in which circumstances and for what decisions.

Definition of Recoverable Value and Deprival Value

'Recoverable Value' is defined as the higher of (i) Net Realisable Value and (ii) Economic Value. 'Deprival Value' is the lower of (a) Replacement Cost and (b) Recoverable Value. The reader may care to check through each of the possibilities 1 to 6 to see why this definition works.

Deprival Value = Lower of

Recoverable Value = Higher of

| Replacement Cost | Realisable Value | Economic Value |

Synonyms For Deprival Value

'Value to the Business' and 'Current Cost' are used as synonyms for 'Deprival Value' and most professional publications[4] make it clear that neither is supposed to be a synonym for the more restricted concept of 'Replacement Cost'. However both are unfortunate terms because 'Value *to* the business' confuses those who think it must relate to Value *of* the Business and 'Current Cost' sounds as if it means simply 'Replacement Cost' without the alternative possibilities of Economic or Realisable Values.

CCA Balance Sheets

It is intended that Assets are shown at Deprival Value ('current cost') - normally assumed to be the replacement cost - the cost that would have been incurred if the item had been purchased at the Balance Sheet date. This is normally linked to a Capital Maintenance Concept whereby Capital is seen in physical terms rather than in money terms (see next Chapter) but it can be linked to a 'Financial Capital' Maintenance Concept (see pages 88/9).

CCA Double Entry Records

In theory a complete set of CCA ledgers could be kept (as well as the standard Historic Cost ledgers). In practice the entries in both would be very similar except for those relating to (i) Fixed Assets at cost, (ii) Depreciation on Fixed Assets, (iii) Stocks, (iv) the Profit and Loss Account and (v) Reserves. Separate analysis of these areas will be needed; it is probably best kept on a computer spreadsheet.

Try to answer the following question before looking at the answer (which is at the end of this chapter).

Modern Accounting 2

Question 3.1 (Answer 3.1 is on page 92)

The following assets are owned by different companies :

1. Beta Ltd manufactures Car Wash Machines which it sells to Petrol Forecourt Operators. On its Balance Sheet it has one completed Car Wash Machine in stock which had cost £10,000 to manufacture. Beta operate a thriving business and their current selling price per Car Wash Machine is £30,000. They believe that most forecourt operators should achieve returns that would give an economic value of £40,000. However, were Beta to try to operate a forecourt with a Car Wash, they would have to switch resources from their current business. Taking account of the opportunity costs of these resources, they estimate that the economic value of a Car Wash Machine to them would be £20,000. They estimate that the cost of manufacturing a Car Wash Machine today (the replacement cost) would be £15,000.

2. Alpha plc owns nearly-new Textile Plant and Machinery which it has just bought from the liquidator of a failed competitor for £4m. This machinery is used in a part of the textile business which is currently in recession and, were Alpha to try to re-sell this equipment, there would be few potential customers. In current conditions it would take a long time to sell but it might raise £6m. This purchase from the liquidator was a special situation and, if the equipment were to be replaced, it would have to be ordered from the original manufacturers. Because of current market conditions these manufacturers have ceased production of this type of plant but they could restart production and would probably charge £15m for equivalent machines. When deciding how to negotiate with the liquidator the management of Alpha plc estimated the returns they expected from this equipment and they estimated its economic value as £8m.

3. Omega Frozen Speciality Foods Ltd freeze carratoes (a cross between a carrot and a tomato). These are harvested in September and cannot be bought fresh except in that month. They make up their accounts to 31st December in each year and, on their latest balance sheet date, they hold 10,000 packs of frozen carratoes. They sell the packs at 50p per pack and there is no economic value to holding the packs. The cost of

fresh carratoes this harvest was the equivalent of 30p per pack which was 10% more expensive than the previous harvest.

4   Sigma Ltd own jigs and dies which would cost £50,000 to replace and would have a negligible value to anybody else. They estimate the economic value of those jigs and dies (together with the knowledge as to how they are used) as £1m.

5   Epsilon plc own a machine which would cost £30,000 to replace and they estimate its economic value at £10,000. They have just received an offer from a theme park which wants to buy the machine for a display of Amusing Historic Manufacture. The theme park are willing to pay £20,000 for the machine.

6   Lambda Car Hire plc believe that it would cost £3m to replace their current fleet of cars. They could probably sell the fleet for £4m net of the costs of such sale and the economic value of the fleet to Lambda is £6m.

7   Iota Parts Ltd make steel drums for domestic washing machines. Their stock of drums awaiting sale would cost £40,000 to replace, has a selling price value of £60,000 and no economic value.

8   The management of Theta Ventures plc have just bought equipment for £450,000 and they claim that the current replacement cost would be £600,000. You suspect that this management is incompetent and that they cannot purchase or negotiate. It is probably true that, if they were to replace the equipment, they would spend £600,000. However a shrewder management would probably be able to buy equivalent equipment for £300,000. The equipment has no resale value and its economic value depends on how well the business is run. The current management of Theta have budgets implying that the economic value is £1m. However you suspect that (a) under the current management, Theta will be lucky if it ever makes a profit and (b) under good management, the equipment has an economic value of £400,000.

REQUIRED : Discuss how you would determine the Deprival Value for each of these assets.

Modern Accounting 2

(i) CCA Balance Sheets : <u>Non-Depreciating Fixed Assets</u>

It is almost always assumed that Deprival Value is Replacement Cost which cannot be ascertained directly for each asset but has to be estimated with the use of Specific Indexes. In the UK the Government Statistical Service publish "Price Index Numbers for Current Cost Accounting" (PINCCA) which is available from H M Stationery Office or the Business Statistics Office, Newport, Gwent. These are Price Indexes for assets held by various broad categories of industries. The next Chapter contains a discussion on whether these are likely to be more or less accurate as estimates of replacement cost than a Consumer Index such as the Index of Retail Prices; advocates of CCA generally assume that they are reasonably accurate.

As with CPP, to index up to 'Current Cost" take the original number of pounds spent in year 1 and multiply by the ratio by which the Specific Price Index has increased between year 1 and the Balance Sheet date (year n). In other words, multiply by the factor SPI_n/SPI_1.

Example
The company bought land near Chelmsford for £100,000 on 1st January 1990 when the specific index for land near Chelmsford was 103. The company wish to produce a Balance Sheet as at 31st December 2000 when they still retain this land and the index stands at 532. The current cost is estimated at

$$100{,}000 \times \frac{532}{103} = £516{,}505$$

If this Balance Sheet is the first CCA Balance Sheet, then the whole of the increase from original cost of £100,000 to Current Cost at 31.12.2000 of £516,505 will have to be credited to the 'Current Cost Reserve'. The double entry will be to Debit the increase of £416,505 to the Asset account and to Credit the Current Cost Reserve with £416,505.

In future years only the increase in Current Cost this year over the Current Cost last year will be credited to the Current Cost Reserve. If the current cost of the land at 31.12.2001 is £600,000, then the increase between 31.12.00 and 31.12.01 has been £83,495. The double entry to effect this increase will be Debit the Asset £83,495 and Credit the Current Cost Reserve with the same sum.

Realised and Unrealised Holding Gains

The Current Cost Reserve contains 'holding gains' which would not form part of those earnings which the advocates of CCA would view as available for distribution. The advocates of CCA wish to maintain the 'operating capacity' of the business and one of the purposes of CCA is to restrict dividends. However, there are several views as to what constitutes the most sensible distribution policy and some would hold that CCA results of past periods should be only one factor among many to be taken into account. Most forms of CCA that have been considered for practical adoption would divide the Current Cost Reserve between 'Realised Holding Gains' and 'Unrealised Holding Gains'. The legal barriers restricting distributions to realised profits are not perfectly defined but it is almost certainly an offense against the law to debit a dividend against unrealised holding gains and it is not a legal offense to debit dividends against realised holding gains (though debiting a dividend payment against *either* causes offense against to keen advocates of CCA).

An unrealised holding gain arises from increases in the CCA values of assets which have not been tested in the market place. Thus the example of holding the land near Chelmsford from 1.1.90 to 31.12.2001 gives rise to an unrealised holding gain which will remain unrealised until the land is sold. When the land is sold, the difference between the original cost and the replacement cost at the date of sale will be a Realised Holding Gain and the difference between the original cost and the last CCA value before sale should be removed from the Unrealised Holding Gains.

Example
It has already been stated that the land near Chelmsford had originally cost £100,000 and had a current cost of £600,000 on 31.12.2001. On 1.7.2002 the land was sold for net proceeds of £750,000 and it is assumed that these Net Proceeds are an indication of the Replacement Cost at 1.7.2002.

The Realised Holding Gain on the land is £650,000 and Unrealised Holding Gains need to be reduced by £500,000. The double entry will be to Debit the Cash Book with £750,000 when the proceeds are received, to Credit the CCA Land account with £600,000 and to Credit the Current Cost Reserve with £150,000. Within the

Current Cost Reserve the whole of the new credit of £150,000 should be added to Realised Holding Gains and £500,000 should be subtracted from Unrealised and added to Realised Holding Gains.

The Difference Between NRV and RC

In this example of the disposal of Land near Chelmsford, the whole of the gain between the original cost and the final net proceeds eventually reached the Current Cost Reserve. The Current Cost Reserve is supposed to contain holding gains - that is, the gains made between (i) historic and (ii) replacement cost during the time the asset is held. An assumption in the Land example is that the net proceeds at disposal are the same as the Replacement Cost at the same date. With land this is probably true but, for most other assets there is normally a difference.

Anybody trading in assets of a particular type normally has a Net Realisable Value (NRV) above Replacement Cost (RC). All other individuals and firms normally have a RC above NRV. This must be generally true or the traders in those assets could not survive.

If the RC of the Land was assumed to be £50,000 below the NRV, then the Holding Gain in the Current Cost Reserve should be reduced by £50,000 and the CCA Profit and Loss Account (Revenue Reserve) should be increased by £50,000.

(ii) CCA Balance Sheets : Depreciating Fixed Assets

Under the purest form of CCA the replacement cost of a 2 year old machine would be the cost of buying an identical machine of exactly the same age. In practice there are very imperfect markets for most of the items which are held as business Fixed Assets - the exception being the markets for second-hand motor vehicles. 'Very imperfect markets' means that it is difficult to find anybody trying to sell identical machines of exactly the same age and, even where such potential replacements exist, the prices sought can vary widely. In the case of equipment made to the owner's own design there may be no possibility of a second-hand market.

Therefore practical attempts to introduce CCA require estimates of the current replacement cost of *new* equivalent assets and then deduct the equivalent of 'accumulated depreciation' from these replacement costs. 'Accumulated depreciation' is in inverted commas because the amount will not have 'accumulated' from charges to the Income Statement nor is it 'depreciation' under the normal definition of the spreading of an incurred cost. Unfortunately the advocates of CCA have not so far developed an adequate vocabulary to cover the concepts that they wish to introduce. This lack of a vocabulary - and the wish to use words that are already in common use with quite different definitions - is one reason why these advocates have been somewhat unsuccessful but it must not stop us from examining what is a useful system of accounting.

To distinguish the concept of 'Depreciation on Replacement Cost' separate from standard Depreciation it would be better to call it by another name. 'Replaciation', for example, would be a good word to suggest the new meaning and that is what we will call it here. Even if the proportion of the replacement cost deducted on CCA Balance Sheets has not been accumulated, it still represents the proportion of the original asset which is estimated to have been 'used' at the Balance Sheet date. Thus the nature of the 'Accumulated Depreciation' on CCA Balance Sheets would be clearer if it is termed 'Used Replaciation'.

Example

Rho plc purchased a fork lift truck for £11,000 on 12.4.2000. The management of the company reckon that fork lift trucks have a life of approximately 10 years and they have a negligible residual value. Therefore, in their raw Historic Cost accounts, they depreciate such items by 10% pa straight line with a full year's charge in the year of purchase and none in the year of disposal. The company's accounting year end is 31st December. On 15.4.00 an index based on the cost of fork lift trucks was 110, on 31.12.04 it was 200 and by 31.12.05 it had grown to 250. (An index number for 15.4.00 can be considered to cover prices throughout that month.)

On the raw Historic Cost Balance Sheets the figures would appear as follows :

as at	31.12.04	31.12.05
	£	£
Cost	11,000	11,000
Accumulated Depreciation	5,500	6,600
Net Book Value	5,500	4,400

Modern Accounting 2

The replacement cost of a new fork lift truck on 31.12.04 can be estimated using the index as

$$11{,}000 \times \frac{200}{110} = £20{,}000$$

At 31.12.04 five years of the ten year life has been used. Thus the Used Replaciation amounts to

$$20{,}000 \times \frac{5}{10} = £10{,}000$$

The replacement cost of a new fork lift truck on 31.12.05 can be estimated using the index at

$$11{,}000 \times \frac{250}{110} = £25{,}000$$

At 31.12.05 six years of the ten year life has been used. Thus the Used Replaciation amounts to

$$25{,}000 \times \frac{6}{10} = £15{,}000$$

On the CCA Balance Sheets the figures would appear as follows:

as at	31.12.04	31.12.05
	£	£
Replacement Cost	20,000	25,000
Used Replaciation	10,000	15,000
CCA Book Value	10,000	10,000

If the Balance Sheet on 31.12.04 was the first CCA Balance Sheet, then the entries required to convert Cost to Replacement Cost and Accumulated Depreciation to Used Replaciation would be:

£ £
Debit Cost/Replacement Cost 9,000 Credit Current Cost Reserve 9,000
(£9,000 is the difference between cost and replacement cost at 31.12.04.)

Debit Current Cost Reserve 4,500 Credit Dep'n/Replaciation 4,500
(£4,500 is the difference between accumulated depreciation and used replaciation at 31.12.04.)

Both these adjustments to the Current Cost Reserve would be treated as affecting the Unrealised Holding Gains.

Current Cost Accounting

Most people assume that, if 2004 was the first CCA Balance Sheet, there should be some neat way of reconciling subsequent Balance Sheets with this 'opening position'. Unfortunately CCA Balance Sheets are expressed in prices ruling at their individual dates and they are not comparable one with another. Thus there need be no relationship between the Used Replaciation shown in the Balance Sheet on 31.12.04, the Replaciation charged in the 2005 CCA Income Statement and the Used Replaciation shown in the Balance Sheet at the end of that year.

In the case of Rho plc, assume that the replaciation charged in the CCA Income Statement on this fork lift truck for the year to 31st December 2005 was £2,300. (This is above 10% of the replacement cost at the start of the year and below 10% of the replacement cost at the end of the year and it cannot be calculated from the data so far given. The calculation will be explained on page 70.) The entries required to adjust the CCA Balances from 31.12.04 to 31.12.05 are:

	£		£
Debit CCA Income Statement	2,300	*Credit Used Replaciation*	2,300

(The charge to the Income Statement. Note that this does not directly affect the Current Cost Reserve. It may be made in two stages - normal historic depreciation plus a 'depreciation adjustment' - see pages 70/1)

Debit Replacement Cost	5,000	*Credit Current Cost Reserve*	5,000

(The increase in the Replacement Cost of new trucks over the year.)

Debit Current Cost Reserve	2,700	*Credit Used Replaciation*	2,700

(The difference between the Used Replaciation at the end and start of the year less the charge in the CCA Income Statement. Sometimes this figure (of £2,700) is called 'Backlog Depreciation on Replacement Cost'. It would be less confusing to call it 'Backlog Replaciation'.)

Once again all the entries to the Current Cost Reserve have affected *Un*realised Holding Gains.

On 28.2.06 the fork lift truck was sold for net proceeds of £5,200. It is recognised that, since the company is not a trader in used fork lifts, these proceeds are probably well below the replacement cost of the asset at the date of disposal. The CCA book value at 31.12.05 is considered to be a better indication of the replacement cost at the date of disposal.

The loss on disposal for the CCA Income Statement will be the difference between the replacement cost at the date of disposal (assumed to be CCA book value at 31.12.05 which is £10,000) and the net proceeds (£5,200). Thus, in this case, the CCA loss on disposal will be £4,800 (whereas, in the raw Historic Cost Profit and Loss Account, the profit on disposal is £800).

Within the Current Cost Reserve the accumulated holding gain on this asset is no longer unrealised. It is possible to calculate the accumulated holding gain by summing the different entries made over the life of the asset but it easier to subtract the raw Historic Cost Net Book Value from the CCA Book Value at the date of disposal. In this case £10,000 - 4,400 = £5,600. £5,600 should be added to realised gains and subtracted from unrealised gains within the Current Cost Reserve. The double entries required on this disposal will be :

	£		£
Debit Cash Book	5,200	Credit Disposal of Fork Lift	5,200

(Banking the proceeds on disposal.)

	£		£
Debit Disposal of Fork Lift	25,000	Credit Repl't Cost - Fork	25,000
Debit Used Replac'n - Fork LT	15,000	Credit Disposal of Fork Lift	15,000

(Writing off the CCA Balances relating to this asset.)

	£		£
Debit CCA P & L	4,800	Credit Disposal of Fork Lift	4,800

(Posting the final loss on the Disposal Account to the CCA Income Statement.)

(iii) CCA Balance Sheets : Stocks

As with other tangible assets, stocks should be shown at Deprival Value (Current Cost). Obsolete stock and very unsuccessful purchases will have to be shown at Net Realisable Value but most stocks will have a Deprival Value that is Replacement Cost. Businesses with many suppliers may have to use a specific index to estimate Replacement Cost at the Balance Sheet date but, since most businesses regularly re-order the same lines, they are more likely (than with Fixed Assets) to be able to identify accurately individual price changes. So a Main Dealer for a single motor manufacturer ought to have the accurate replacement cost information to hand for each item in stock whereas a Department Store carrying many lines from many suppliers may have to use an index. Most manufacturers can accurately identify replacement costs for the high value items of stock and may use a specific index for the rest.

Current Cost Accounting

Example

Theta Ltd holds stock the volume of which has always been purchased evenly over the previous 3 months. At 31.12.99 Theta held stock with a FIFO raw historic cost of £30,000 and at 31.12.2000 Theta held stock with a FIFO raw historic cost of £40,000. A specific index based on items in Theta's stock showed the following:

Date		Date	
15.10.99	112	15.10.2000	124
15.11.99	112	15.11.2000	125
15.12.99	114	15.12.2000	127
15.1.2000	116	15.1.2001	127

The average index for the 3 months to 31.12.99 is $(112+112+114)/3 = 112.67$. The average index for the 3 months a year later is $(124+125+127)/3 = 125.33$. The index at 31.12.99 is $(114+116)/2 = 115$ and the index a year later is $(127+127)/2 = 127$. Thus the replacement cost of stock at 31.12.99 will be

$$30{,}000 \times \frac{115}{112.67} = £30{,}620$$

and the replacement cost of stock a year later will be

$$40{,}000 \times \frac{127}{125.33} = £40{,}533$$

The double entry required to show stock at replacement cost on Balance Sheets will be to Debit Stock and Credit the Current Cost Reserve with the difference between the Replacement and Historic Cost at the end of the year (after the income statement has been prepared) and then to reverse that entry at the start of the next year. In this case on 31.12.99:

		£		£
Debit Stock		620	*Credit Current Cost Reserve*	620

and on 1.1.00:

	£		£
Debit Current Cost Reserve	620	*Credit Stock*	620

on 31.12.00:

	£		£
Debit Stock	533	*Credit Current Cost Reserve*	533

and on 1.1.01:

	£		£
Debit Current Cost Reserve	533	*Credit Stock*	533

Modern Accounting 2

CCA Balance Sheets : Monetary Assets and Liabilities

Monetary Assets such as Debtors, Bank Balances and Cash need no adjustment for CCA Balance Sheets nor do Monetary Liabilities such as creditors.

CCA Balance Sheets : Current Cost Reserve

The entries affecting the Current Cost Reserve that have been covered so far in this Chapter have been those that directly affect other items in the Balance Sheet. There are other entries between the Current Cost Reserve and the CCA Income Statement but these are covered on pages 77 and 78.

Try to answer the following question before looking at the answer (which is at the end of this chapter).

Question 3.2 (Answer 3.2 is on page 93)

The following Raw Historic Cost Balance Sheets have been prepared for Tau Ltd which has not yet produced any CCA Accounts :

As at	31.12.99	31.12.00
	£	£
Fixed Assets		
Cost	56,000	78,000
Accumulated Depreciation	23,000	45,000
	33,000	33,000
Current Assets		
Stock	16,000	20,000
Debtors	20,000	22,000
Bank	3,000	2,000
	39,000	44,000
less Creditors due within 1 year	15,000	14,000
Net Current Assets	24,000	30,000
	57,000	63,000
Share Capital	10,000	10,000
Revenue Reserves	47,000	53,000
	57,000	63,000

An analysis of Fixed Assets shows the following :

As at	31.12.99 Cost	31.12.99 Acc Depn	31.12.00 Cost	31.12.00 Acc Depn
Date of Purchase :	£	£	£	£
May 92	12,000	8,000	10,000	9,000
Oct 94	8,000	5,000	4,000	3,000
Jan 96	26,000	8,000	26,000	18,000
Jun 99	10,000	2,000	10,000	8,000
Mar 00			28,000	7,000
	56,000	23,000	78,000	45,000

Two disposals of Fixed Assets were made during the year. Items purchased in May 1992 at a cost of £2,000 were sold as were items purchased in October 1994 at a cost of £4,000.

Stocks at the start and end of the year to 31 December 2000 had been purchased evenly over the previous two months.

Specific price indexes for Stock and Fixed Assets give the following readings :

Date	Stock	Fixed Assets	Date	Stock	Fixed Assets
15.5.92	101	102	15.1.00	106	139
15.10.94	103	112	15.3.00	100	143
15.1.96	105	120	15.11.00	112	151
15.6.99	99	134	15.12.00	112	155
15.11.99	105	137	15.1.01	114	160
15.12.99	106	137			

REQUIRED :   CCA Balance Sheets for 31 December 1999 and 31 December 2000. Do not attempt to analyse reserves or show a separate Current Cost Reserve.

CCA Income Statements

The general principle behind CCA calculations of 'earnings' is that the deprival value of the resources being consumed should be charged against the revenue generated by their consumption. Once again, in practice, deprival value is almost always assumed to be replacement cost and this means that it is prices of expenses at the date of sale that should affect results and *not* prices at the date at which expenses were purchased. The two areas which are normally most affected are (1) Depreciation or Replacation of Fixed Assets and (2) Stocks and their impact on the Cost of Sales.

(ii) CCA Income Statements : Depreciation

If (a) sales (in terms of physical units of product) were made on an even basis throughout the year and (b) no significant purchases or sales of Fixed Assets were made during the year, then replaciation could be charged to the CCA Income Statement as a proportion of the Replacement Costs of Fixed Assets *on average* during the year. If a specific index is going to be used, this requires averaging the 12 index numbers for the mid-point of each month of the year.

The conditions relating to the even pattern of sales and the stability of Fixed Assets are rarely met completely. Strictly if depreciation is to allocate costs in proportion to benefits, the raw Historic Cost Depreciation should be weighted according to the seasonal pattern of Sales (in physical units). In theory, each month's raw Historic Cost Depreciation would reflect the Fixed Assets in use in that month and each month's Depreciation would be indexed to Replaciation at price levels for that particular month. This is rarely considered as a practical proposal and, not only is it assumed that Replaciation can be charged at average price levels during the year, but where price increases are moderate it is not unusual for price levels at the end of the year to be used as a surrogate for average price levels during the year. This use of a surrogate does seem to be an unnecessary laziness because it is hardly difficult to add 12 index numbers together and divide the total by 12 to produce a simple average.

The difference between Replaciation and the Depreciation charged in raw Historic Cost Accounts is frequently called the 'Depreciation Adjustment' and commonly abbreviated to 'DA'. Several proposals for CCA Accounts charge standard raw Historic Cost Depreciation and then make a second charge for the 'Depreciation Adjustment'. The two charges together are, in effect, Replaciation (or 'Depreciation on Replacement Cost') charged at average price levels during the accounting year.

Used Replaciation can be calculated from the Accumulated Depreciation figures by indexing them in the same way as Historic Cost is indexed up to Replacement Cost.

Example
During the year to 30th June 2000 Iota Ltd charged £67,000 Depreciation in the company's raw historic cost accounts. This has been analysed as follows :

	£
Depreciation on Assets purchased in	
October 1995	15,000
November 1997	27,000
July 1999	25,000
	67,000

A Specific Price Index based on the Fixed Assets held by Iota showed the following :

Date	Index	Date	Index
15.10.95	120	15.7.99	145
15.11.97	135	Average for year to 30.6.00	150

Replaciation can be calculated as follows :

Date of Purchase	Depreciation £	Index Factor	Replaciation £
Oct 1995	15,000	150/120	18,750
Nov 1997	27,000	150/135	30,000
Jul 1999	25,000	150/145	25,862
	67,000		74,612

Thus, in the CCA Income Statement, £74,612 should be charged as Replaciation. This could be charged in two parts - £67,000 as Depreciation and £7,612 as 'Depreciation Adjustment'. (This use of a 'Depreciation Adjustment' is sadly half-hearted and one reason why the professional proposals incorporating it have not attracted sufficient support.) Note that Replaciation charged in a CCA Income Statement will not necessarily reconcile with Used Replaciation on CCA Balance Sheets because the Opening Balance Sheet will be in replacement costs at the start of the year and the Closing Balance Sheet will be in replacement costs at the *end* of the year.

Modern Accounting 2

CCA Income Statements : Disposal of Fixed Assets

The 'book value' of Fixed Assets in a CCA Balance Sheet will normally differ from that in a Historic Cost Balance Sheet and so the surplus or loss on disposal will normally also differ. In theory the replacement cost at the actual point of disposal should be charged against the proceeds but, in practice, this replacement cost will usually be assumed to be the same as the book value on the last CCA Balance Sheet before the disposal.

Example of a Disposal of Plant :

Chaotic Manufacturing plc bought a widget inserter for £40,000 on 15.1.95 and sold it for £4,000 on 15.3.00. They depreciate all plant and machinery by 10% pa straight line charging a full year's depreciation in the year of purchase and none in the year of disposal. They make up their accounts to 30th June in each year. The specific index used by the company to estimate the replacement cost of plant in its CCA Accounts read 110 on 15.1.95 and 200 on 30.6.99.

	£
Historic Cost - Loss on Sale :	
Cost	40,000
Accumulated Depreciation :	
5 accounting years '95, '96, '97, '98 and '99	
50% of cost	20,000
Net Book Value	20,000
Proceeds	4,000
Loss on Sale	16,000

CCA - Loss on Sale - Based on Preceding Balance Sheet Values :

Replacement Cost 40,000 X $\frac{200}{110}$ = 72,727

Used Replaciation (50% as above)	36,364
	36,363
Proceeds	4,000
Loss on CCA Book Value	32,363

If a 'Depreciation Adjustment' is going to be used - rather than straight-forwardly charging replaciation - then the same approach will be used with surpluses and losses on disposal of Fixed Assets. Charge the Historic Cost Loss on Disposal of £16,000 to the CCA Income Statement and then add the difference between that and the Loss on CCA Book Value (32,363 - 16,000 = 16,363) to the 'Depreciation Adjustment'.

(iii) CCA Income Statements : Stocks and The Cost of Sales

The following is a typical Trading Account :

	£000	£000
Sales		12,000
Opening Stock	1,500	
Purchases	6,400	
	7,900	
less Closing Stock	1,700	
Historic Cost of Sales		6,200
Gross Profit		5,800

Under CCA the Historic Cost of Sales must become the cost of replacing items at the date on which they are sold. We will assume that the volume of sales and the volume of purchases both took place evenly throughout the year and thus both could be assumed to take place at average price levels during the year. The two figures in this trading account that cannot have taken place at average price levels are (a) Opening Stock and (b) Closing Stock. If both stock figures were restated at average price levels, then the Historic Cost of Sales would become the *Replacement* Cost of Sales - that is the cost of replacing goods at the date of sale. A specific price index based on the cost of items held in stock gives the following readings :

	Index
At the date of purchase of Opening Stock	130
At the date of purchase of Closing Stock	200
On Average for the year	150

Opening Stock restated to average price levels becomes

$1,500 \times \frac{150}{130} = 1,731$ (in £000)

Closing Stock restated to average price levels becomes

$1,700 \times \frac{150}{200} = 1,275$ (in £000)

Thus the original trading account converted into average price levels appears as follows :

Modern Accounting 2

	£000		£000
Sales			12,000
Opening Stock (av prices)	1,731		
Purchases	6,400		
	8,131		
less Closing Stock (av prices)	1,275		
Replacement Cost of Sales			6,856
Gross Profit over cost of replacing sales			5,144

The difference between the raw Historic Cost of Sales and the Replacement Cost of Sales is frequently called the 'Cost of Sales Adjustment' and commonly abbreviated to 'COSA'. If it can be assumed that Sales and Purchase volumes were both constant throughout the year, then the formula for COSA is

$$O \times \frac{I_a}{I_o} - C \times \frac{I_a}{I_c} - (O - C)$$

where O is FIFO Historic Cost Opening Stock
C is FIFO Historic Cost Closing Stock
I_a is the Specific Index on average during the year
I_o is the Specific Index on average during the purchase period for opening stock
I_c is the Specific Index on average during the purchase period for closing stock

In this case the Historic Cost of Sales was 6,200 (£000) and the Replacement Cost of Sales was 6,856 (£000). COSA will be the difference between the two or 656 (in £000). Substituting in the formula gives

$$1,500 \times \frac{150}{130} - 1,700 \times \frac{150}{200} - (1,500 - 1,700) = 656 \; (\text{£000})$$

COSA for a Seasonal Business

However it is rare for the volume of sales and purchases to be approximately constant throughout the year because almost all businesses are strongly seasonal affected by holidays at Christmas, Easter and August and changing weather between the months. Some large UK retail chains make 50% of their annual gross profit in a 6 week period before Christmas. Most shops attempt to keep their premises busy by stocking different lines in different seasons.

Manufacturers may try to make complementary products - one UK manufacturer of wheel-barrows stamps out shelving systems during the slack months for garden tools.

Many businesses deliberately choose accounting year-ends during their slackest period because that is the time when stocks are lowest, there are fewest half-complete transactions and it is easiest to prepare the accounts. Many publicly quoted companies make up their accounts to 31st December or 31st March and neither date is likely to give a stock figure which is representative of average stocks during the year. Thus using the formula (above) to calculate COSA is normally inaccurate - it may give a figure that is less than 10% of the true figure.

To produce an accurate COSA for most businesses, information on both selling and purchase prices is needed. Many manufacturers can isolate the valuable purchase and wage costs and use a general index on the many less important items. With the important costs there may only have been one or two price changes in the year. Where certain lines are sold or purchased only in certain months, these will have to be treated separately from the rest of the business.

Example
In the year to 30th September 2001 Upsilon plc made the following Purchases and Sales :

	Index based on Purchase Prices	Purchases £m	Sales £m
Oct	112	150	10
Nov	113	10	5
Dec	115	8	9
Jan	117	7	8
Feb	120	6	11
Mar	125	5	12
Apr	126	6	13
May	130	7	14
Jun	133	8	15
Jul	136	10	17
Aug	140	11	200
Sep	141	1	400
		__229__	__714__

Modern Accounting 2

Selling prices were constant from October 1st 2000 to May 31st 2001 when they increased by 35%. They then remained constant from 1st June until the end of the accounting year. FIFO Opening Stock had a historic cost of £2m and was purchased when the index was 106. FIFO Closing Stock had a historic cost of £3m and was purchased when the index was 140. The raw Historic Cost Trading Account is as follows :

	£m	£m
Sales		714
Opening Stock	2	
Purchases	229	
	231	
less Closing Stock	3	
Historic Cost of Sales		228
Gross Profit		486

If the formula on page 74 were to be used to estimate COSA, the following calculations would be made :

Average Purchase Price Index :
(112+113+115+117+120+125+126+130+133+136+140+141)/12
= 125.67

COSA under the formula on page 71 :

$2 \times \dfrac{125.67}{106} - 3 \times \dfrac{125.67}{140} - (2 - 3) = 0.678$ (£m)

To work out an accurate COSA the *volumes* of Sales and Purchases in each month need to be calculated. We have details of the *values* and we have details of price movements. To calculate volumes divide the values by unit prices (or by a price index) as in the following table :

Column	a	b	c	d	b/a	d/c
Month	Index based on Purchase Prices	Purchases in £m	Index based on Sales Prices	Sales in £m	Purchase Volume units	Sales Volume units
Oct	112	150	100	10	1.3393	0.1000
Nov	113	10	100	5	0.0885	0.0500
Dec	115	8	100	9	0.0696	0.0900
Jan	117	7	100	8	0.0598	0.0800
Feb	120	6	100	11	0.0500	0.1100
Mar	125	5	100	12	0.0400	0.1200
Apr	126	6	100	13	0.0476	0.1300
May	130	7	100	14	0.0538	0.1400
Jun	133	8	135	15	0.0602	0.1111
Jul	136	10	135	17	0.0735	0.1259
Aug	140	11	135	200	0.0786	1.4815
Sep	141	1	135	400	0.0071	2.9630
		229		714	1.9680	5.5015
Open Stock	106	2			0.0189	
		231			1.9869	
Close Stock	140	3			0.0214	
		228			1.9655	

This table shows that 5.5015 'Sales Volume Units' (SVU) and 1.9655 'Purchase Volume Units' (PVU) were sold in this year. What are these 'volume units'? If sales had a value of £100 and each unit had a selling price of £2, then logically a volume of 50 units were sold. However this logic depends on knowing a unit selling price (or unit purchase price) - £2 per unit - and, in this case and in many practical circumstances, we can construct a price index but we do not have easy access to unit prices because the business does not trade in just one line of goods. We have to make do with 'volume units' which give us a way of estimating volume movements but would need further analysis into individual lines of goods before they could be expressed in boxes, kilos or cubic centimetres.

If 1.9655 PVU were used in the sale of 5.5015 SVU in this year, then 1.9655/5.5015 = 0.357266 PVUs were used in the sale of one SVU. From this figure we can calculate the Replacement Cost of Sales.

If the Sales for each month in SVU are multiplied by 0.357266, we can obtain the Sales for each month in PVU. The original PVU

Modern Accounting 2

figures were obtained by *dividing* values by the relevant purchase price indexes and so it must be possible to get back to values by *multiplying* by the relevant purchase price index numbers. If the Sales in PVU for each month are multiplied by the Purchase Price Index for that month, the result should be the Replacement Cost of Sales for that month.

Column	a	b	c	d
		a X 0.357266		b X c
	Sales	Sales	Purchase	Replacement
	in SVU	in PVU	Price	cost of
Month			Index	sales
Oct	0.1000	0.0357	112	3.9984
Nov	0.0500	0.0179	113	2.0227
Dec	0.0900	0.0322	115	3.7030
Jan	0.0800	0.0286	117	3.3462
Feb	0.1100	0.0393	120	4.7160
Mar	0.1200	0.0429	125	5.3625
Apr	0.1300	0.0464	126	5.8464
May	0.1400	0.0500	130	6.5000
Jun	0.1111	0.0397	133	5.2801
Jul	0.1259	0.0450	136	6.1200
Aug	1.4815	0.5293	140	74.1020
Sep	2.9630	1.0586	141	149.2626
	5.5015	1.9656		270.2599

If the Replacement Cost of Sales for the whole year is £m270.2599 (as at the bottom right of the last table) and the Historic Cost of Sales is £m228 (as in the raw Historic Cost account on page 76), then the COSA = 270.2599 - 228 = £m42.2599.

This is over 62 times the estimated COSA obtained by using the formula based solely on end-year stocks but that is because this example had very low end-year stocks compared with the stocks held during the year. Most businesses will find that the formula gives a gross underestimate of COSA but the extent of the underestimate will not be as extreme as in this example.

One key assumption behind the use of SVU and PVU is that the different lines of goods included in the figures, are purchased and sold with approximately the same seasonality. The manufacturer of both wheelbarrows and shelving systems will have to calculate two separate COSAs because the sales and production of each of these lines follow different patterns over the year. A second key assumption is that purchase prices of the different lines of goods follow approximately the same pattern throughout the year. A third key assumption is that selling prices of the different lines of goods follow approximately the same pattern throughout the year. Many lines carried in the same business have common elements and use the same resources and so the second and third assumptions are more likely to be met than the first.

The tables on the previous two pages are ideally suited to computer spreadsheets. In most businesses the data should not be difficult to collect. Indeed if it is difficult to collect, there must be some doubt as to the competence of the current management and instituting systems to collect the information for COSA calculations may encourage managers to use selling price, cost price and stock information to take more rational decisions.

CCA Income Statements : Double Entry

As was indicated for CCA Balance Sheets, the double entry for Replaciation (or Depreciation plus the Depreciation Adjustment) is to Debit the CCA Income Statement and Credit Used Replaciation (which will be deducted from Fixed Assets on the Balance Sheet). Sometimes the Depreciation Adjustment is credited to the Current Cost Reserve but, if this is done, it will just increase the 'backlog depreciation' that has to be debited to the Current Cost Reserve.

The double entry for COSA is Debit the CCA Income Statement and Credit the Current Cost Reserve with the value of the Cost of Sales Adjustment.

The Current Cost Reserve

In exam questions (and in practice) it is probably best to concentrate on the figures required for assets on a CCA Balance Sheet and as adjustments in a CCA Income Statement letting the Current Cost Reserve act as a 'reservoir' absorbing the changes required by the other figures. Trying to calculate the Current Cost Reserve and then making the other figures fit is unlikely to be successful. The T account on the next page is an example of how the Current Cost Reserve adjustments for a year might be shown :

Modern Accounting 2

Current Cost Reserve

	£		£
1.1.00 Stock (Difference v Cost and Replacement Cost of Opening Stock)	800	1.1.00 Balance b/f	20,500
		31.12.00 Replacement Cost of Fixed Assets (Increase in the Replacement Cost of New Fixed Assets Over the Year)	5,300
31.12.00 Used Replaciation (Backlog Replaciation)	2,100		
		31.12.00 CCA Income Statement - COSA	1,400
31.12.00 Balance c/f	25,200	31.12.00 Stock (Difference v Cost and Replacement Cost of Closing Stock)	900
	__28,100__		__28,100__

CCA Income Statements : Professional Proposed Formats

New proposals (if any) will come from the Accounting Standards Board (ASB). In the past the Accounting Standards Committee (ASC) and their predecessors, the Accounting Standards Steering Committee (ASSC), made a number of similar proposals for CCA Income Statement formats. This adaption from a 1986 document[5] is representative :

"

	£	£
Historic Cost Operating Profits		32,314,567
Depreciation Adjustment	2,154,789	
Cost of Sales Adjustment	3,543,758	
Total current cost operating adjustments		5,698,547
Earnings attributable to ordinary shareholders adjusted for the effects of price changes		__26,616,020__

The total current cost operating adjustments represent the aggregate amount required to be set aside out of the reported historical cost profit to compensate for the effects of specific price changes on the company's activities during the year. It is made up of additional amounts required to replace fixed assets and stock consumed during the year (i.e. the depreciation and cost of sales adjustments)."

Current Cost Accounting

Proposals earlier than 1986 had used terms such as 'Current Cost Operating Profit' and this unfortunate use of the term *profit*, which almost all business people use to mean historic cost profit, did not lead to a fruitful debate. The term *earnings* is used above; another word that has been used to separate this statistic from its cousins with different definitions is *surplus*.

CCA Income Statements : Rent on Leasehold Premises

The replacement cost of most expenses at the date of consumption - apart from stock and depreciation - will be the same as their historic cost. Expenses such as Electricity and Telephone are normally charged and paid for close to the date at which they are consumed. However rent payable can be an exception because many businesses operate under leases with 5 year upward-only rent reviews. When prices are rising, this means that the rent in the first two years of the five year period can be difficult for the business to meet whereas the rent of the last two years is a minor expense.

If no account is taken of this, the CCA Earnings of any one year may be a poor indicator of 'future maintainable earnings' and - as is discussed in the next Chapter - some argue that this is a major advantage of CCA. Few proposals for introducing CCA have tackled this problem. Any solution would involve redistributing the rent charge between the years in order that less was charged in the early years and more in the later years. This would mean that an additional asset (prepayment) would appear on Balance Sheets during the initial four years of the five year period. For retail groups this might be significant and controversial.

Try to answer the following questions before looking at the answers (which are at the end of this chapter).

Question 3.3 (Answer 3.3 is on page 94)

Opening Stock cost £45,000 when the specific index based on stock prices was 112. Closing Stock cost £53,000 when the same specific index was 132. An average of this specific index for the year was 127.

REQUIRED : Estimate COSA on the basis of the information above and state any assumptions that you need to make.

Question 3.4 (Answer 3.4 is on page 95)

Nu Ltd has not yet produced its first set of CCA figures. Its raw historic cost accounts for the year to 30th June 2000 appear as follows:

Profit and Loss Account for the year to 30th June 2000

	£	£
Sales		550,000
Opening Stock	25,000	
Purchases	230,000	
	255,000	
less Closing Stock	30,000	
Cost of Sales		225,000
Gross Profit		325,000
General Expenses	205,000	
Loss on sale of Fixed Asset	5,000	
Depreciation	52,000	
		262,000
Net Operating Profit before Taxation		63,000
Taxation		23,000
Profit for the year after taxation		40,000
Dividends :		
Paid	5,000	
Proposed	6,000	
		11,000
Unappropriated Profit for the year		29,000

Balance Sheets as at

	30.6.99	30.6.00
Fixed Assets	£	£
Cost	610,000	675,000
Depreciation	350,000	380,000
Net Book Value	260,000	295,000
Current Assets		
Stock	25,000	30,000
Debtors	55,000	49,000
Bank	2,000	-
	82,000	79,000
less Creditors :		
Amounts due within one year	30,000	33,000
Net Current Assets	52,000	46,000
	312,000	341,000

Current Cost Accounting

	£	£
Share Capital	20,000	20,000
Revenue Reserves	<u>292,000</u>	<u>321,000</u>
	<u>312,000</u>	<u>341,000</u>

Analysis of <u>Cost</u> of Fixed Assets :

Purchased on	Price Index based on Fixed Assets	Cost at 30.6.99 £	Cost of Disposal £	Cost at 30.6.00 £
Jan 96	113	150,000	35,000	115,000
Oct 97	125	160,000		160,000
Mar 99	143	300,000		300,000
30.6.99	149			
Jul 99	151			100,000
30.6.00	160			
Avg for year	155	<u>610,000</u>	<u>35,000</u>	<u>675,000</u>

Analysis of <u>Accumulated Depreciation</u> on Fixed Assets

Purchased on	Acc Depn 30.6.99 £	Charged in year £	Acc Depn on Disposals £	Acc Depn 30.6.00 £
Jan 96	110,000	6,000	22,000	94,000
Oct 97	90,000	11,000		101,000
Mar 99	150,000	25,000		175,000
Jul 99		10,000		10,000
	<u>350,000</u>	<u>52,000</u>	<u>22,000</u>	<u>380,000</u>

Index based on Prices of Items held in Stock :

At date of purchase of Stock held at 30.6.99	110
30.6.99	120
On average over year to 30.6.00	140
At date of purchase of Stock held at 30.6.00	150
30.6.00	160

Assume that the replacement cost of the Fixed Assets disposed of in the year was the same at the date of disposal as shown on the previous CCA Balance Sheet. Assume that the volume of Sales and Purchases was even throughout the year.

REQUIRED : CCA Balance Sheets at 30 June 1999 and 2000 and a CCA Income Statement for the year to 30 June 2000.

Question 3.5 (Answer 3.5 is on page 98)

Pi Ltd already produces CCA figures. Its available accounts for the year to 30th September 2000 appear as follows:

<u>Profit and Loss Account</u> for the year to 30th September 2000

	Historic Cost £	Historic Cost £
Sales		890,000
Opening Stock	40,000	
Purchases	670,000	
	710,000	
less Closing Stock	50,000	
Cost of Sales		660,000
Gross Profit		230,000
General Expenses	81,000	
(Profit) on sale of Fixed Asset	(1,000)	
Depreciation	35,000	
		115,000
Net Operating Profit before Taxation		115,000
Taxation		53,000
Profit for the year after taxation		62,000
Dividends : Paid		27,000
Unappropriated Profit for the year		35,000

	CCA	Historic Cost
<u>Balance Sheets</u> as at	30.9.99	30.9.00
	£	£
Fixed Assets		
Replacement Cost/Cost	710,000	362,000
Replaciation/Depreciation	345,000	191,000
	365,000	171,000
Current Assets		
Stock at Rep Cost/Cost	42,000	50,000
Debtors	75,000	105,000
Bank	359	20,000
	117,359	175,000
less Creditors :		
Amounts due within one year	40,000	13,000
Net Current Assets	77,359	162,000
	442,359	333,000

Current Cost Accounting

	£	£
Share Capital	40,000	40,000
Current Cost Reserve	352,000	
Revenue Reserves	50,359	293,000
	442,359	333,000

Analysis of <u>Cost</u> of Fixed Assets :

Purchased on	Price Index based on Fixed Assets	Cost at 30.9.99 £	Cost of Disposal £	Cost at 30.9.00 £
Jan 95	110	269,000		269,000
May 97	160	149,680	100,680	49,000
30.9.99	210			
Dec 99	220			44,000
30.9.00	230			
Avg for year	224	418,680	100,680	362,000

Analysis of <u>Accumulated Depreciation</u> on Fixed Assets

Purchased on	Acc Depn 30.9.99 £	Charged in year £	Acc Depn on Disposals £	Acc Depn 30.9.00 £
Jan 97	147,000	27,000		174,000
May 97	49,039	4,000	40,039	13,000
Dec 99		4,000		4,000
	196,039	35,000	40,039	191,000

Index based on Prices of Items held in Stock :

At date of purchase of Stock held at 30.9.99	120
30.9.99	126
On average over year to 30.9.00	132
At date of purchase of Stock held at 30.9.00	134
30.9.00	140

Assume that the replacement cost of the Fixed Assets disposed of in the year was the same at the date of disposal as shown on the previous CCA Balance Sheet. Assume that the volume of Sales and Purchases was even throughout the year.

REQUIRED : CCA Balance Sheet at 30 September 2000 and a CCA Income Statement for the year to the same date.

Modern Accounting 2

Question 3.6 (No Answer to this Question has been Included in This Book)

Lambda Ltd already produces CCA figures. Its available accounts for the year to 31st December 2000 appear as follows:

Profit and Loss Account for the year to 31st December 2000

	Historic Cost £000	Historic Cost £000
Sales		3,354
Opening Stock	1,457	
Purchases	1,629	
	3,086	
less Closing Stock	1,123	
Cost of Sales		1,963
Gross Profit		1,391
General Expenses	45	
Depreciation	810	
		855
Net Operating Profit		536

	CCA	Historic Cost
Balance Sheets as at	31.12.99	31.12.00
Fixed Assets	£000	£000
Replacement Cost/Cost	7,235	8,101
Replaciation/Depreciation	2,617	2,971
	4,618	5,130
Current Assets		
Stock at Rep Cost/Cost	1,515	1,123
Debtors	588	595
Bank	361	5
	2,464	1,723
less Creditors :		
Amounts due within one year	231	252
Net Current Assets	2,233	1,471
	6,851	6,601
Share Capital	500	500
Current Cost Reserve	5,060	
Revenue Reserves	1,291	6,101
	6,966	6,601

Current Cost Accounting

Analysis of Cost of Fixed Assets :

Purchased on	Price Index based on Fixed Assets	Cost at 31.12.99 £000	Cost at 31.12.00 £000
Jul 96	130	4,754	4,754
Jan 98	150	1,297	1,297
31.12.99	160		
Sep 00	165		2,050
31.12.00	170		
Avg for year	163	6,051	8,101

Analysis of Accumulated Depreciation on Fixed Assets

Purchased on	Acc Depn 31.12.99 £000	Charged in year £000	Acc Depn 31.12.00 £000
Jul 96	1,902	475	2,377
Jan 98	259	130	389
Sep 00		205	205
	2,161	810	2,971

Index based on Prices of Items held in Stock :
At date of purchase of Stock held at 31.12.99	125
31.12.99	130
On average over year to 31.12.00	140
At date of purchase of Stock held at 31.12.00	145
31.12.00	150

Assume that the volume of Sales and Purchases was even throughout the year.

REQUIRED : A CCA Balance Sheet at 31 December 2000 and a CCA Income Statement for the year to the same date.

Question 3.7 (Answer 3.7 is on page 101)

In the year to 31st March 2001 Theta plc made the following Purchases and Sales :

	Index based on Purchase Prices	Purchases £m	Sales £m
1.4.00 - 30.6.00	121	20	4
1.7.00 - 30.9.00	135	15	7
1.10.00 - 31.12.00	150	3	9
1.1.01 - 31.3.01	180	1	58
		39	78

Selling prices were constant from April 1st 2000 to September 30st 2000 when they increased by 50%. They then remained constant from 1st October until the end of the accounting year. FIFO Opening Stock had a historic cost of £12m and was purchased when the index was 110. FIFO Closing Stock had a historic cost of £15m and was purchased when the index was 140.

REQUIRED : Calculate a COSA taking account of the seasonality of this business with as much accuracy as is possible from the data provided.

The Monetary Working Capital Adjustment (MWCA)

Some proponents of CCA contend that "monetary working capital is for many companies an integral part of the net operating assets and is as much involved in the day to day operating activities as stock. As such, a given level of monetary working capital will be held in order to sustain a given level of operating capacity."[6] This argument leads them to deduct a further adjustment from the Income Statement to take account of the funds required to maintain a given level of Monetary Working Capital when prices rise.

However, even among those who would accept the last paragraph, there are disputes as to what should be included in Monetary Working Capital and how (a) negative Monetary Working Capital and (b) falling prices should be handled. Monetary Working Capital

(MWC) must start with Trade Debtors less Trade Creditors. Some would include certain bank and cash balances. Some would deduct *all* current liabilities and not just trade creditors. Some would increase CCA Earnings if the Monetary Working Capital is negative or prices fall but most proponents of the MWCA would drop their advocacy immediately it ceases to reduce the final CCA Earnings figure.

The formula for calculating the MWCA is normally shown as

$$(C - O) - I_a \times \left(\frac{C}{I_c} - \frac{O}{I_o}\right)$$

where O is MWC at the start of the year
       C is MWC at the end of the year
       I_a is the Specific Index at the average point during the year
       I_o is the Specific Index at the start of the year
       I_c is the Specific Index at the end of the year

This formula is similar to that shown on page 72 for COSA but the elements have been rearranged in a less logical fashion and, indeed, the logic of applying the formula is much more difficult to fathom.

If the intention of the MWCA is to retain profit (and prevent it from being paid as dividend) in order to maintain the Operating Capacity at the *start* of the year, it could be achieved by calculating the addition needed to index up the opening MWC to what it would be at the end of the year if MWC had remained constant in real terms. Thus it might be more logical for

$$\text{MWCA} = O \times \frac{I_c}{I_o} - O$$

The specific index used in the calculation of MWCA will normally be based on the firm's selling prices (which would normally determine the level of Debtors that the business must support). However, if purchase prices do not move in harmony with selling prices, the Trade Creditors may have to be indexed in one way and the Debtors in another. The disputes surrounding the MWCA mean that it is less likely to be a part of serious proposals in the future.

The Gearing Adjustment (GA)

This adjustment would reverse a part of the other three CCA Earnings Adjustments - Depreciation (DA), Cost of Sales (COSA) and Monetary Working Capital (MWCA). The part would be determined by the proportion of net operating assets (at Current Cost) funded by loans rather than by ordinary shareholders.

Thus, if interest-bearing loans amount to half of the company's net operating assets, the DA was £5m, the COSA was £3m and no MWCA was provided, then the Gearing Adjustment would be £4m - one half of £5m + £3m.

If a business is partly funded with borrowed money and it maintains a constant operating capacity as prices rise, the borrowing can also rise in currency terms without the business being any worse off. In a sense, the lenders are bearing a part of the other CCA adjustments. If a purpose in calculating CCA Earnings is to determine the dividend that can be paid to ordinary shareholders to keep an unchanged operating capacity, then the Gearing Adjustment is needed. However, like the MWCA, the Gearing Adjustment is contentious and unlikely to be a part of serious proposals in the future.

The Financial Capital Maintenance Concept

The Financial Capital Maintenance Concept is not part of traditional CCA and is an unusual way of partly combining CCA with CPP (introduced by the ASC in the mid-80s). It involves :

(a) Take the shareholders' funds from the CCA Balance Sheet at the start of the period. In other words, the figure of current cost assets less liabilities at the beginning of the year.

(b) Restate the figure from (a) with a consumer price index such as the retail prices index to $£CPP_{end\ of\ the\ year}$. In other words multiply the opening CCA shareholders' funds by the RPI at the end of the year and divide by the RPI at the start of the year.

(c) If any capital has been raised from shareholders in the year, index that additional capital to $£CPP_{end\ of\ year}$.

(d) If any dividends have been paid to shareholders in the year, index those dividends to £CPP$_{end\ of\ year}$. (Ignore any ACT associated with those dividends.)

(e) Add (b) to (c) and deduct (d). In other words adjust the opening CCA shareholders' funds in £CPP$_{end\ year}$ by any funds paid in or taken out in £CPP$_{end\ year}$.

(f) Take the shareholders' funds from the CCA Balance Sheet at the <u>end</u> of the period. In other words, the figure of current cost assets less liabilities at the close of the year.

(g) Deduct (e) from (f) to determine the surplus under this system.

If consumer prices have been rising at a slower rate than prices of the assets held by the company, then a full distribution of the surplus (g) to the shareholders by way of dividend will reduce the 'operating capacity' of the business. Most proponents of CCA view the maintenance of operating capacity as paramount and thus this concept will not satisfy them. Many opponents of CCA would not use the CCA net assets and thus they will be equally unsatisfied by the Financial Capital Maintenance Concept.

References

[1] W T Baxter; Inflation Accounting; published by Philip Allan; 1984; Pages 287/8

[2] Accounting Standards Committee; Accounting for the Effects of Changing Prices : a Handbook; 1986; Para A1.7; Page 61

[3] Ibid; Para A1.72; Page 75

[4] Ibid; Para A1.4; Page 59

[5] Ibid; Table 8; Page 48

[6] Ibid; Para A4.3; Page 87

Modern Accounting 2

Answers to Questions 3.1 to 3.7

Answer 3.1

1. Net Realisable Value : £30,000. Economic Value : £20,000. Replacement Cost : £15,000. If Beta lost the asset, they would replace it because they can make a profit holding it and an even larger profit selling it. Therefore Deprival Value : £15,000 (Replacement Cost).

2. Net Realisable Value : £6m. Economic Value : £8m. Replacement Cost : £15m. If Alpha lost the asset, they would not replace it because they cannot make a profit either holding it or selling it. However it is not worth selling because the economic value is higher than net realisable value. Therefore Deprival Value : £8m (Economic Value).

3. Net Realisable Value : £5,000. Economic Value : 0. Replacement Cost : ?. It is not possible to replace this seasonal crop at the Balance Sheet date. If prices rise at the same rate up to next season, the cost of the next season's crop should be 10% higher than this year. Only 3 months of the year between seasons has passed between purchase and the year end. If Deprival Value is fudged as being 2.5% higher than historic cost, this will not charge the full cost of the eventual replacement. Most advocates of CCA would say that Deprival Value should be taken as 33p per pack - or £3,300. The next Chapter (Chapter 4) considers the advantages of CCA; note that a major advantage - that of charging the cost borne by new capacity in a business - cannot be true of this situation. No new competitor could buy the seasonal crop at the Balance Sheet date.

4. Replacement Cost : £50k. Net Realisable Value : 0. Economic Value : £1m. If Sigma lost the asset, they would replace it because they can make an excellent profit holding it. Therefore Deprival Value : £50k (Replacement Cost).

5. Replacement Cost : £30k. Economic Value : £10k. Net Realisable Value : £20k. If Epsilon lost the asset, they would not replace it because they cannot make a profit either holding it or selling it. In the current situation, they should sell. Therefore Deprival Value : £20k (Net Realisable Value). This situation is more usual with obsolete stock than with machinery.

6. Replacement Cost : £3m. Net Realisable Value : £4m. Economic Value : £6m. If Lambda lost the asset, they would replace it because they can make profits either selling or - even better - holding the assets. Therefore Deprival Value : £3m (Replacement Cost).

Current Cost Accounting

7   Replacement Cost : £40k. Net Realisable Value : £60k. Economic Value : 0. If Iota lost the asset, they would replace it because they can make a profit selling it. Therefore Deprival Value : £40k. (Replacement Cost).

8   This case highlights the point that all 3 values that make up Deprival Value are dependant on the skill and judgment of those doing the replacing, selling and holding. They are all subjective values and a company management will normally have excellent reasons to be biased in estimating them. The management in this case would estimate Deprival Value as £600k (their estimate of replacement cost). You would estimate Deprival Value as zero with the current management (who would continue to operate at a loss) and £300k with a shrewder management (who could replace at that cost and operate at a profit).

Answer 3.2

WORKINGS
Fixed Asset SPI at 31.12.00 = (155+160)/2 = 157.5
Fixed Asset SPI at 31.12.99 = (137+139)/2 = 138

Fixed Assets at Replacement Cost and Used Replaciation :

As At Date of Purchase :	31.12.99 Replacement Cost £	31.12.99 Used Replaciation £	31.12.00 Replacement Cost £	31.12.00 Used Replaciation £
May 92	16,235	10,824	15,441	13,897
Oct 94	9,857	6,161	5,625	4,219
Jan 96	29,900	9,200	34,125	23,625
Jun 99	10,299	2,060	11,754	9,403
Mar 00			30,839	7,710
	66,291	28,244	97,784	58,854

Stock SPI at 31.12.00 = (112+114)/2 = 113
Stock SPI at 31.12.99 = (106+106)/2 = 106
Average Stock SPI for Nov and Dec 99 = (105+106)/2 = 105.5
Average Stock SPI for Nov and Dec 00 = (112+112)/2 = 112

Current Cost of Stock at 31.12.99 = 16,000 X 106/105.5 = £16,076
Current Cost of Stock at 31.12.00 = 20,000 X 113/112 = £20,179

Modern Accounting 2

Balance Sheet as at	31.12.99	31.12.00
	£	£
Fixed Assets		
Replacement Cost	66,291	97,784
Used Replaciation	28,244	58,854
	38,047	38,930
Current Assets		
Stock	16,076	20,179
Debtors	20,000	22,000
Bank	3,000	2,000
	39,076	44,179
less Creditors	15,000	14,000
Net Current Assets	24,076	30,179
	62,123	69,109
Share Capital	10,000	10,000
Reserves (including Current Cost Reserve)		
	52,123	59,109
	62,123	69,109

Answer 3.3

Using the formula on page 72 :

$$O \times \frac{I_a}{I_o} - C \times \frac{I_a}{I_c} - (O - C)$$

where O is FIFO Historic Cost Opening Stock (In this case £45,000)
C is FIFO Historic Cost Closing Stock (In this case £53,000)
I_a is the Specific Index at the average point during the year (In this case 127)
I_o is the Specific Index at the average point during the purchase period for opening stock (In this case 112)
I_c is the Specific Index at the average point during the purchase period for closing stock (In this case 132)

Substituting in the formula :

$$45,000 \times \frac{127}{112} - 53,000 \times \frac{127}{132} - (45,000 - 53,000) = £8,034$$

This formula assumes that (a) the volume of sales and (b) the volume of purchases are even throughout the year. The use of the index assumes that it accurately reflects prices of the specific goods being bought and sold.

Answer 3.4

WORKINGS :
Replacement Cost of Fixed Assets

	Replacement Cost at 30.6.99	Replacement Cost of Disposal	Replacement Cost at 30.6.00
Items Purchased			
on Jan 96	197,788	46,150	162,832
Oct 97	190,720		204,800
Mar 99	312,587		335,664
Jul 99			105,960
	<u>701,095</u>	<u>46,150</u>	<u>809,256</u>

Depreciation/Replaciation on Fixed Assets

	Accumulated Depreciation 30.6.99	Used Replaciation 30.6.99	Depreciation Charge	Replaciation Charge
Items Purchased				
on Jan 96	110,000	145,044	6,000	8,230
Oct 97	90,000	107,280	11,000	13,640
Mar 99	150,000	156,294	25,000	27,098
Jul 99			10,000	10,265
	<u>350,000</u>	<u>408,618</u>	<u>52,000</u>	<u>59,233</u>

	Accumulated Depreciation on Disposals	Used Replaciation on Disposals	Accumulated Depreciation at 30.6.00	Used Replaciation at 30.6.00
Items Purchased				
on Jan 96	22,000	29,009	94,000	133,097
Oct 97			101,000	129,280
Mar 99			175,000	195,804
Jul 99			10,000	10,596
	<u>22,000</u>	<u>29,009</u>	<u>380,000</u>	<u>468,778</u>

Disposal of Fixed Asset

Historic Cost	35,000
Accumulated Depreciation at date of disposal	<u>22,000</u>
Net Book Value	13,000
Loss on Historic Cost P & L	<u>5,000</u>
Therefore Proceeds from disposal	<u>8,000</u>

Modern Accounting 2

Disposal of Fixed Asset continued
Proceeds (see previous page)		8,000
Replacement Cost at date of disposal	46,150	
Used Replaciation at date of disposal	29,009	
CCA Book Value		17,142
CCA Loss on Disposal		9,142

COSA - Cost of Sales Adjustment
Substituting in the formula on page 72 :

$$25,000 \times \frac{140}{110} - 30,000 \times \frac{140}{150} - (25,000 - 30,000) = £8,818$$

	Historic Cost	Factor	Replacement Cost Yr ends	Factor	Replacement Cost Av Prices
Stock at					
30.6.99	25,000	120/110	27,273	140/110	31,818
30.6.00	30,000	160/150	32,000	140/150	28,000

Depreciation Adjustment
Depreciation charged in Historic Cost P & L	52,000	
Replaciation charged in CCA Income Statement	59,233	
		7,233
Loss on Sale of FA charged in Historic Cost P & L	5,000	
Loss on Sale of FA charged in CCA Income Statement	9,142	
		4,142
		11,374

Current Cost Reserve
Replacement Cost of Fixed Assets at 30.6.99	701,095	
Historic Cost of Fixed Assets at 30.6.99	610,000	91,095
Used Replaciation on Fixed Assets at 30.6.99	408,618	
Accumulated Depreciation at 30.6.99	350,000	58,618
Holding Gains on Fixed Assets		32,477
Replacement Cost of Stock	27,273	
Historic Cost of Stock	25,000	
Holding Gain on Stock		2,273
Current Cost Reserve at 30.6.99 (first CCA Balance Sheet)		34,750
From This Year's Income Statement : COSA		8,818
Holding Gains in year on the Replacement Cost of Fixed Assets		
Replacement Cost of Fixed Assets 30.6.99	701,095	
Replacement Cost of Disposal	46,150	
	654,945	
Cost of Additions	100,000	
	754,945	
Replacement Cost of Fixed Assets 30.6.00	809,256	54,312
carried forward to next page		97,880

Current Cost Accounting

brought forward from the last page		97,880
Backlog Replaciation :		
Used Replaciation at 30.6.99	408,618	
less Used Replaciation on Fixed Asset Disposal	29,009	
	379,609	
Replaciation charged in CCA Income Statement	59,233	
	438,842	
Used Replaciation at 30.6.00	468,778	(29,936)
Holding Gain on Stock at 30.6.00	2,000	
Holding Gain on Stock at 30.6.99	2,273	(273)
		67,672

<u>Full CCA Income Statement</u>	£	£
Sales		550,000
Opening Stock at average prices for year	31,818	
Purchases	230,000	
	261,818	
Closing Stock at average prices for year	28,000	
Replacement Cost of Sales		233,818
		316,182
General Expenses	205,000	
Loss on Disposal of Fixed Asset	9,142	
Replaciation	59,233	273,374
CCA Earnings before taxation		42,807
*Taxation		23,000
		19,807
Dividends :		
Paid	5,000	
Proposed	6,000	11,000
Unappropriated CCA Earnings of the year		8,807
Balance brought forward		292,000
		300,807
<u>Adjusted HC to CCA Statement</u>		
Net Operating Profit before Taxation		
per Historic Cost Accounts		63,000
Cost of Sales Adjustment	8,818	
Depreciation Adjustment	11,374	20,193
CCA Earnings before Taxation		42,807

This statement continues as from the asterisk in the full statement above.

Modern Accounting 2

CCA Balance Sheets as at	30.6.99	30.6.00
Fixed Assets	£	£
Replacement Cost	701,095	809,256
Used Replaciation	408,618	468,778
	292,477	340,479
Current Assets		
Stock at Replacement Cost	27,273	32,000
Debtors	55,000	49,000
Bank	2,000	
	84,273	81,000
less Creditors	30,000	33,000
	54,273	48,000
	346,750	388,479
Share Capital	20,000	20,000
Revenue Reserves	292,000	300,807
Current Cost Reserve	34,750	67,672
	346,750	388,479

Answer 3.5

Replacement Cost of Fixed Assets

Purchased on	At 30.9.99	Disposal	At 30.9.00
Jan 95	513,545		562,455
May 97	196,455	132,143	70,438
Dec 99			46,000
	710,000	132,143	678,892

Depreciation/Replaciation on Fixed Assets

	Accumulated Depreciation at 30.9.99	Used Replaciation at 30.9.99	Depreciation Charge	Replaciation Charge
Jan 95	147,000	280,636	27,000	54,982
May 97	49,039	64,364	4,000	5,600
Dec 99			4,000	4,073
	196,039	345,000	35,000	64,655

	Accumulated Depreciation on Disposals	Used Replaciation on Disposals	Accumulated Depreciation at 30.9.00	Used Replaciation at 30.9.00
Jan 95			174,000	363,818
May 97	40,039	52,551	13,000	18,688
Dec 99			4,000	4,182
	40,039	52,551	191,000	386,688

Current Cost Accounting

Disposal of Fixed Asset
Historic Cost		100,680
Accumulated Depreciation at the date of disposal		40,039
Net Book Value		60,641
Profit on Historic Cost P & L		1,000
Therefore Proceeds from disposal		61,641
Resplacement Cost at date of disposal	132,143	
Used Replaciation at date of disposal	52,551	
CCA Book Value		79,591
CCA Loss on Disposal		17,950

COSA - Cost of Sales Adjustment
Substituting in the formula on page 72 :

$40,000 \times \frac{132}{120} - 50,000 \times \frac{132}{134} - (40,000 - 50,000) = £4,746$

	Historic Cost	Factor	Replacement Cost Yr ends	Factor	Replacement Cost Av Prices
Stock at					
30.9.99	40,000	126/120	42,000	132/120	44,000
30.9.00	50,000	140/134	52,239	132/134	49,254

Depreciation Adjustment
Replaciation charged in CCA Income Statement	64,655	
Depreciation charged in Historic Cost P & L	35,000	
		29,655
Profit on Sale of FA in Historic Cost P & L	1,000	
Loss on Sale of FA in CCA Income Statement	17,950	
		18,950
		48,605

Current Cost Reserve
Balance as at 30.9.99		352,000
From this year's income statement : COSA		4,746
Holding Gains this year on the Replacement Cost of Fixed Assets :		
Replacement Cost of Fixed Assets 30.9.99	710,000	
Replacement Cost of Disposal	132,143	
	577,858	
Cost of Additions	44,000	
	621,858	
Replacement Cost of Fixed Assets 30.9.00	678,892	
		57,035
carried forward to next page		413,781

99

Modern Accounting 2

brought forward from last page		413,781
Backlog Replaciation :		
Used Replaciation 30.9.99	345,000	
Used Replaciation on Disposal	52,551	
	292,449	
Replaciation in CCA Income Statement	64,655	
	357,103	
Used Replaciation 30.9.00	386,688	
		(29,584)
Holding gain on stock 30.9.00	2,239	
Holding gain on stock 30.9.99	2,000	
		239
		384,435

Full CCA Income Statement	£	£
Sales		890,000
Opening stock at average prices over year	44,000	
Purchases	670,000	
	714,000	
Closing stock at average prices over year	49,254	
		664,746
		225,254
General Expenses	81,000	
Loss on Sale of Fixed Asset	17,950	
Replaciation	64,655	
		163,605
CCA Earnings before taxation		61,649
*Taxation		53,000
		8,649
Dividends : Paid		27,000
		(18,351)
Balance brought forward		50,359
		32,008

Adjusted HC to CCA Statement		
Net Operating Profit before Taxation		
per Historic Cost Accounts		115,000
Cost of Sales Adjustment	4,746	
Depreciation Adjustment	48,605	
		53,351
CCA Earnings before Taxation		61,649

This statement continues from the asterisk in the full statement above.

Current Cost Accounting

CCA Balance Sheet as at 30 September 2000
	£	£
Fixed Assets		
Replacement Cost		678,892
Used Replaciation		386,688
		292,205
Current Assets		
Stock at Replacement Cost	52,239	
Debtors	105,000	
Bank	20,000	
	177,239	
less Creditors : Amounts due within one year	13,000	
		164,239
		456,443
Share Capital		40,000
Current Cost Reserve		384,435
Revenue Reserves		32,008
		456,443

Answer 3.7

Quarter	Purchases	Purchase Price Index	Purchases in PVU	Sales	Sales Price Index	Sales in SVU
1	20	121	0.1653	4	100	0.0400
2	15	135	0.1111	7	100	0.0700
3	3	150	0.0200	9	150	0.0600
4	1	180	0.0056	58	150	0.3867
	39		0.3020	78		0.5567
Open Stock	12	110	0.1091			
	51		0.4110			
Close Stock	15	140	0.1071			
	36		0.3039			

Conversion factor of SVU to PVU = 0.3039/0.5567 = 0.5459

Quarter	Sales in PVU	Replacement Cost of Sales
1	0.021837	2.642
2	0.038215	5.159
3	0.032756	4.913
4	0.211094	37.997
		50.712

COSA = 50.7 - 36 = £m14.7

Chapter Four

The Uses and Shortcomings of CCA and CPP

Section A - A Discussion on the Merits of CCA

The arguments for CCA Income Statements fall into three main groups :

(a) First it is contended that holding gains cannot be distributed to shareholders without reducing the operating capacity of the business. "Income from ordinary operations should represent an amount ... available for distribution outside the firm without contraction of the level of its operating capacity."[1]

(b) Secondly it is claimed that holding gains are of a different nature from normal trading profits, are less likely to recur and are less predictable. "The concept of dichotomizing NI (Holding Gains and CCA Earnings) into Holding Gains and RI (Residual Income or CCA Earnings) is based on the assumption that the business enterprise has two revenue gathering activities : holding and operating. Furthermore the claim that RI is a measure of long run performance increased academic interest in the predictive ability of the measure."[2]

(c) Thirdly it is argued that, if CCA Statements are the main financial accounts, managements will make better decisions. In particular they will be prepared to accept replacement cost as the 'true cost' and will set selling prices accordingly. "An important aspect of the controversy over asset valuation methods has been the relevance of reported asset values to management decisions."[3]

(a) Dividends and Operating Capacity - COSA

Let us look at a business that operates in the simplest and most stable conditions. Only one product line is bought and sold. The volume of sales and the volume of purchases are completely even over time. Each day the same fixed number of units are both sold and purchased. Hence the volume of stock never changes.

All sales and purchases are for cash. In other words, (a) there is no time lag between (i) selling and (ii) receiving the cash and (b) there is no time lag between (i) buying and (ii) paying for the goods.

In these circumstances the Cost of Sales Adjustment (COSA) will adjust the FIFO Historic Cost Gross Profit to the cash generated by trading.

Example
Assumptions :
a   Every day is a working day and every day 100 units are bought and 100 units are sold. 1,000 units remains the constant level of stock.
b   Purchase prices have been £5 per unit for many years until 16th November when they changed to £7 per unit. They then remained at £7 per unit for some months.
c   Selling prices have been £10 per unit for many years until 16th November when they changed to £14 per unit. They then remained at £14 for some months.

Sales for November are 15 days of 100 units per day @ £10 plus 15 days of 100 units per day @ £14 which equals £36,000. Purchases for November amount to 15 days of 100 units per day @ £5 plus 15 days of 100 units per day @ £7 which equals £18,000. Opening Stock is 1,000 units @ £5 which equals £5,000 and Closing Stock is 1,000 units @ £7 which equals £7,000. A raw Historic Cost Trading account for November (30 days) would appear as follows :

	£	£
Sales		36,000
Opening Stock	5,000	
Purchases	18,000	
	23,000	
less Closing Stock	7,000	16,000
		20,000

In this example, ignoring any other expenses or income, payments and receipts are the same as purchases and sales. Thus the funds generated by trading are £36,000 minus £18,000 which equals £18,000. This is the same as the CCA Earnings because the replacement cost of Sales is the same as the Purchases for the month.

According to the Operating Capacity Argument, £18,000 is the maximum that should be distributed to the owners of this business if they wish to maintain its 'Operating Capacity'. Distributing the full Historic Cost Profit of £20,000 would mean (i) reducing stock, (ii) increasing borrowing or (iii) reducing funds held in the business elsewhere at the start of the period. Presumably stock levels are set on some rational basis and, if they are destroyed, it will reduce the ability of the business to maintain sales at the current level.

The Effect of Debtors and Creditors

Few businesses both buy and sell on a pure cash basis. Businesses selling to other businesses have to sell on credit and they are lucky to receive their money within 30 days of the sale. If we assumed that the business in the example above has a debtor turnover and a creditor turnover both of 30 days, then the Receipts and Payments of November would all relate to the Sales and Purchases of October. In this case the cash generated in November would be only £15,000 (Sales of £30,000 minus Purchases of £15,000).

If the business retailed to the public, the sales may be for cash and the purchases may be on 30 days credit. Then the cash generated in November rises to £21,000 - Sales of £36,000 minus Purchases of £15,000.

This appears to undermine the Operating Capacity Argument for all but pure cash traders. However advocates of CCA would claim that this can be handled by the Monetary Working Capital Adjustment (MWCA) - see pages 88 and 89 of the last Chapter. Some keen advocates even demand *negative* MWCAs for retailers. However the various proposals for implementing MWCA have attracted little general support - perhaps because they have been ill-explained.

The Effect of Seasonality

An accurately prepared COSA should adjust the cost of Sales so that it becomes the Replacement Cost of Sales - or the cost of replacing the goods at the point of sale. However most businesses do not always replace goods at that point. Stocks fluctuate and there can be significant delays before replacement is made. These are delays while replacement costs may rise or fall. The Operating Capacity argument would be improved if COSA was redefined so that the Replacement Cost of Sales became the cost of replacement *not* at the point of sale but instead at the time when the goods are <u>actually</u> next purchased. However, although this would help the Operating Capacity argument, it would increase the cost of collecting the data and it would delay publication of CCA accounts.

Dividends and Operating Capacity - Replaciation

If, in each year, the same proportion of each category of Fixed Assets was replaced and this proportion was the same as the proportion of Replacement Cost charged as Replaciation, then the 'Fixed Asset spend' each year would be the same as the Replaciation charged in the CCA Income Statement. If Fixed Assets are bought on cash terms with no prepayments or credit, then 'Fixed Asset spend' will be the same as the actual cash paid for Fixed Assets.

Example

Regularprint Ltd own 10 offset litho presses. Each of these presses produces identical output and lasts for 10 years from new. At the start of each accounting year they have one new press, one 1 year old press, one 2 year old press and so on. Their oldest press at the start of each accounting year is 9 years old.

At the end of each accounting year their youngest press is 1 year old, they scrap the oldest press (which is now 10 years old) and buy another press. The 10 year old presses have no scrap (or residual value). In Regularprint's historic cost accounts they charge depreciation at the rate of 10% pa on cost (straight line). In the company's CCA Income Statement, Replaciation (or the Depreciation Adjustment) will be based on the replacement costs at the *end* of the year and not on average during the year.

For Regularprint the Replaciation charged in a CCA Income Statement in any year would precisely match the amount spent on Fixed Assets in that year. If the company paid a dividend which exceeded CCA Earnings, it would have to (a) not buy a new press that year - which would reduce the operating capacity of the business, (b) obtain the cash from squeezing other assets held by the business (which, if they are legitimate business assets, should also reduce operating capacity) or (c) raise fresh capital through borrowing (or from shareholders).

However the Regularprint example does not prove that 'CCA Replaciation will ensure that a business can always replace its Fixed Assets'. Replaciation like Depreciation is a mere accounting entry; it has no direct impact on cash. Its only indirect impact is that it changes the final CCA Earnings figure and that may influence dividend decisions. Even if this indirect influence does occur, it will not prevent the business from spending the money elsewhere or from making CCA trading losses.

Most businesses do not buy their Fixed Assets with the mechanical regularity of Regularprint. For example, in a chemical works Fixed Assets may consist of certain large items of plant which are bought only once in twenty years and many small items which are less specific to that particular process and are bought in quantity during boom years and meagrely during slumps. (Half of the large items with a twenty year life may be fully depreciated because they have been subject to a 10% straight line depreciation policy and they may never be 'replaced' because either their product or their process is judged obsolete - or close to the end of its life.)

If Regularprint had just one press that was replaced every 10 years, then each year's CCA Income Statement during the life of that single press would have a charge based on replacement costs *during that year*. It is most unlikely that the sum of those individual yearly charges would equal that amount that has to be spend on a new press at the end of the old one's life.

Should Dividends be Determined by the Results of Prior Periods?

The Operating Capacity argument implies that Dividend decisions are (or should be) determined by the stated 'profits' or 'earnings' for the period that has just ended. In the UK there are legal restrictions designed to prevent companies from distributing more than their stated raw historic cost earnings. Do these legal restrictions make economic sense? Should they be changed so that only CCA Earnings can be distributed? Should it be the lower of CCA Earnings and raw historic cost profits? What is in the best interest of shareholders? Can the best interests of employees and managers be identified?

Merton H Miller and Franco Modigliani[4] are the best-known academic authors on this topic and they concluded that dividend policy was irrelevant because there was no such thing as an optimal policy. They reached this conclusion by assuming that there was no taxation and there were perfect capital markets (with perfect information); unfortunately both assumptions invalidate their conclusion as a basis for practical decisions.

Chapter 13 of the previous book in this series (Modern Accounting 1) on UK Business Taxation contains a short section on "Dividends in the Hands of Shareholders" which explains that Pension Funds can reclaim tax when a dividend is paid but wealthy individual shareholders have to pay additional higher rate taxation on dividends. This means that there is a conflict of interest between the two classes of shareholders with Pension Funds wanting maximum dividend payouts and most wealthy individual shareholders preferring minimum dividends in the hope that they can take their gains as more lightly taxed 'capital gains' when they eventually sell the shares (see Realising Profits from Limited Companies in Chap 14 Book 1).

In the UK in the 1980s as Pension Funds increased their equity stakes in companies, dividend 'cover' (see Chapter 16 of Book 1) reduced. In other words, companies paid a higher proportion of their profits out by way of dividend as logic would suggest they should. In theory the Pension Funds might encourage companies both to increase dividends and to recover part of the money with immediate rights issues.

Assuming Perfect Capital Markets implies that, for a given level of risk, there will be a single 'market' level of return. All managers should try to forecast risks and returns and the more accurate their forecasts, the more perfect the market will be. Most managers try to find some area where there is market imperfection in order that they can excel. Logically the harder they work at this, the fewer such areas will remain and the closer capital markets get to being 'perfect'.

In practice most fund managers who act for institutional shareholders make assumptions as to the likely opportunities available *within* a company and the opportunities available *outside* that company. They frequently believe (rightly or wrongly) that there is a difference between the two. If the opportunities available within the company are judged better than those outside, the fund managers will not press the company to pay dividends. If the outside opportunities look better to the fund managers, they will pressure the company to pay more - even if they are aware of the company's results and know that trading profits have come from holding gains and that higher dividends would in part be repayment of 'capital' - however 'capital' is defined - and the same would be true of well-informed individual shareholders. This judgement as to opportunities relates to *future* opportunities, future investment and future returns. The results of the immediately past period are irrelevant except in so far as they aid forecasts of the future.

Thus it appears that legal restrictions on the payment of dividends do not make economic sense. It is difficult to argue that they are in the interests of shareholders - as long as shareholders are aware of the company's results and whether the dividends are repayment of 'capital' - however 'capital' is defined. The interests of employees and managers are more complicated. Free capital markets may well reduce the operating capacity of managements judged to be incompetent and increase that of those judged to be successful. In the long run this should increase the employment opportunities available across the whole economy - if the fund managers and investors are good judges.

However, while this may benefit employees in general, the interests of an individual director of a company may be to reinvest and to replace even where better opportunities outside that company exist. The pay and status of directors may be more dependant on the absolute size of their business rather than the return on capital employed. They may believe that their own self-interest is best served by finding more inside opportunities and exaggerating the prospects of these opportunities. In the 'long run' such a firm is likely to sacrifice efficiency, profits and shareholder confidence but the 'long run' may occur after an individual director has moved on.

(b) Predictive Abilities of CCA Earnings

This proposition states that holding gains are of a different nature from normal trading profits and they are less likely to recur. If they are excluded from the primary measure of trading performance, then readers of accounts will be left with a statistic that is a better indicator of future results.

Why should past profits - however defined - be any indicator of future profit-making capacity? There are at least three reasons. First, it may be that some businesses operate in a semi-mechanical fashion. Large businesses with large numbers of customers and suppliers develop a momentum of their own. Once patterns of activity have been established it takes time for the patterns to change. If customers are used to buying a particular good or service from a particular business, then the next time they require that particular item they are quite likely to return to their established habits.

Secondly, past results may be an indicator of the business acumen of the management of the business. It seems logical that those who have done well in the past are more likely to do well in the future.

Thirdly past profits may be an indicator of the level of capital within the business and that level may be an indicator of future profit making capacity.

Sometimes holding gains are referred to as 'windfall profits'. There are two ideas behind this term. One idea is that such profits are once and for all. But there is also the implication that they were unplanned and outside the control of management. This might be true if purchase price levels are random and impossible to forecast. Yet why should they be more difficult to forecast than selling prices or market demand? In other words, holding gains may be an indication of good management.

A builder who believed that the price of sand was about to rise and the price of bricks was about to fall, would be wise to increase his stock of sand and run down his stock of bricks. However there may be limits to the extent that this may be done. If it was bagged cement (instead of bricks) that was going to get more expensive, then the builder would be unable to make much of a stock holding gain because cement in bags goes hard if held for more than a few days. Equally there are limits on the storage space controlled by most businesses. On the other hand, if stocks must be limited, then the holding gains should be less important and the argument for excluding them less convincing.

Holding gains on fixed assets are less likely to indicate the acumen of the *current* management because it is more likely that the original purchase of the assets was made by managers who have retired or are now working elsewhere.

Abdel-Khalik and McKeown[5] and Frank[6] did empirical studies in this area and they were *unable* to show that CCA Earnings were a better predictive measure than raw Historic Cost Profit. In fact, in their samples, holding gains themselves turned out to be a better predictive measure than either CCA Earnings or HC Profit. Perhaps this is not wholly surprising because their measurements were made in raw currency and not CPP units and in an economy with consistent general inflation in every year of their study. The main element in most firms' holding gains is more likely to be changes in the value of currency rather than changes in 'real' relative prices. The Predictive Measure argument is more plausible when holding gains are expressed in CPP units (the details of which are explained in the next Chapter on CCA in CPP).

Under CCA in CPP, Holding Gains are made only if a price rises in real terms - over and above the rise needed to keep pace with general inflation. Are such real price rises likely to repeat in subsequent years? The best known example of a specific price rise exceeding the rate of general inflation is that of oil. After the second large price hike in 1979 there were commentators suggesting that fossil fuels were a finite resource and price rises above the rate of inflation could be expected for the indefinite future. It has not happened. The price of oil behaves similarly to the price of agricultural commodities and metals. Real rates of price increase stimulate economy in the use by consumers, the search for substitutes and the search for alternative sources of supply. Whether this pattern can continue in the case of oil is a matter of debate. There are time lags to these processes and those commodities - on which real holding gains have been made - appear most susceptible to future real holding losses. Some of the large oil companies do publish CCA accounts and, in their case, they may be especially useful although they could be even more useful if they were CCA in CPP.

Perhaps the only resource which can maintain indefinite price increases above the rate of general inflation is human brain-work. Human beings never stop developing new products and different ways of making the same products. Continuing increases in productivity should eventually lead to higher pay rates for labour (although it may initially lead to unemployment and it may change the demand for different skills). Some services are almost pure labour and it is difficult to see how the labour content could be reduced. Higher real pay rates imply that the price of many of these services will rise in real terms and thus the price of most goods must decline in real terms.

(c) CCA for Management Decisions

In the UK it was the results of a 1975 government enquiry - normally called the Sandilands Report[7] - which made practitioners face CCA as a practical proposition. The terms of reference for that enquiry[8] required them to consider "the effects upon ... management decisions" and in their report they state[9] that "although management may not actually use the published accounts for the day-to-day managing of the company, it is clearly desirable that the published accounts and those used by management should be drawn up on the same basic principles..."

There are two contentious assumptions in that quotation. The first is that only *one* set of accounts with one set of basic principles can be published externally as financial accounts (and possibly also internally as management accounts). The second is that it is clear to all the readers of the report why it is desirable that internal and external publications should be drawn up on the same principles.

Many users of financial accounts are passive recipients of the information with little opportunity to demand further disclosures. They need legislation and accounting standards to determine the content and format of financial accounts.

Whereas those inside a business taking management decisions are usually able to collect all the data that is both available internally and also might have a bearing on those decisions. It would be odd for legislation to try to prescribe management accounting statements - almost as odd as law-makers laying down rules for any private correspondence. If the law laid down *minimum* contents for such statements, how would it be enforced when such material is not for general publication and nobody outside the company would know if the law had been obeyed? If the law laid down *maximum* contents, would managers be allowed to collect 'unapproved data' and discuss it between themselves as long as it was not committed to paper?

One might wonder why the Sandilands committee had terms of reference referring to internal management decisions. And given such terms of reference, why was their report not split into (i) a section for action relating to Financial Accounts and (ii) a section relating to

Management Accounts that could consist of worthy thoughts and pleas for improved business education?

These problems all stem from a condescending attitude to the users of accounting data. It is assumed that users will be 'confused' if they are presented with more than one sort of Balance Sheet or Income Statement. It is assumed that managers inside a business might not trust either the internal or external data if they appear to show 'different pictures'.

If someone expresses 'confusion' over financial documents, it is frequently a polite way of asking for an explanation. Knowing that one are confused is better than mistakenly believing that one understands the meaning of a financial statistic. Recognising confusion is the first stage in most processes of education and discovery.

This book and its predecessor (Modern Accounting 1) have explained that there are several different ways of measuring assets and results. Most of those different ways have advantages for different purposes and no one of those ways tells the whole story. A simplified unrealistically clear picture will not help managers, shareholders or bankers take sensible decisions. The search for a single system of accounting that will measure all aspects of business performance is more in the nature of a religious quest than a scientific endeavour.

Do CCA Income Statements Improve Management Decisions?

(i) Setting Selling Prices

This subject was discussed in Chapter 15 of Modern Accounting 1 where the concepts of demand curves and sunk costs were introduced. If selling prices are being set for goods that are already in stock, then the historic cost of those goods is a sunk cost and should have no direct bearing on the current decisions. A profit-maximising business will take account of 'relevant costs' and the quantity that it can sell in the current period at different prices and the impact that those different prices will have on future prices and future demand. Usually the business will want to replace the goods and the 'relevant costs' will indeed be replacement costs; the cost incurred by the action of sending goods out of our warehouse may well be the cost of restocking our warehouse with similar products.

However the last paragraph may be misleading. It is true that the historic cost is a sunk cost and should have no *direct* bearing on the current decisions but it may have an *indirect* bearing on customer demand in two ways. Firstly our competitors may hold equivalent stocks to our own, they may use historic cost-plus pricing and their prices will influence the market for our product. Secondly our customers may be aware of their suppliers' stock levels and how their suppliers' costs have moved and they may have views on the 'fairness' of replacement cost pricing.

Thus it may not be good advice to suggest that an individual management should entirely ignore historic costs when setting selling prices. However some of those that have argued that 'business should make selling prices reflect replacement costs' have not been giving unbiased advice to an *individual* business. They have wanted to influence the climate of opinion amongst *all* businesses and customers. There is many an industrialist whose after-dinner speeches consist of a plea that his competitors should raise their prices; any debate over inflation accounting encourages variations on this theme.

Current replacement costs may almost always be a factor to be considered when setting selling prices, but why should that influence internal management statements of profit or earnings? Statements of CCA Earnings for the month just ended do not show today's replacement costs for individual items. However, although CCA Accounts may not contain the information needed for these specific management decisions, it can be argued that they help to legitimise the idea of replacement costs in the minds of managers and make them more willing to accept replacement costs when they appear in other contexts.

(ii) Costs that Rise in Real Terms

It has already been said that it is rare for the cost of an individual good - as opposed to certain services - to rise continuously by more than a general consumer index because productivity in manufacturing rises over time and so manufacturing prices fall relatively to other prices. If it does happen in any period, it is unlikely to recur and much more likely that there will be a future fall in real terms.

Real price rises have occurred with commodities such as oil and coffee. Should a producer of instant coffee or of oil-derived plastics vary his selling prices so that they reflect current replacement costs?

In these cases the impact of this period's selling prices on customers' behaviour in *future* periods can be the most important factor. If a single season's poor coffee crop raises prices so that consumers find an alternative drink, they may never return to their former addiction to instant coffee.

(iii) Costs that Fall in Real Terms

A falling real cost is a more common problem. Here the competitors that can both carry minimum stocks and yet satisfy their customers must have an advantage. If a certain level of stock-holding is unavoidable and the real price decline is constant and can be forecast, then a perfect capital market would ensure that it is still possible to obtain a reasonable return on the original historic cost (in CPP) even though that is above the current replacement cost. In theory, if that reasonable return is not available, capacity and capital would be removed from that business area until the return rises back to that reasonable level.

(iv) The Depreciation/Replaciation Element in Costs

If (a) new capital and capacity are being attracted into an industry or - as a minimum - existing obsolete capacity is being replaced, (b) there is perfect information available to all existing and potential competitors in that industry and (c) the current replacement costs of fixed assets are the same for all potential competitors, then it is logical to assume that the market for that industry's output will be affected by current replaciation (replacement costs of fixed assets) and not by depreciation (based on the historic costs of the individual assets that happen to owned by an individual firm).

Once managers believe that all three conditions in the last sentence were met, they would be wise to consider replaciation costs when setting selling prices. They would almost certainly be wise to ignore depreciation costs because the reasons why other sunk costs can influence a market are unlikely to be present. One producer is unlikely to hold a portfolio of fixed assets with proportions bought as the same dates as another producer. And customers - whatever their views on the 'fairness' of replacement cost pricing - are less likely to know the details of the original costs of fixed assets than they are of more recently incurred costs.

(v) Judging the Performance of Individual Managers and Teams

CCA Earnings are useful in evaluating the performance of those managers who have little influence over decisions to (i) invest in Fixed Assets or (ii) increase or decrease levels of stock. Subject to the conditions stated in the preceding paragraphs, the market for a company's products is more likely to be influenced by current replacement costs rather than original historic costs. Thus CCA Earnings may be the best measure of performance for many Sales Departments.

The Limitations of Sole Reliance on CCA Earnings Statements

At the start of this Chapter three arguments for CCA Earnings were presented and they have been discussed above. However the debate on CCA in the UK in the 1970s was influenced by more doubtful claims. The most important of these was that the Taxation burden on business would be reduced if CCA Earnings were presented as the only true measure of business performance. The terms of reference of the Sandilands Committee made it clear that the then government had no intention of reducing the total tax burden on companies but few business people have read that detail. Talk of a 'more equitable' distribution of the tax burden strikes most practical people as implying that their business will pay less tax.

In Chapter 13 of Modern Accounting 1 there are examples of Corporation Tax computations which show that, in the UK, legislation and the practice of the Inland Revenue will ensure that modifications are made to published accounting profits before they are accepted as taxable profits. The Inland Revenue can demand what information they require from businesses. If The Treasury wished to tax businesses on CCA Earnings - which they have not wished to up until now and they are unlikely to wish to in the future - they can do so without affecting published financial accounts.

Some would argue against any taxation of business profits, earnings or surpluses (however computed) on the basis that (a) it is not equitable compared with 'immediately spendable' and stable income such as wages and salaries and (b) it harms the economy to the detriment of all. Several authors have argued that businesses should be taxed instead on uninvested cash flow. Kaldor's essays on taxation[10] contain similar arguments.

However these are broad political and economic questions which need to be separated from discussions over the statistics that should be included in Financial Accounts. Politicians may decide to reintroduce window tax - but that should not persuade anyone that the best performance measure is obtained by counting the number of windows in business premises!

Another factor that influenced early discussions on CCA was that, in the 1970s, the UK had a Prices and Incomes Board that attempted to control inflation by restricting the selling prices of individual companies. Such a policy could return and CCA Financial Accounts might influence public opinion in favour of allowing prices to be set on the basis of replacement costs.

Wage and salary negotiations are influenced by the reported profits or earnings of employers and the three legitimate arguments for CCA Income Statements are excellent reasons why the negotiators may need to study CCA statements. However any employee representatives will be suspicious (probably rightly) if they are denied access to accounts produced on alternative bases.

The following questions should help in the evaluation of any system of accounting for inclusion in published financial reports :

(i)   Does it provide *additional* information?
(ii)   Are readers unlikely to be misled by the new information?
(iii)   Is the cost of collecting, computing and distributing the information insignificant?
(iv)   Is the information unlikely to help competitors and potential competitors of the business?
(v)   Could the additional information be useful to some readers?

If each of these questions can be answered positively, then it is difficult to criticise the system.

(i) Does CCA Provide *Additional* Information?

The Sandilands Report and the professional publications that followed it were clear that CCA statements were meant to be the primary financial statements, CPP statements were not welcome and, during a transitionary period only, raw Historic Cost statements would be published 'on sufferance' as an appendix behind the CCA figures. If these proposals had been accepted, CCA would *not* be in addition to other systems. Some of the anger directed at CCA arose because its proponents wished it to hold a monopoly.

Companies that were unwilling to identify replacement costs directly could use a Government publication, PINCCA, which contained indexes for different industry sectors. The price index numbers published in PINCCA followed the index of retail prices (RPI) with remarkable sympathy and several studies suggested that variations from the RPI were not statistically significant[11]. This implies that CCA statements that made use of PINCCA did not provide information that was in addition to CPP Historic Cost Accounts and, *if* a choice has to be made, full CPP figures were more complete and logical than CCA adjustments.

(ii) Are Readers Unlikely to be Misled by CCA?

(a) The Impact of Change

It has already been contended that, because the cost of certain labour-intensive services can be expected to rise at rates above an average measure such as the RPI, so the cost of most physical goods must be expected to rise at rates below those of the average measure. (Elements contained in an average that are heavier than that average must be counter-balanced by those that are lighter. Otherwise the average measure could not be a true average of all of its elements.) Thus the Fixed Assets (other than land) and the Stock of most businesses will have unit costs which do not keep pace with general inflation.

This is not the situation perceived by many practical business managers. Prior to the publication of the Sandilands Report there were several articles in the business and accountancy press from those who believed that their own sectors suffered worse rates of price increase than that measured by the RPI.

One possible reason for this contradiction is that the practical managers were looking at what they believed needed to be spent on revised *new* designs whereas a price index is intended to measure increases in the cost of the *same* items. How many businesses always replace Fixed Assets with identical copies of what will be scrapped? How many businesses never revise their product range and always replace Stock with an identical copy of what has just been sold?

Some businesses are in a continuous state of flux. Indeed a business will not be amongst the most profitable if it is not continually trying to beat the competition by redesigning its products, looking for new markets and products and productivity gains by changing the materials used in its present product line and the way in which it is produced. New methods and new products mean new investment and probably a change of scale. The firm in the 'stable equilibrium' state of an economics textbook would not change its methods, nor change or grow and, since a living world is a changing world, that is not possible. Simply maintaining current production levels and methods may not be an option.

CCA depends on the assumption that Deprival Value is almost always Replacement Cost. However, the faster that technologies, designs, production methods, fashions and materials change, the more often that the Deprival Value of Fixed Assets will be Economic Value and the Deprival Value of Stock will be Net Realisable Value.

(b) Replacement Philosophy

CCA may lull managers into a false sense of security and reinforce a 'replacement philosophy'. The businesses associated with the keenest practical advocates of CCA have been strikingly unsuccessful - while those advocates have been in charge. The years when Sandilands was chairman of Commercial Union were most unfortunate for that insurance company. Philips, the electronics giant, has had a change of management and is no longer at the forefront of replacement cost accounting but their poor financial performance during their replacement cost period raises questions.

Why would an electronics company - of all businesses - have espoused replacement costs? Was it a plea for help from those managers? A desperate attempt to persuade themselves that the pace of change in their industry could be slowed? CCA by insisting on replacement cost to the exclusion of Economic Value and Net Realisable Value in calculating Deprival Value may allow managers to avoid choices they should be forced to make.

(c) Difficulties in Determining Replacement Costs

Can businesses in a state of change follow the advice to search out the replacement cost of new assets "with equivalent service potential"[12]? What is equivalent? Newspapers used to be printed in black and white but now most titles print in colour. Each generation of newspaper presses prints faster with better resolution, less wastage and less labour input. Our business may own old presses. Is 'equivalent service potential' the ability to print the previous quantity of what is now used for newspapers (high resolution colour) or is it the ability to print the previous quantity of what was previously normal for a newspaper? How can adjustments be made for the higher wastage and labour input on the older plant?

Another example would be a business stamping out a metal part that will change to plastic when the stamping equipment is scrapped. Is the 'equivalent' to the stamping equipment a plastic injection moulder? Does it depend on whether the revised part will be produced in-house or bought in?

Replacement Costs are easiest to determine for items bought 'off the shelf' whereas, if a company has equipment built to a special design, the first unit normally costs more than the second, the second more than the third and so on. Some knowledge and design work incurred in the first unit can be used in the production of the later units. How should replacement costs for such equipment be determined? It is the costs of competitors that affect the market and these need not be the same as the costs necessary for a single firm to maintain physical capital.

(d) Subjectivity

Replacement Costs have been criticised as being 'subjective' whereas, in comparison, Historic Costs have been claimed to be objective[13]. There are likely to be areas of estimation in both but presumably most would accept the proposition that, in many circumstances, the variation in possible values for replacement costs is wide. A company's directors have a vested interest in the impression given in the financial accounts and this degree of flexibility may encourage misleading financial statements. A counter-argument is that full details of the evidence and assumptions behind replacement cost valuations would sometimes allow readers to make their own judgements.

(e) Comparability Between Years

CCA Income Statements are expressed in raw currency of the mid-point (or average point) of the trading year. Thus one year's results

Pros and Cons of CCA and CPP

are not directly comparable with those for prior periods or with any CCA Balance Sheet and this could mislead any reader who thought that CCA adjusted for inflation. This problem is overcome by CCA in CPP.

(iii) Is the Cost of Collecting, Computing and Distributing CCA Information Insignificant?

These costs are difficult to quantify and will be greater in the early years of implementation than later. If those preparing the figures are not convinced of their utility or the underlying logic, then they will not work with enthusiasm or speed. Attempts to calculate statistics such as COSA on the basis of year-end stocks and PINCCA index numbers will satisfy few and much time will be wasted by those charged with the task.

On the other hand, some oil companies and some public utilities operating in stable environments make more serious attempts to calculate the Replacement Cost of Sales. They collect the data as part of their normal management accounting system and, so far as it is possible to isolate this cost, it is not significant.

(iv) Is CCA Information Unlikely to Help Competitors and Potential Competitors of the Business?

Many large public companies own several different businesses and their consolidated accounts are not particularly helpful to a competitor of any individual business. In theory the separate company accounts of a subsidiary should be more helpful but, in practice, real or suspected inter-group transactions may make these difficult to interpret.

Groups that are dominated by a single business are more likely to produce figures that help competitors. CCA figures for the current cost of Fixed Assets should be particularly helpful but this is rarely argued - perhaps because those CCA figures that have been published have been of doubtful accuracy.

(v) Could CCA Information be Useful to Some Readers?

If CCA Income Statements are prepared conscientiously and restricted to very stable situations where there is reason to believe that certain prices will not follow general inflation, then it is probable that CCA information could help some readers with certain decisions. These conditions are met by some oil company and public utility accounts. CCA in CPP is even more likely to be helpful.

The second and third arguments at the start of this chapter (page 103) may have counter-arguments but they are sufficiently valid for many readers to want to see CCA information in addition to Historic Cost in CPP information.

CCA Balance Sheets

Given a choice between knowing the Replacement Cost, the Net Realisable Value or the Economic Value of an asset, most users of accounting data would vote for Realisable or Economic Value. Replacement Cost may or may not be the same as Deprival Value but it is not immediately apparent to everyone that it produces useful Balance Sheets.

In support of CCA Balance Sheets it can be argued :

(a)　　If the 'Replacement Cost of Goodwill' is added to the CCA Net Assets of a business in a thriving industry, this may indicate the realisable value of the business as a whole.

(b)　　CCA Net Assets may give more satisfactory performance ratios (such as Return on Capital Employed).

(c)　　The Replacement Costs of individual assets may be indicators of their Realisable Values.

and (d)　The Replacement Costs of assets may help readers to estimate future cash flows.

(a) The Realisable Value of the Business as a Whole

Usually a business is more than the collection of net assets shown on its Balance Sheet. A potential competitor could buy equivalent assets but that would not be sufficient to buy the equivalent stream of profits because there may be many intangible hidden assets. For example the business may benefit from teams of employees with specialist knowledge and established patterns of work. The business may hold the rights to brand names, designs and patents and may have established valuable habits amongst customers and suppliers.

If one believed that it was possible to identify each one of these intangible hidden assets and to calculate the cost to a new entrant to the market of establishing equivalent benefits, then one would believe that it was possible to estimate the 'Replacement Cost of Goodwill'. Behind this concept is the theory that, in perfect capital markets, the market value of successful businesses must be the cost to a potential competitor of establishing the same conditions that the business currently enjoys. If the expected future profits of the business rose above a market return on such a value, then additional competition would arrive to drive those profits down.

This is not a theory that will be taken seriously by all users of accounts because, in most situations, there must be doubts as to (a) whether a sensible estimate of the 'replacement cost of goodwill' can be made and (b) whether there are perfect capital markets.

(b) CCA Balance Sheet Ratios

Performance ratios based on CCA Balance Sheets are particularly relevant when judging teams of managers who were not in position when most of the Fixed Assets were purchased.

(c) Replacement Costs as Indicators of Realisable Values

It is not unreasonable to assume that, in many markets, the price of new assets will have some bearing on the price of equivalent second-hand assets. However the market for certain specialised Business Fixed Assets can be very thin. Many people find it difficult to understand the consequences of thin markets because, in their private lives, they are used to buying consumer products at set retail prices and they have no experience of haggling over the price of unique items. There are millions of purchasers of bags of sugar and the price of sugar does not differ greatly from one retail chain to another. However, for some specialised Business Fixed Assets, there may, at times, be no purchaser and the maximum possible potential purchasers may be below ten.

Recently in the UK, after a business failure, the liquidator tried to sell a brand name. He assumed that nobody would be very interested but that an established business in that area might be prepared to pay £500 to stop anyone else using that brand name. To his surprise two companies were interested and the brand name was eventually sold for £500,000.

It has already been said that there is some subjectivity in most estimates of the replacement costs of Fixed Assets and this is even more true of their realisable values (partly because most businesses have less experience of selling than buying Fixed Assets). A single point estimate may be less useful than knowing the range of possible values and the evidence and assumptions on which the estimate is based.

Unscrupulous managers - who wish to maximise apparent earnings - would arrange holding losses on stock and those fixed assets (like plant) subject to depreciation. To cover those holding losses on the Balance Sheet they would try to boost the holding gains on those Fixed Assets (like land) not subject to depreciation.

Section B - A Discussion on the Merits of CPP

It is easy for discussions on CPP to confuse two separate issues : (a) Translations of statistics from raw currency into CPP and (b) Historic Cost Accounting in CPP. Translations into CPP do not imply Historic Cost Accounts and the next chapter illustrates how CCA can be translated into CPP. However many accountants associate CPP with Historic Cost because of the proposals prior to the Sandilands Report and because that report assumed that CPP meant Historic Cost.

Arguments in Favour of CPP Translations

Business investment is raised from human-beings. Although the shareholders of a company may be a pension fund, a unit trust and a life insurance fund, these 'institutional investors' are conduits channelling the savings of private individuals. In the years in which individuals invest they do so by restricting their consumption and their usual reason for investing is that they hope to increase their future consumption. Frequently they invest during their years of employment in order to consume during their years of retirement.

Let us assume that a couple own and run a business and they consume only one product - say eggs. Presumably each investment would be made by reducing their present consumption of eggs and the returns from investment (unless reinvested) would increase their future consumption of eggs. If they invest £100 when each egg costs

10p and they later realise their investment for £150 when each egg costs 20p, is it reasonable to say that they have made a profit of £50? They restricted their consumption of eggs by 1,000 eggs and the later proceeds would enable them to increase their consumption by only 750 eggs.

Considerable resources are put into the production of a general index such as the Retail Prices Index while the underlying methods and assumptions are the subject of public scrutiny and debate. The RPI is the best understood measure of the value of money both with ordinary members of the public and with more sophisticated groups.

Other Users

The Sandilands committee listed users of financial accounts apart from shareholders, analysts and other intermediaries (advising and acting for present and potential shareholders). They identified (a) Lenders such as banks, (b) Suppliers and Customers, (c) Employees, (d) the Government and (e) the General Public. What sorts of decisions might these users take on the basis of accounting data? What information would help them take those decisions?

Lenders, Suppliers, Customers and Employees are interested in the stability of the business and its ability to fulfil its contractual obligations to them. Thus they are interested in the future cash flow of the business and, in so far as this can be determined from the data relating to past periods, they wish to see comparisons between Balance Sheets and Profit Statements over several years. The economies of democracies usually experience inflation and those comparisons will not be valid without some translation using a price index. Is there a price index that these users would prefer to a consumer price index?

There have been no sensible proposals for any other price index for translation. (The use of specific indexes in CCA does not involve *translation* of the statistics.) These users are either individuals or corporations with their own shareholders and this business's successes and failures (in so far as they affect these users) will have an eventual impact on the consumption of individuals in their own constituencies.

The Government is a special case. The various arms of central and local government demand information from businesses and are not restricted by the contents of financial accounts. In fact some of the information demanded on official forms is repeated in the financial accounts but, although the civil servants could obtain the data without troubling the business, they still demand completion of their own questionnaires and they do not make much use of what has already been published for other users.

In so far as the Government has an interest in financial accounts, it is the interest of a censor. Civil servants and politicians may well wish to prevent the use of CPP translations because they wish to hide the consequences of inflation. It has been argued that publication of inflation adjusted data 'reminds' readers to raise their prices and wages and thus produces further inflationary pressure. It has also been argued that investors should not be reminded that their 'true' gains are not their money gains and that CPP data will discourage investment. These arguments depend on assuming an ignorant and passive population.

Including 'the General Public' as a user of financial accounts is hardly helpful. It is like adding 'etc' to the end of a list. Of course, with any authors on this topic, there must be interests and decisions which they have not identified. No list of users can be exhaustive and there must arise situations with decisions which one has not foreseen. But until those interests and decisions have been separately analysed, it is impossible to discuss what accounting data they will need.

Monetary Gains and Losses

Grand Metropolitan produced one of the UK's earliest sets of published CPP accounts. There was considerable controversy over the figures because Grand Metropolitan had borrowed to take over companies such as Express Diaries, Berni Inns, Watney Mann and Trumans. All these companies were rich in Freehold property at a time of rising real property prices and high rates of general inflation. This borrowing with high inflation ensured that the CPP profits were much higher than the raw currency profits due to Monetary Gains.

This was not a result that many commentators expected because they had assumed that higher depreciation charges would always reduce the inflation adjusted figures. Once the effect of Monetary Gains was clear it was suggested that they were dangerous, illusory and would encourage companies to over-borrow. It is instructive to note that Grand Metropolitan is today a highly successful group of companies that has been grown from small beginnings.

The CPP figures gave readers of the accounts an indication of the growth being achieved whereas the unadjusted figures misled readers because all the interest paid on the borrowing was charged as an expense without recognising that most of that interest was really recompense for a drop in the true value of the capital sums owing.

There are companies that over-borrow (or over-gear) and they cannot meet their capital and interest payments on the due dates but this is a separate point to be considered when judging the company's cash flow. There are also companies which borrow to invest in assets which do not retain their value in 'real terms'. However this can be dealt with as holding losses.

Interest rates have a weak correlation with actual inflation and a stronger correlation with expected inflation. Rates of exchange between currencies are also linked to actual and expected inflation. Currencies with low inflation tend to have strong exchange rates and low rates of interest. Currencies with high inflation tend to have weak exchange rates and high rates of interest. International investors have to trade off expected inflation and exchange rates against the rate of interest. Lenders would like to (a) keep the value of their loans intact and (b) receive a high rate of interest but, in practice, they normally have to choose one or the other.

The advantage of Monetary Gains and Losses is that they remove the element of interest paid and received which relates to compensation for the drop in the real value of capital sums and they leave just that element which relates to the charge for the use of borrowed spending power in the period.

Economies with Hyper-Inflation

Once rates of inflation are above 20% pa, raw currency Accounts (under any convention) are very difficult to interpret. In these circumstances some companies have produced their accounts in a currency other than their own (normally dollars) and some companies have used CPP translations. CPP might appear to be preferable because (a) there are no currencies which do not lose some of their value over time and (b) the rate of exchange between currencies will not perfectly match changes in spending power and may be difficult to determine if there are artificial exchange controls. However the countries with hyper-inflation are those most likely to have governments publishing fraudulent price index data.

Arguments Against CPP Translations

If the rate of inflation is very low (say, below half a percent per annum) and has remained at that low rate for the whole of the life of all large companies in the economy, the cost of producing CPP data (although small) may not be justified.

Those shareholders who have another relationship with the business may have reasons for their investment apart from the wish for additional future consumption. Some businesses may be perceived by some of their investors as providing benefits that cannot be measured in strict commercial terms.

Occasionally investment is made by restricting consumption during high earning years to provide savings for years of misfortune. In these cases the consumption foregone may be different in nature from the additional consumption achieved and neither may be perfectly represented by the RPI. The consumption forgone may be a luxury world cruise and the additional consumption may be many meals of bread and dripping.

The RPI is based on average expenditure patterns over a large group of households surveyed. It is not a perfect measure for any particular household. Each individual has a slightly different pattern of spending from every other individual and that pattern changes over time.

Nonetheless the RPI may be the best index available and is, in practice, accepted by most of those who invest as a reasonable indicator of inflation. Most of these investors both increase and realise their investments during years of approximately equivalent moderate comfort. And it is difficult to believe that motives for investment unconnected with consumption are of major significance.

Arguments in Favour of Historic Cost in CPP

Historic Cost accounts in CPP show the costs in terms of units of consumption foregone. It is a form of opportunity cost - looking at the alternative if no investment had taken place - but it is also still Historic Cost which normally indicates the last time the value was tested outside the business assuming that the buyer wanted to pay as little as possible and the vendor wanted to charge as much as possible. With unscrupulous or incompetent managers this value may be a better indicator of current realisable value and replacement cost than asking for direct estimates of those measures.

Professional firms and consultancies are employed to value assets at their current realisable values or replacement costs and their involvement can give the impression of independent expertise. With any valuation one needs to know the number of recent similar transactions that the valuer is using as evidence for his figure. How recent were these other transactions? How similar were the assets? What assumptions is the valuer making of his own volition and what assumptions were demanded in his brief?

Sometimes a company's directors arrange for several firms of surveyors to value a property. The directors then publish just one of those valuations - presumably the one that is closest to the figure they want to show. Valuers know that it is the company's directors and senior managers who arrange their remuneration and decide whether they get future work. Those senior managers may indicate to the valuer prior to his report what they wish to read.

If the company's fixed asset and stock cost behave in approximate accordance with general inflation, Historic Cost in CPP achieves the effect of the Cost of Sales Adjustment (COSA) and the Depreciation Adjustment (DA) of CCA. At high rates of general inflation relative price movements become a lower proportion of individual price changes and become more difficult to measure.

Businesses that are unwilling to construct their own specific indexes have been encouraged to use indexes published for broad classifications of industries and call the result 'CCA'. In practice these broad indexes have followed the RPI but, whether they do or not. it would be difficult to prove that they were any better than the RPI at indicating the current replacement costs of an individual business. Broad industrial classifications raise complicated problems of definition and hide the diversity of the individual businesses grouped together.

Arguments Against Historic Cost in CPP

Historic Costs (HC) on Balance Sheets are Sunk Costs. If managers are deciding the fate of assets and have access to perfect forecasts of Realisable Value (NRV), Replacement Cost (RC) and Economic Value (EV), then they should ignore Historic Costs.

(However published *financial* accounts are not produced solely for the managers of businesses. Too often a false choice is implied between HC, NRV, RC and EV. Where reasonably accurate information is available, why not publish them all? A comparison of HC with the other values gives readers an indication of the competence of those who incurred the Historic Costs.)

Historic Costs can be manipulated when companies under the same control trade with each other. Robert Maxwell was a master at arranging misleading trades between his private and public companies. (However Historic Costs are less likely to be manipulated than estimates of the other values and it is easier to prove that such fraud has taken place.)

References

[1] Committee on Concepts and Standards for Long Lived Assets, American Accounting Association (Accounting Review, July 1964) discussed in Contemporary Inflation Accounting (Abacus Dec 1975) Petri and Minch

[2] Disclosures of Estimates of Holding Gains and the Assessment of Systematic Risk (Journal of Accounting Research Suppl 1978) Abdel-Khalik and McKeown

[3] Fixed Asset Prices and Economic Production Theory (Abacus Dec 1979) Catt and Rivett

[4] Dividend Policy, Growth and the Valuation of Shares (Journal of Business, October 1961) Merton H Miller and Franco Modigliani

[5] Disclosures of Estimates of Holding Gains and the Assessment of Systematic Risk (Journal of Accounting Research Suppl 1978) Abdel-Khalik and McKeown

[6] A Study of the Predictive Significance of Two Income Measures (Journal of Accounting Research, Spring 1969) Frank
also
An Investigation of the Effects of Differing Accounting Frameworks on the Prediction of Net Income (The Accounting Review, October 1969) Simmons and Gray

[7] Inflation Accounting, Report of the Inflation Accounting Committee, Cmnd.6225, HMSO September 1975

[8] Ibid, page iv

[9] Ibid, para 189, page 52

[10] Reports on Taxation, Vol 1, Papers Relating to the United Kingdom (Duckworth, London 1980) Nicholas Kaldor

[11] How Well Does a Single Index Represent the Nineteen Sandilands Plant and Machinery Indexes? (Journal of Accounting Research, Spring 1977) Peasnell and Skerratt

[12] Accounting Standards Committee; Accounting for the Effects of Changing Prices : a Handbook; 1986; Para A1.7; Page 61

[13] On a Cloth Untrue, Inflation Accounting : the way forward (Woodhead-Faulkner, London 1984) D R Myddleton

Further Reading

Inflation Accounting (Philip Allan, 1984) W T Baxter

Current Cost Accounting, the benefits and costs (Prentice Hall/ICAEW, 1984) ed B Carsberg and M Page

Accounting Under Inflationary Conditions (Allen and Unwin, 1974) P R A Kirkman

Inflation Accounting, an introduction to the debate (Cambridge University Press, 1983) G Whittington

Inflation Accounting (Longman, 1984) P Clayton and J Blake

Modern Accounting 2

Chapter Five

CCA in CPP

As with CCA-in-raw-currency, expenses are charged to the income statement at their replacement cost at the date of consumption. But both revenue and expenses are indexed with a consumer price index to £CPP at the Balance Sheet date and the CPP monetary gain or loss on holding monetary liabilities or assets is added or subtracted from the trading surplus to give a CCA-in-CPP figure for earnings.

The net assets on the closing Balance Sheet should be identical to those shown on the CCA-in-raw-currency Balance Sheet at the same date. Last year's Balance Sheet to be shown as comparative figures this year, will show net assets which are the CCA-in-raw-currency figures indexed up to this year's £CPP.

Thus, the comparative figures will show how much would have been needed in terms of *today's currency* to have replaced the assets *last year*. This year and last year's Balance Sheets can now be validly shown side by side because they are both expressed in the same CPP currency (unlike CCA-in-raw-currency). But they are still CCA Balance Sheets and therefore they show replacement costs at their individual Balance Sheet dates.

One effect of conversion into CPP is that, below the Net Assets on the Balance Sheets, the Current Cost Reserve will be less than that shown in raw currency. The holding gains or losses will depend on whether specific prices have edged ahead or dropped behind general inflation and this should make the holding gains (or losses) a much more interesting figure. If those gains are random and outside of management control, then the remaining earnings should be a better indicator of future maintainable profit. On the other hand, if future prices can be forecast and stock levels are under management control, then differing holding gains between direct competitors may indicate differing qualities of management.

Modern Accounting 2

There follow 4 examples - of increasing complexity - of CCA in CPP. Alpha holds stock (below). Beta has just bought a Fixed Asset (page 137). Gamma owns several older Fixed Assets (page 139) and Delta holds both Stock and Fixed Assets (page 145).

Example of a Company Holding Stock - CCA in CPP

Alpha Ltd has produced the following Historic Cost in raw currency accounts :

Balance Sheets as at   31 Dec 2000   31 Dec 2001
                                        £   £
Stock, at cost   <u>10,000</u>   <u>20,000</u>
Share Capital   10,000   10,000
Revenue Reserves   -   10,000
                                   <u>10,000</u>   <u>20,000</u>

Profit and Loss Account for the year to 31 December 2001

                                        £   £
Sales   30,000
Opening Stock, 1.1.2001   10,000
Purchases   <u>30,000</u>
                                   40,000
less Closing Stock   <u>20,000</u>
                                                      20,000
Net Profit   <u>10,000</u>

Both sales and purchases took place evenly over the year. Stocks were purchased evenly over the last 3 months of each year. The following indexes are relevant :

	Specific Index based on items held in Stock	Consumer Price Index
Date :		
average for 3 months to 21.12.2000	105	110
1.1.2001	107	111
average for year to 31.12.2001	117	115
average for 3 months to 31.12.2001	120	117
31.12.2001	123	119

First some CCA figures both in raw currency and in CPP are needed:

CCA in CPP

[A] Stocks at Replacement Cost   31 Dec 2000   31 Dec 2001
                                        £   £
Stock, at replacement cost
10,000 X 107/105   10,190
  in £CPP   £CPP$_{31.12.01}$
10,190 X 119/111   10,925
20,000 X 123/120   20,500

[B] Replacement Cost of Sales for the year to 31 December 2001
                                        £   £
Opening Stock, at mid-year prices
10,000 X 117/105   11,143
Purchases   30,000
                                   41,143
less Closing Stock at mid-year prices
20,000 X 117/120   19,500
Replacement Cost of Sales   21,643
Replacement Cost of Sales in £CPP   £CPP$_{31.12.01}$
21,643 X 119/115   22,396

Secondly some Historic Cost in CPP figures are needed :

[C] Stock at Historic Cost as at   31 Dec 2000   31 Dec 2001
                                  £CPP$_{31.12.01}$ £CPP$_{31.12.01}$
Stock, at historic cost in CPP
10,000 X 119/110   10,818
20,000 X 119/117   20,342

[D] Historic Cost of Sales for the year to 31 December 2001
                                  £CPP$_{31.12.01}$ £CPP$_{31.12.01}$
Opening Stock [C]   10,818
Purchases 30,000 X 119/115   31,043
                                   41,861
less Closing Stock [C]   20,342
Historic Cost of Sales   21,519

It is now possible to calculate the stock holding gains. The Cost of Sales Adjustment (COSA) is the difference between the Replacement Cost (in CPP) and the Historic Cost of Sales (in CPP).

Modern Accounting 2

The Holding Gains for the year are summarised below :

	£CPP$_{31.12.01}$	£CPP$_{31.12.01}$
COSA in CPP :		
Replacement Cost of Sales in CPP [B]	22,396	
Historic Cost of Sales in CPP [D]	21,519	
		877

less Holding Gain on Opening Stock made in the previous year :
Replacement Cost at 31.12.00 of Opening Stock [A]
                                            10,925
Historic Cost of Opening Stock [C]   10,818
                                                                107
                                                                770

add Holding Gain on Closing Stock made this year :
Replacement Cost at 31.12.01 of Closing Stock [A]
                                            20,500
Historic Cost of Closing Stock [C]   20,342
                                                                158
Holding Gains in the year to 31 Dec 2001   928

In this case Holding *Gains* were made because the specific index climbed at a faster rate than the general index. The final CCA in CPP accounts will appear as follows:

Balance Sheets as at	31 Dec 2000	31 Dec 2001
	£CPP$_{31.12.01}$	£CPP$_{31.12.01}$
Stock at replacement cost [A]	10,925	20,500
Net Assets at 1.1.2001	10,925	10,925
Holding Gains of the year		928
Surplus on Income Statement		8,647
		20,500

Income Statement for the Year to 31 December 2001

	£CPP$_{31.12.01}$
Sales 30,000 X 119/115	31,043
Replacement Cost of Sales [B]	22,396
Surplus	8,647

CCA in CPP

Example of Initial Depreciation of a Fixed Asset - CCA in CPP

Beta Ltd has produced the following Historic Cost in raw currency accounts :

<u>Balance Sheets</u> as at

	31 Dec 2002 £	31 Dec 2003 £
Fixed Asset, at cost	100,000	100,000
less Accumulated Depreciation	-	20,000
		80,000
Current Asset		
Cash	-	40,000
	100,000	120,000
Share Capital	100,000	100,000
Revenue Reserves	-	20,000
	100,000	120,000

<u>Profit and Loss Account</u> for the year to 31 December 2003

	£
Sales	40,000
Depreciation on Fixed Asset	20,000
Net Profit	20,000

Sales took place evenly over the year. The Fixed Asset was bought on 31st December 2002. It is estimated to have a 5 year life with no residual value. The following indexes are relevant :

	Specific Index based on the Fixed Asset	Consumer Price Index
Date :		
1.1.2002	107	111
average for year to 31.12.2003	117	115
31.12.2003	123	119

[E] Replaciation in the Income Statement

Replaciation in £ terms :
20,000 X 120/110 £21,818
Replaciation in CPP terms :
21,818 X 121/113 £CPP$_{31.12.03}$23,363

[F] Fixed Assets on the Balance Sheets as at

	31 Dec 2002 £CPP$_{31.12.03}$	31 Dec 2003 £CPP$_{31.12.03}$
Replacement Cost :		
100,000 X 121/105	115,238	
Since purchase was on 31.12.02, only a CPP adjustment needed.		
100,000 X 130/110		118,182
Since replacement cost is at 31.12.03, no CPP adjustment needed.		
Used Replaciation :		
118,182 / 5 (one fifth of replacement cost)	−	23,636
	115,238	94,546

[G] Monetary Loss

On holding £40,000 while the RPI rises from 113 to 121

$$40{,}000 \times \frac{(121 - 113)}{113} = \text{£CPP}_{31.12.03}2{,}832$$

[J] Holding Gain in year to 31 Dec 2003 :

	£CPP$_{31.12.03}$	£CPP$_{31.12.03}$
Replacement Cost of Fixed Asset at 31.12.03 [F]		118,182
Replacement Cost of Fixed Asset at 31.12.02 [F]		115,238
		2,944
Used Replaciation at 31.12.03 [F]	23,636	
less Used Replaciation at 31.12.02	−	
	23,636	
Replaciation Charged in year [E]	23,363	
		273
Holding Gain		2,671

As with the previous example (Alpha Ltd), the specific index has risen faster than the general index and thus there are positive holding gains. The final CCA in CPP accounts appear on the next page.

CCA in CPP

Balance Sheets as at   31 Dec 2002   31 Dec 2003
                                    £CPP$_{31.12.03}$ £CPP$_{31.12.03}$
Fixed Assets
  Replacement Cost [F]   115,238   118,182
  less Used Replaciation [F]   -   23,636
                                                        94,546
Current Asset
  Cash   -   40,000

                                    115,238   134,546

Net Assets at 1.1.2003   115,238   115,238
Holding Gains of the year [J]   2,671
Surplus on Income Statement   16,637
                                                       134,546

Income Statement for the Year to 31 December 2003
                                    £CPP$_{31.12.03}$ £CPP$_{31.12.03}$
Sales 40,000 X 121/113   42,832

Replaciation [E]   23,363
Monetary Loss [G]   2,832
                                                        26,195

Surplus   16,637

Example of Depreciating Several Fixed Assets - CCA in CPP

Gamma Ltd has produced the following Historic Cost in raw currency accounts :

Modern Accounting 2

Balance Sheets as at

	31 Dec 2004 £	31 Dec 2005 £
Fixed Assets, at cost	300,000	600,000
less Accumulated Depreciation	190,000	250,000
	110,000	350,000
Current Assets		
Debtors	70,000	100,000
Cash	2,000	1,000
	72,000	101,000
less Creditors Due Within One Year	20,000	100,000
Net Current Assets	52,000	1,000
	162,000	351,000
Share Capital	100,000	100,000
Revenue Reserves	62,000	251,000
	162,000	351,000

Profit and Loss Accounts
for the year to

	31 Dec 2004 £	31 Dec 2005 £
Sales	150,000	329,000
Depreciation on Fixed Assets	30,000	60,000
Sundry Expenses	70,000	80,000
	100,000	140,000
Net Profit	50,000	189,000

Both Sales and Sundry Expenses took place evenly over the respective years. No dividends have ever been paid by this company. Ignore taxation. No Fixed Assets have ever been sold by this company. Assume that the only movements in Net Monetary Assets are those indicated above. The following indexes are relevant :

Date :	Specific Index on Fixed Assets	Consumer Price Index
15.7.98	120	110
15.3.99	122	130
1.1.04	123	160
average for year to 31.12.04	124	165
1.1.05	125	170
15.6.05	126	174
average for year to 31.12.05	126	175
31.12.05	127	180

CCA in CPP

Analysis of Fixed Assets at Cost as at   31.12.04   31.12.05
                                              £   £
Date of Purchase :
15.7.98   100,000   100,000
15.3.99   200,000   200,000
15.6.05   -   300,000
                                         _____   _____
                                         300,000   600,000

All Fixed Assets are Depreciated at 10% pa on cost (straight line) with a full year's depreciation in the year of purchase.

Analysis of Accumulated Depreciation on Fixed Assets
as at   31.12.04   31.12.05
                                              £   £
Date of Purchase :
15.7.98   70,000   80,000
15.3.99   120,000   140,000
15.6.05   -   30,000
                                         _____   _____
                                         190,000   250,000

[E] Replaciation in the Income Statements
Year to 31.12.04 in £s   £
10,000 X 124/120   10,333
20,000 X 124/122   20,328
                                                          _____
                                                          30,661

                                                      £CPP$_{31.12.05}$
in CPP : 30,661 X 180/165   33,448

Year to 31.12.05 in £s   £
10,000 X 126/120   10,500
20,000 X 126/122   20,656
30,000 X 126/126   30,000
                                                          _____
                                                          60,156

                                                      £CPP$_{31.12.05}$
in CPP : 60,156 X 180/175   61,875

Modern Accounting 2

[F] <u>Fixed Assets on the Balance Sheets</u> as at

	31 Dec 2004	31 Dec 2005
	£	£
Replacement Cost at the Balance Sheet dates :		
100,000 X 125/120	104,167	
100,000 X 127/120		105,833
200,000 X 125/122	204,918	
200,000 X 127/122		208,197
300,000 X 127/123		309,756
	<u>309,085</u>	<u>623,786</u>
Used Replaciation at the Balance Sheet dates :		
70,000 X 125/120	72,917	
80,000 X 127/120		84,667
120,000 X 125/122	122,951	
140,000 X 127/122		145,738
30,000 X 127/123		30,975
	<u>195,868</u>	<u>261,380</u>
In CPP :	£CPP$_{31.12.05}$	£CPP$_{31.12.05}$
Replacement Cost :		
309,085 X 180/170	327,266	
as above (already in prices at 31.12.05)		623,786
Used Replaciation :		
195,868 X 180/170	207,390	
as above (already in prices at 31.12.05)		261,381
	<u>119,876</u>	<u>362,406</u>

[G] <u>Net Monetary Assets</u> as at	31.12.04	31.12.05
	£	£
Debtors	70,000	100,000
Cash	2,000	1,000
	72,000	101,000
less Creditors	20,000	100,000
	<u>52,000</u>	<u>1,000</u>

The movements in the year to 31.12.04 must have been Sales (£150,000) less Sundry Expenses (£70,000) which is an increase of £80,000. Thus the Net Monetary Assets (NMA) at 31.12.03 must have been the NMA a year later (£52,000) less the positive movement of £80,000. In other words, there must have been Net Monetary Liabilities of £28,000.

Movements of Net Monetary Assets

Year to	31.12.04 £	31.12.05 £
brought forward	(28,000)	52,000
15.6.05 Purchase of Fixed Asset		300,000
		(248,000)
Av Point Sales less Sundry Expenses	80,000	249,000
	52,000	1,000

Using method 1 (as described on pages 25, 26 and 27) for calculating the monetary loss and gain :

Monetary Loss for the year to 31.12.04 in $£CPP_{31.12.04}$

$$-28,000 \times \frac{(170 - 160)}{160} + 80,000 \times \frac{(170 - 165)}{165}$$

$= £CPP_{31.12.04} 674$

in $£CPP_{31.12.05}$: $674 \times 180/170 = £CPP_{31.12.05} 714$

Monetary Gain for the year to 31.12.05

$$-52,000 \times \frac{(180-170)}{170} + 300,000 \times \frac{(180-174)}{174} - 249,000 \times \frac{(180-175)}{175}$$

$= £CPP_{31.12.05} 172$

[H] <u>Translating into $£CPP_{31.12.05}$</u>

Item	£	Factor	$£CPP_{31.12.05}$
Sales in year to 31.12.04	150,000	180/165	163,636
Sundry Exp's yr to 31.12.04	70,000	180/165	76,364
Sales in year to 31.12.05	329,000	180/175	338,400
Sundry Exp's yr to 31.12.05	80,000	180/175	82,286
Debtors at 31.12.04	70,000	180/170	74,117
Cash at 31.12.04	2,000	180/170	2,118
Creditors at 31.12.04	20,000	180/170	21,176
Addition to Fixed Assets on 15.6.05	300,000	180/174	310,345

Modern Accounting 2

[J] Holding Losses in year to 31 Dec 2005 :

	£CPP$_{31.12.05}$	£CPP$_{31.12.05}$
Replacement Cost of Fixed Assets at 31.12.04 [F]		327,266
Cost of Addition on 15.6.05 [H]		310,345
		637,611
Replacement Cost of Fixed Assets at 31.12.05 [F]		623,786
		13,825
Used Replaciation at 31.12.04 [F]	207,390	
Replaciation Charged in year [E]	61,875	
	269,265	
Used Replaciation at 31.12.05 [F]	261,380	
		7,885
Holding Losses		5,940

In this example, the general index has risen faster than the specific index and thus there are holding losses. The final CCA in CPP accounts appear below.

Balance Sheets as at	31 Dec 2004	31 Dec 2005
	£CPP$_{31.12.05}$	£CPP$_{31.12.05}$
Fixed Assets		
Replacement Cost [F]	327,266	623,786
less Used Replaciation [F]	207,390	261,380
	119,876	362,406
Current Assets		
Debtors [H]	74,117	100,000
Cash [H]	2,118	1,000
	76,235	101,000
less Creditors Due Within One Year [H]	21,176	100,000
	55,059	1,000
	174,935	363,406
Net Assets at 1.1.2005	174,935	174,935
Holding Losses of the year [J]		(5,940)
Surplus on Income Statement		194,411
		363,406

Income Statements

Year to	31 Dec 2004	31 Dec 2005
	£CPP$_{31.12.05}$	£CPP$_{31.12.05}$
Sales [H]	163,636	338,400
Replaciation [E]	33,448	61,875
Sundry Expenses [H]	76,364	82,286
Monetary Loss (Gain) [G]	714	(172)
	110,526	143,989
Surplus	53,110	194,411

Example with Stock and Several Fixed Assets - CCA in CPP

Delta Ltd has produced the following Historic Cost in raw currency accounts :

Balance Sheets as at	31 Dec 1999	31 Dec 2000
	£	£
Fixed Assets, at cost	270,000	300,000
less Accumulated Depreciation	105,000	155,000
	165,000	145,000
Current Assets		
Stock	90,000	100,000
Debtors	80,000	70,000
Cash	2,000	3,000
	172,000	173,000
less Creditors Due Within One Year	30,000	40,000
Net Current Assets	142,000	133,000
	307,000	278,000
Share Capital	100,000	100,000
Revenue Reserves	207,000	178,000
	307,000	278,000

Modern Accounting 2

Profit and Loss Account
for the year to 31 Dec 2000

	£	£
Sales		300,000
Opening Stock	90,000	
Purchases	176,000	
	266,000	
less Closing Stock	100,000	
		166,000
Gross Profit		134,000
Sundry Expenses	50,000	
Depreciation on Fixed Assets	75,000	
Loss on sale of Fixed Asset	5,000	
		130,000
Net Profit		4,000
Taxation		3,000
		1,000
Dividends Paid		30,000
		(29,000)
Brought forward		207,000
		178,000

Sales, Purchases and Sundry Expenses took place evenly over the year. Assume that Taxation and Dividends Paid took place at the 'average point' of the year. Stocks were purchased over the final 7 months of the respective years. The following indexes are relevant :

Date :	Specific Index on Stock	Specific Index Fixed Assets	Consumer Price Index
15.1.98	110	103	115
15.3.99	106	107	120
average for the last 7 months of 1999			
	105	109	122
1.1.00	100	112	125
average for year to 31.12.00	95	118	130
average for the last 7 months of 2000			
	90	120	133
15.9.00	87	122	134
1.10.00	86	123	135
31.12.00	84	124	136

146

Analysis of Fixed Assets at Cost
as at   31 Dec 1999   31 Dec 2000
Date of Purchase :   £   £
15.1.98   150,000   100,000
15.3.99   120,000   120,000
15.9.00   -   80,000
                                           270,000   300,000

All Fixed Assets are Depreciated at 25% pa on cost (straight line) with a full year's depreciation in the year of purchase and none in the year of sale. On 1.10.00 a Fixed Asset that had cost £50,000 on 15.1.98 was sold for £20,000.

Analysis of Accumulated Depreciation on Fixed Assets
as at   31 Dec 1999   31 Dec 2000
Date of Purchase :   £   £
15.1.98   75,000   75,000
15.3.99   30,000   60,000
15.9.00   -   20,000
                                           105,000   155,000

[A] Stocks at Replacement Cost   31 Dec 1999   31 Dec 2000
                                                £   £
Stock, at replacement cost
90,000 X 100/105   85,714
 in £CPP   £CPP$_{31.12.00}$
85,714 X 136/125   93,257
100,000 X 84/90   93,333

[B] Replacement Cost of Sales for the year to 31 December 2000

Opening Stock, at mid-year prices   £   £
90,000 X 95/105   81,429
Purchases   176,000
                                           257,429
less Closing Stock at mid-year prices
100,000 X 95/90   105,556
Replacement Cost of Sales   151,873
Replacement Cost of Sales in £CPP   £CPP$_{31.12.00}$
 151,873 X 136/130   158,883

Modern Accounting 2

[C] <u>Stock at Historic Cost</u> as at 31 Dec 1999 31 Dec 2000
Stock, at historic cost in CPP £CPP$_{31.12.00}$ £CPP$_{31.12.00}$
90,000 X 136/122 <u>100,328</u>
100,000 X 136/133   <u>102,256</u>

[D] <u>Historic Cost of Sales</u> for the year to 31 December 2000
                             £CPP$_{31.12.00}$ £CPP$_{31.12.00}$
Opening Stock [C]   100,328
Purchases 176,000 X 136/130   <u>184,123</u>
                                 284,451
less Closing Stock [C]   <u>102,256</u>
Historic Cost of Sales   <u>182,195</u>

[E] <u>Replaciation in the Income Statement</u>
Depreciation must be the difference between the accumulated depreciation on 31.12.00 and that on 31.12.99 adjusted for the £25,000 accumulated on the item sold.

Depreciation charged on items purchased on :   £
15.1.98 (£75,000 - 75,000 + 25,000)   25,000
15.3.99 (£60,000 - 30,000)   30,000
15.9.00 (£20,000 - 0)   <u>20,000</u>
                                               <u>75,000</u>

Replaciation charged on items purchased on :   £
15.1.98 25,000 X 118/103   28,641
15.3.99 30,000 X 118/107   33,084
15.9.00 20,000 X 118/122   <u>19,344</u>
                                               <u>81,069</u>
                                            £CPP$_{31.12.00}$
in CPP : 81,069 X 136/130   <u>84,811</u>

[F] <u>Fixed Assets on the Balance Sheets</u> as at
                                 31 Dec 1999   31 Dec 2000
                                     £   £
Replacement Cost at the Balance Sheet dates :
150,000 X 112/103   163,107
100,000 X 124/103   120,388
120,000 X 112/107   125,607
120,000 X 124/107   139,065
80,000 X 124/122   81,311
                                  <u>288,714</u>   <u>340,764</u>

CCA in CPP

	31 Dec 1999	31 Dec 2000
	£	£
Used Replaciation at the Balance Sheet dates :		
75,000 X 112/103	81,553	
75,000 X 124/103		90,291
30,000 X 112/107	31,402	
60,000 X 124/107		69,533
20,000 X 124/122		20,328
	112,955	180,152
In CPP :	£CPP$_{31.12.00}$	£CPP$_{31.12.00}$
Replacement Cost :		
288,714 X 136/125	314,121	
as previous page (already in prices at 31.12.00)		340,764
Used Replaciation :		
112,955 X 136/125	122,895	
as above (already in prices at 31.12.00)		180,152
	191,226	160,612

[G] <u>Net Monetary Assets</u> as at 31.12.99 and 31.12.00

	£	£
Debtors	80,000	70,000
Cash	2,000	3,000
	82,000	73,000
less Creditors	30,000	40,000
	52,000	33,000

<u>Movements of Net Monetary Assets</u>
Year to 31 Dec 2000

		£	£
brought forward			52,000
Av Point	Sales	300,000	
	Purchases	(176,000)	
	Sundry Expenses	(50,000)	
	Taxation	(3,000)	
	Dividend	(30,000)	41,000
			93,000
15.9.00	Purchase of Fixed Asset		80,000
			13,000
1.10.00	Proceeds from Sale of Fixed Asset		20,000
Carried forward			33,000

Modern Accounting 2

Using method 1 (as described on pages 25, 26 and 27) for calculating the monetary loss and gain :
Monetary Loss for the year to 31.12.00 in £CPP$_{31.12.00}$
52,000 X (136-125)/125 + 41,000 X (136-130)/130
- 80,000 X (136-134)/134 + 20,000 X (136-135)/135 =
£CPP$_{31.12.00}$5,422

[H] Translating into £CPP$_{31.12.00}$

Item	£	Factor	£CPP$_{31.12.05}$
Sales	300,000	136/130	313,846
Purchases	176,000	136/130	184,123
Sundry Expenses	50,000	136/130	52,308
Taxation	3,000	136/130	3,138
Dividends	30,000	136/130	31,385
Debtors at 31.12.99	80,000	136/125	87,040
Cash at 31.12.99	2,000	136/125	2,176
Creditors at 31.12.99	30,000	136/125	32,640
Addition to Fixed Assets on 15.9.00	80,000	136/134	81,194
Proceeds from the sale of a Fixed Asset on 1.10.00	20,000	136/135	20,148

[I] Loss on Disposal of Fixed Asset

	£
Historic Cost of Fixed Asset sold	50,000
Replacement Cost at the date of disposal : 50,000 X 123/103	£59,708
Accumulated Depreciation at the date of disposal	25,000
Used Replaciation at the date of disposal : 25,000 X 123/103	£29,854

in CPP	£CPP$_{31.12.00}$
Replacement Cost 59,708 X 136/135	60,150
Used Replaciation 29,854 X 136/135	30,075
	30,075
less Proceeds from Sale [H]	20,148
Loss on sale	9,927

CCA in CPP

[J] <u>Holding Gains on Fixed Assets</u> in year to 31 Dec 2000 :

	£CPP_{31.12.00}	£CPP_{31.12.00}
Replacement Cost of Fixed Assets at 31.12.00 [F]		340,764
Replacement Cost of Fixed Assets at 31.12.99 [F]	314,121	
Cost of Addition on 15.9.00 [H]	<u>81,194</u>	
	395,315	
Replacement Cost of Disposal [I]	<u>60,150</u>	<u>335,165</u>
		5,599
Used Replaciation at 31.12.99 [F]	122,895	
Used Replaciation on Disposal [I]	<u>30,075</u>	
	92,820	
Replaciation Charged in year [E]	<u>84,811</u>	
	177,631	
Used Replaciation at 31.12.00 [F]	<u>180,152</u>	<u>2,521</u>
Holding Gains on Fixed Assets		<u>3,078</u>

[K] <u>Holding Losses on Stock</u> in year to 31 Dec 2000 :

	£CPP_{31.12.00}	£CPP_{31.12.00}
COSA in CPP :		
Historic Cost of Sales in CPP [D]	182,195	
Replacement Cost of Sales in CPP [B]	<u>158,883</u>	23,312
less Holding Loss on Opening Stock made in the previous year :		
Historic Cost of Opening Stock [C]	100,328	
Replacement Cost at 31.12.99 of Opening Stock [A]	<u>93,257</u>	<u>7,071</u>
		16,241
add Holding Loss on Closing Stock made this year :		
Historic Cost of Closing Stock [C]	102,256	
Replacement Cost at 31.12.00 of Closing Stock [A]	<u>93,333</u>	<u>8,923</u>
Holding Losses on Stock		<u>25,164</u>
Holding Losses on Stock [K]		25,164
less Holding Gains on Fixed Assets [J]		<u>3,078</u>
		<u>22,086</u>

The final CCA in CPP accounts appear on the next page.

Modern Accounting 2

Balance Sheets as at   31 Dec 1999   31 Dec 2000
                                            £CPP$_{31.12.00}$ £CPP$_{31.12.00}$
Fixed Assets
  Replacement Cost [F]   314,121   340,764
  less Used Replaciation [F]   122,895   180,152
                                            191,226   160,612
Current Assets
  Stock [A]   93,257   93,333
  Debtors [H]   87,040   70,000
  Cash [H]   2,176   3,000
                                            182,473   166,333
less Creditors Due Within One Year [H]   32,640   40,000
Net Current Assets   149,833   126,333

                                            341,059   286,945
                                            £CPP$_{31.12.00}$ £CPP$_{31.12.00}$
Net Assets at 1.1.2000   341,059   341,059
Holding Losses of the year [K]-[J]   (22,086)
Deficit on Income Statement   (32,028)
                                                               286,945

Income Statement
for the Year to 31 Dec 2000
                                            £CPP$_{31.12.00}$ £CPP$_{31.12.00}$
Sales [H]   313,846
Replacement Cost of Sales [B]   158,883
                                                               154,963

Sundry Expenses [H]   52,308
Replaciation [E]   84,811
Loss on Sale of Fixed Asset [I]   9,927
Monetary Loss [G]   5,422   152,468
Trading Surplus   2,495
Taxation [H]   3,138
                                                               (643)
Dividend Paid [H]   31,385

(Deficit)   (32,028)

Delta's CCA in CPP figures give substantial additional information to that contained in the Historic Cost in raw currency figures. On the Balance Sheet at 31 December 2000 the Holding Losses show the *net* figure of £CPP$_{31.12.00}$22,086 and the full analysis would be needed for a reader to grasp the full extent of the Stock Holding Losses. Why is Delta holding so much stock? How are stock prices forecast to perform in the future?

If Delta's competitors perform as badly, it may be that little fresh capacity is being attracted to this business and the Deprival Value of Fixed Assets may not be their Replacement Cost. Was the addition to Fixed Assets in this year merely replacement or was it an attempt to move in a new direction?

Try to answer the following questions before looking at the answers (which are at the end of this chapter).

Question 5.1 (Answer 5.1 is on page 160)

Mozart Ltd has produced the following Historic Cost in raw currency accounts :

Balance Sheets as at   31 Dec 1999   31 Dec 2000
                                    £   £
Stock   2,000   1,000
Debtors   30,000   260,000
Cash   1,000   27,000
                                33,000   288,000

Share Capital   1,000   1,000
Revenue Reserves   32,000   287,000
                                33,000   288,000

Profit and Loss Account for the year to 31 Dec 2000
                                    £   £
Sales   560,000
Opening Stock   2,000
Purchases   304,000
                               306,000
less Closing Stock   1,000
                                              305,000
Net Profit   255,000

Stocks at the end of each year were purchased in the last quarter of that year. Sales and purchases have been analysed into quarters as follows :

Quarter to	Sales	Purchases
	£	£
31.3.00	10,000	300,000
30.6.00	20,000	1,000
30.9.00	30,000	1,000
31.12.00	500,000	2,000
	560,000	304,000

The following indexes are relevant :

Date	Price Index based on Selling Prices	Price Index based on Purchase Prices	Consumer Price Index
Average for quarter to 31.12.99	100	110	120
At 31.12.99	100	112	124
Average for quarter to :			
31.3.00	100	114	125
30.6.00	105	118	126
30.9.00	110	120	130
31.12.00	120	123	140
At 31.12.00	120	126	145

REQUIRED : Redraft the above accounts for Mozart Ltd into CCA in CPP.

Question 5.2 (Answer 5.2 is on page 163)

Schubert Ltd has produced the following Historic Cost in raw currency accounts :

Balance Sheets as at

	31 Dec 2000 £	31 Dec 2001 £
Fixed Assets, at cost	275,000	355,000
less Accumulated Depreciation	135,000	198,000
	140,000	157,000
Current Assets		
Stock	130,000	160,000
Debtors	50,000	78,000
Cash	10,000	20,000
	190,000	258,000
less Creditors Due Within One Year	40,000	50,000
Net Current Assets	150,000	208,000
	290,000	365,000
Share Capital	10,000	10,000
Revenue Reserves	280,000	355,000
	290,000	365,000

Profit and Loss Account for the year to 31 Dec 2001

	£	£
Sales		800,000
Opening Stock	130,000	
Purchases	485,000	
	615,000	
less Closing Stock	160,000	455,000
Gross Profit		345,000
Sundry Expenses	82,000	
Depreciation on Fixed Assets	71,000	
(Profit) on sale of Fixed Asset	(3,000)	
		150,000
Net Profit		195,000
Taxation		80,000
		115,000
Dividends Paid		40,000
		75,000
Brought forward		280,000
		355,000

Sales, Purchases and Sundry Expenses took place evenly over the year. Assume that Taxation and Dividends Paid took place at the 'average point' of the year. Stocks were purchased over the final 4 months of the respective years. The following indexes are relevant:

Date :	Specific Index on Stock	Specific Index Fixed Assets	Consumer Price Index
15.4.98	104	111	125
15.7.99	110	121	130
average last 4 months of 2000	120	131	133
1.1.01	125	132	136
15.2.01	126	135	137
15.3.01	128	137	138
average for year to 31.12.01	130	140	142
average last 4 months of 2001	135	143	144
31.12.01	140	145	146

Analysis of Fixed Assets at Cost

as at	31 Dec 2000	31 Dec 2001
Date of Purchase :	£	£
15.4.98	125,000	125,000
15.7.99	150,000	130,000
15.2.01	-	100,000
	275,000	355,000

All Fixed Assets are Depreciated at 20% pa on cost (straight line) with a full year's depreciation in the year of purchase and none in the year of sale. On 15.3.01 a Fixed Asset that had cost £20,000 on 15.7.99 was sold for £15,000.

Analysis of Accumulated Depreciation on Fixed Assets

as at	31 Dec 2000	31 Dec 2001
Date of Purchase :	£	£
15.4.98	75,000	100,000
15.7.99	60,000	78,000
15.2.01	-	20,000
	135,000	198,000

REQUIRED : Redraft the above accounts for Mozart Ltd into CCA in CPP.

Question 5.3 (No Answer to this question has been included in this book)

Wagner Ltd has produced the following Historic Cost in raw currency accounts :

Balance Sheets as at

	31 Dec 2001 £	31 Dec 2002 £
Fixed Assets, at cost	400,000	400,000
less Accumulated Depreciation	180,000	150,000
	220,000	250,000
Current Assets		
Stock	80,000	150,000
Debtors	90,000	60,000
Cash	3,000	3,000
	173,000	213,000
less Creditors Due Within One Year	40,000	50,000
Net Current Assets	133,000	163,000
	353,000	413,000
Share Capital	100,000	100,000
Revenue Reserves	253,000	313,000
	353,000	413,000

Profit and Loss Account for the year to 31 Dec 2002

	£	£
Sales		500,000
Opening Stock	80,000	
Purchases	304,000	
	384,000	
less Closing Stock	150,000	234,000
Gross Profit		266,000
Sundry Expenses	100,000	
Depreciation on Fixed Assets	40,000	
Loss on sale of Fixed Asset	6,000	146,000
Net Profit		120,000
Taxation		50,000
		70,000
Dividends Paid		10,000
		60,000
Brought forward		253,000
		313,000

Sales, Purchases and Sundry Expenses took place evenly over the year. Assume that Taxation and Dividends Paid took place at the 'average point' of the year. Stocks were purchased evenly over the final 9 months of the respective years.

Date :	Specific Index on Stock	Specific Index Fixed Assets	Consumer Price Index
15.2.95	110	103	115
15.6.00	106	107	120
average last 9 months of 2001	105	109	122
1.1.02	100	112	125
average for year to 31.12.02	95	118	130
15.7.02	87	122	134
average last 9 months of 2002	90	120	133
15.9.02	86	123	135
31.12.02	84	124	136

Analysis of Fixed Assets at Cost

as at	31 Dec 2001	31 Dec 2002
Date of Purchase :	£	£
15.2.95	200,000	100,000
15.6.00	200,000	200,000
15.7.02	-	100,000
	400,000	400,000

All Fixed Assets are Depreciated at 10% pa on cost (straight line) with a full year's depreciation in the year of purchase and none in the year of sale. On 15.9.02 a Fixed Asset that had cost £100,000 on 15.2.95 was sold for £24,000.

Analysis of Accumulated Depreciation on Fixed Assets

as at	31 Dec 2001	31 Dec 2002
Date of Purchase :	£	£
15.2.95	140,000	80,000
15.3.99	40,000	60,000
15.9.00	-	10,000
	180,000	150,000

REQUIRED : Redraft the above accounts for Mozart Ltd into CCA in CPP.

Modern Accounting 2

Answers to Questions 5.1 to 5.2

Answer 5.1

[A] Stocks at Replacement Cost	31 Dec 1999	31 Dec 2000
Stock, at replacement cost	£	£
2,000 X 112/110	2,036	
in £CPP	£CPP$_{31.12.00}$	
2,036 X 145/124	2,381	
1,000 X 126/123		1,024

[B] Replacement Cost of Sales for the year to 31 December 2000

	a	b	c = a/b	d	e	f = d/e
Quarter	Purchases £	Purchase Price Index	Purchases in PVU	Sales £	Sales Price Index	Sales in SVU
1	300,000	114	2,632	10,000	100	100
2	1,000	118	8	20,000	105	190
3	1,000	120	8	30,000	110	273
4	2,000	123	16	500,000	120	4,167
	304,000		2,664		78	4,730
add Opening Stock	2,000	110	18			
	306,000		2,682			
less Closing Stock	1,000	140	8			
	305,000		2,674			

Conversion factor of SVU to PVU = 2,674/4,730 = 0.5653

	g = f X 0.5653	h = b	i = g X h	j	k = i X145/j
Quarter	Sales in PVU	Purchase Price Index	Replacement Cost of Sales in £	Consumer Price Index	Replacement Cost in £CPP$_{31.12.00}$
1	56.6	114	6,452.4	125	7,485
2	107.4	118	12,673.2	126	14,584
3	154.4	120	18,528.0	130	20,666
4	2,355.6	123	289,738.8	140	300,087
	2,674.0		327,392.4		342,822

160

CCA in CPP

[C] Stock at Historic Cost as at   31 Dec 1999   31 Dec 2000
Stock, at historic cost in CPP $£CPP_{31.12.00}$ $£CPP_{31.12.00}$
2,000 X 145/120   <u>2,417</u>
1,000 X 145/140   <u>1,036</u>

[D] Historic Cost of Sales for the year to 31 December 2000

Purchases	£	Factor	$£CPP_{31.12.00}$
Q1	300,000	145/125	348,000
Q2	1,000	145/126	1,151
Q3	1,000	145/130	1,115
Q4	<u>2,000</u>	145/140	<u>2,071</u>
	<u>304,000</u>		<u>352,333</u>

	$£CPP_{31.12.00}$	$£CPP_{31.12.00}$
Opening Stock [C]	2,417	
Purchases (above)	<u>352,333</u>	
	354,750	
less Closing Stock [C]	<u>1,036</u>	
Historic Cost of Sales		<u>353,718</u>

[G] Net Monetary Assets as at   31.12.99   31.12.00

	£	£
Debtors	30,000	260,000
Cash	<u>1,000</u>	<u>27,000</u>
	<u>31,000</u>	<u>287,000</u>

Movements of Net Monetary Assets
Year to 31 Dec 2000   £   £
brought forward   31,000

Q1	Purchases	300,000	
	Sales	<u>10,000</u>	<u>290,000</u>
			(259,000)
Q2	Sales	20,000	
	Purchases	<u>1,000</u>	<u>19,000</u>
			(240,000)
Q3	Sales	30,000	
	Purchases	<u>1,000</u>	<u>29,000</u>
			(211,000)
Q4	Sales	500,000	
	Purchases	<u>2,000</u>	<u>498,000</u>
Carried forward			<u>287,000</u>

Modern Accounting 2

Monetary Gain for the year to 31.12.00 in £CPP$_{31.12.00}$
- 31,000 X (145 - 124)/124 + 290,000 X (145 - 125)/125
- 19,000 X (145 - 126)/126 - 29,000 X (145 - 130)/130
- 498,000 X (145 - 140)/140 =
£CPP$_{31.12.00}$17,153

[H] <u>Translating into £CPP$_{31.12.00}$</u>

Item	£	Factor	£CPP$_{31.12.05}$
Sales Q1	10,000	145/125	11,600
Sales Q2	20,000	145/126	23,016
Sales Q3	30,000	145/130	33,461
Sales Q4	500,000	145/140	517,857
	560,000		585,934
Debtors at 31.12.99	30,000	145/124	35,081
Cash at 31.12.99	1,000	145/124	1,169

[K] <u>Holding Losses on Stock</u> in year to 31 Dec 2000 :

	£CPP$_{31.12.00}$	£CPP$_{31.12.00}$
COSA in CPP :		
Historic Cost of Sales in CPP [D]	353,718	
Replacement Cost of Sales in CPP [B]	<u>342,822</u>	10,896

less Holding Loss on Opening Stock made in the previous year :
  Historic Cost of Opening Stock [C]   2,417
  Replacement Cost at 31.12.99 of Opening Stock [A]
    <u>2,381</u>   <u>36</u>
    10,860

add Holding Loss on Closing Stock made this year :
  Historic Cost of Closing Stock [C]   1,036
  Replacement Cost at 31.12.00 of Closing Stock [A]
    <u>1,024</u>   <u>12</u>
Holding Losses on Stock   <u>10,872</u>

Final CCA in CPP Accounts :

<u>Balance Sheets</u> as at

	31 Dec 1999	31 Dec 2000
	£CPP$_{31.12.00}$	£CPP$_{31.12.00}$
Stock [A]	2,381	1,024
Debtors [H]	35,081	260,000
Cash [H]	1,169	27,000
	<u>38,631</u>	<u>288,024</u>

CCA in CPP

	$£CPP_{31.12.00}$	$£CPP_{31.12.00}$
Net Assets at 1.1.2000	38,631	38,631
Holding Losses of the year [K]		(10,872)
Surplus on Income Statement		260,265
		288,024

Income Statement
for the Year to 31 Dec 2000

	$£CPP_{31.12.00}$
Sales [H]	585,934
Replacement Cost of Sales [B]	342,822
	243,112
Monetary Gain [G]	17,153
Surplus	260,265

Answer 5.2

[A] Stocks at Replacement Cost	31 Dec 2000	31 Dec 2001
	£	£
Stock, at replacement cost		
130,000 X 125/120	135,417	
in £CPP	$£CPP_{31.12.01}$	
135,417 X 146/136	145,374	
160,000 X 140/135		165,926

[B] Replacement Cost of Sales for the year to 31 December 2001

	£	£
Opening Stock, at mid-year prices		
130,000 X 130/120	140,833	
Purchases	485,000	
	625,833	
less Closing Stock at mid-year prices		
160,000 X 130/135	154,074	
Replacement Cost of Sales		471,759
Replacement Cost of Sales in £CPP		$£CPP_{31.12.01}$
471,759 X 146/142		485,048

[C] Stock at Historic Cost as at	31 Dec 2000	31 Dec 2001
Stock, at historic cost in CPP	$£CPP_{31.12.01}$	$£CPP_{31.12.01}$
130,000 X 146/133	142,707	
160,000 X 146/133		162,222

Modern Accounting 2

[D] Historic Cost of Sales for the year to 31 December 2001

	$£CPP_{31.12.01}$	$£CPP_{31.12.01}$
Opening Stock [C]	142,707	
Purchases 485,000 X 146/142	498,662	
	641,369	
less Closing Stock [C]	162,222	
Historic Cost of Sales		479,147

[E] Replaciation in the Income Statement
Depreciation must be the difference between the accumulated depreciation on 31.12.01 and that on 31.12.00 adjusted for the £8,000 accumulated on the item sold.

Depreciation charged on items purchased on :	£
15.4.98 (£100,000 - 75,000)	25,000
15.7.99 (£78,000 - 60,000 + 8,000)	26,000
15.2.01 (£20,000 - 0)	20,000
	71,000

Replaciation charged on items purchased on :	£
15.4.98 25,000 X 140/111	31,531
15.7.99 26,000 X 140/121	30,083
15.2.01 20,000 X 140/135	20,741
	82,355

	$£CPP_{31.12.01}$
in CPP : 82,355 X 146/142	84,675

[F] Fixed Assets on the Balance Sheets as at

	31 Dec 2000	31 Dec 2001
	£	£
Replacement Cost at the Balance Sheet dates :		
125,000 X 132/111	148,649	
125,000 X 145/111		163,288
150,000 X 132/121	163,636	
130,000 X 145/121		155,785
100,000 X 145/135		107,408
	312,285	426,481

	31 Dec 2000	31 Dec 2001
	£	£
Used Replaciation at the Balance Sheet dates :		
75,000 X 132/111	89,189	
100,000 X 145/111		130,631
60,000 X 132/121	65,455	
78,000 X 145/121		93,471
20,000 X 145/135		21,481
	154,644	245,583

CCA in CPP

	£CPP$_{31.12.01}$	£CPP$_{31.12.01}$
In CPP :		
Replacement Cost :		
312,285 X 146/136	335,247	
as previous page (already in prices at 31.12.01)		426,481
Used Replaciation :		
154,644 X 136/125	166,015	
as above (already in prices at 31.12.00)		245,583
	<u>169,232</u>	<u>180,898</u>

[G] <u>Net Monetary Assets</u> as at	31.12.00	31.12.01
	£	£
Debtors	50,000	78,000
Cash	10,000	20,000
	60,000	98,000
less Creditors	40,000	50,000
	<u>20,000</u>	<u>48,000</u>

<u>Movements of Net Monetary Assets</u>
Year to 31 Dec 2001

		£	£
brought forward			20,000
15.2.01	*Purchase of Fixed Asset*		100,000
			(80,000)
15.3.01	*Proceeds from Sale of Fixed Asset*		15,000
			(65,000)
Av Point	*Sales*	800,000	
	Purchases	(485,000)	
	Sundry Expenses	(82,000)	
	Taxation	(80,000)	
	Dividend	<u>(40,000)</u>	113,000
Carried forward			<u>48,000</u>

Monetary Gain for the year to 31.12.01 in £CPP$_{31.12.01}$

-20,000 X (146-136) + 100,000 X (146-137)/137 - 15,000 X (146-138)/138
-113,000 X (146-142)/142 =

£CPP$_{31.12.01}$1,046

Modern Accounting 2

[H] Translating into £CPP$_{31.12.01}$

Item	£	Factor	£CPP$_{31.12.05}$
Sales	800,000	146/142	822,535
Purchases	485,000	146/142	498,662
Sundry Expenses	82,000	146/142	84,310
Taxation	80,000	146/142	82,253
Dividends	40,000	146/142	41,127
Debtors at 31.12.00	50,000	146/136	53,677
Cash at 31.12.00	10,000	146/136	10,735
Creditors at 31.12.00	40,000	146/136	42,941
Addition to Fixed Assets on 15.2.01	100,000	146/137	106,569
Proceeds from the sale of a Fixed Asset on 15.3.01	15,000	146/138	15,870

[I] Gain on Disposal of Fixed Asset

	£
Historic Cost of Fixed Asset sold	20,000
Replacement Cost at the date of disposal : 20,000 X 137/121	£<u>22,645</u>
Accumulated Depreciation at the date of disposal	8,000
Used Replaciation at the date of disposal : 8,000 X 137/121	£<u>9,058</u>

in CPP	£CPP$_{31.12.01}$
Replacement Cost 22,645 X 146/138	23,958
Used Replaciation 9,058 X 146/138	<u>9,583</u>
	14,375
less Proceeds from Sale [H]	<u>15,870</u>
Gain on sale	<u>1,495</u>

166

CCA in CPP

[J] Holding Gains on Fixed Assets in year to 31 Dec 2001 :

	£CPP₃₁.₁₂.₀₁	£CPP₃₁.₁₂.₀₁
Replacement Cost of Fixed Assets at 31.12.01 [F]		426,481
Replacement Cost of Fixed Assets at 31.12.00 [F]	335,247	
Cost of Addition on 15.9.00 [H]	106,569	
	441,816	
Replacement Cost of Disposal [I]	23,957	
		417,859
		8,622
Used Replaciation at 31.12.00 [F]	166,015	
Used Replaciation on Disposal [I]	9,583	
	156,432	
Replaciation Charged in year [E]	84,675	
	241,107	
Used Replaciation at 31.12.01 [F]	245,583	
		4,476
Holding Gains on Fixed Assets		**4,146**

[K] Holding Gains on Stock in year to 31 Dec 2001 :

	£CPP₃₁.₁₂.₀₁	£CPP₃₁.₁₂.₀₁
COSA in CPP :		
Replacement Cost of Sales in CPP [B]	485,048	
Historic Cost of Sales in CPP [D]	479,147	
		5,902
less Holding Loss on Opening Stock made in the previous year :		
Replacement Cost at 31.12.00 of Opening Stock [A]		
	145,374	
Historic Cost of Opening Stock [C]	142,707	
		2,667
		3,234
add Holding Loss on Closing Stock made this year :		
Replacement Cost at 31.12.01 of Closing Stock [A]		
	165,926	
Historic Cost of Closing Stock [C]	162,222	
		3,704
Holding Gains on Stock		**6,938**

Holding Gains on Fixed Assets [J]	4,146
Holding Gains on Stock [K]	6,938
	11,084

Modern Accounting 2

Balance Sheets as at

	31 Dec 2000 £CPP$_{31.12.01}$	31 Dec 2001 £CPP$_{31.12.01}$
Fixed Assets		
Replacement Cost [F]	335,247	426,481
less Used Replaciation [F]	166,015	245,588
	169,232	180,898
Current Assets		
Stock [A]	145,374	165,926
Debtors [H]	53,677	78,000
Cash [H]	10,735	20,000
	209,786	263,926
less Creditors Due Within One Year [H]	42,941	50,000
Net Current Assets	166,845	213,926
	336,077	394,824

	£CPP$_{31.12.01}$	£CPP$_{31.12.01}$
Net Assets at 1.1.2001	336,077	336,077
Holding Gains of the year [J]+[K]		11,084
Surplus on Income Statement		47,663
		394,824

Income Statement
for the Year to 31 Dec 2001

	£CPP$_{31.12.01}$	£CPP$_{31.12.01}$
Sales [H]		822,535
Replacement Cost of Sales [B]		485,048
		337,487
Gain on Sale of Fixed Asset [I]		1,495
Monetary Gain [G]		1,046
		340,028
Sundry Expenses [H]	84,310	
Replaciation [E]	84,675	
		168,985
Trading Surplus		171,043
Taxation [H]		82,253
		88,790
Dividend Paid [H]		41,127
Surplus		47,663

Chapter Six

Discounted Cash Flow

Let us assume that a company has a large overdraft on which the bank charges 10% per annum in arrears. The overdraft limit is so high that the company will always be able to borrow more money.

If the company spends a further £1 today (Year 0), then that will increase the current overdraft by £1. The overdraft after one year (Year 1) will be increased by £1.10 which is the £1 spent plus interest for one year. The overdraft after two years (Year 2) will be increased by £1.21. The extra penny arises because, in the second year, there is interest on interest. We could say that £1 in year 0 is equivalent to £1.10 in year 1 and £1.21 in year 2.

Let us assume that the company has a choice between either (a) spending some money today (Year 0) or (b) spending £800 in two years time (Year 2). Unfortunately we do not know how much money has to be spent under option (a) but how much *would* we be prepared to spend today to avoid spending £800 in two years time?

We know that £1 today is equivalent to £1.21 in two years. How many £1.21s are there in £800? In other words, divide £800 by £1.21 which gives an answer of £661. We would be indifferent between spending £661 today (Year 0) or £800 in two years time (Year 2). The 'Present Value' (PV) of £800 in Year 2 discounted at 10%pa is £661.

Compound Interest

If any figure is multiplied by 1, then it is unchanged. Thus charging interest is equivalent to multiplying the sum borrowed by 1 plus the rate of interest. Interest is normally expressed as a percentage (which is 100 times the decimal). In this case the rate of interest is 10% which is one tenth (or 0.1). So charging interest at 10% is the same as multiplying the 'capital sum' (the sum borrowed) by 1.1

Modern Accounting 2

If the overdraft was £100 before the interest was charged, then charging interest increases the overdraft from £100 to £100 X 1.1 - which is £110. If money is neither paid from or to the bank account, then after a year of the balance being £110, more interest will be charged. This time £110 multiplied by 1.1 will leave a balance of £121. This process is called 'compound' interest because of the compounding effect of interest on interest.

By convention, in formulas, the rate of interest is normally called 'r' and the year number is called 'y'. 'r' is the rate of interest as a decimal (in this case 0.1) and not as a percentage. A 'factor' is a number which when multiplied by the previous figure gives the next figure. The formula for the compound interest factor is

$$(1 + r)^y$$

In this case, if r is 0.1 and y is year 2, then

$$(1 + r)^y = (1 + 0.1)^2 = 1.21$$

Discount Factors

On the last page, to work out the present value of £800 in 2 years time we had to divide £800 by 1.21. Dividing by 1.21 is the same as multiplying by the reciprocal of 1.21 (or 1/1.21) which equals 0.826 to 3 decimal places. Use a calculator to check that this is correct. Scientific calculators have a separate button for reciprocals - normally labelled '1/x'.

The present value of £1 in Year y at rate of interest r is the reciprocal of the compound interest factor formula :

$$\frac{1}{(1 + r)^y}$$

This is the same as $(1 + r)^{-y}$. The present values of one unit of currency in the future are often called discount factors. The discount factors at 10% (r= 0.1) are as follows :

Year	Discount factor
0	1
1	0.909
2	0.826
3	0.751

Discounted Cash Flow

The greater the year number, the lower is the discount factor. Also the greater the rate of interest, the lower is the discount factor. The table below gives discount factors at rates of interest of 5% and 40% for years 2 and 6. Notice that money in the future is worth less at high rates of interest and this is more noticeable the longer into the future one looks.

rate of interest (r) :	5%	40%
year (y)		
2	0.907	0.510
6	0.746	0.133

This means that (other things being equal) it is more difficult to justify business investment in economies with high rates of interest and businesses in such economies will tend to have shorter time horizons. In other words, they will not be prepared to invest today for a return that will arrive much later; they will want the return within a year or two of the investment.

To calculate the discount factors for year 6, one needs to calculate a figure to the power of 6. On a scientific calculator the button to use is normally labelled ' x^y '. Thus the factor where r = 0.4 and y = 6 can be obtained by tapping in '1.4', pressing the ' x^y ' button, tapping '6', the '=' button and finally the '1/x' button. Check that this works. There are tables of discount factors published but these may not be provided in exams and they are unlikely to be conveniently by your hand when you need them in practical situations.

A table of discount factors is on page 220 of this book.

Year Numbers

By convention, the start of the project (normally assumed to be the present time) is called 'Year 0', a year after the start is called 'Year 1', a year after that 'Year 2' and so on. In theory these are all points in time; they do not represent periods of time. Thus, with most business projects, perfect accuracy could only be achieved by having many points in time because there may be receipts and payments every single working day. In exam questions it is normally assumed that a whole year's cash transactions occur at the end of the year.

In practical situations, tedious calculations may be done with a computer and it is possible that more time points will be set -

perhaps at the end of each month, week or day. When this happens the 'y' in formulas may be replaced with a 't' - short for 'time'.

Net Present Value (NPV)

A company operates on the 10%pa overdraft already explained. It is considering buying a fruit machine with a two year life. The fruit machine will cost £900 today. It will be emptied in a years time when the takings will be £600. It will be emptied for the second and last time at the end of its life in two years time when the takings will be £500. The machine will have no scrap value. The cash flows may be listed in a table as follows :

Year	(a) Amount in £s	(b) Discount factor
0	(900)	1
1	600	0.909
2	500	0.826

The £ figures in brackets in such a table represent payments. The £ figures without brackets represent receipts.

To determine whether it is worth making the investment, multiply each item in column (a) to the discout factor on the same row in column (b) to get the present value (PV).

Year	(a) Amount in £s	(b) Discount factor	Present Value
0	(900)	1	-900
1	600	0.909	545
2	500	0.826	413
		Net Present Value (NPV)	58

The Net Present Value (NPV) is the sum of the present values of the payments and receipts. If it is positive (as in this case), then the project might be accepted. If it is negative, then the project should be rejected. The NPV is not a sum of money that will appear in a bank account or be shown as a profit in the accounts. The NPV is only useful when deciding whether to accept or reject a project.

Try to answer the following questions before looking at the answers (which are at the end of this chapter).

Question 6.1 (Answer 6.1 is on page 221)
Calculate discount factors for years 1 to 5 (inclusive) at 37% pa. (Use a calculator and do not simply read the answer from tables.)

Question 6.2 (Answer 6.2 is on page 221)
Jane Austen forecasts that her cost of capital will be 10% in the year from year 0 to year 1, 20% in the year from year 1 to year 2 and 30% in the year from year 2 to year 3. Jane is considering a project that involves a payment in year 0 and receipts in each of years 1, 2 and 3.
REQUIRED : Calculate discount factors that will enable Jane to compute the Net Present Value (NPV) of her project.

Question 6.3 (Answer 6.3 is on page 221)
Charles Dickens is considering whether to invest in a project with the following cash flows :

Year	£
0	(12,000)
1	(3,000)
2	15,000
3	5,000

Charles' cost of capital throughout this period will be 20% pa.
REQUIRED : Compute the Net Present Value (NPV) of this project.

Question 6.4 (Answer 6.4 is on page 222)
William Shakespeare is considering whether to invest in a project with the following cash flows :

Year	£
0	(19,000)
1	9,000
2	12,000
3	4,000

William's cost of capital throughout this period will be 15% pa.
REQUIRED : Compute the Net Present Value (NPV) of this project.

Modern Accounting 2

Depreciation and DCF

Discounted Cash Flow (DCF) techniques work with actual payments and receipts of cash (or cheques) and these are not normally the same as figures of accounting Profit or Loss. In particular, when a Fixed Asset is purchased, it is the date of payment that affects DCF calculations and dates on which Depreciation are charged are irrelevant for DCF calculations.

As was explained in Chapter 7 of Modern Accounting 1, depreciation is an accounting adjustment and it is not a cash payment. The cash payment is normally a large sum paid to the supplier close to the date on which the Fixed Asset is purchased whereas depreciation spreads that payment over several accounting years.

Therefore, if future profits have been forecast, those profit figures should be analysed before they are used in any DCF calculations. If the profits are stated after depreciation charges, then they should be increased by adding back the depreciation to work towards an estimate of future cash flows.

Working Capital and DCF

'Working Capital' means Current Assets less Current Liabilities. In Current Assets are Stocks and Debtors (Customers) while Current Liabilities contain Creditors (Suppliers). Many investments in Fixed Assets are made to expand a business. More Sales usually means more debtors. It may also imply more stock and more creditors.

Stock, Debtors and Creditors are 'delaying mechanisms'. The goods have to be produced and go into stock before they can be sold. After a sale there is a delay while the customer is a debtor before the receipt arrives. A compensating delay may be the credit our business receives from suppliers.

These working capital delays should not affect the total net receipts over the whole life of a project. The *total* profits before depreciation will normally equal the *total* net receipts ignoring the payments for Fixed Assets. However these delays will affect the *dates* on which receipts and payments are made during the life of a project and those dates are important to DCF techniques.

In theory, the dates of each payment and each receipt should be forecast but, in practice, this may be difficult. It is normally easier to estimate (a) future sales, (b) then future expenses and profits and lastly (c) to adjust the profit figures to approximate cash flow equivalents with 'Working Capital Adjustments'. Estimating working capital requirements can be helped by looking at the relationships that obtain in the rest of the business or with competitors.

Example
Blue Rinses Ltd is considering whether to spend £2m on new plant now in order to launch a new product in their range of commercial laundry driers. They estimate that unit sales of the new product would be as follows :

Year	1	2	3	4
Units	5,000	8,000	9,000	3,000

The product will be dropped after four years when the equipment and any rights to the product are estimated to have negligible value. Each unit would be sold for £500 and would have variable costs of £300. 50% of the variable costs are represented by the raw material content of the product. Fixed costs (excluding Depreciation) are expected to be £100,000 pa higher if the launch takes place than if it does not.

There are not expected to be any bad debts and, during the life of the product (except for the fourth year), sales debtors are expected to be 20% of the sales for the year just ended. Because sales will be run down in the fourth year, at the end of that year there should be negligible sales debtors.

There should be no work-in-progress at any year-end. Stock of raw materials should be 10% of the raw materials to be used in production in the following year. Stock of finished goods should be 15% of the units estimated to be sold in the following year. At year ends creditors are likely to be 20% of the raw material purchased in the previous year - except at the end of year 4 because production will have been progressively wound down over that final year and there will be no creditors still outstanding at the end of the project. Assume that the Accruals and Prepayments on Fixed Costs at the end of each year can be ignored because they will counterbalance each other.

These working capital assumptions are fairly realistic. It is logical to assume that stocks will be maintained on the basis of estimated

Modern Accounting 2

future activity and debtors and creditors will relate to *past* activity. In this example it will be assumed that all cash flows occur at year ends and that the cost of capital to Blue Rinses Ltd is 25%pa.

(a) Sales can be calculated by multiplying the unit sales by the unit selling price :

Year	1	2	3	4
Sales in £s	2,500,000	4,000,000	4,500,000	1,500,000

(b) Variable Costs can be calculated by multiplying the unit sales by the variable cost per unit :

Raw Materials	750,000	1,200,000	1,350,000	450,000
Other	750,000	1,200,000	1,350,000	450,000

Sales ((a) above) minus variable costs gives Contribution :

| £s | 1,000,000 | 1,600,000 | 1,800,000 | 600,000 |

Depreciation on £2m equipment that lasts 4 years with no residual value can be calculated as 25% pa straight line.

Fixed Costs in £s :

Depreciation	500,000	500,000	500,000	500,000
Other	100,000	100,000	100,000	100,000

Profit can be calculated as Contribution less all Fixed Costs :

| £s | 400,000 | 1,000,000 | 1,200,000 | 0 |

In practice some of the fixed costs may be absorbed into the Finished Goods stocks at the ends of years 1, 2 and 3. This would not change the total charge for Fixed Costs over the 4 years but it would change the allocation between the years. For the present let us ignore this point and assume that Finished Goods stock is to be costed on a variable cost basis only. At the end of the workings for this example it will be shown that different valuation methods for Finished Goods stock have no effect on the final DCF calculations.

We can now calculate the working capital required at the end of each year.

(c) Stock of Finished Goods in units (15% of sales of next year) :

| units | 1,200 | 1,350 | 450 | 0 |

Units Produced must be the Units Sold this year plus the Units in Closing Stock this year less the Units in stock last year :

| units | 6,200 | 8,150 | 8,100 | 2,550 |

Discounted Cash Flow

<u>Raw Materials Used in Production</u> must be the Units Produced multiplied by the Raw Material cost per unit :

Year	1	2	3	4
£s	930,000	1,222,500	1,215,000	382,500

<u>Stock of Raw Materials</u> (10% of usage in next year) :

| £s | 122,250 | 121,500 | 38,250 | 0 |

<u>Purchases</u> of Raw Materials must be the usage plus the closing stock less the opening stock :

| | 1,052,250 | 1,221,750 | 1,131,750 | 344,250 |

<u>Working Capital</u> :
Stock of Raw Materials (above) :

| £s | 122,250 | 121,500 | 38,250 | 0 |

Stock of Finished Goods (units multiplied by variable cost) :

| £s | 360,000 | 405,000 | 135,000 | 0 |

Sales Debtors (20% of Sales of this year)

| £s | 500,000 | 800,000 | 900,000 | 0 |
| | 982,250 | 1,326,500 | 1,073,250 | 0 |

less Creditors (20% of Purchases of this year)

| £s | 210,450 | 244,350 | 226,350 | 0 |

Working Capital at the end of each year

| £s | <u>771,800</u> | <u>1,082,150</u> | <u>846,900</u> | <u>0</u> |

Change in Working Capital (this year minus last year)

| £s | <u>771,800</u> | <u>310,350</u> | <u>(235,250)</u> | <u>(846,900)</u> |

The changes in working capital summed across the columns should come to zero. In other words, working capital is only delaying the receipt of cash from the early years to the later years; it is not changing the total amount of cash.

CASH FLOWS :   £   £   £   £
Profit for the year
              400,000   1,000,000   1,200,000   0
Add Depreciation
              <u>500,000</u>   <u>500,000</u>   <u>500,000</u>   <u>500,000</u>
              900,000   1,500,000   1,700,000   500,000
Less Change in Working Capital
              <u>771,800</u>   <u>310,350</u>   <u>(235,250)</u> <u>(846,900)</u>
CASH   <u>128,200</u>   <u>1,189,650</u> <u>1,935,250</u> <u>1,346,900</u>

Discounted Cash Flow Calculations :

Year	Cash Flow £	Discount Factors @ 25%	Present Values £
0	(2,000,000)	1.000	(2,000,000)
1	128,200	0.800	102,560
2	1,189,650	0.640	761,376
3	1,935,250	0.512	990,848
4	1,346,900	0.410	551,690
			406,474

The final Net Present Value is positive. On the basis of the information given, Blue Rinses Ltd should undertake this project.

The Effect of Absorbing Fixed Costs into Finished Goods Stock

Earlier it was stated that different valuation methods for Finished Goods stock have no effect on the final DCF calculations. Although increased Finished Goods stock figures would affect the allocation of accounting profits between the years, it would also have a counterbalancing effect on the Changes in Working Capital figures.

The Fixed Costs incurred in each year were £600,000. In year 1 5,000 units were sold and 6,200 units were produced. If FG stock is increased by £100 per unit for 'overheads', then with 1,200 units in stock at the end of year 1, profits of year 1 will increase by £12,000 to £412,000. However the Change in Working Capital will also rise by £12,000 and thus the Cash Flow in year 1 must remain at £128,200.

In exam questions on DCF it normally makes sense to value Finished Goods stock at Variable Cost alone unless the question makes it clear that an alternative basis is required.

Try to answer the following questions before looking at the answers (which are at the end of this chapter).

Discounted Cash Flow

Question 6.5 (Answer 6.5 is on page 222)

Snooty Fashions Ltd is considering whether to open another shop in premises due for redevelopment. If they do open this new outlet, they would immediately spend £0.8m on alterations and shopfitting. They estimate that sales at the new location would be as follows :

Year £000	1	2	3	4
	700	1,000	1,200	1,400

The lease lasts for only four years and it is unlikely that it will be renewed because the landlord has plans to demolish the present building and redevelop. Snooty sets selling prices to ensure that gross profits as a percentage of sales are 50%. Fixed costs (such as rent, electricity and wages but excluding depreciation) are expected to be £100,000 pa on this shop.

All sales will be for cash. Stocks at the start of trading (Year 0) and at the end of each year are expected to be 20% of the estimated cost of sales of the following year. At the end of year 4 stock can be assumed to be zero. (What little stock is left in this shop will be transferred to the other outlets in the chain.) At year-ends creditors are likely to be 10% of the stock purchased in the previous year. The creditors at year 1 will be 10% of the purchases of the first year <u>excluding</u> the initial stock purchased at the start of trading (Year 0). Assume that there are no creditors at the end of year 4 when the new shop is vacated. Assume that the Accruals and Prepayments on Fixed Costs at the end of each year can be ignored because they will counterbalance each other.

Assume that receipts from sales, payments to suppliers and all fixed costs occur at year ends apart from payments to suppliers for the initial stock at the start of trading that will be paid for at year 0. The cost of capital to Snooty Fashions Ltd is 30%pa.

REQUIRED : Calculate the NPV of this proposed venture to aid the company in the decision as to whether to go ahead or not.

Question 6.6 (No answer to this question has been included in this book)

Microwave Developments Ltd is considering whether to spend £1m on new equipment now in order to launch a new microwave water heater to replace the boiler in central heating systems. They estimate that unit sales of the new product would be as follows :

Year	1	2	3	4
Units	2,000	9,000	9,000	2,000

After four years it is expected that new designs and developments will make this product obsolete and this product will be dropped. Then the equipment and any rights to the product are estimated to have negligible value.

If the product is launched, each unit would be sold for £600 and would have variable costs of £400. 60% of the variable costs are represented by the raw material content of the product. Fixed costs (excluding Depreciation) are expected to be £200,000 pa higher if the launch does take place.

There are not expected to be any bad debts and, during the life of the product (except for the fourth year), sales debtors are expected to be 15% of the sales for the year just ended. Because sales will be run down in the fourth year, at the end of that year there should be negligible sales debtors.

There should be no work-in-progress at any year-end. Stock of raw materials should be 20% of the raw materials to be used in production in the following year. Stock of finished goods should be 25% of the units estimated to be sold in the following year. At year ends creditors are likely to be 10% of the raw material purchased in the previous year - except at the end of year 4 because production will have been progressively would down over that final year and there will be no creditors still outstanding at the end of the project. Assume that the Accruals and Prepayments on Fixed Costs at the end of each year can be ignored because they will counterbalance each other.

Assume that all cash flows occur at year ends and that the cost of capital to Microwave Developments Ltd is 15%pa.

REQUIRED : Calculate the NPV of this proposed venture to aid the company in the decision as to whether to go ahead or not.

Discounted Cash Flow

Interest Paid and DCF

Just as Depreciation should not be a part of the Cash Flows subjected to DCF analysis, so Interest Paid should almost always be also excluded. Discounting itself should take account of the cost of capital. To use cash flows that are net of interest paid is almost always to double count.

The exception arises with 'connected financing' which is where low interest finance is available only if a particular project is pursued. Governments may encourage businesses into a depressed region with 'soft' loans. Aircraft manufacturers may refuse to cut stated prices beyond a certain point but they may still be prepared to give an effective further price cut with cheap loans. Connected financing means that (a) the finance is not available without the project and (b) the finance would be used if the project is accepted.

Situations with connected financing can be evaluated by stating projects net of (i) the sum borrowed as a soft loan, (ii) the interest paid on the soft loan and (iii) repayments of the soft loan.

Example of Connected Financing

Jim Ruthless is considering two projects. They are *mutually exclusive* because he does not have time to do both. He could become an international arms dealer and the cash flows associated with this option are shown as Project A below. Or he could become a publisher of romantic fiction and the cash flows associated with this option are shown as Project B below.

Year	Project A £000	Project B £000
0	(10)	(20)
1	7	12
2	7	13

The cost of capital to Jim Ruthless is 20%pa and any surplus funds can always be reinvested to gain 20%pa. The NPVs of the projects discounted at 20% are £694 for A and -£972 for B and, if money is Jim's only objective, he will choose A (arms dealing).

However Jim's Aunt Dotty has other views and will lend him £10,000 @ 5%pa interest for 2 years only if he becomes a publisher of romantic fiction.

The cash flows of the soft loan are £10,000 receipt in year 0, interest paid of £500 in year 1 and repayment of capital and interest in year 2 totalling £10,500. Project B can be shown net of this financing in the right hand column below :

Year	Project B Gross	Connected Financing	NET
	£	£	£
0	(20,000)	10,000	(10,000)
1	12,000	(500)	11,500
2	13,000	(10,500)	2,500

The NPV @20% of the final Net column is £1,319. On the basis of the information given, it appears that publishing romantic fiction with the borrowing @ 5% is the better option.

Incremental Figures

Most of the examples in this chapter so far have been of self-contained projects where the cash flows could be easily isolated from those of any other continuing business. However many practical investments involve cash flows which are intimately tied to those of existing businesses. DCF analysis should be done on the *incremental* impact of the new investment.

In other words, (a) a forecast should first be made of the cash flows without the possible new investment, (b) a forecast should then be made of the cash flows with the new investment and (c) the difference between the two will form the basis of the DCF analysis. This need for two forecasts is one reason why many businesses find it difficult to audit the efficiency of investment decisions. If a business has done well after new investment, it may be because of the new investment - or it may be that it would have done well without it.

Perpetuities

A perpetuity is an interest-bearing loan that will never be repaid. UK Government War Loan is an example of a quoted perpetuity. If an investor puts £100 in a deposit account that pays interest at a constant 10%pa and the investor leaves that money on deposit 'for ever', then he would receive £10 a year after the deposit (Year 1), £10 in year 2, £10 in year 3 and so on to infinity. We could say that the Present Value of a stream of receipts of £10 pa starting in year 1 and continuing to infinity (discounting @10% pa) is £100.

Discounted Cash Flow

The interest return of investing £1 at interest rate r p.a. is £r p.a. starting a year from the investment. The present value of £1 p.a. received every year from year 1 to infinity is £1/r where r is the discount rate.

If the stream of annual payments started in year 2 rather than in year 1, then since each payment is deferred by one year, the present value would be £1/r discounted for one year by dividing by (1 + r). If the stream of annual payments started in year 3, then the present value would be £1/r divided by $(1 + r)^2$. Thus if the stream of annual payments started in year y rather than in year 1, then the present value would be £1/r discounted for y-1 years by dividing by $(1 + r)^{(y-1)}$.

The Present Value of a stream of receipts of £1 starting year y and continuing to infinity is

$$\frac{1}{r(1+r)^{(y-1)}}$$

Example

Sunshine Developments plc are considering an office development which would take some 3 years to fully let. Once fully let it should yield a constant return until the indefinite future. The cash flows are estimated as follows:

Year	£000
0	(3,000)
1	200
2	250
3	300
4 to ∞	350

Discount rates at 10% pa can be calculated as follows:

Year	Formula			
0	1	=	1 =	1.000000
1	$\frac{1}{(1+r)}$	=	$\frac{1}{1.1}$ =	0.909090
2	$\frac{1}{(1+r)^2}$	=	$\frac{1}{1.1^2}$ =	0.826446
3	$\frac{1}{(1+r)^3}$	=	$\frac{1}{1.1^3}$ =	0.751314
4 to ∞	$\frac{1}{r(1+r)^3}$	=	$\frac{1}{0.1 \times 1.1^3}$ =	7.513148

Modern Accounting 2

The NPV can be calculated as follows :

Year	£	Discount Rate	Present Values
0	(3,000)	1.000000	(3,000)
1	200	0.909090	182
2	250	0.826446	207
3	300	0.751314	225
4 to ∞	350	7.513148	2,630
			244

This project has a positive NPV discounting at 10%. Because the project is assumed to have an indefinite life and the largest positive cash flows are in the indefinite stream, the NPV will be very sensitive to changes in the discount rate. (In this example the NPV at 11% is negative.)

Try to answer the following questions before looking at the answers (which are at the end of this chapter).

Question 6.7 (Answer 6.7 is on page 223)

Interpropco plc is considering whether to buy the freehold of a building let on a long lease with 999 years to run. (This lease is so long that it can be considered to run to infinity.) The vendor is asking for three payments of £30,000. The first payment would have to be made now, the second in a year's time and the third in two year's time. Interpropco would receive ground rents of £20,000 pa for the remaining life of the lease starting with the first receipt in five year's time. The cost of capital to Interpropco is 15% pa.

REQUIRED : Compute the NPV of this project to aid the company make a decision as to whether to make this purchase.

Question 6.8 (Answer 6.8 is on page 223)

Relocate Ltd are considering whether to move their business to a development area. Such a move would involve :
(a) Purchase of a freehold site for £0.2m payable immediately with £6m building costs payable in a year's time.
(b) Sale of the existing building for £4m receivable in two year's time.
(c) Relocation and redundancy payments to the existing staff estimated at £1.7m payable in a year's time and £2m payable in two year's time.
(d) A soft loan from a Government agency of £1m for 4 years from a year's time at an interest rate of 5% pa.
(e) Increased fixed costs (telephone, travel and other communication costs) of £5m pa starting in a year's time and continuing indefinitely.

A major reason for considering this move is that they are unable to expand on their present site. They are using the present site to capacity with sales of £60m pa. Sales are expected to increase by 10% pa compound from one year's time (Year 1) to Year 4. Sales should then remain constant at their year 4 level indefinitely.

Variable Costs amount to 50% of sales. 30% of Variable Costs are accounted for by Raw Materials. At present Raw Material Stocks amount to 10% of expected usage in the following year, Finished Goods Stocks amount to 20% of expected unit sales in the following year, Debtors amount to 10% of last year's sales and Creditors amount to 10% of last year's purchases of raw materials.

The new site is further from both suppliers and customers and both Finished Goods and Raw Material Stock Levels will be kept 20% above those that would have been necessary for the same volumes (if those had been possible) from the old site. These increased stock levels will start from Year 1. Since the decision whether to move has not yet been taken, stock levels today (Year 0) have been set on the basis of expected raw material usage and expected sales if the company remains in its present premises and activity continues to be constrained. The cost of capital to Relocate Ltd is 25% pa.

REQUIRED : Compute the NPV of this project.

Inflation

The impact of inflation should benefit most business investments because they involve payments now in today's prices for benefits that will be received later at future (higher) prices.

Example

Snappy Forecourts are considering whether to buy a car wash machine for £70,000 payable now. They expect the machine to last for 5 years and to be used for 10,000 car washes in each of those years. Assume that the costs of operating the machine are minimal. The current selling price of each car wash is £2 but Snappy expect to be able to raise their selling prices by 5% pa. For the purposes of this analysis assume that all sales are made at the end of each year (and thus the first sales of year 1 will be made at £2.10 per car wash). The cost of capital to Snappy Forecourts is 15% pa.

Many large businesses in the UK are wary of allowing their managers to take account of expected price increases when evaluating new investments. If Snappy Forecourts insisted that inflation should be ignored, their DCF analysis would appear as follows :

Year	Cash Flow	Discount Factor @ 15%	Present Value
0	(70,000)	1.0000	(70,000)
1	20,000	0.8696	17,392
2	20,000	0.7561	15,122
3	20,000	0.6575	13,150
4	20,000	0.5718	11,436
5	20,000	0.4972	9,944
Net Present Value			(2,957)

Thus, without inflation, they would reject the investment. If they did take account of the expected price increases, then their analysis would appear as follows :

Year	Cash Flow	Discount Factor @ 15%	Present Value
0	(70,000)	1.0000	(70,000)
1	21,000	0.8696	18,261
2	22,050	0.7561	16,672
3	23,153	0.6575	15,223
4	24,310	0.5718	13,900
5	25,526	0.4972	12,691
Net Present Value			6,747

Now the NPV is positive and the investment might be accepted.

Economies with high rates of price inflation tend to have high rates of interest. In those economies if managers are unable to take account of inflation but they do have to take account of high costs of capital, then they will find it difficult to justify most business investments.

In the Snappy Forecourts example the benefits in current prices were £20,000 for each of years 1 to 5. To find the actual benefit for year 1, the £20,000 had to be multiplied by 1.05. The actual benefit for year 2 was £20,000 multiplied by 1.05 squared. For year 3 the 1.05 was cubed. Thus the current price benefit was multiplied by the price increase factor to the power of the year number.

If £M is the benefit in current prices,
y is the year in which the benefit was received,
and i is the rate of price inflation

The actual benefit in prices of the year in which it will be received is

$$M(1+i)^y$$

By convention, when considering the impact of inflation on investment appraisal, the cost of capital is called the *'money* cost of capital' and given the letter 'm' (rather than r). Thus the discounting process divides each benefit by $(1+m)^y$ where m is the cost of capital. The Present Value of each benefit will be

$$\frac{M(1+i)^y}{(1+m)^y}$$

The *'real* cost of capital' is the net impact of the money cost and inflation and is given the letter 'r'. The value of r must be such that the Present Value of each benefit is

$$\frac{M}{(1+r)^y}$$

If

$$\frac{M(1+i)^y}{(1+m)^y} = \frac{M}{(1+r)^y}$$

then

$$r = \frac{(1+m)}{(1+i)} - 1$$

Sometimes journalists refer to the real cost of capital and they may imply that it can be found by simple subtraction. In other words, if the money rate of interest is 26% and the rate of inflation is 5%, then they may state that the real rate of interest is 21%. At low rates of inflation taking one figure from the other gives a reasonable approximation of the real rate of interest but at high inflation rates it is misleading.

Modern Accounting 2

If m = 0.26 and i = 0.05, then r = (1.26/1.05) -1 = 0.2 or 20%. This is not far from m - i = 21% but if prices double each year and money rates of interest are 120% pa, then m = 1.2 and i = 1 and r = (2.2/2) - 1 = 0.1. There is a big difference between a real rate of interest of 10% and m - i which gives 20%.

Try to answer the following questions before looking at the answers (which are at the end of this chapter).

Question 6.9 (Answer 6.9 is on page 225)

If the rate of inflation is 15% pa and the money rate of interest is 25% pa, what is the real rate of interest?

Question 6.10 (Answer 6.10 is on page 225)

Mr Moneybags has agreed to lend some money to Miss Worthy and he wishes to charge the money rate of interest that will give him a real rate of 10% pa. If the rate of inflation is 35% pa, what is the money rate of interest that he should charge?

Question 6.11 (Answer 6.11 is on page 225)

Picasso Projects Ltd is considering whether to open an art gallery. The cash flows from this project have been estimated in terms of prices at today's date (Year 0) as follows :

Year	£
0	(90,000)
1	8,000
2	30,000
3	40,000
4	30,000
5	20,000

All the factors underlying this cash projection are likely to be affected by the same general rate of inflation which is estimated to be 4% pa. The money cost of capital is 15% pa.

REQUIRED : Calculate the NPV of this project to aid the company make its decision.

The Real Cost of Capital and Working Capital Adjustments

Unfortunately Working Capital Adjustments have the effect of delaying the cash effects of transactions of one period until the next period. This means transactions incurred in the prices of Period 1 can have their cash impact in Period 2. Hence if Working Capital Adjustments are significant, (a) keeping cash flows in current price levels and using the real cost of capital as a discount rate will be less accurate than (b) inflating the cash flows and then discounting by the money cost of capital.

Specific Price Increases

Most business projects involve several streams of payments and receipts each of which is subject to different price changes at different times. If one could forecast the future with certainty, the best way of calculating NPVs would be to build the individual price changes into the cash flows and discount with the money cost of capital. In the real world it may not be possible to do this but it may be worth extracting particular streams of payments and receipts and subjecting them to different 'real discount rates'.

Example

Snodgrass Gardening Ltd is considering buying a seed spraying machine for £80,000 payable immediately that would enable it to accept contracts to plant the verges of motorways. Such a seed spraying machine will last for 4 years and have no residual value. The expenses of this project are all Fixed Expenses. The labour expense would cost £20,000 pa at today's wage rates and such wage rates are expected to increase by 15% pa. Other expenses should amount to £30,000 pa at today's price levels and such price levels are expected to increase by 5% pa. Both labour costs and other expenses can be assumed to start from Year 1. Annual income from the project at today's price levels would be £60,000 in year 1, £70,000 in year 2, £80,000 in year 3 and £50,000 in year 4. The expected rate of price increase on this annual income is expected to be 10% pa. The cost of capital to Snodgrass Gardening Ltd is 12% pa.

3 sets of discount factors can be calculated as follows:

	Wages	Other Expenses	Income
Price Increase	15%	5%	10%
Real Cost of Capital	(1.12/1.15)-1	(1.12/1.05)-1	(1.12/1.1)-1
	= -2.61%	= 6.67%	= 1.82%
Year	$(1 - 0.0261)^y$	$(1 + 0.0667)^y$	$(1 + 0.0182)^y$
0	1.000	1.000	1.000
1	1.027	0.938	0.982
2	1.054	0.879	0.965
3	1.083	0.824	0.947
4	1.112	0.772	0.930

The rate at which wages increase (15%) is assumed to be higher than the money cost of capital (12%). Therefore the real cost of capital is negative and the 'discount' factors are increasing with the year numbers. The cash flows (in Year 0 price levels) will be as follows:

£ Year	Equipment	Wages	Other Expenses	Income
0	(80,000)			
1		(20,000)	(30,000)	60,000
2		(20,000)	(30,000)	70,000
3		(20,000)	(30,000)	80,000
4		(20,000)	(30,000)	50,000

Discounted Cash Flow

Multiplying the cash flows by the discount factors gives :

Year	£	£	£	£
0	(80,000)			
1		(20,536)	(28,125)	58,929
2		(21,086)	(26,367)	67,522
3		(21,651)	(24,719)	75,790
4		(22,231)	(23,174)	46,523
PVs	(80,000)	(85,503)	(102,386)	248,764

Summing these 4 present values, the whole project has a Net Present Value of £(19,124). Since the NPV is negative the project should be rejected.

Try to answer the following question before looking at the answer (which is at the end of this chapter).

Question 6.12 (Answer 6.12 is on page 226)

Dave's Nite Club Ltd is considering buying a juke box for £5,000 payable immediately. Such a juke box will last for 4 years and have no residual value. The expenses of this project are all Fixed Expenses. The cost of buying new records would cost £1,000 pa at today's prices and such prices are expected to increase by 10% pa. Other expenses should amount to £500 pa at today's price levels and such price levels are expected to increase by 7% pa. Both the cost of records and the other expenses can be assumed to start from Year 1. Annual income from the project at today's price levels would be £3,000 in year 1, £4,000 in year 2, £4,000 in year 3 and £3,500 in year 4. The expected rate of price increase on this annual income is expected to be 9% pa. The cost of capital to Dave's Nite Club Ltd is 20% pa.

REQUIRED : Calculate the NPV of this project to aid the company make its decision.

Modern Accounting 2

Taxation and DCF

Almost all U.K. business projects will affect the taxes that have to be paid by the business. There are some projects where the tax impact is a mirror image of the primary cash flows. In these the initial cash payments are treated as expenses for tax and no working capital delays prevent the later receipts being taxed in the period in which they are received.

Example
Temp Employment Agencies Ltd are considering whether to open another branch in property with only 3 years to run on the lease. No investment in Fixed Assets will be required but most branches take a year to become established during which time they make losses. To simplify this example it is assumed that the rate of Corporation Tax is 50% and the delay between making taxable profits and paying tax is one year. The cash flows have been estimated as follows :

Year £	Primary Cash Flows	Taxation Cash Flows	Net Cash Flows
0	(30,000)	-	(30,000)
1	(10,000)	15,000	5,000
2	50,000	5,000	55,000
3	40,000	(25,000)	15,000
4	-	(20,000)	(20,000)

The initial losses are causing positive tax cash receipts because it is assumed that they can be set against the profits of the rest of the business reducing the total tax that would otherwise have to be paid. It is not unusual to find that the post-tax cash flows of a project are improved if it is undertaken by a company with taxable profits from other activities.

The delay between profits being made and tax becoming payable means that most projects will show tax payments after the last receipt from the primary cash flows. (This will have an effect on IRRs which are explained on page 198).

Discounting the primary pre-tax cash flows at 10% pa gives an NPV of £32,284. Discounting the net post-tax cash flows at 10% pa gives an NPV of £17,609. Both are positive and this appears to be a very attractive project.

If tax follows the primary cash flows in this 'mirror image' fashion, then both the pre- and the post-tax analysis will always give the same decision. In other words, if the primary cash flows give a positive NPV, then so will the net post-tax cash flows. Equally if one gives a negative NPV, then so will the other.

Unfortunately the tax on most projects will not be a mirror image of the primary cash flows. Some of the payments may never get tax relief and some will be relieved slowly with Capital Allowances. Stock and Debtor working capital delays mean that the receipts of one year are taxed as profits of the previous year. Expenditure in the last days of an accounting year normally gets tax relief a year earlier than expenditure at the start of the next accounting year and so it rarely makes economic sense to invest at the start of accounting periods.

Tax relief is given on interest paid. Thus the discount rate used in calculating NPVs should be based on post-tax interest costs (amongst other costs - see below and the next page). Strictly the post-tax cost of interest should take account of the delay between paying the interest and receiving relief. If gross interest is 10%, the tax rate is 50% and the delay between paying interest and receiving relief is a year, then the effective net rate of interest is 5.25%. (The calculation behind this figure is explained on page 200.)

The Cost of Equity

Equity means the stake in the business held by the ordinary shareholders (or partners in the case of an unincorporated business). This stake is not just the nominal value of their shares because that nominal value normally relates to capital raised many years ago and the figures are likely to be irrelevant to current decisions. The stake must also take account of retained reserves because these relate to profits that were not taken as dividend and, by not taking full dividends, the ordinary shareholders were implicitly making further investments in the business. However even adding reserves to the nominal value of ordinary shares may not be enough because reserves are dependent on the Balance Sheets figures for identified assets and (a) those figures may not be the best way of valuing those particular assets and (b) the assets identified may be an incomplete selection of the 'true assets' excluding most intangible assets and any asset that has arisen without a separate expenditure of cash.

For a quoted company in reasonably efficient capital markets with a reasonable flow of information available to most of the operators in that market, it may be that the current market price given to the shares is the best indicator of the current value of the equity stake in the business.

Given a value of the equity stake, what can be meant by the 'Cost of Equity'? The Ordinary Shareholders are the owners of the business and they may assume that the object of the company's management is to maximise the return to them. Talk of a *cost* of equity appears to imply that the business has a separate identity with objectives that may not coincide with those of its ostensible owners.

The concept of cost may be difficult in this context but it is not wholly without validity in the sense of an *opportunity* cost. If a shareholder was not investing in this business, then presumably the investment would be placed elsewhere. What return would be achieved elsewhere? It is in the interests of the shareholders (and probably in the interests of the economy as a whole) that the management of this business see that alternative return as their minimum target.

Sometimes the cost of equity is said to follow the Gordon Growth Model[1] :

$$\frac{d_1}{m_0} + g$$

where d_1 is the next dividend to be paid, m_0 is the market price of the shares immediately after the last dividend was paid and g is the growth factor of dividends over time such that the dividend at time t will be $d_1(1 + g)^{(t-1)}$. This model is a simplification of reality because it assumes that dividends are paid at equal time intervals and that they grow by a constant factor. However equity investors invest for capital gain as well as immediate dividend and (ignoring liquidations and take-over bids) growth in dividends has to be assumed for the prospect of capital gain to be rational.

Taxation and the Cost of Equity

The payment of a dividend in the UK triggers a further payment of Advanced Corporation Tax (ACT) (see Chapter 13 of Modern Accounting 1). This ACT is normally recoverable against Mainstream Corporation Tax (MCT) 9 months after the end of the company's accounting year-end. If the basic rate of income tax is 25% and the rate of ACT is 1/3, the payment of the dividend at time t would become 4/3rds of the net and at some later point 1/3rd of the net would be returned. It is possible to adjust the cost of equity for ACT but the formula has to take account of the actual delays in each case and so is specific to that case alone. For the questions in this book (and in examinations unless the question states otherwise) assume that d_t in the cost of equity formula is the *net* of ACT dividend and that ACT and its set-off can be ignored. The extra accuracy with a more complicated formula will not be significant at low to moderate costs of equity.

Risk and the Cost of Capital

Capital has different costs when raised from different sources. It is normally assumed that the growth demanded by equity holders makes the cost of equity the most expensive source of capital and the cost of fully secured loans should be one of the least expensive sources. It is assumed that the equity holders 'demand' (or expect) this higher return because of the increased risk that they have to bear in comparison to the other providers of capital.

'Risk', in this context, relates to the prospect of the return being lower or higher than the average estimate. Most courses in statistics explain 'Probability Distributions'. The measure of risk in an investment must be connected to the 'Standard Deviation' of the probability distribution as a proportion of the 'Mean'.

Unfortunately most estimates of future business returns are more likely to be closer to the mode of the probability distribution than the mean. In other words, most people will give an estimate of the *most likely* outcome rather than of the pure average. Since most investment probability distributions are 'skewed', this mode is an unsatisfactory substitute for the mean. In particular most business projects have limits on their possible success that are closer to the mode than the limits on their possible failure. In other words, in a restaurant with 50 places one might estimate the most likely number of diners at 45. However the capacity of the restaurant prevents more than 50 whereas the worst that could happen in that zero customers arrive. 50 is only just above 45 but zero is a long way from either.

It is wise to 'spread risk' by investing a little in many projects rather than putting everything into just one project. In other words, don't put all your eggs in one basket. Unfortunately most businesses are affected by the same factors and this will prevent risk-spreading from eliminating 'market risk'. General economic recessions depress the returns from almost *all* equity investments and general economic booms have the converse effect. So the risks affecting an individual share are not disconnected from the risks affecting the other shares. The 'Capital Asset Pricing Model'[2] is an academic analysis of this area but it is outside the scope of this book.

The Weighted Average Cost of Capital (WACC)

Usually decisions are best taken on the basis of the *marginal* effect. That is looking at the differences between the situation with and without the proposed project. In Chapter 15 (Costs for Decision Making) of Modern Accounting 1 this point was made with Pricing Decisions and Product Elimination Decisions. Average measures rarely lead to optimal decisions.

Yet the Weighted Average Cost of Capital (WACC) is recommended as the discount rate for DCF appraisal because it is assumed that different costs for capital from different sources mostly arise from the different sources accepting different levels of risk. If fresh capital is raised from the cheapest source, this increases the risk undertaken by the other source(s) and increased risk should lead to increased cost from that source. There are different theories in this area but this is the most commonly held amongst academics and is associated with Modigliani and Miller[3].

Let us assume that there only two sources of capital : (a) borrowing which costs 5% and (b) equity which costs 15%. Our company has net business assets worth £2m and these have been financed by £1m borrowing and £1m equity. If both returns were absolutely certain, it is difficult to see why anyone would lend at 5% when they could obtain 15% through the equity market. In practice we know that there are different risks associated with the two forms of capital and it is logical to assume that at least one factor explaining the different returns is risk.

If more funds are raised by borrowing but the level of equity remains the same, then the level of 'gearing' (see Chapter 16 of Modern Accounting 1) increases. This increases the risk undertaken by the equity holders (assuming that the risk of the project on which the loan will be spent has the same risk profile as that of the existing

Discounted Cash Flow

business). If the return to the ordinary shareholders does not increase (and they are aware of this situation), then the market value of the ordinary shares should fall. Since the market value (m_0) is part of the formula for the 'cost' of equity, this will increase that cost and the average cost of capital will remain approximately the same.

Let us assume that there are only two forms of capital raised by our company : (a) Equity and (b) Loan Capital. If M_e is the market capitalisation of all equity, M_l is the market capitalisation of all loan capital, C_e is the cost of equity and C_l is the cost of loan capital, then the Weighted Average Cost of Capital will be

$$\frac{M_e C_e + M_l C_l}{M_e + M_l}$$

Example

Structure plc has 3m ordinary shares (nominal value 10p) in issue and the market price per share just after the last dividend was £2. The next dividend is expected to be 10p (net) per share payable in a year's time. The company only pays one dividend annually and dividends are expected to grow by 15% pa. The company has also issued 10% pa loan stock with a nominal value of £1m. The current market price of this Loan Stock is 80% of the nominal value. The redemption date for this loan stock is so distant that it can be ignored. The rate of corporation tax against which the loan stock interest can be relieved is 30%. (Ignore the delay between paying interest and obtaining tax relief.)

In this case, the market capitalisation of equity (M_e) will be 3m shares at £2 each. M_e = £6m. The market capitalisation of loan capital (M_l) will be 80% of £1m. M_l = £0.8m.

Gross interest of £0.1m will be paid which will cost £0.07m post-tax. £0.07 is 8.75% of £0.8m and so C_l = 0.0875. Note that the cost of loans has to take account of *current* market values and not original nominal values. If the company wanted to reduce its gearing it would buy back the loan stock in the market and this would be cheaper than redeeming at par. Evidently either interest rates have risen since the stock was issued or the credit rating of this company has fallen.

The cost of equity (C_e) will be 10p/200p + 0.15. Thus C_e = 0.2 (or 20%) and the weighted average cost of capital (WACC) =

$$\frac{6 \times 0.2 + 0.8 \times 0.0875}{6 + 0.8} = 0.1868 \text{ (or } 18.7\%)$$

Modern Accounting 2

Try to answer the following question before looking at the answer (which is at the end of this chapter).

Question 6.13 (Answer 6.13 is on page 226)

Manet Artwork Ltd has 1m ordinary shares (nominal value 20p) in issue and the market price per share just after the last dividend was £1.50. The next dividend is expected to be 8p (net) per share payable in a year's time. The company only pays one dividend annually and dividends are expected to grow by 12% pa. The company has also issued 14% pa loan stock with a nominal value of £0.8m. The current market price of this Loan Stock is 120% of the nominal value. The redemption date for this loan stock is so distant that it can be ignored. The rate of corporation tax against which the loan stock interest can be relieved is 25%. (Ignore the delay between paying interest and obtaining tax relief.)

REQUIRED : Calculate the Weighted Average Cost of Capital for Manet Artwork Ltd.

Internal Rate of Return (IRR or DCF Yield)

The Internal Rate of Return is an alternative to Net Present Value (NPV) as a performance measure for projects. It is the discount rate of interest that sets the NPV to zero. As the rate of interest rises, so the NPV of an investment will fall. Let us return to the example on page 172 :

Year	Amount in £s	Discount factor @ 10%	Present Value
0	(900)	1	(900)
1	600	0.909	545
2	500	0.826	413
	Net Present Value (NPV)		58

It appears that the NPV discounting at 10% is +£58. Thus the IRR of that project must be above 10%. Let us test the NPV discounted at 20% :

Year	Amount in £s	Discount factor @ 20%	Present Value
0	(900)	1	(900)
1	600	0.833	500
2	500	0.694	347
	Net Present Value (NPV)		(53)

Discounted Cash Flow

At 20% the NPV is negative. So the IRR must be between 10% and 20%. Let us test the NPV discounted at 15%:

Year	Amount in £s	Discount factor @ 15%	Present Value
0	(900)	1	(900)
1	600	0.870	522
2	500	0.756	378
		Net Present Value (NPV)	0

Thus, in this example, the IRR has been conveniently close to 15%. The NPV 5% below the IRR was not the same positive figure as the NPV 5% above was negative. Therefore the relationship between the NPV and the discount rate cannot be a simple linear relationship. It would be possible to formulate the IRR for this example that only extends to year 2, but most real projects have longer lives and formulas are not used to calculate IRRs. In practice finding the IRR means continuing to calculate NPVs using different rates of interest until one finds the rate that gives an NPV close to zero.

Multiple IRRs

A project with just 2 time points can only have one IRR. Consider the following project:

Year	Amount in £s
0	(100)
1	110

The discount factor for year 1 contains no values of r^2 or r to any higher power. Rather obviously the IRR of this project is 10%.

However a project with 3 time points (such as that at the top of this page) must have two IRRs. The discount factor for year 2 does contain an r^2 and those who have done maths will recognise that solving for r must involve a quadratic equation and that implies two possible solutions. In the case of the cash flows shown at the top of the page, the second solution is $r = -1.483$ (or -148%). A minus rate of interest is difficult to interpret and most practical people are happy to ignore any negative IRRs. However these freak negative IRR solutions are one reason why most academic opinion is wary of IRR as an objective measure.

If (a) the sum of a project's undiscounted receipts exceeds the sum of the undiscounted payments and (b) the first receipt arrives after the last payment, then there can only be one positive IRR.

However, if condition (b) in the last paragraph is broken, there can be more than one positive 'IRR'. Business projects with 'mixed receipts and payments' can arise (i) if they are evaluated after taxation, (ii) if they are evaluated with frequent time points (say every month) or (iii) if there are costs of reinstating an environment at the end of the project (as can arise in mining and oil production). The following cash flows are an example :

Year	Amount in £s
0	(669)
1	1,639
2	(1,000)

In this case the discount rates that set the NPV to zero are both positive : 15% and 30%. Neither of these 'IRRs' is a valid measure on which to judge this project. Projects with mixed receipts and payments are partly investments and partly a means of raising finance. Before evaluating the IRR the cash flows need to be restated so that payments and receipts are not intermingled. This can be done by discounting the later payments back to an earlier year where they can be netted against receipts. If the WACC is 10%, then the final payment of £1,000 in year 2 can be discounted back one year (divided by 1.1) and becomes £909 in year 1. The receipt of £1,639 netted with a payment of £909 becomes a receipt of £730. The cash flows are restated as follows :

Year	Amount in £s
0	(669)
1	730

Now the IRR is 9.1% and (assuming that the WACC is correct) it is a valid measure of the project. Since the IRR is below the WACC, this project should be rejected.

The Cost of Loan Interest - Net of Tax

On page 193 it was stated that if gross interest is 10%, the tax rate is 50% and the delay between paying interest and receiving tax relief is a year, then the effective net rate of interest is 5.25%. The

Discounted Cash Flow

cash flows of borrowing £100 (a) for one year, (b) for two years, (c) for three years and (d) for the indefinite future would be as follows :

Year	(a) £	(b) £	(c) £	(d) £
0	100	100	100	100
1	(110)	(10)	(10)	(10)
2	5	(105)	(5)	(5)
3		5	(105)	(5)
4			5	(5)
5 to ∞				(5)

If the sum is borrowed for just one year (a), then the receipt in year 0 is the £100 borrowed, the payment in year 1 is the return of the capital plus interest for a year and the receipt in year 2 is tax relief on the interest paid. If the sum is borrowed for 2 years (b), then the cash flows will be equivalent to an (a) starting in year 0 added to a second (a) starting in year 1. In other words, the receipt in year 0 is the £100 borrowed, the payment in year 1 is interest for a year, the payment in year 2 is interest for a year plus the return of the capital less tax relief on the interest paid in year 1 and the receipt in year 3 is tax relief on the interest paid in year 2. The same logic can be used for (c).

If the sum is borrowed indefinitely (d), then the receipt in year 0 is the £100 borrowed, the payment in year 1 is interest for a year and the payment in every year from year 2 onwards is interest for a year less tax relief on the interest paid in the previous year.

So far, in calculating IRRs, it has been assumed that investments were being evaluated and the cash flows had to arrange all payments before all receipts in order to avoid mixed investment and borrowing. However IRRs are valid for 'pure' borrowing cash flows as long as all receipts occur before all payments. Looking at the cash flows above, only (d) meets this condition. The formula for the discount factor for a perpetuity from years y to ∞ has already been given on page 183 as

$$\frac{1}{r(1+r)^{(y-1)}}$$

In this case the factor needs to run from year 2 and so $y = 2$. Using that formula and testing for different values of r, there is only one positive value of r that gives a zero NPV and that is close to

5.25%. (Cash flows (a), (b) and (c) also have only one positive IRR and that is also 5.25%, but it is good practice to avoid calculating the IRRs of 'mixed cash flows'.)

Annuity Factors (Cumulative Discount Factors)

Since we have a formula for calculating the PV of a perpetuity starting in year y and continuing indefinitely, it must be possible to derive a formula for a stream of identical cash sums starting in year 1 and continuing to year y.

Adjusting the formula on the previous page to start a year later, the PV of £1 received every year from year *y+1* is

$$\frac{1}{r(1+r)^y}$$

The PV of £1 received every year from year 1 to ∞ is 1/r. If the PV of receipts from year y+1 were subtracted from 1/r, it should give the PV of £1 received every year from year 1 to year y :

$$\frac{1}{r} - \frac{1}{r(1+r)^y}$$

Sometimes this is restated as $r^{-1}(1 - (1+r)^{-y})$. There is a table of these factors on page 220. They are normally called 'Annuity Factors' but they can be called 'Cumulative Discount Factors'. The annuity factor for year 1 must be the same as the standard discount factor for year 1. The annuity factor for year 2 could be calculated using the above formula but it could also be found by adding the discount factor for year 1 to the discount factor for year 2. The annuity factor for year 3 can be found by adding the discount factors for years 1, 2 and 3 together.

Using Annuity Factors to Find the IRR

It was earlier stated that 'in practice finding the IRR means continuing to calculate NPVs using different rates of interest until one finds the rate that gives an NPV close to zero'. The exception to this rule arises where a single payment is followed by a stream of constant receipts as in the following example :

Discounted Cash Flow

Year	£
0	(1,000)
1	350
2	350
3	350
4	350

Since the receipts are identical in each year from year 1 to year 4, the NPV can be found by multiplying the receipt by the annuity factor for year 4. If a is the annuity factor, then the NPV is -1,000 + 350a. The IRR sets the NPV to zero; so at the IRR 1,000 = 350a. Or a = 1,000/350 = 2.86. Looking across the annuity tables for y = 4, the figure closest is where r = 15%. Thus the IRR of these cash flows is 15%.

Try to answer the following questions before looking at the answers (which are at the end of this chapter).

Question 6.14 (Answer 6.14 is on page 227)

Pissarro Retail Designs Ltd is considering a project with the following cash flows :

Year	£
0	(1,200)
1	1,100
2	500

REQUIRED : Find the IRR of these cash flows. (Tip : discount at 20%. If that does not give a zero NPV, add or subtract 10%.)

Question 6.15 (Answer 6.15 is on page 227)

Canneletto Boating Ltd is considering a project with the following cash flows :

Year	£
0	(750)
1	1,840
2	(1,000)

The WACC of Caneletto Boating is 25%.

REQUIRED : Find the IRR of these cash flows.

Question 6.16 (Answer 6.16 is on page 227)

Velazquez Colour Ltd is considering a project with the following cash flows :

Year	£
0	(2,500)
1	782
2	782
3	782
4	782
5	782

REQUIRED : Use annuity tables to find the IRR of these cash flows.

Economic Values

The 'Economic Value' of an asset is the NPV of the stream of receipts and payments that will arise from continuing to hold the asset. That stream of cash transactions should be calculated on an incremental basis. In other words, the stream should be the difference between (a) what will happen *with* the asset and (b) what will happen *without* the asset.

As has already been explained, CCA is logically dependent on the belief that the Replacement Cost will almost always be the Deprival Value of a business asset. For most Fixed Assets, other than land and buildings, the Net Realisable Value is likely to be low and so this belief rests on a comparison of Economic Value with Replacement Cost. If Economic Values are always greater than Replacement Costs, then CCA is based on reasonable foundations. On the other hand, if there are significant numbers of instances where Replacement Costs are greater than Economic Values, then the case for CCA (at least for the companies with those situations) is very dubious.

Advocates of CCA envisage a stable business world where technical developments are rare. Some opponents of CCA envisage a dynamic business world with booms and slumps where technical developments are rapid.

It might be thought that empirical evidence could adjudicate between these two views. If all the companies included in the FT100 index (and a selection of smaller businesses) were prepared to publish both the economic values and the replacement costs of all their assets every year for a period that included both an economic boom and a slump, then one side might be the clear winner. Academics would certainly enjoy such an exercise (but they would not have to bear the costs). However the reaction outside academic circles would be less favourable.

It is difficult to get managers to put figures on paper for forecasts to support a real business investment. Individual managers may be emotionally committed to a project and want to persuade their colleagues and yet they find the idea of forecasting incremental cash flows difficult. And that involves scenarios which are real and which might actually occur.

To forecast what will happen if one of the assets were to be removed is to envisage a scenario which is most unlikely. It will strike most practical businesspeople as completely unreal.

Of course there are many examples where, on a tour of a factory, one of the directors may casually say that certain machinery will never be replaced. The market for the product is no longer strong enough or a better machine has been developed or the original investment proved unwise. However to demand that the director then compute the economic value - not just in the broad terms required to judge when to cease using the equipment but in figures on paper to be published to the outside world - would make most such directors consider what possible benefit they or their businesses would gain from such an exercise.

Companies buy equipment over a period of time and sometimes items bought separately are attached together and sometimes items bought together are separated. What constitutes a 'separate asset' is not always easy to define. The more the assets are separated the higher the total of all the economic values is likely to be.

10 separate assets may be needed to produce a stream of income with an NPV of £1m. Without any one of those assets the whole stream of income will stop. So if each of the assets had its economic value determined separately, the total economic value of all 10 assets would be £10m. But if the assets are grouped together the economic value is only £1m.

Most managers do not view their businesses as just a collection of tangible assets. The streams of income may be dependent on many other factors such as the team of employees, relationships with customers and suppliers, brand names and patents. It may be unwise to list the additional factors because the list can never be complete and it may encourage demands that these intangible assets be also given dubious valuations.

Changing from One Time Period to Another

So far in this Chapter all the examples have assumed that a year is the time period. So each receipt or payment had to be made (or computed *as if* it was made) on one day of the year. The costs of capital have been given as annual percentage rates.

In practice most banks charge interest each quarter or each month and many loan stocks pay interest each half year. Trading payments and receipts occur on every working day and there are considerable variations in most businesses between the different seasons of the year.

In the UK, consumer lending institutions use the initials 'APR' which stands for Annual Percentage Rate and consumer deposit-taking institutions use the initials 'CAR' which stands for Compound Annual Rate. The formula for converting from a rate of interest for one time period to a rate of interest for another is

$$(1 + r)^m - 1$$

where r is the rate of interest for the old time period and m is the multiple between the old and the new time period.

Example 1

The Grabbit Credit Card charges interest at 3% per month. What is this as an annual percentage rate (APR)?

There are 12 months in a year and so $m = 12$. In this case the rate per old time period (month) is 3% and so $r = 0.03$. The APR will be

$$(1 + r)^m - 1 = (1 + 0.03)^{12} - 1 = 0.426 \text{ or } 42.6\%$$

Example 2

The Secure Building Society credits interest on share accounts every quarter at the rate of 3% per quarter. What is the compound annual rate (CAR)?

There are 4 quarters in a year and so $m = 4$. In this case the rate per old time period (quarter) is 3% and so $r = 0.03$. The CAR will be

$$(1 + r)^m - 1 = (1 + 0.03)^4 - 1 = 0.126 \text{ or } 12.6\%$$

Example 3

A zero coupon bond with 5 years left before redemption at par is currently quoted at 50% of par. What is the implied compound annual rate (CAR)? (A zero coupon bond is a security which does not pay interest during its life but which is redeemed at a higher value than the money raised by issue.)

In this case the old time period is greater than the new and so m will equal one fifth or 0.2. A purchaser of the bond today will double their money over five years. So the redemption value will be the return of the investment plus 100% interest and so r will equal 1. The CAR will be

$$(1 + r)^m - 1 = (1 + 1)^{0.2} - 1 = 0.149 \text{ or } 14.9\%$$

The formula for moving from one time period to another is linked to the compound interest formula given on page 170.

Receipts and Payments paid Every Cycle

Evaluating projects with shorter time periods leads to 'cycles' of payments and receipts. Rents are normally paid every quarter and, if a project is being evaluated with monthly time breaks, then rent will be paid every third time period. The formula for a perpetuity starting year y (page 183) can be combined with the formula for changing from one time period to another.

The Present Value of £1 paid (or received) every c time periods starting at period t and continuing to infinity is

$$\frac{(1 + r)^{(c-t)}}{(1 + r)^c - 1}$$

Example

Propinvest Ltd is considering buying a freehold of a property let on a 999 year lease (a freehold reversion). This lease yields a ground rent of £10,000 p.a. The first receipt of ground rent will arise 2 months after the purchase. The cost of capital to Propinvest is 2% per month. Assume that the length of the lease is equivalent to infinity.

In this case the time periods for evaluation should be monthly. c will equal 12 because the ground rent is received annually and t will equal 2 because the first receipt will be in 2 months time. The present value of £1 received every 12 months starting in month 2 :

$$\frac{(1 + r)^{(c-t)}}{(1 + r)^c - 1} = \frac{(1 + 0.02)^{(12-2)}}{(1 + 0.02)^{12} - 1} = 4.544$$

The ground rent will be £10,000 pa and so the Present Value of this freehold reversion is £45,440. This is the maximum sum that Propinvest should be prepared to pay for this asset.

Cycle Payments with a Starting and Finishing Date

Just as the formula for a perpetuity can be converted to that for an annuity (see page 202); so the last formula must be capable of adaption so that the cycle of payments (or receipts) does not continue to infinity. If the final payment is made at time f, then the stream of payments starting at time (f + c) will *not* be made. Such a stream of payments of £1 will have a present value of

$$\frac{(1 + r)^{(c-f-c)}}{(1 + r)^c - 1} = \frac{(1 + r)^{-f}}{(1 + r)^c - 1}$$

If the starting payment is made at time 's', then the present value of the stream actually received must be the PV of an infinite stream starting at year 's' less the PV of the sums not paid starting year (f + c). The Present Value of £1 paid (or received) every c time periods starting at period s and continuing until the final payment at period f is

$$\frac{(1 + r)^{(c-s)}}{(1 + r)^c - 1} - \frac{(1 + r)^{-f}}{(1 + r)^c - 1} = \frac{(1 + r)^{(c-s+f)} - 1}{(1 + r)^f ((1 + r)^c - 1)}$$

Example

Chapter 7 in Modern Accounting 1 covered Depreciation and there was a section on the 'Time Value of Money'. In this section it was explained that taking account of time values would lead one to charge more depreciation to the later years of an asset's life and less to the early years. This conclusion will be discussed in greater detail in the next chapter but here let us consider the initial workings of the example of Andrew Bloggs who could (a) buy an router for £10,000 or (b) lease it for 5 years paying the hire charge in the *middle* of each year. This router has a five year life with no scrap value at the end of those five years.

How much would Andrew pay under the lease each year if the implied interest charge in that lease is 5% per 6 months? Often these lease facilities are provided by finance houses and such leases are essentially means of borrowing money. Each payment will be partly repayment of the capital sum borrowed and partly interest.

Discounted Cash Flow

Let us assume that the asset is delivered on 1st Jan 2000 and that is the date on which the supplier of the router has to be paid. The payments under the lease would be made on 1st July 2000, 2001, 2002, 2003 and 2004. These cash flows will have to be analysed using half yearly time breaks. If the payments under the lease were £1,000 (which is not correct) then the cash flows of the finance house providing the lease facility would be as follows :

Time (t)	Date	Discount Factor			£
0	1.1.00	1.05^{-0} =	1.000		(10,000)
1	1.7.00	1.05^{-1} =	0.952		1,000
2	1.1.01	1.05^{-2} =	0.907		-
3	1.7.01	1.05^{-3} =	0.864		1,000
4	1.1.02	1.05^{-4} =	0.823		-
5	1.7.02	1.05^{-5} =	0.784		1,000
6	1.1.03	1.05^{-6} =	0.746		-
7	1.7.03	1.05^{-7} =	0.711		1,000
8	1.1.04	1.05^{-8} =	0.677		-
9	1.7.04	1.05^{-9} =	0.644		1,000

The lease receipt (for the finance house) or payment (for Andrew) should be set so that there is a zero NPV discounting at 5% per time interval. Let us add the discount factors for t = 1, 3, 5, 7 and 9 together : 0.952 + 0.864 + 0.784 + 0.711 + 0.644 = 3.955 At a zero NPV the annual lease payment multiplied by 3.955 has to equal £10,000. If the annual lease payment is £x :

$$3.955 x = 10,000$$
Therefore
$$x = 2,528$$

The annual payments under the lease will be £2,528. Let us check that the formula on the previous page gives the same result. The rate of interest (r) is 0.05, the Cycle Length (c) is 2 (every second time interval), the Start of the stream (s) is 1 and the Final payment (f) is 9. So the discount factor for a stream of payments starting in t_1 and continuing every second year until the final payment in t_9 is

$$\frac{(1+r)^{(c-s+f)} - 1}{(1+r)^f((1+r)^c - 1)} = \frac{(1+0.05)^{(2-1+9)} - 1}{(1+0.05)^9((1+0.05)^2 - 1)}$$

$$= 3.955$$

So the formula will give the same answer as adding up all the separate discount factors. In this case, because the lease lasted only

5 years, it was possible to add up the individual factors but a longer problem would need the formula.

Try to answer the following questions before looking at the answers (which are at the end of this chapter).

Question 6.17 (Answer 6.17 is on page 227)

Refinance Ltd is considering raising money by means of a sale and leaseback of their current premises. They have been offered £6m for their freehold on condition that, immediately after sale, they sign a 999 year lease to take the premises back. This lease provides for a rent-free period for the first year and two months and then requires rent each quarter payable in advance. Thus the first payment will be made 14 months after the sale, the second payment 17 months after the sale, the third payment 20 months after the sale and so on. You can assume that 999 years is so long that the lease can be considered to be infinite.

REQUIRED : Compute the rent that would have to be charged each quarter after the rent-free period to give an APR of 15%.

Question 6.18 (Answer 6.18 is on page 228)

Yum Yum Catering Ltd are considering whether to accept a fixed price contract for running a staff restaurant. This contract would start in 15 months time and would run for 5 years from its start. The receipts to Yum Yum would be a fixed £200,000 per annum received at the end of each year of the contract. The only costs to Yum Yum would be wages which would be paid monthly starting with the first payment in 13 months time and continuing until the end of the contract with the last payment of wages being made in 75 months time. (Staff have to prepare prior to the start of the contract.) The cost of capital to Yum Yum is 14% pa and the cost of labour is expected to increase by 0.5% per month. At today's labour rates the monthly wage bill (from a year and a month's time) is £10,000.

REQUIRED : Compute the Net Present Value of the cash flows from this contract to help the company in its decision.

Terminal Values

The Net Terminal Value of a project is the value of the cash flows compounded (rather than discounted) to their value at the end of the project. Any project with a positive NPV will have a positive NTV (and any project with a negative NPV will have a negative NTV). Many students prefer the concept of Terminal Value to that of Present Value because it is possible to envisage a bank account charging interest on overdrafts and granting interest on positive balances that would finally have the terminal value as its balance. However Terminal Values are rarely used in practice or in examinations. They have the major drawback of being dependent on the length of the project.

Example
A project lasts for 2 years with cash flows as follows :

Year	£
0	(10,000)
1	6,000
2	7,000

The cost of capital is 10%. To find the terminal value (a) multiply £(10,000) by 1.1^2 and (b) multiply £6,000 by 1.1^1. Then add the result of (a), (b) and the final cash flow (£7,000) together.

Net Terminal Value = £-10,000 X 1.21 + 6,000 X 1.1 + 7,000
= £1,500

Purchase and Replacement Models

Different businesses can have widely differing policies on how long assets should be kept. Commonly used equipment can be bought new or on the second hand market although, in practice, some businesses always buy new (and some P & R models also make that assumption). There is often a trade-off between (a) the cost of the asset, (b) the costs of maintaining it and (c) the value of its output. Purchase and replacement models deal with assets that will be in constant demand and so will always need to be replaced when one is sold or scrapped. They try to answer the problems of when assets should be bought and when they should be sold.

Modern Accounting 2

Example
Metal Bashing Ltd will require oxycutters for the indefinite future. Oxycutters have a life three years and have no scrap value at the end of that life. At present the machines cost : £5,000 new, £3,000 one year old and £1,250 two years old. The current costs of maintenance on the machine are : £1,300 for the first year, £1,500 for the second year and £3,000 for the third year of life of the machine. Assume that these maintenance payments are made in one lump sum half way through the relevant year. Oxycutters give equivalent output in every year of their life.

It is possible to sell a second-hand one year old oxycutter for £2,100 and a two year old oxycutter for £875. The money cost of capital is 25% pa and all cost and revenue prices are likely to rise by 3% pa for the indefinite future.

There are six possible options in the circumstances outlined above and the cash flows of each option are shown in the table below :

		A Buy : New	B 1 year old	C 2 years old
Age at disposal :				
1 year old	Entry Payment	5,000	Option not possible	Option not possible
	Repeating Cycle	1,300 2,900		
2 years old	Entry Payment	5,000	3,000	Option not possible
	Repeating Cycle	1,300 0 1,500 4,125	1,500 2,125	
3 years old	Entry Payment	5,000	3,000	1,250
	Repeating Cycle	1,300 0 1,500 0 3,000 5,000	1,500 0 3,000 3,000	3,000 1,250

Looking at the top left cell of this table (Cell A1 - Buying new and disposing at 1 year old) the 'entry payment' of £5,000 is made just once in t_0 when the first new oxycutter is bought. Six months

Discounted Cash Flow

after that (t_1) a 2 period repeating cycle starts with a maintenance payment of £1,300. Six months after that (t_2) the first machine is sold for £2,100 and a replacement bought for £5,000. This 2 period cycle will repeat indefinitely. Every odd time interval £1,300 maintenance will be paid and every even time interval £2,900 will be paid to sell and replace.

Looking at the bottom left cell of this table (Cell A3 - Buying new and disposing at 3 years old) the 'entry payment' of £5,000 is made in t_0 when the first new oxycutter is bought. Six months after that (t_1) a 6 period repeating cycle starts with a maintenance payment of £1,300. The other maintenance payments are first made in periods 3 and 5. Six months after that (t_2) the first machine is scrapped and a replacement bought for £5,000. This 6 period cycle will repeat indefinitely. In period 1, 7, 13, 19 etc £1,300 maintenance will be paid. In period 3, 9, 15, 21 etc £1,500 maintenance will be paid. And so on.

Since we are given a money rate of interest and a rate of price inflation, the formula from page 187 can be used with m = 0.25 and i = 0.03. r = 1.25/1.03 - 1 = 21.359% pa which is equivalent to $1.21359^{0.5} - 1$ = 10.163% per half year. The Present Value of £1 paid (or received) every c time periods starting at period t and continuing to infinity is

$$\frac{(1 + r)^{(c-t)}}{(1 + r)^c - 1}$$

A table of such factors can be constructed:

c =	2	4	6
t = 1	5.158	2.828	2.061
t = 2	4.682	2.567	1.871
t = 3		2.330	1.698
t = 4		2.115	1.541
t = 5			1.399
t = 6			1.270

Thus the PVs of each option can be calculated:

PV_{A1} = £5,000 + 1,300 X 5.158 + 2,900 X 4.682 = £25,282
PV_{A2} = £5,000 + 1,300 X 2.828 + 1,500 X 2.330 + 4,125 X 2.115 = £20,895
PV_{A3} = £5,000 + 1,300 X 2.061 + 1,500 X 1.698 + 3,000 X 1.399 + 5,000 X 1.270 = £20,773
PV_{B2} = £3,000 + 1,500 X 5.158 + 2,125 X 4.682 = £20,685
PV_{B3} = £3,000 + 1,500 X 2.828 + 3,000 X 2.330 + 3,000 X 2.115 = £20,577
PV_{C3} = £1,250 + 3,000 X 5.158 + 1,250 X 4.682 = £22,575

Since these are all PVs of payments, the lowest option would be chosen. In this case, buying a year old machine and holding it for the remaining 2 year life before replacement (Cell B3) is the best option.

Modern Accounting 2

Try to answer the following question before looking at the answer (which is at the end of this chapter).

Question 6.19 (Answer 6.19 is on page 228)

Jiffy Storage Ltd will require fork lift trucks for the indefinite future. Fork Lift Trucks have a life three years and have a scrap value at the end of that life of ₤600. At present the trucks cost : ₤10,000 new, ₤6,000 one year old and ₤2,000 two years old. The current costs of maintenance on the truck are : ₤1,000 for the first year, ₤1,200 for the second year and ₤4,000 for the third year of life of the truck. Assume that these maintenance payments are made in one lump sum half way through the relevant year. Trucks give equivalent output in every year of their life.

It is possible to sell a second-hand one year old truck for ₤5,000 and a two year old truck for ₤1,000. The money cost of capital is 20% pa and all cost and revenue prices are likely to rise by 5% pa for the indefinite future.

REQUIRED : Advise Jiffy Storage as to the best purchase and replacement police for fork lift trucks.

Using a Computer Spreadsheet to Calculate NPVs and IRRs

Most spreadsheet programs (like Lotus 123 and Excel) have functions such as @NPV and @IRR. Before using any of these functions (a) study the manual for that spreadsheet and (b) use a paper, pencil and calculator on a simple problem to check that the spreadsheet function gives the answer that you expect. There are a number of errors and quirks built into some of these spreadsheet functions.

Typically the range used for the NPV function must start at t_1 (or Year 1) and *not* from the present time. Whereas the IRR function will use a range starting from t_0 (Year 0).

Sensitivity Analysis

A major advantage of using a computer spreadsheet is that many NPV calculations can be done at speed. All the assumptions behind the forecasts can be kept constant apart from one factor. Repetitive

NPVs can be calculated for all possible variations of that factor. The result can be a graph showing how sensitive the project is to variations in just that factor.

Difficulties in Forecasting the Future

Many business projects are developed from previous successful experiences. The closer the new project is to previous experiences, the easier it is to forecast the cash flows. The more it is new or experimental, the more difficult those forecasts become.

The examples in this chapter have asked for calculations based on given forecasts. NPVs can also be used to 'work backwards'. Given a required NPV, what do the uncertain cash flows have to be before the project can be accepted? Once the required values for these uncertain factors are known, they can be studied and their reasonableness evaluated.

NPV versus IRR

For a single project an NPV evaluation should give the same result as an IRR evaluation. If the NPV discounted at the cost of capital is positive, then the IRR must be above the cost of capital.

However sometimes two projects are mutually exclusive. Project A has a higher NPV than Project B but Project B has a higher IRR than Project A. Which project should be preferred above the other?

Example

Perplex Limited is considering two mutually exclusive projects - Project A and Project B. The cost of capital to Perplex Limited is 10% pa. The cash flows of the two projects are as follows :

£ Year	Project A	Project B
0	(10,000)	(10,000)
1	2,750	6,000
2	2,750	6,000
3	2,750	-
4	2,750	-
5	2,750	-

Annuity factors at 10% : Yr 5 - 3.790; Yr 2 - 1.737.

$NPV_A = -10{,}000 + 2{,}750 \times 3.790 = 423$
$NPV_B = -10{,}000 + 6{,}000 \times 1.737 = 410$

The Internal Rate of Return is the Discount Rate that sets the NPV of a project to zero. In this case the IRR of A is very close to 11.5% and the IRR of B is very close to 13% and yet A has a higher NPV than B.

In cases like this the project with the higher NPV and lower IRR must always be larger than the other project. 'Larger' means that it must consume more capital or (as in this case) run for a longer time.

Most academic analysis of this problem concludes that the higher NPV project should be accepted. Most practical business people conclude that the higher IRR project should be accepted. Both views may be correct because they are each making different assumptions.

Academic Analysis

For the academics 'capital rationing' is a 'market imperfection' and is assumed to be rare. For them the reason why the projects are mutually exclusive should not be because of shortage of capital. In perfect capital markets a higher return is associated with higher risk. Thus Project A is the best choice if the following conditions hold true :

(a) Either (i) the cash flows are certain and we can ignore risk or (ii) Project B has more risk than Project A because it has a higher IRR.
(b) It is certain that as much money as we will require within the next five years can be raised at (or below) 10%pa.
(c) Neither of these projects has any effect on future business opportunities. In other words, the full incremental impact is included in the stated cash flows.

Business Analysis

But most business people assume that 'capital rationing' is the normal situation and its absence is unusual. If there is no capital rationing, then the earlier return from Project B has no impact on any other future projects we could pursue. However if the company is short of capital and found Project C with the following cash flows:

Year	0	1	2	3	4	5
£	-	(3,250)	(3,250)	2,750	2,750	2,750

then Project B together with Project C is precisely equivalent to Project A. The IRR of Project C is below that of either of the other two (but still above the cost of capital). It will always be the case that the difference between two projects in this situation (of conflict between positive NPVs and IRRs) has an IRR below that of either of them and above the cost of capital.

Many business people could not state how they could reinvest the surplus funds from B over A. They do not know what opportunities will be available in a year's time. But they would consider it most pessimistic to assume that such opportunities will have a lower IRR than either of those currently available. (Most academic analysts would prefer to assume that unknown future opportunities will yield no more than the cost of capital.)

Business people tend to assume that risk is correlated to the size of the project and has little relationship to the IRR of the project. Surprisingly, text book examples in this area have been (a) of different degrees of automation in the same factory and (b) of different volumes of property development on the same site. With automation and property projects, the business (rather than the academic) assumptions as to risk are probably valid.

Thus Project B is the best choice if the following conditions hold true :
(a) Either (i) the cash flows are certain and we can ignore risk or
(ii) Project B has less risk than Project A because it is smaller.
(b) It is doubtful whether as much money as we will require within the next five years can be raised at (or below) 10%pa.
(c) We are optimistic as to unknown future business opportunities.

Capital Rationing

Perfect solutions to capital rationing problems can only be achieved if a full analysis can be made of all available opportunities during the period of capital rationing. There are two main linear programming models in this area. They are interesting but rarely used in practice and outside the scope of this book.

Why DCF and NPVs are Not Universally Accepted in Business

Some top managers see successful capital investment as a behavioural exercise. They concentrate less on their *own* forecasts of

Modern Accounting 2

outcomes than on ensuring that their subordinates sponsoring projects are personally committed to them and will work as hard and long as is necessary to ensure that the project meets its targets.

Unfortunately not all business people enjoy mathematics. Frequently many of those whose efforts will materially affect the cash flows are not able (or willing) to calculate NPVs or to appreciate their meaning. This implies that they are not likely to be emotionally committed to ensuring that targets expressed as NPVs are achieved.

The concept of a 'return' as a percentage is much easier to grasp and IRRs are normally calculated for the managers in most large companies. Yet although IRRs may be included in the formal documentation that companies keep in their filing systems, it is the simple idea of Payback which sways many business meetings.

Payback

The Payback of a project is the length of time that it takes to recover the initial investment.

Example

A project with the following cash flows is being evaluated :

Year	£
0	(10,000)
1	5,000
2	5,000
3	5,000

The Payback of this project is 2 years.

Payback takes no account of (a) cash flows received after the payback period and (b) the timing of cash flows within the payback period. Its use partly stems from the firmly fixed belief in many companies that Capital Rationing is the normal state.

Discounted Payback

Discounted Payback is the illegitimate result of mixing NPV with Payback. If NPV is too complicated a concept to be understood from the shop-floor to the board-room and Payback is too crude a measure to give optimal decisions, then Discounted Payback neatly combines the disadvantages of both.

Example

The cost of capital is 10% pa. A project with the following cash flows is being evaluated :

Year	£	Discount Factors at 10%	PVs	Cumulative
0	(10,000)	1.000	(10,000)	(10,000)
1	5,000	0.909	4,545	(5,455)
2	5,000	0.826	4,130	(1,325)
3	5,000	0.751	3,755	2,430

The Discounted Payback is between 2 and 3 years. Sometimes the precise proportion of the final year is calculated. In this case the proportion would be 1,325/3,755.

References

[1] The Cost of Equity Capital (Journal of Finance, June 1978) Myron J Gordon and Lawrence I Gould

[2] An introduction to Risk and Return (Financial Analysts Journal, March-April 1974) Franco Modigliani and Gerald A Pogue

[3] The Cost of Capital, Corporation Finance and the Theory of Investment (American Economic Review, June 1958) Franco Modigliani and Merton H Miller

Further Reading

Principles of Financial Management (Prentice Hall, 1988) Haim Levy and Marshall Sarnat

Investment Appraisal and Financing Decisions (Chapman and Hall, 1990) Stephen Lumby

Modern Accounting 2

Discount Factors

r =	5%	6%	7%	8%	9%	10%	11%	12%	13%	14%	15%	16%	17%	18%
y =														
1	0.952	0.943	0.935	0.926	0.917	0.909	0.901	0.893	0.885	0.877	0.870	0.862	0.855	0.847
2	0.907	0.890	0.873	0.857	0.842	0.826	0.812	0.797	0.783	0.769	0.756	0.743	0.731	0.718
3	0.864	0.840	0.816	0.794	0.772	0.751	0.731	0.712	0.693	0.675	0.658	0.641	0.624	0.609
4	0.823	0.792	0.763	0.735	0.708	0.683	0.659	0.636	0.613	0.592	0.572	0.552	0.534	0.516
5	0.784	0.747	0.713	0.681	0.650	0.621	0.593	0.567	0.543	0.519	0.497	0.476	0.456	0.437

r =	19%	20%	21%	22%	23%	24%	25%	26%	27%	28%	29%	30%	31%	32%
y =														
1	0.840	0.833	0.826	0.820	0.813	0.806	0.800	0.794	0.787	0.781	0.775	0.769	0.763	0.758
2	0.706	0.694	0.683	0.672	0.661	0.650	0.640	0.630	0.620	0.610	0.601	0.592	0.583	0.574
3	0.593	0.579	0.564	0.551	0.537	0.524	0.512	0.500	0.488	0.477	0.466	0.455	0.445	0.435
4	0.499	0.482	0.467	0.451	0.437	0.423	0.410	0.397	0.384	0.373	0.361	0.350	0.340	0.329
5	0.419	0.402	0.386	0.370	0.355	0.341	0.328	0.315	0.303	0.291	0.280	0.269	0.259	0.250

Annuity Factors

r =	5%	6%	7%	8%	9%	10%	11%	12%	13%	14%	15%	16%	17%	18%
y =														
1	0.952	0.943	0.935	0.926	0.917	0.909	0.901	0.893	0.885	0.877	0.870	0.862	0.855	0.847
2	1.859	1.833	1.808	1.783	1.759	1.736	1.713	1.690	1.668	1.647	1.626	1.605	1.585	1.566
3	2.723	2.673	2.624	2.577	2.531	2.487	2.444	2.402	2.361	2.322	2.283	2.246	2.210	2.174
4	3.546	3.465	3.387	3.312	3.240	3.170	3.102	3.037	2.974	2.914	2.855	2.798	2.743	2.690
5	4.329	4.212	4.100	3.993	3.890	3.791	3.696	3.605	3.517	3.433	3.352	3.274	3.199	3.127

r =	19%	20%	21%	22%	23%	24%	25%	26%	27%	28%	29%	30%	31%	32%
y =														
1	0.840	0.833	0.826	0.820	0.813	0.806	0.800	0.794	0.787	0.781	0.775	0.769	0.763	0.758
2	1.547	1.528	1.509	1.492	1.474	1.457	1.440	1.424	1.407	1.392	1.376	1.361	1.346	1.331
3	2.140	2.106	2.074	2.042	2.011	1.981	1.952	1.923	1.896	1.868	1.842	1.816	1.791	1.766
4	2.639	2.589	2.540	2.494	2.448	2.404	2.362	2.320	2.280	2.241	2.203	2.166	2.130	2.096
5	3.058	2.991	2.926	2.864	2.803	2.745	2.689	2.635	2.583	2.532	2.483	2.436	2.390	2.345

Discounted Cash Flow

Answers to Questions 6.1 to 6.19

Answer 6.1
Discount factors for years 1 to 5 at 37% pa :

Year		
1	$\frac{1}{(1 + 0.37)^1} =$	0.729927
2	$\frac{1}{(1 + 0.37)^2} =$	0.532793
3	$\frac{1}{(1 + 0.37)^3} =$	0.388900
4	$\frac{1}{(1 + 0.37)^4} =$	0.283868
5	$\frac{1}{(1 + 0.37)^5} =$	0.207203

Answer 6.2
Discount factors for varying rates of interest :

Year		
1	$\frac{1}{1.1} =$	0.909090
2	$\frac{1}{(1.1 \times 1.2)} =$	0.757575
3	$\frac{1}{(1.1 \times 1.2 \times 1.3)} =$	0.582750

Answer 6.3

Year	(a) Cash	(b) Discount Factor	(a) X (b) Present Value
0	(12,000)	1	(12,000)
1	(3,000)	0.833333	(2,500)
2	15,000	0.694444	10,417
3	5,000	0.578703	2,893
			(1,190)

The NPV is negative. If no further information is available, this project should be rejected.

Answer 6.4

Year	(a) Cash	(b) Discount Factor	(a) X (b) Present Value
0	(19,000)	1	(19,000)
1	9,000	0.869565	7,826
2	12,000	0.756143	9,074
3	4,000	0.657516	2,630
			530

The NPV is positive. This project can still be considered.

Answer 6.5

Year	0	1	2	3	4
	£	£	£	£	£
Sales		700,000	1,000,000	1,200,000	1,400,000
Cost of Sales		350,000	500,000	600,000	700,000
Gross Profit		350,000	500,000	600,000	700,000
Fixed Costs		100,000	100,000	100,000	100,000
Depreciation		125,000	125,000	125,000	125,000
Net Profit		125,000	275,000	375,000	475,000

Stocks (20% of next year's Cost of Sales)
        70,000   100,000   120,000   140,000   0

Purchases (Cost of Sales plus Closing Stock less Opening Stock)
        70,000   380,000   520,000   620,000   560,000

Creditors (10% of Purchases)
        -    38,000   52,000   62,000   0

Working Capital (Stock less Creditors)
        -    62,000   68,000   78,000   0

Changes in Working Capital
        62,000   6,000   10,000   (78,000)

CASH FLOWS

Profit for the year		125,000	275,000	375,000	475,000
Add Depreciation		125,000	125,000	125,000	125,000
		250,000	400,000	500,000	600,000
Less Change in Working Capital		62,000	6,000	10,000	(78,000)
CASH		188,000	394,000	490,000	678,000

Year 0 Cash Payment = Shopfitting + Stock = £800,000 + 70,000

Discounted Cash Flow

Year	Cash Flow	Discount Factors @ 30%	Present Values
0	(870,000)	1.0000	(870,000)
1	188,000	0.7692	144,615
2	394,000	0.5917	233,136
3	490,000	0.4552	223,031
4	678,000	0.3501	<u>237,387</u>
			<u>(31,830)</u>

The NPV is negative and thus, on the basis of the information given, this project should be rejected.

Answer 6.7

Year	Cash Flow £	Discount Factors @ 15%	Present Values £
0	(30,000)	1.00000	(30,000)
1	(30,000)	0.86957	(26,087)
2	(30,000)	0.75614	(22,684)
3		0.65752	0
4		0.57175	0
5 to ∞	20,000	3.81169	76,234
Net Present Value			<u>(2,537)</u>

Since the NPV is negative, this project should be rejected.

Answer 6.8

Year £m	(A) Contribution (increase 10% yrs 1 to 4) Same as V Cost	(B) Finished Goods Stock (1.2 X 20% of Next yr's Var Cost - except yr 0)	(C) Finished Goods Produced (Var Cost + $B_0 - B_{-1}$)
0	30.000	6.000	30.000
1	33.000	8.712	35.712
2	36.300	9.583	37.171
3	39.930	10.542	40.888
4	43.923	10.542	43.923
5	43.923	10.542	43.923
6 to ∞	43.923	10.542	43.923

Modern Accounting 2

Year £m	(D) Raw Mat Used in Production (30% of C)	(E) Raw Mat Stocks (1.2 X 10% of use next yr - except yr 0)	(F) Raw Mat Purchased (D + E₀ - E₋₁)
0	9.000	0.900	9.000
1	10.714	1.338	11.152
2	11.151	1.472	11.285
3	12.266	1.581	12.376
4	13.177	1.581	13.177
5	13.177	1.581	13.177
6 to ∞	13.177	1.581	13.177

Year £m	(G) Creditors (10% of F)	(H) Debtors (10% of Sales or 20% of A)	(I) Working Capital (E + B + H - G)
0	0.900	6.000	12.000
1	1.115	6.600	15.535
2	1.129	7.260	17.187
3	1.238	7.986	18.871
4	1.318	8.785	19.590
5	1.318	8.785	19.590
6 to ∞	1.318	8.785	19.590

Cash effects of paras :

Year	a	b	c	d	e
0	(0.200)				
1	(6.000)		(1.700)	1.000	(5.000)
2		4.000	(2.000)	(0.050)	(5.000)
3				(0.050)	(5.000)
4				(0.050)	(5.000)
5				(1.050)	(5.000)
6 to ∞					(5.000)

Year £m	J Summary of paras (a) to (e)	K Increased Contribution	L Working Capital Change
0	(0.200)		
1	(11.700)	3.000	3.535
2	(3.050)	6.300	1.652
3	(5.050)	9.930	1.685
4	(5.050)	13.923	0.718
5	(6.050)	13.923	-
6 to ∞	(5.000)	13.923	-

Discounted Cash Flow

Year £m	M Cash Flows (J + K - L)	N Discount Factors @ 25%	O Present Values (M X N)
0	(0.200)	1.0000	(0.200)
1	(12.235)	0.8000	(9.788)
2	1.598	0.6400	1.023
3	3.195	0.5120	1.636
4	8.155	0.4096	3.340
5	7.873	0.3277	2.580
6 to ∞	8.923	1.3107	11.696

Net Present Value <u>10.286</u>
Since the NPV is positive, this project is worth considering.

Answer 6.9

r = (1.25/1.15) - 1 = 8.70%

Answer 6.10

If r = (1 + m)/(1 + i) - 1
then m = (1 + r)(1 + i) - 1 = 48.50%

Answer 6.11

r = (1.15/1.04) - 1 = 10.577%

Year	Cash Flows	Discount Factors @ 10.577%	Present Values
0	(90,000)	1.00000	(90,000)
1	8,000	0.90435	7,235
2	30,000	0.81784	24,535
3	40,000	0.73962	29,585
4	30,000	0.66887	20,066
5	20,000	0.60489	12,098

Net Present Value <u>3,519</u>

Modern Accounting 2

Answer 6.12

	Records	Other Expenses	Income
Price Increase	10%	7%	9%
Real Cost of Capital	(1.2/1.1)-1	(1.2/1.07)-1	(1.2/1.09)-1
	9.09%	12.15%	10.09%

Discount Factors :

Year			
0	1.0000	1.0000	1.0000
1	0.9167	0.8917	0.9083
2	0.8403	0.7951	0.8251
3	0.7703	0.7089	0.7495
4	0.7061	0.6321	0.6808

Cash Flows :

Year	Juke Box	Records	Other Expenses	Income
0	(5,000)			
1		(1,000)	(500)	3,000
2		(1,000)	(500)	4,000
3		(1,000)	(500)	4,000
4		(1,000)	(500)	3,500

Present Values (Cash Flows multiplied by the Discount Factors) :

Year				
0	(5,000)			
1		(917)	(446)	2,725
2		(840)	(398)	3,300
3		(770)	(354)	2,998
4		(706)	(316)	2,383
PVs	(5,000)	(3,233)	(1,514)	11,406

Summing these 4 present values, the whole project has a Net Present Value of £1,658. Since the NPV is positive the project might be accepted.

Answer 6.13

M_e = £1.50 X 1m = £1.5m C_e = 8/150 + 0.12 = 17.33%
M_l = £0.8m X 1.2 = £0.96m C_l = 0.75 X 14/120 = 8.75%

$$\frac{M_e C_e + M_l C_l}{M_e + M_l} = \frac{1.5 \times 17.33 + 0.96 \times 8.75}{1.5 + 0.96} = 13.98\%$$

or close to 14%

Discounted Cash Flow

Answer 6.14

The NPV discounting @ 20% = +£64
So add 10% to the discount rate.
The NPV discounting @ 30% = -£58
So the IRR must be above 20% and below 30%. Discounting @ 25% gives an NPV very close to zero.

Answer 6.15

The payment in year 2 must be discounted back to year 1. £1,000/1.25 = £800
So the cash flows can be restated :

Year	£
0	(750)
1 1,840-800 =	1,040

This gives an IRR of 39%

Answer 6.16

If a is the annuity factor for year 5, the NPV is -2,500 + 782a.
When the NPV is zero   a = 2,500/782 = 3.197

Annuity factor tables say that r = 17% when y = 5 and a = 3.199
Therefore the IRR is very close to 17%

Answer 6.17

15% pa can be converted into a monthly interest rate using the formula on page 206 :
$(1 + r)^m - 1 = (1 + 0.15)^{(1/12)} - 1 = 0.011714$ or 1.17%

The rent payable starts in month 14 and continues every 3rd month to infinity. Using the formula on page 207 with r = 0.0117, c = 3 and t = 14 :

$$\frac{(1 + r)^{(c-t)}}{(1 + r)^c - 1} = \frac{(1 + 0.0117)^{(3-14)}}{(1 + 0.0117)^3 - 1} = 24.74127$$

So £6m should be a multiple of 24.74 of the quarterly rent.

$$\frac{£6,000,000}{24.74} = £242,510$$

Modern Accounting 2

Answer 6.18

14% pa can be converted into a monthly interest rate using the formula on page 206 :
$(1 + r)^m = (1 + 0.14)^{(1/12)} - 1 = 0.010978$ or 1.10%

Receipts under the contract would arise in months 27, 39, 51, 63 and 75. Using the formula on page 208 with $r = 0.0110$, $c = 12$, $s = 27$ and $f = 75$:

$$\frac{(1 + r)^{(c-s+f)} - 1}{(1 + r)^f((1 + r)^c - 1)} = \frac{(1 + 0.0110)^{(12-27+75)} - 1}{(1 + 0.0110)^{75}((1 + 0.0110)^{12} - 1)}$$

$$= 2.911508$$

Since each receipt will be £200,000, the PV of the receipts will be
£200,000 X 2.912 = £582,302

Price rises on labour amount to 0.5% per month. Using the formula on page 187 to obtain the real rate of interest :

$$\frac{(1 + m)}{(1 + i)} - 1 = \frac{(1 + 0.011)}{(1 + 0.005)} - 1 = \quad 0.005949 \text{ or } 0.59\%$$

Since the wage payments are made monthly (c=1), we could use annuity tables to calculate their NPV. (Find the annuity factor for the final payment and subtract the annuity factor for the month prior to the first payment.) However we may as well continue to use the same formula from page 208 with $r = 0.0059$, $c = 1$, $s = 13$ and $f = 75$:

$$\frac{(1 + r)^{(c-s+f)} - 1}{(1 + r)^f((1 + r)^c - 1)} = \frac{(1 + 0.0059)^{(1-13+75)} - 1}{(1 + 0.0059)^{75}((1 + 0.0059)^1 - 1)}$$

$$= 48.91149$$

Since (at current prices) each payment will be £10,000, the PV of the payments will be
£10,000 X 48.911 = £489,115

The NPV of this contract must be £582,302 - 489,115 = £93,187. Since this is positive, the contract may be worth accepting.

Answer 6.19

Real cost of capital = 1.2/1.05 - 1 = 14.29% pa

14.29% pa = $(1 + 0.1429)^{0.5} - 1$ per half year = 6.9% per half year

Discounted Cash Flow

	A	B	C
Buy :	New	1 year old	2 years old
Age at disposal :			
1 year old Entry Payment	10,000	Option not	Option not
Repeating Cycle	**1,000** **5,000**	possible	possible
2 years old Entry Payment	10,000	6,000	Option not
Repeating Cycle	1,000 0 1,200 9,000	**1,200** **5,000**	possible
3 years old Entry Payment	10,000	6,000	2,000
Repeating Cycle	1,000 0 1,200 0 4,000 9,400	1,200 0 4,000 5,400	**4,000** **1,400**

	c =	2	4	6
t = 1		7.483	3.991	2.834
t = 2		7.000	3.733	2.651
t = 3			3.480	2.480
t = 4			3.267	2.320
t = 5				2.170
t = 6				2.030

Thus the PVs of each option can be calculated :

PV_{A1} = £10,000 + 1,000 X 7.483 + 5,000 X 7.000 = £52,483
PV_{A2} = £10,000 + 1,000 X 3.991 + 1,200 X 3.480 + 9,000 X 3.267 = £47,582
PV_{A3} = £10,000 + 1,000 X 2.834 + 1,200 X 2.480 + 4,000 X 2.170 + 9,400 X 2.030 = £43,557
PV_{B2} = £3,000 + 1,500 X 7.483 + 2,125 X 7.000 = £49,980
PV_{B3} = £3,000 + 1,500 X 3.991 + 3,000 X 3.480 + 3,000 X 3.267 = £42,398
PV_{C3} = £1,250 + 3,000 X 7.483 + 1,250 X 7.000 = £41,733

Option C3 (Buying 2 year old trucks and holding for a year) has the lowest NPV and hence is the best option.

Modern Accounting 2

Chapter Seven

Definitions of Economic Income

This area is normally associated with the work of Fisher[1] and Hicks[2]. Economic Income in their writings related to individuals (rather than companies) and they assumed that its main function was to determine the amount that an individual can consume in a period without increasing or reducing 'Capital'. Economic income is defined by the formula :

$Y_e = C + (K_n - K_{n-1})$

where Y_e is economic income;
C is the maximum possible consumption in the year assuming continuation of the investment - C would normally be the net cash flow of the year from investments;
K_n is the 'Capital' at the end of the period;
and K_{n-1} is the 'Capital' at the start of the period.

Sometimes it is suggested that this is similar to the underlying concept of traditional accounting profit with only the definition of 'Capital' altered. The next two chapters on Consolidations and Foreign Currency Translations should throw doubts on this apparent similarity because modern ideas on 'movements on reserves' for Goodwill and Currency Adjustments distance accounting profit from comparisons of Capital at the start and end of a period.

The Definition of 'Capital' for Economic Income

K_n and K_{n-1} are defined as the Discounted Present Values of expected net returns from existing investments. Thus the calculation of 'Capital' will depend on (a) forecasts of future cash flows and (b) the rate of interest used as a discount rate.

Ideal Income

To measure Ideal Income one needs conditions of perfect certainty as to future events and it would normally be assumed that, if all players in a market have this perfect forecasting capability, this will lead to perfect competition with one unchanging market rate of interest (charged to and obtainable by everybody) that can be used as a discount rate.

Example of Ideal Income

The cash flows that will arise from Ideala's existing portfolio of business investments are as follows:

Year	£
1	2,000
2	2,000
3	2,000

Ideala's current investments have a three year life and are then worthless. The constant market rate of interest is 10% pa. Thus the 'Capital' of Ideala today (K_0) is:

Year	£	Discount factor	PV
1	2,000	0.909	1,818
2	2,000	0.826	1,652
3	2,000	0.751	1,502
			4,972

In a year's time her 'Capital' (K_1) in these investments will be 1,818 + 1,652 = 3,470

In two year's time her 'Capital' (K_2) in these investments will be 1,818

And in three year's time there will be no future benefit from these investments and thus $K_3 = 0$

The economic income for Ideala from these investments will be:

Year	C	K_n	K_{n-1}	Economic Income
1	2,000	3,470	4,972	2,000+3,470-4,972= 498
2	2,000	1,818	3,470	2,000+1,818-3,470= 348
3	2,000	0	1,818	2,000+0-1,818= 182

This apportionment of economic income has two striking features. Firstly a constant cash flow of £2,000 per annum has produced a stream of income that *reduces* in each year from £498 to £348 to £182. Secondly the income for each year gives a constant return on the 'Capital' employed at the start of that year and that constant return is the same as the discount rate. In this case the discount rate was 10% pa and £498 is 10% of £4,972, £348 is (approximately) 10% of £3,470 and £182 is 10% of £1,818.

Economic Definitions of Income

Expressed on a more traditional income statement with 'depreciation' of the original 'Capital', these income calculations would appear as follows :

Year	1	2	3	Total
Receipts	2,000	2,000	2,000	6,000
Depreciation	1,502	1,652	1,818	4,972
	498	348	182	1,028

This form of 'depreciation' of the original 'Capital' is similar to 'Depreciation Taking Account of the Time Value of Money' (see Chapter 7 of Modern Accounting 1).

New Investments

If Ideala were to consume just the economic income shown above, then the figures of 'depreciation' would be available for investment in new projects. In this world of perfect knowledge and competition the new projects would return precisely 10% pa and Ideala's total economic income from both the existing investments and any new investments would stay constant at £498 per annum.

Let us assume that Ideala's new projects all have an infinite life and return constant cash flows each year from the anniversary of investment to infinity. In Year 1 Ideala will invest £1,502 in new projects, in Year 2 £1,652 and in Year 3 £1,818. In Year 2 the cash receipts from the new projects will be £150 which will all arise from the investment at Year 1. At Year 3 the cash receipts from the new projects will be £316 which will be £150 from the investment in Year 1 and almost £166 from the investment at Year 2. In every year from Year 4 onwards the cash receipts from the new projects will be £498 (£150 + £166 + £182). The full income will be as follows :

Year	1	2	3	4 and onwards
Economic Income :				
from existing investments	498	348	182	0
from new investments	0	150	316	498
Total Economic Income	498	498	498	498

Problems with the Ideal Economic Income Model

This model is not likely to appeal to those who think that employees play a part in a company's success. It would appear that

Modern Accounting 2

'income' is solely a function of capital invested and the efforts and skills of individual humans have no part to play.

And in real business investments it is not possible to forecast the future with absolute certainty and different observers would produce different forecasts.

Income Ex Ante

Income ex ante is measured at the start of each year. The formula can be shown as :

$Y_e = C' + (K'_n - K_{n-1})$

where C' is the cash flow of the year (forecast at the start of the year) and K'_n is the 'Capital' at the end of the year (also forecast at the start of the year) and K_{n-1} is the 'Capital' at the start of the year (once again forecast at the start of the year).

Example of Ex Ante Income

The discount rate remains at 10% pa. At Year 0 Antea believes that her cash flows from existing investments will be receipts of £3,000 at Year 1, a further £3,000 at Year 2 and a final £3,000 at Year 3. Thus at Year 0 Antea believes her 'Capital' at that date to be :

Year	£	Discount factor	PV
1	3,000	0.909	2,727
2	3,000	0.826	2,478
3	3,000	0.751	2,253
			7,458

At Year 0 she would believe that her 'Capital' at Year 1 to be £2,727 + 2,478 = £5,205. Thus her ex-ante economic income for Year 1 will be $C' + (K'_n - K_{n-1}) = 3,000 + (5,205 - 7,458) = 747$.

However the actual cash receipt at Year 1 turned out to be £2,000. The difference between the forecast £3,000 and the actual cash receipt is referred to in academic literature as a 'windfall' loss. At Year 1 Antea believes that future cash flows will amount to £1,000 on both Year 2 and Year 3. Antea's 'Capital' (in existing investments) at Year 1 (forecast at Year 1) will be :

Year	£	Discount factor	PV
2	1,000	0.909	909
3	1,000	0.826	826
			1,735

The difference between the Year 1 'Capital' forecast a year earlier and that forecast at the same date will be another 'windfall' loss. The windfall losses at Year 1 will be £3,000 - 2,000 = 1,000 (on the Year 1 receipt) and £5,205 - 1,735 = 3,470 (on 'Capital' at Year 1). Together the two windfall losses at Year 1 are £4,470. Her forecast 'Capital' at Year 2 (forecast a year earlier) will be just £909. Thus her ex-ante economic income for Year 2 will be C' + (K'$_n$ - K$_{n-1}$) = 1,000 + (909 - 1,735) = 174.

However the actual cash receipt at Year 2 turned out to be £2,000. The difference between the forecast £1,000 and the actual cash receipt is now a 'windfall' profit. At Year 2 Antea believes that future cash flows will amount to just £3,000 at Year 3. Antea's 'Capital' (in existing investments) at Year 2 (forecast at Year 2) will be

£3,000 X 0.909 = 2,727. This gives rise to another windfall profit of £2,727 - 909 = £1,818. Together the total windfall profits at Year 2 are £2,818.

Antea's 'Capital' (in existing investments) at Year 3 (forecast at Year 2) will be zero. Thus her ex-ante economic income for Year 3 will be C' + (K'$_n$ - K$_{n-1}$) = 3,000 + (0 - 2,727) = 273. The actual cash receipt at Year 3 is £2,000 and thus the windfall loss at Year 3 is £1,000.

Income Ex Post

Income ex post is measured at the end of each year. The formula can be shown as :

$Y_e = C + (K_n - K'_{n-1})$

where C is the actual cash flow of the year and K_n is the forecast 'Capital' at the end of the year (forecast at the end of the year) and K'_{n-1} is the 'Capital' at the start of the year (also forecast at the end of the year).

Example of Ex Post Income

The discount rate remains at 10% pa. At Years 0, 1 and 2 Postia holds the same beliefs as to her cash flows from existing investments as does Antea on the same dates. However, as with Ideala and Antea, the actual cash receipts at each of the three years was £2,000. Postia's 'Capital' (in existing investments) at Year 0 (based on forecasts at Year 1 and the known receipt at Year 1) will be :

Year	£	Discount factor	PV
1	2,000	0.909	1,818
2	1,000	0.826	826
3	1,000	0.751	751
			<u>3,395</u>

Postia's estimate of 'Capital' at Year 1 (forecast at that date) will be :

Year	£	Discount factor	PV
2	1,000	0.909	909
3	1,000	0.826	826
			<u>1,735</u>

Thus her ex-post income for Year 1 will be $C + (K_n - K'_{n-1})$ = £2,000 + (1,735 - 3,395) = £340

Postia's estimate of 'Capital' at Year 1 (based on a forecast at Year 2 and the known receipt at Year 2) will be :

Year	£	Discount factor	PV
2	2,000	0.909	1,818
3	3,000	0.826	2,478
			<u>4,296</u>

This gives rise to a 'windfall' profit of £4,296 - 1,735 = 2,561 at Year 1. Her estimate of 'Capital' at Year 2 (based on a forecast at the same date will be £3,000 X 0.909 = £2,727.

Thus her ex-post income for Year 2 will be $C + (K_n - K'_{n-1})$ = £2,000 + (2,727 - 4,296) = £431

Postia's 'Capital' at Year 2 (forecast at Year 3) is £2,000 X 0.909 = £1,818. This gives rise to a 'windfall' loss of £2,727 - 1,818 = 909 at Year 2. Her 'Capital' at Year 3 is zero (whenever forecast).

Thus her ex-post income for Year 3 will be the same as Ideala's income for the same year at $C + (K_n - K'_{n-1})$ = £2,000 + (1,818 - 0) = £182

Summarising the Values of K and C :

Column	a	b	c	d	e	f
	K :				C :	
	Perfect Knowlege	Forecast 1 year earlier	Forecast at date	Forecast 1 year later	Actual	Forecast 1 year earlier
Year						
0	4,972	-	7,458	3,395	-	-
1	3,470	5,205	1,735	4,296	2,000	3,000
2	1,818	909	2,727	1,818	2,000	1,000
3	0	0	0	0	2,000	3,000

Summarising the 'Income' Streams :

Year	Ideal	Ex Ante		Ex Post	
	Income $e+a-a_{-1}$	Income $f+b-c_{-1}$	Windfall $e-f+c-b$	Income $e+c-d_{-1}$	Windfall $d-c$
1	498	747	(4,470)	340	2,561
2	348	174	2,818	431	(909)
3	182	273	(1,000)	182	-
	<u>1,028</u>	<u>1,194</u>	<u>(2,652)</u>	<u>953</u>	<u>1,652</u>

Adding total windfalls to the total ex-ante (or ex-post) economic incomes will not reconcile these figures to total Ideal income without taking account of the initial misforecasts of K_0. K_0 with perfect knowlege is £4,972 but the ex-ante income stream starts with an estimate of K_0 of £7,458 which is £2,486 too much. The ex-post income stream starts with an estimate of K_0 of £3,395 which is £1,577 too little. The three versions of economic income can be reconciled as follows :

	Total Ex Ante	Total Ex Post
Economic Income	1,194	953
Windfalls	(2,652)	1,652
	(1,458)	2,605
Initial misforecast K_0	2,486	1,577
Total Ideal Income	<u>1,028</u>	<u>1,028</u>

Try to answer the following question before looking at the answer (which is at the end of this chapter).

Question 7.1 (Answer 7.1 is on page 242)

The cost of capital to Joe Soap is 15% pa. He has entered into a venture which at 1.1.00 he believes will produce receipts of £1,000 on 1.1.01, £2,000 on 1.1.02 and £3,000 on 1.1.03. His estimates of the receipts on 1.1.01 and 1.1.02 prove correct but the actual receipt on 1.1.03 is £4,000. Joe's estimates remain constant until 1.1.02 when he believes that the receipt on 1.1.03 will be £5,000.

REQUIRED : Determine Ideal, Ex Ante and Ex Post Economic Income for each of the remaining years of this venture. Reconcile the totals of these three income streams.

What Decisions are Aided by These Statistics?

We have defined the statistics of Ideal Income, Ex Post and Ex Ante Income but how would anyone benefit from their computation? Ostensibly they exist to determine drawings or dividends on the assumption that individuals wish to keep their 'capital' constant. But, as was discussed in Chapter 4, there are good reasons why investors may not wish to keep their 'capital' (however defined) in a particular business constant. However if rational investors had taken the conscious decisions to (a) increase investment in one business and (b) reduce it in another, they would want to know whether their dividend and share purchase and/or sale decisions were having the effects they desired.

The definitions of 'capital' used in the computation of economic income are based on *future* benefits. If the forecasts on which they are based are believed, they would affect quoted share prices. If estimates of replacement costs are also believed, the comparison of economic capital with replacement cost would affect capital allocation decisions. In other words, those businesses with economic values in excess of their replacement costs would be granted more capital to expand and vice versa those businesses with economic values below replacement costs would not be granted more capital but would be pressed to provide details of realisable values in order that decisions could be taken on whether they should return capital and contract.

The obvious problem is that this all depends on belief and trust. A single figure for economic capital is unlikely to satisfy many investors. They would want to know when the future cash flows are expected to arise, what assumptions were behind those estimates and what discount rates had been used in the final NPV calculation.

Positive cash flows in a single period can be achieved by selling the fixed assets or incurring liabilities to make later payments. Encouragements to publish estimates of future cash flows without details as to how they will arise are an invitation for unscrupulous company promoters to defraud portfolio investors.

However a *comparison* between Economic Income, Historic Cost Profit in CPP and CCA Earnings would be interesting. It would lead readers of accounts to question the differences and more of those readers would understand the limitations of any single one of those statistics.

It is estimates of the future and not the certainties of the past that should affect most management and investing decisions. The past is of interest only in so far as it aids those estimates of the future. However no honest estimate of the future can be made that is not based on past experience. And all estimates and estimating abilities need to be tested against actualities.

The Political Implications of Constant Capital Models

When the ideas behind the economic definitions of income were developed, it would have been normal to assume that capital was owned by wealthy individuals who had inherited it and intended to pass it on to their own offspring. The general sentiment behind the notion of consuming just sufficient to maintain capital would have been natural and unquestioned.

This may strike modern readers as likely to lead to an unstable and strife-ridden society where only a small self-perpetuating group control capital and the rest of the population has to survive on the fruits of immediate labour.

Current attitudes are affected by a financial climate where the major equity holders are pension funds, unit trusts and other financial intermediaries for middle income individuals. It is now more natural to assume that most capital arises from savings from income during middle age and will be consumed after retirement.

However this recognition of the accumulated savings of the middle incomed has not changed everybody's attitude towards 'old' and 'new' money as this extract from a recent newspaper article[3] shows :

"...while the having of money ... can be a gracious thing, the making of it (at least in very large sums) is almost always tawdry. Even when the wealth has not come from villainous or immoral pursuits, the single-minded dedication to profit is a crass preoccupation. Being rich can be benign, but getting rich is almost always ugly. And those who are seen by their contemporaries to be making fortunes are thought beyond the pale. ... The hatred for those who have become rich by their own efforts goes too deep to be cancelled by good works. Unworthy and crudely snobbish as it may be, the loathing of new wealth is almost as universal in our democratic age as it was in the Renaissance, when the vulgar money came from trade with the New World."

Situations Where Near-Perfect Forecasts Can be Made

Forecasting the future is much easier with many property and financial transactions than is normal in business. A property investment company that has let a building on a long lease to a government department can forecast future cash flows with more certainty than a concert promoter.

In circumstances where a known income or expenditure stream has to be allocated to different accounting periods the allocations implied by the ideal economic income model are more rational and will lead to better decisions.

The amortisation of lease premiums is the example that has already been given (see Chapter Seven of Modern Accounting 1 and pages 208-209 of Chapter Six of this book). There are other cases involving sale and leaseback and more esoteric forms of financing where the ideal economic income model should be used.

Publication of Budgets

Most large businesses produce budgets for use by the managers within the company. These are partly targets and partly forecasts (see Chapter Thirteen) of the coming year's results. If these were published for shareholders, this might improve the pricing of the company's shares. If managers knew that their budgets would be published, this might alter the figures within those budgets. It might also increase the pressure on auditors and the accountants within the company to allow dubious accounting adjustments in order to show actual results close to those budgeted.

Creating Shareholder Value

Alfred Rappaport argues that company managers should attempt to maximise the gains of their equity holders[4]. He has faith in the ability of stock markets to correctly price shares at the ideal economic capital value of the businesses. Without this faith there is an unfortunate conflict between different groups of shareholders who hold the shares at different times. If the share price can be 'talked up' with over-optimistic forecasts, then those who bought the shares before they were over-valued and then sell at over-value will gain at the expense of those who buy their holdings.

Strategic Value

David Allen, Roger Mills and John Robertson argue in favour of managements attempting to maximise 'Strategic Value'[5]. There are a number of ideas behind this concept one of which is similar to economic capital. If managers are set targets in terms of traditional accounting profits, they may cut expenditures like training, advertising and product development which are treated as expenses in the year in which they are incurred but produce their benefits over an extended period. It is argued that profit targets make managers think only of the short term and ignore the longer term. Demanding that managers maximise the present value of estimated future cash flows may avoid this problem if :

a   they know who will estimate the future cash flows and on what basis this estimate will be made,

b   they trust the estimator,

c   they themselves believe in the concept and they understand the discounting calculations,

d   the discount rate is set in advance and agreed by all parties and

Modern Accounting 2

e   they believe that this measure of their performance will *really* be the measure determining their future salary and career and that they will not be blamed for this year's poor accounting profits.

References

[1] The Theory of Interest, I Fisher, Macmillan, 1930
[2] Value and Capital, J R Hicks, Clarendon Press, 1946
[3] Janet Daley, The Times, 5 May 1992
[4] Creating Shareholder Value, Alfred Rappaport, The Free Press (Macmillan Inc), 1986
[5] Management Accounting (UK Journal), November 1991, December 1991 and January 1992

Further Reading

Income and Value Measurement : Theory and Practice 3rd Ed, T A Lee, Van Nostrand Reinhold (UK), 1985

Answer 7.1

	K :				C :	
	Perfect Knowlege	Forecast 1 year earlier	Forecast at date	Forecast 1 year later	Actual	Forecast 1 year earlier
Year						
0	5012		4354	4354		
1	4764	4008	4008	5520	1000	1000
2	3478	2609	4348	3478	2000	2000
3	0	0	0	0	4000	5000

		Ex Ante		Ex Post	
	Ideal	Income	Windfalls	Income	Windfalls
Year					
1	752	654	0	654	1512
2	714	601	1739	828	(870)
3	522	652	(1000)	522	0
Economic Income	1988	1907	739	2004	642
Windfalls		739		642	
		2646		2646	
Initial Misforecast K_0		658		658	
		1988		1988	

Chapter Eight

Consolidations

Sometimes this topic is called 'Consolidated Accounting' and sometimes it is called 'Group Accounts'. Almost all companies with a quotation on a stock exchange own subsidiaries and a surprising number of medium-sized and large family held businesses operate through groups of companies. One company is a subsidiary of another if either (a) more than 50% of the equity of the first company is owned by the second company or (b) the second company has voting control of the first company (S736 CA1985[1]). Usually only the equity (or ordinary shares) have votes, each ordinary share carries one vote and thus the two definitions of a subsidiary - (a) and (b) above - amount to the same thing.

Example of a Newly Formed 100% Subsidiary

Hold plc has arranged for Sub Ltd to be incorporated on 31 December 1999. At that date the Balance Sheets of the two companies appeared as follows :

	Hold £000	Sub £000
Fixed Assets		
Land, at cost	100	
10,000 ordinary shares in Sub, at cost	10	
	110	
Current Assets		
Cash	20	10
	130	10
Share Capital		
Ordinary shares of £1 each	30	10
Revenue Reserves	100	
	130	10

Modern Accounting 2

The consolidated Balance Sheet of Hold and its subsidiary will appear as follows :

	£000
Fixed Assets	
Land, at cost (100 + 0)	100
Current Assets	
Cash (20 + 10)	30
	130
Share Capital	
Ordinary shares of £1 each (all Hold)	30
Consolidated Revenue Reserves (all Hold)	100
	130

In this example the cash in Sub was substituted for the asset 'Shares in Subsidiary' in Hold's Balance Sheet to produce a consolidated Balance Sheet.

Example of a Formed 100% Subsidiary With Post-Acquisition Reserves

Continuing the saga of Hold plc and Sub Ltd, let us assume that on 31 December 2000 the Balance Sheets of the two companies appeared as follows :

	Hold £000	Sub £000
Fixed Assets		
Land, at cost	100	5
10,000 ordinary shares in Sub, at cost	10	
	110	
Current Assets		
Cash	40	55
	150	60
Share Capital		
Ordinary shares of £1 each	30	10
Revenue Reserves	120	50
	150	60

Their Profit and Loss Accounts for the Year to 31 December 2000 appeared as follows :

	Hold	Sub
	£000	£000
Sales	155	175
less Expenses	110	120
Trading Profit	45	55
Dividends Received	5	
	50	55
Dividends Paid	30	5
Unappropriated Profit	<u>20</u>	<u>50</u>

The consolidated Balance Sheet of Hold and its subsidiary will appear as follows :

	£000
Fixed Assets	
Land, at cost (100 + 5)	105
Current Assets	
Cash (40 + 55)	95
	200
Share Capital	
Ordinary shares of £1 each (all Hold)	30
Consolidated Revenue Reserves (120 + 50)	170
	200

The consolidated Profit and Loss Account of Hold and its subsidiary will appear as follows :

	£000
Sales (155 + 175)	330
less Expenses (110 + 120)	230
Trading Profit	100
Dividends Paid (all Hold)	30
Unappropriated Profit	<u>70</u>

In this example the consolidated accounts appear as if they are largely the two sets of individual company accounts added together. Once again the asset in Hold's Balance Sheet for the shares in Sub disappears as does the Share Capital in Sub's Balance Sheet. Note how the dividend paid by Sub (in Sub's Profit & Loss) has been cancelled against its receipt (in Hold's Profit & Loss). Since Sub was created by Hold, all its profits are 'post-acquisition' and can be included in the consolidated reserves. If Sub had made profits before its shares had been acquired by Hold, then these profits would have been 'pre-acquisition' and could not have been included in the consolidated reserves (under normal rules - see page 278).

Example of an Acquired 100% Subsidiary With Pre-Acquisition Reserves

Step-parent plc acquired the whole of Child Ltd's shares on 31 December 1999. At that date the Balance Sheets of the two companies appeared as follows :

	Step-parent £000	Child £000
Fixed Assets		
Land, at cost	250	
30,000 ordinary shares in Child, at cost	70	
	320	
Current Assets		
Cash	40	70
	360	70
Share Capital		
Ordinary shares of £1 each	50	30
Revenue Reserves	310	40
	360	70

In this case the cost of the shares in Child Ltd equalled the net asset backing behind those shares. Child was a shell company with £70,000 in cash as its only asset and Step-parent paid just £70,000 for the shares. With trading companies it is more common to find that the cost of the shares does not precisely equal the net asset backing at the date of acquisition and this problem will be dealt with later (see page 256). The consolidated Balance Sheet of Step-parent and its subsidiary will appear as follows :

	£000
Fixed Assets	
Land, at cost (250 + 0)	250
Current Assets	
Cash (40 + 70)	110
	360

Consolidations

	£000
Share Capital	
Ordinary shares of £1 each (all Step)	50
Consolidated Revenue Reserves (all Step)	310
	360

Note that the Consolidated Revenue Reserves do not include any of the Reserves (or profits) of the subsidiary made before it was acquired by its parent company. Pre-acquisition profits are almost always excluded from consolidated accounts except where 'merger accounting' is used (see page 278).

The cost of the shares in Child (in Step-parent's Balance Sheet) has been cancelled against the Share Capital and Reserves in Child's Balance Sheet. Apart from that, the Consolidated Balance Sheet is the sum of the two underlying Balance Sheets.

Example of an Acquired 100% Subsidiary With Both Pre and Post-Acquisition Reserves

Continuing the story of Step-parent plc and Child Ltd, one year later on 31 December 2000 their two Balance Sheets appeared as follows :

	Step-parent £000	Child £000
Fixed Assets		
Land, at cost	250	50
30,000 ordinary shares in Child, at cost	70	
	320	
Current Assets		
Cash	80	65
	400	115
Share Capital		
Ordinary shares of £1 each	50	30
Revenue Reserves	350	85
	400	115

Their Profit and Loss Accounts for the Year to 31 December 2000 appeared as follows :

Modern Accounting 2

	Step-parent £000	Child £000
Sales	100	360
less Expenses	40	295
Trading Profit	60	65
Dividends Received	20	
	80	65
Dividends Paid	40	20
Unappropriated Profit of the year	40	45
Balance brought forward	310	40
	350	85

The consolidated Balance Sheet of Step-parent and its subsidiary will appear as follows :

	£000
Fixed Assets	
Land, at cost (250 + 50)	300
Current Assets	
Cash (80 + 65)	145
	445

	£000
Share Capital	
Ordinary shares of £1 each (all Step)	50
Consolidated Revenue Reserves (350 + 45)	395
	445

The consolidated Profit and Loss Account of Step-parent and its subsidiary will appear as follows :

	£000
Sales (100 + 360)	460
less Expenses (40 + 295)	335
Trading Profit	125
Dividends Paid (all Step)	40
Unappropriated Profit	85
Balance brought forward (all Step)	310
	395

In this example the reserves of the subsidiary were partly pre-acquisition (£40K) and partly post-acquisition (£45K).

Consolidations

Try to answer the following questions before looking at the answers (which are at the end of this chapter).

Question 8.1 (Answer 8.1 is on page 292)

On 31 December 2000 the Balance Sheets of Paris Ltd and its subsidiary Toulouse Ltd appeared as follows:

	Paris £000	Toulouse £000
Fixed Assets		
Land, at cost	100	500
50,000 ordinary shares in Toulouse, at cost	300	
	400	500
Share Capital		
Ordinary shares of £1 each	10	50
Revenue Reserves	390	450
	400	500

When Paris bought its shares in Toulouse, the Revenue Reserves of Toulouse were 250 (£000). Their Profit and Loss Accounts for the Year to 31 December 2000 appeared as follows:

	Paris £000	Toulouse £000
Sales	2,010	6,000
less Expenses	1,800	5,700
Trading Profit	210	300
Dividends Received	200	-
	410	300
Dividends Paid	300	200
Unappropriated Profit of the year	110	100
Balance brought forward	280	350
	390	450

REQUIRED: The consolidated Balance Sheet of Paris Ltd at 31 December 2000 and the Consolidated Profit and Loss Account for the year to that date.

Question 8.2 (No Answer to this Question has been Included in This Book)

On 31 December 2000 the Balance Sheets of Rome plc and its subsidiary Milan Ltd appeared as follows :

	Rome £000	Milan £000
Fixed Asset		
40,000 ordinary shares in Milan, at cost	500	
Current Asset		
Cash	100	1,000
	600	1,000
Share Capital		
Ordinary shares of £1 each	100	40
Revenue Reserves	500	960
	600	1,000

When Rome bought its shares in Milan, the Revenue Reserves of Milan were 460 (£000). Their Profit and Loss Accounts for the Year to 31 December 2000 appeared as follows :

	Rome £000	Milan £000
Sales	1,000	2,000
less Expenses	540	1,600
Trading Profit	460	400
Dividends Received	240	-
	700	400
Dividends Paid	400	240
Unappropriated Profit of the year	300	160
Balance brought forward	200	800
	500	960

REQUIRED : The consolidated Balance Sheet of Rome plc at 31 December 2000 and the Consolidated Profit and Loss Account for the year to that date.

Example of an Acquired Partly Held Subsidiary With Pre-Acquisition Reserves

Foster plc acquired some of Infant Ltd's shares on 31 December 1999. At that date the Balance Sheets of the two companies appeared as follows :

	Foster £000	Infant £000
Fixed Assets		
Land, at cost	125	
15,000 ordinary shares in Infant, at cost	45	
	170	
Current Assets		
Cash	35	60
	205	60
Share Capital		
Ordinary shares of £1 each	30	20
Revenue Reserves	175	40
	205	60

Once again the cost of the shares in Infant Ltd equalled the net asset backing behind those shares. Foster owns three quarters of Infant and thus the 'minority interest' in this subsidiary must be one quarter. There are two obvious ways of handling the problem of a partly held subsidiary :

(a) Only the holding company's proportion of each asset and liability of the subsidiary could be added into the figures on the consolidated Balance Sheet. This would have the disadvantage that it would not show the value of the whole group but it would have the advantage that it would show the value attributable to the holding company. Sometimes this method is called the 'equity method' of consolidating Balance Sheets. In most countries it is rarely used and it is never used in the UK (for consolidating subsidiaries).

(b) The whole of the net assets of the subsidiary could be added into the figures on the consolidated Balance Sheet and counterbalanced by an additional 'liability' labelled 'Minority Interests' representing the proportion of the subsidiary's net assets not owned by the holding company. This has the

Modern Accounting 2

disadvantage that it does not show which particular assets and liabilities are partly owned but it has the advantage that it does show the value of the group as a whole. This method is standard for the consolidation of subsidiaries.

The consolidated Balance Sheet of Foster and its subsidiary will appear as follows :

	£000	£000
Method	(a) rarely used	(b) normal
Fixed Assets : Land, at cost (125 + 0)	125	125
Current Assets		
Cash (35 + 45) or (35 + 60)	80	95
	205	220
	£000	£000
Share Capital		
Ordinary shares of £1 each (all Foster)	30	30
Consolidated Revenue Reserves (175 + 0)	175	175
	205	205
Minority Interests (25% of Infant's Net Assets)	-	15
	205	220

Example of an Acquired Partly Held Subsidiary With Both Pre and Post-Acquisition Reserves

Continuing the story of Foster plc and Infant Ltd, one year later on 31 December 2000 their two Balance Sheets appeared as follows :

	Foster	Infant
	£000	£000
Fixed Assets		
Land, at cost	125	40
15,000 ordinary shares in Infant, at cost	45	
	170	
Current Assets		
Cash	200	100
	370	140
Share Capital		
Ordinary shares of £1 each	30	20
Revenue Reserves	340	120
	370	140

Their Profit and Loss Accounts for the Year to 31 December 2000 appeared as follows:

	Foster £000	Infant £000
Sales	585	460
less Expenses	400	300
Trading Profit	185	160
Dividends Received	60	
	245	160
Dividends Paid	80	80
Unappropriated Profit of the year	165	80
Balance brought forward	175	40
	340	120

The consolidated Balance Sheet of Foster and its subsidiary (under method (b)) will appear as follows:

	£000
Fixed Assets	
Land, at cost (125 + 40)	165
Current Assets	
Cash (200 + 100)	300
	465
Share Capital	£000
Ordinary shares of £1 each (all Foster)	30
Consolidated Revenue Reserves (340 + 75% of 80)	400
	430
Minority Interests (25% of 140)	35
	465

The consolidated Profit and Loss Account of Foster and its subsidiary will appear as follows:

	£000
Sales (585 + 460)	1,045
less Expenses (400 + 300)	700
Trading Profit	345
Minority Interests (25% of 160)	40
	305
Dividends Paid (all Foster)	80
Unappropriated Profit	225
Balance brought forward (all Foster)	175
	400

Modern Accounting 2

Note that in the UK the total Sales and Expenses of the group are shown with the net minority interest in the profit of the subsidiary deducted lower down the Profit and Loss Account.

Try to answer the following questions before looking at the answers (which are at the end of this chapter).

Question 8.3 (Answer 8.3 is on page 292)

On 31 December 2000 the Balance Sheets of Los Angeles Ltd and its subsidiary San Francisco Ltd appeared as follows:

	L A £000	S F £000
Fixed Assets : Land, at cost	80	600
30,000 ordinary shares in S F, at cost	240	
	320	600
Share Capital		
Ordinary shares of £1 each	20	50
Revenue Reserves	300	550
	320	600

When Los Angeles bought its shares in San Francisco, the Revenue Reserves of San Francisco were 350 (£000). Their Profit and Loss Accounts for the Year to 31 December 2000 appeared as follows:

	L A £000	S F £000
Sales	110	2,000
less Expenses	90	1,750
Trading Profit	20	250
Dividends Received	60	-
	80	250
Dividends Paid	20	100
Unappropriated Profit of the year	60	150
Balance brought forward	240	400
	300	550

REQUIRED : The consolidated Balance Sheet of Los Angeles Ltd at 31 December 2000 and the Consolidated Profit and Loss Account for the year to that date using (a) normal methods of handling minority interests and (b) the equity method.

Consolidations

Question 8.4 (No Answer to this Question has been Included in This Book)

On 31 December 2000 the Balance Sheets of Berlin plc and its subsidiary Frankfurt Ltd appeared as follows:

	Berlin £000	Frankfurt £000
Fixed Asset		
80,000 ordinary shares in Frankfurt, at cost	200	
Current Asset		
Cash	200	2,000
	400	2,000
Share Capital		
Ordinary shares of £1 each	100	100
Revenue Reserves	300	1,900
	400	2,000

When Berlin bought its shares in Frankfurt, the Revenue Reserves of Frankfurt were 150 (£000). Their Profit and Loss Accounts for the Year to 31 December 2000 appeared as follows:

	Berlin £000	Frankfurt £000
Sales	1,000	2,600
less Expenses	1,340	1,700
Trading (Loss) Profit	(340)	900
Dividends Received	640	-
	300	900
Dividends Paid	100	800
Unappropriated Profit of the year	200	100
Balance brought forward	100	1,800
	300	1,900

REQUIRED: The consolidated Balance Sheet of Berlin plc at 31 December 2000 and the Consolidated Profit and Loss Account for the year to that date using (a) normal methods of handling minority interests and (b) the equity method.

Example of an Acquired Wholly Owned Subsidiary With Pre-Acquisition Reserves and Goodwill

Oppress Ltd acquired the whole of Victim Ltd's shares on 31 December 1999. At that date the Balance Sheets of the two companies appeared as follows :

	Oppress £000	Victim £000
Fixed Assets		
Land, at cost	250	
14,000 ordinary shares in Victim, at cost	30	
	280	
Current Assets		
Cash	10	20
	290	20
Share Capital		
Ordinary shares of £1 each	10	14
Revenue Reserves	280	6
	290	20

This time the cost of the shares in Victim Ltd is £10,000 more that the net asset backing behind those shares because Victim's only asset is cash of £20,000 and Oppress paid £30,000 for the shares. The difference between (a) the cost of shares in a subsidiary and (b) the net asset backing behind those shares at the date of purchase is called 'Goodwill'. This use of the word (Goodwill) is a technical use and may have nothing to do with the normal meaning of the word. The new subsidiary may be loathed and detested by its customers, suppliers and employees but Oppress still paid £10,000 for 'Goodwill'. There are at least three ways in which this Goodwill can be treated in consolidated accounts :

(a) It could be treated as an intangible asset on the Consolidated Balance Sheet remaining at 'cost' for as long as the shares in this subsidiary are held. This is the treatment that used to be common in the UK.

(b) It could be treated as an intangible asset on the Consolidated Balance Sheet to be depreciated against future profits. This is the treatment that is currently common in the US.

(c)   It could be written off 'against reserves' in the year the shares are acquired. The write-offs (or 'movements in reserves') are normally shown as a note to the accounts and are not normally shown on the face of the Profit and Loss Account. They do not affect the figures for Earnings Per Share and unsophisticated readers of accounting statements may not notice them. This is the treatment that is currently common in the UK.

Let us view these different treatments for both this year and the following year and then consider which treatment is most valid.

The consolidated Balance Sheet at 31st December 1999 of Oppress and its subsidiary will appear as follows :

Treatments	(a) and (b) £000	(c) £000
Fixed Assets		
Goodwill, at cost (30 - 20)	10	
Land, at cost (250 + 0)	250	250
	260	
Current Assets		
Cash (10 + 20)	30	30
	290	280
	£000	£000
Share Capital		
Ordinary shares of £1 each (all Oppress)	10	10
Consolidated Revenue Reserves (all Oppress)	280	270
	290	280

Example of an Acquired Wholly Owned Subsidiary With Both Pre and Post-Acquisition Reserves and Goodwill

Continuing the story of Oppress Ltd and Victim Ltd, one year later on 31 December 2000 their two Balance Sheets appeared as follows :

Modern Accounting 2

31 Dec 2000	Oppress £000	Victim £000
Fixed Assets		
Land, at cost	200	25
14,000 ordinary shares in Victim, at cost	30	
	230	
Current Assets		
Cash	20	10
	250	35
Share Capital		
Ordinary shares of £1 each	10	14
Revenue Reserves	240	21
	250	35

Their Profit and Loss Accounts for the Year to 31 December 2000 appeared as follows :

	£000	£000
Sales	750	380
less Expenses	780	345
Trading (Loss) Profit	(30)	35
Dividends Received	20	-
	(10)	35
Dividends Paid	30	20
Unappropriated (Loss) Profit of the year	(40)	15
Balance brought forward	280	6
	240	21

Under treatment (b) for Goodwill the write-off is to be over 5 years straight line. The Consolidated Balance Sheet of Oppress at 31st December 2000 under the three possible treatments of Goodwill will be as follows :

	(a) £000	(b) £000	(c) £000
Fixed Assets			
Goodwill			
at cost (30 - 20)	10		
at NBV (4/5 of 10)		8	
Land at cost	225	225	225
	235	233	
Current Assets			
Cash (20 + 10)	30	30	30
	265	263	255

258

	£000	£000	£000
Share Capital			
Ordinary Shares of £1 each (all Oppress)	10	10	10
Consolidated Revenue Reserves	<u>255</u>	<u>253</u>	<u>245</u>
	<u>265</u>	<u>263</u>	<u>255</u>

The consolidated Profit and Loss Account of Oppress and its subsidiary will appear as follows :

Treatment	(a)	(b)	(c)
	£000	£000	£000
Sales (750 + 380)	1,130	1,130	1,130
less General Expenses (780 + 345)	<u>1,125</u>	<u>1,125</u>	<u>1,125</u>
	5	5	5
less Depreciation of Goodwill	—	2	—
Trading Profit	5	3	5
Dividend Paid (all Oppress)	<u>30</u>	<u>30</u>	<u>30</u>
	(25)	(27)	(25)
Balance brought forward	<u>280</u>	<u>280</u>	<u>270</u>
	<u>255</u>	<u>253</u>	<u>245</u>

Having seen the impact of each of the three possible treatments of Goodwill on consolidation, let us consider the advantages and disadvantages of each.

(a) Leaving Goodwill at Undepreciated Cost as a Balance Sheet Asset.

> This shows the full cost incurred in acquiring businesses. It does not explain *why* the directors of Oppress were willing to pay more than the Net Asset Value (NAV) to acquire Victim. If the reason relates to a benefit that will continue indefinitely, then this approach may be logical. If the reason relates to a benefit that will be eroded over time, then this approach will overstate future profits. If there was no reason and the overpayment was made mistakenly, recklessly or fraudulently, then net assets will be overstated now and in the future for as long as this subsidiary is retained.
>
> Some marketing consultants have suggested that brand names can be an intangible asset with an indefinite life. They point to

confectionery brand names like 'Kit Kat' and drinks brand names like 'Teachers' Whisky. However such long-lived brand names are heavily advertised every year and their value might soon be eroded in the absence of continued advertising. It is not easy to think of examples of intangible assets with near-infinite lives that would justify the use of this treatment of goodwill.

(b) Depreciating Goodwill Against the Profits of Future Years

If the reason for paying more than the NAV at the date of acquisition, relates to a benefit that will be eroded over time, then this approach is wholly logical. There may be difficulties in determining the correct period over which to depreciate Goodwill but these difficulties are those that apply to all depreciation of tangible fixed assets.

However there are powerful vested interests in the UK that argue against such treatment. It would reduce the stated profits of acquisitive companies and therefore discourage takeovers. There is empirical evidence to show that few takeovers and mergers lead to economic efficiency and the long-term returns to shareholders in acquisitive companies are less than those to shareholders in companies which do not acquire others.[2]

In the UK most bidders concentrate on persuading the shareholders of their target rather than explaining to their own shareholders the rationale behind their bid. Most directors believe (probably correctly) that their salaries, security of employment and future freedom from constraints depend on their company being the parent company of the largest possible group of companies.

Clearing banks and merchant banks obtain substantial fee income from takeover and merger activity. Newspapers - especially quality newspapers - obtain substantial advertising revenue from contested take-over bids. Financial journalists find that acquisitive companies employ the most inventive financial PR consultants to feed them with stories. And, of course, financial commentators and journalists recognise that take-over bids encourage newspaper consumers to read the financial pages. All these powerful vested interests work in favour of continued take-over activity and work against accounting treatments such as treatment (b) which would tend to curb such activity.

(c) Writing Goodwill off Against Reserves.

If the reason for paying above the NBV of the new subsidiary relates to intangible benefits that have resulted from costs which have been - and will in future - be treated as expenses and these costs will continue to be incurred at the same level in the future as they were in the past, then this treatment may be the most sensible. Costs such as staff recruitment and training, advertising and product development can yield benefits over several years but are traditionally written off as expenses in the year in which they are incurred.

If such costs are written off as expenses immediately when they are incurred while the company is within the group, then it can be argued that it is inconsistent to treat them as an asset when they have been paid for in the purchase price of a new business. Equally it appears wrong to charge depreciation on past such costs to a year which will also bear the full amount of those incurred in the same year. Such double charging of expenses will not give readers a good indicator of future maintainable profit.

However this treatment does depend on assuming that these 'semi-asset expenses' will continue to be incurred at the same level in the future as they were in the past. Some groups which regularly grow through acquisition have been accused of buying businesses where many such costs have just been incurred, writing them against their reserves and then running the businesses into the ground by refusing to invest in such costs while the business is in their ownership.

If one can assume that these 'semi-asset expenses' give their benefits over a five year period, then the first five years within the new group will show high stated profits - although there may be almost no business left after the first five years. In 1991 consultants favourable to ICI arranged for stories to appear in newspapers disparaging Hanson while Hanson held a substantial share stake in ICI and the board of ICI was afraid that he might bid. The main theme behind these stories was that Hanson bought companies and then starved them of investment in these semi-asset expenses. It was said that Hanson bought Ever Ready (Berec), sold the research laboratories and product knowledge to a competitor and then refused to invest in the development of new markets and new products. On television (Channel 4) it was argued that the stated profits of this company appeared high during the early years of ownership by Hanson but then fell away.

Some have argued that treatment (b) is the best treatment because no-one knows why sums have been spent on Goodwill. However shareholders might ask whether, if the directors do not care to explain or 'do not know' why they have spent large sums of company money, they should continue in office.

The information as to how much has been paid for Goodwill is shown under treatment (b) even if it is hidden in small type amongst the notes to the accounts. With several years of published accounts it should be possible for the reader to re-state the profits and net assets as they would have been had either of the other two treatments been adopted.

Goodwill in Service Businesses

Some service businesses - such as consultancies, advertising agencies, employment agencies and music businesses - have very low tangible net assets. Most of the cost of buying such a business may be classified as Goodwill and the company may become a valueless shell without the benefit of its current contracts and the services of key executives and employees. The length of the service agreements of key individuals can be a determinant of the price to be paid for the company. Frequently these key individuals are the main vendors of the company's shares and frequently the price to be paid for the shares depends on the profits that the company earns during its first few years within the new group.

In a situation like this only treatment (b) for Goodwill is valid. Evidently the acquiring company is buying a stream of income. The acquiring company may hope that there will still be some value left within the shell when the current contracts with employees and customers expire but reasonable prudence requires that Goodwill should be depreciated over the life of those contracts.

When WPP Group took over J Walter Thompson, there were complaints from the United States that the UK treatment of writing Goodwill direct to reserves was not valid and discriminated against US businesses that were not allowed to use it. There were similar complaints when Blue Arrow took over Manpower (an employment agency) and when Saatchi & Saatchi bought consultancies.

The 'Fair' Value of the New Subsidiary's Assets

The ASC (the predecessor of the ASB - the UK Accounting Standards Board) introduced the unfortunate phrase 'Fair Value' to this debate. Some may ask what is meant by 'fair'? Fair to whom? And who determines this precious equity? Is net realisable value fair? Is replacement cost fair? What assumptions are to be made in determining any of these values?

Under the ASC rules acquiring companies are allowed to revalue the net assets of the new subsidiary. They are not bound to use the accounting policies or net book values that the subsidiary used prior to the take-over.

The ASB now requires companies to show these changes in accounting net book values by way of note and this may curb the grosser abuses that the ASC rules allowed. However few independent companies will have published their accounts up to the date of their take-over before the date of that take-over. This means that there will be a final period of independence where the accounting policies will be under the control of the new management.

If acquisitive companies wish to show the highest group profits, they will reduce the value of the acquired company's equipment because that will reduce future depreciation. They will also set up provisions at the date of takeover to cover for 'reorganisation costs' in amalgamating the new business into the group. These provisions will reduce those expenses of the new subsidiary that will be charged against group profits in the consolidated Profit and Loss Account.

Of course such revaluations of plant and reorganisation provisions will increase the apparent Goodwill. However, as long as treatment (c) is permitted, that Goodwill can be hidden as a movement on reserves.

Example of Fair Values and a New Subsidiary

We have already produced consolidated accounts for Oppress Ltd and it subsidiary, Victim Ltd for the year to 31st December 2000 (see pages 252-5). However the directors of Oppress Ltd are unhappy with the picture shown. They require you to prepare new consolidated Balance Sheets at 31st December 1999 and 2000 and a new consolidated Profit and Loss Account for the year to 31st December 2000 using treatment (c) for Goodwill and setting up a provision for reorganising Victim of £19,000 at 31st December 1999 all of which is to be set against expenses in the following year.

This provision of £19,000 will increase Goodwill from £10,000 to £29,000. The consolidated Balance Sheet at 31st December 1999 will appear as follows :

	£000	£000
Fixed Assets		
Land, at cost (250 + 0)		250
Current Assets		
Cash (10 + 20)	30	
less Creditors : Amounts due within one year		
Provision / Accrual	19	11
		261
Share Capital		
Ordinary Shares of £1 each (all Oppress)		10
Consolidated Revenue Reserves (all Oppress)		251
		261

The consolidated Profit and Loss Account for the Year to 31st December 2000 will appear as follows :

	£000	£000
Sales (750 + 380)	1,130	
less Expenses (780 + 345 - 19)	1,106	
Trading Profit		24
Dividend Paid (all Oppress)		30
		(6)
Balance brought forward		251
		245

The consolidated Balance Sheet at 31st December 2000 will be identical to that shown on page 255 under treatment (c). The effect of this manoeuvre has been to increase the apparent profit of the first year after acquisition. It has been claimed that some acquisitive companies have boosted their profits for several years after a large acquisition by slowly releasing such provisions. When TI Group waged its recent successful but contested take-over battle for Dowty, the Dowty defence documents alleged that TI had set up such provisions after each acquisition and then, in one case, had returned the following year *after* acquisition to increase the original provision through a movement on reserves as 'previously understated' Goodwill. The accounts of TI were sufficiently opaque as to make it difficult to judge the truth of this allegation.

Consolidations

Full Example of Acquired Partly Held Subsidiaries With Both Pre and Post Acquisition Reserves, Goodwill and a Capital Reserve on Acquisition.

The Balance Sheets of Acquire Ltd, Over Ltd and Under Ltd at 31st December 1999 read as follows :

	Acquire Ltd £000	Over Ltd £000	Under Ltd £000
Fixed Assets			
Land, at cost			300
Plant at NBV	50	200	
7,000 ordinary shares in Over Ltd	150		
less Creditors Due After More Than One Year			
20% Loan Stock repayable in 2500			280
	200	200	20
Share Capital			
Ordinary Shares of £1 each	10	10	5
2% Preference Shares of £1 each		180	
Revenue Reserves	190	10	15
	200	200	20

Acquire had bought its stake in Over Ltd when the revenue reserves (after Fair Value adjustments) of Over were £20,000. The preference shares of Over Ltd carry no votes. The draft Profit and Loss Accounts of the three companies for the year to 31st December 2000 read as follows :

	Acquire Ltd £000	Over Ltd £000	Under Ltd £000
Sales	1,000	2,003.6	5,000
less Expenses	800	1,000.0	5,100
Trading Profit	200	1,003.6	(100)
Dividends received	700		
	900		
Preference Dividend Paid		3.6	
		1,000.0	
Ordinary Dividend Paid	800	1,000.0	
	100	-	
Balance brought forward	190	10	15
	290	10	(85)

Modern Accounting 2

The draft Balance Sheets of the three companies at 31st December 2000 read as follows :

	Acquire Ltd £000	Over Ltd £000	Under Ltd £000
Fixed Assets			
Land, at cost			300
Plant at NBV	140	200	
7,000 ordinary shares in Over Ltd	150		
3,000 ordinary shares in Under Ltd	10		
less Creditors Due Within One Year			100
			200
less Creditors Due After More Than One Year :			
20% Loan Stock repayable in 2500			280
	300	200	(80)
Share Capital			
Ordinary Shares of £1 each	10	10	5
2% Preference Shares of £1 each		180	
Revenue Reserves	290	10	(85)
	300	200	(80)

On 1st July 2000 Acquire bought its stake in Under Ltd. The Sales and Expenses of Under in the first half of the year were £2.5m and £2.55m respectively. The above draft accounts do not take account of two fair value adjustments to the accounts of Under Ltd required by the directors of Acquire Ltd. (a) They want Land revalued to £700,000 as from the date of acquisition. (b) They want a reorganisation provision of £200,000 as at the date of acquisition, £50,000 of which will be released in the 6 months to 31st December 2000 and the rest will be released in the following year. Acquire writes all goodwill directly to reserves immediately on the purchase of a new subsidiary.

Since both sides of a Balance Sheet must reach the same total, the shareholders' funds must equal the net assets of the company. Acquire does not own any preference shares in Over Ltd. In consolidations preference shares are traditionally treated as having their nominal value. Thus the net asset backing behind all the ordinary shares at the date of acquisition must be the nominal value (£10,000) plus the reserves (£20,000).

Consolidations

Workings [A] - Goodwill arising on Acquire's purchase of 70% of Over

	£000	£000
Cost of Shares		150
Net Asset Backing Behind Those Shares		
0.7 X (10 + 20)		21
		129

Workings [B] - Net Assets of Under Ltd on 1.7.00 (date of acquisition)

	£000	£000
Net Assets per Balance Sheet 31.12.99		20
Loss for the first half of the year :		
Sales	2,500	
Expenses	2,550	50
		(30)
Fair Value Adjustments :		
Revaluation of Land	400	
Reorganisation Provision	200	200
		170

The cost of 60% of Under Ltd was £10,000. 'Negative Goodwill' is treated as a 'Capital Reserve arising on consolidation'.

60% of Net Assets above :		
0.6 X 170	102	
Cost of shares	10	
Capital Reserve arising on consolidation		92

Workings [C] - Consolidated Revenue Reserves at 31.12.99 (Under not yet part of group)

Since Over's Reserves were £20,000 at the date when Acquire bought the shares and they had fallen to £10,000 by 31.12.99, the post-acquisition loss of Over must have been £10,000.

	£000	£000
Reserves of Acquire Ltd	190	
70% of Post-Acquisition Loss of Over		
0.7 X (20 - 10)	7	183
Goodwill on Over Ltd written off - see [A]		129
		54

Modern Accounting 2

Workings [D] - Balance Sheet Minority Interests (in Over) at 31.12.99

		£000	£000
	Preference Shares	180	
	Ordinary Shares : 30% of Nominal Value plus reserves :		
	0.3 X (10 + 10)	6	186

Workings [E] - Profit and Loss Minority Interests (in Over and Under) for the Year to 31.12.00

			£000	£000
Over Ltd	Ord - 30% of (1,003.6 - 3.6)		300	
	Pref		3.6	
Under Ltd	40% of second half of year - loss plus release of provision:			
	0.4 X (2,500 - 2,550 + 50) = 0		-	303.6

Workings [F] - Balance Sheet Minority Interests (in Over and Under) at 31.12.00

		£000	£000
Over Ltd	Preference Shares	180	
	Ordinary Shares : 30% of Nominal Value plus reserves :		
	0.3 X (10 + 10)	6	186
Under Ltd	Net Assets at 31.12.00 Restated :		
	Per Draft Balance Sheet	(80)	
	Revaluation of Land	400	
		320	
	Unreleased Provision	150	
		170	
	40% Minority : 0.4 X 170		68
			254

Consolidated Balance Sheet at 31 Dec 1999

	£000	£000
Fixed Assets :		
Plant at NBV (50 + 200)		250
Share Capital		
Ordinary Shares of £1 each (all Acquire)	10	
Consolidated Revenue Reserves [C]	54	
		64
Minority Interests [D]		186
		250

Consolidated Profit and Loss Account
for the Year to 31st December 2000

	£000	£000
Sales (1,000 + 2,003.6 + 2,500)	5,503.6	
less Expenses(800 + 1,000 + 2,550 - 50*)	4,300	
Group Trading Profit		1,203.6
less Minority Interests [E]		303.6
		900
Dividends Paid (all Acquire)		800
		100
Balance brought forward [C]		54
		154

* Release of provision

Consolidated Balance Sheet at 31 Dec 2000

	£000	£000
Fixed Assets :		
Land, at valuation		700
Plant at NBV (140 + 200)		340
		1,040
less Creditors Due within One Year		
Sundry (Over Ltd)	100	
Provision / Accrual	150	250
		790
less Creditors Due After More than One Year		
20% Loan Stock Repayable 2500		280
		510
Share Capital		
Ordinary Shares of £1 each (all Acquire)	10	
Capital Reserve arising on consolidation [B]	92	
Consolidated Revenue Reserves [P & L]	154	256
Minority Interests [F]		254
		510

Minority Interests, Preference Shares and Loan Stock

The single figures for Minority Interests that appeared on the above Balance Sheets were calculated on the assumption that both the Preference Shares in Over Ltd and the Loan Stock in Under Ltd were worth their nominal values. This is the assumption that is

Modern Accounting 2

normally made in practice and it could be misleading. If current rates of interest are 10%, the market value of the preference shares is likely to be below their nominal value and the market value of the loan stock is likely to be above its nominal value.

Consolidations and T Accounts

Sometimes students learn a rote method of doing simple consolidated Balance Sheet problems using T accounts. Unfortunately most of these rote methods are not helpful for more complicated problems and they can obscure the meanings and definitions of (a) Goodwill (or its negative - Capital Reserve arising on Consolidation), (b) Consolidated Revenue Reserve and (c) Minority Interests. Using T accounts can also slow examinees down and make it difficult to produce an answer to a problem in the limited time allowed.

The main advantage of using T accounts is that it should produce a consolidated Balance Sheet that balances (but possibly has an even number of compensating errors within it). T accounts for Acquire's consolidated Balance Sheet at 31 December 2000 would appear as follows :

Land

	£000		£000
Under's Draft BS	300		
Under's Reserves	400		

Plant

	£000		£000
Acquire's BS	140		
Over's BS	200		

Goodwill on Over

	£000		£000
Acquire BS - Cost of Shares	150	Over - Share Capital	7
		Over - Reserves	7
		Consolidated Rev Reserves - Post Acq Loss	7
		Consolidated Rev Reserves - Goodwill	<u>129</u>

270

Consolidations

Capital Reserve on Under

	£000		£000
Acquire's BS - Cost of Shares	10	Under's Share Capital	3
		Under's Reserves	99

Creditors Due Within One Year

		£000
	Under's BS	100

Loan Stock

		£000
	Under's BS	280

Share Capital

		£000
	Acquire's BS	10

Minority Interests

	£000		£000
		Over's BS - Ord Sh Cap	3
		Over's BS - Pref Sh Cap	180
		Over's BS - Rev Reserves	3
		Under's BS - Share Cap	2
		Under Reserves	66

Consolidated Revenue Reserves

	£000		£000
Goodwill on Over - Post Acq Loss	7	Acquire's BS	290
Goodwill on Over	129		

Under Reserves

	£000		£000
Under's Draft BS	85	Land	400
Re-org Provision	150		
Minority Interests	66		
Capital Reserve on consol	99		—

Reorganisation Provision

	£000		£000
		Under Reserves	150

Definitions for Consolidated Balance Sheets

Goodwill (and it's negative : Capital Reserve arising on Consolidation) is defined as the difference between (a) the Cost of Shares in a Subsidiary and (b) the Net Asset Backing behind those shares *at the date of acquisition*.

Minority Interests on a Consolidated Balance Sheet are the Net Asset backing behind the shares *at the Balance Sheet date* in a subsidiary not owned by its parent company.

Consolidated Revenue Reserves are the Revenue Reserves of the holding (parent) company plus (a) the retained post-acquisition profits of subsidiaries (and associated companies - see page 278) less (b) any Goodwill on consolidation written against profits and directly to revenue reserves.

Try to answer the following questions before looking at the answers (which are at the end of this chapter).

Question 8.5 (Answer 8.5 is on page 293)

The Balance Sheets of Washington plc and New York Ltd at 30th June 2000 read as follows :

	Washington £000	Washington £000	New York £000	New York £000
Fixed Assets				
Freehold Property		2,500		1,100
Plant at NBV		1,500		900
400,000 shares in NY, at cost		2,000		
		6,000		2,000
Current Assets				
Stock	3,200		4,000	
Debtors	1,800		2,500	
Bank	500		-	
	5,500		6,500	
less Creditors due within 1 year	2,000	3,500	4,000	2,500
		9,500		4,500
Share Capital				
Ordinary Shares of £1 each		2,000		500
Revenue Reserves		7,500		4,000
		9,500		4,500

Washington bought the shares in New York on 1st July 1995 when the reserves of New York were £700,000.

REQUIRED : Consolidated Balance Sheets for Washington plc at 30th June 2000 assuming that -
(a)   Goodwill is depreciated against profits on a straight line basis over 10 years from the date of purchase

and then
(b)   Goodwill is written directly against reserves immediately on purchase.

Modern Accounting 2

Question 8.6 (No Answer to This Question has been Included in This Book)

The Balance Sheets of Sydney plc and Brisbane Ltd at 30th September 2000 read as follows:

		Sydney		Brisbane
	£000	£000	£000	£000
Fixed Assets				
Freehold Property		-		1,700
Plant at NBV		4,500		200
300,000 shares in Brisbane, at cost		4,000		
		8,500		1,900
Current Assets				
Stock	2,600		1,000	
Debtors	2,300		1,400	
Bank	100		300	
	5,000		2,700	
less Creditors due within 1 year	3,000	2,000	3,000	(300)
		10,500		1,600
Share Capital				
Ordinary Shares of £1 each		2,000		400
Revenue Reserves		8,500		1,200
		10,500		1,600

Sydney bought the shares in Brisbane on 1st October 1999 when the reserves of Brisbane were £100,000.

REQUIRED: Consolidated Balance Sheets for Sydney plc at 30th September 2000 assuming that -

(a) Goodwill is depreciated against profits on a straight line basis over 5 years from the date of purchase

and then

(b) Goodwill is written directly against reserves immediately on purchase.

Question 8.7 (Answer 8.7 is on page 294)

The Balance Sheets of Cardiff plc and Swansea Ltd at 31st December 2000 read as follows :

	Cardiff £000	Swansea £000
Fixed Assets		
Plant at NBV	1,700	3,900
500,000 shares in Swansea, at cost	200	
	1,900	3,900
Working Capital	1,000	3,000
	2,900	6,900
Share Capital		
Ordinary Shares of £1 each	1,000	600
Revenue Reserves	1,900	6,300
	2,900	6,900

The Profit and Loss Accounts of Cardiff plc and Swansea Ltd for the year to 31st December 2000 read as follows :

	Cardiff £000	Swansea £000
Sales	36,000	5,000
less Expenses	30,000	5,900
Trading Profit (Loss)	6,000	(900)
Taxation	2,300	(300)
Profit after taxation	3,700	(600)
Dividend Paid	2,000	-
	1,700	(600)
Balance brought forward	200	6,900
	1,900	6,300

Cardiff bought the shares in Swansea on 1st January 2000.

REQUIRED : A Consolidated Balance Sheet for Cardiff plc at 31st December 2000 and a Consolidated Profit and Loss Account for the year to that date.

Question 8.8 (Answer 8.8 is on page 295)

The Balance Sheets of London Ltd, Birmingham Ltd and Manchester Ltd at 31st December 1999 read as follows :

	London £000	Birmingham £000	Manchester £000
Fixed Assets			
Land, at cost			200
Plant at NBV	90	100	
8,000 ordinary shares in Birmingham Ltd	200		
less Creditors Due After More Than One Year			
20% Loan Stock repayable in 2500		80	
	290	20	200
Share Capital			
Ordinary Shares of £1 each	10	10	10
3% Preference Shares of £1 each			180
Revenue Reserves	280	10	10
	290	20	200

London had bought its stake in Birmingham Ltd when the revenue reserves (after Fair Value adjustments) of Birmingham were £30,000. The draft Profit and Loss Accounts of the three companies for the year to 31st December 2000 read as follows :

	London £000	Birmingham £000	Manchester £000
Sales	1,200	5,000	3,005.4
less Expenses	800	3,000	2,500
Trading Profit	400	2,000	505.4
Dividend received	1,200		
	1,600		
Preference Dividend Paid			5.4
			500.0
Ordinary Dividend Paid	900	1,500	-
	700	500	500
Balance brought forward	280	10	10
	980	510	510

Consolidations

The draft Balance Sheets of the three companies at 31st December 2000 read as follows :

	London £000	Birmingham £000	Manchester £000
Fixed Assets			
Land, at cost			700
Plant at NBV	600	600	
8,000 ordinary shares in Birmingham Ltd	200		
7,000 ordinary shares in Manchester Ltd	190		
less Creditors Due After More Than One Year :			
20% Loan Stock repayable in 2500		80	
	990	520	700
Share Capital			
Ordinary Shares of £1 each 10		10	10
2% Preference Shares of £1 each			180
Revenue Reserves	980	510	510
	990	520	700

On 1st July 2000 London bought its stake in Manchester Ltd. The preference shares of Manchester Ltd carry no votes. The Sales and Expenses of Manchester in the first half of the year were £1,002,700 and £1.5m respectively. The above draft accounts do not take account of a fair value adjustment to the accounts of Manchester Ltd required by the directors of London Ltd. They want a reorganisation provision of £300,000 as at the date of acquisition, £100,000 of which will be released in the 6 months to 31st December 2000 and the rest will be released in the following year. London writes all goodwill directly to reserves immediately on the purchase of a new subsidiary.

REQUIRED : Consolidated Balance Sheets for London Ltd at 31st December 1999 and 2000 and a Consolidated Profit and Loss Account for the year to 31st December 2000.

Modern Accounting 2

Associated and Related Companies

This topic is not covered in this book. Some companies which are not subsidiaries may be partly consolidated on the 'equity' basis. Generally these are companies where the holding company has a stake at or above 20% but below 50%.

Merger Accounting

This topic is not covered in this book. This chapter has used the normal method of consolidating subsidiaries which can be called the 'acquisition' method (as apposed to the 'merger' method). Where a subsidiary has been purchased by the holding company issuing its own shares in exchange for the shares in the subsidiary, it may be possible to use the merger method (although, in practice, this is rare).

Unrealised Inter-Group Profit

If a company within a group sells goods to another company within the same group, then no group profit should be taken on those goods until the sale is realised outside the group. The major argument for historic cost is that it is a value agreed by traders independent of each other where the vendor wanted to charge as much as possible and the purchaser wanted to pay as little as possible. Two companies under the same control put this independence in question.

Thus, if a company holds stock from other group companies at the balance sheet date, the unrealised profit should be eliminated from the consolidated figures in order that the stock can be shown 'at cost to the group'.

It used to be suggested that, if either the vendor or purchaser company were not a wholly owned subsidiary, then a proportion of the profit could be treated as realised to or from the Minority Interests. However this is a suspect argument because the Minority Interests do not have control and are unlikely to have agreed (or rejected) the inter-group prices. In any case, realising a proportion of inter-group profit leaves a stock figure that is not true cost to any company. It is better practice to eliminate *all* inter-group profit on stock. Sales and Purchases on Consolidated Profit and Loss Accounts should show only those transacted outside the group.

Example of eliminating Inter-Group Profit on Stock

Square Ltd is a manufacturer selling goods both to its subsidiary Circle Ltd and to outside customers. All of Square's purchases are made from outside the group. Square sets its selling prices so that each sale gives a mark-up on manufacturing costs of 100%. In Square's accounts stock is valued at manufacturing cost with no element of administrative or selling overhead.

Circle Ltd makes all of its purchases from its holding company, Square, and makes all of its sales to outside customers. Circle is not a manufacturer and, in Circle's accounts, stock is valued at the direct cost (to that company) of purchase. Square bought its stake in Circle some years ago when the reserves of Circle were £10,000. Any goodwill was immediately written to group reserves.

The Balance Sheets of both companies at 31st December 1999 read as follows :

	Square £000	Circle £000
5,500 Ordinary Shares in Circle at cost	100	
Stock, at cost to the company	100	100
Cash	-	900
	200	1,000
Share Capital		
Ordinary Shares of £1 each	10	10
Revenue Reserves	190	990
	200	1,000

The Profit and Loss Accounts of both companies for the year to 31 December 2000 read as follows :

	Square £000	Square £000	Circle £000	Circle £000
Sales		4,000		4,000
Opening Stock	100		100	
Purchases	1,000		3,500	
Other manufacturing costs	1,000		-	
	2,100		3,600	
less Closing Stock	100	2,000	2,000	1,600
Gross Profit		2,000		2,400
Administrative and selling costs		1,800		2,300
Trading Profit		200		100
Balance brought forward		190		990
		390		1,090

Modern Accounting 2

The Balance Sheets of both companies at 31st December 2000 read as follows :

	Square £000	Circle £000
5,500 Ordinary Shares in Circle at cost	100	
Stock, at cost to the company	100	2,000
Cash	200	
less Creditors due within one year		
Bank Overdraft		900
	400	1,100
Share Capital		
Ordinary Shares of £1 each	10	10
Revenue Reserves	390	1,090
	400	1,100

Circle's Balance Sheets can be restated to show stock at cost to the group eliminating the inter-group profit from reserves :

At	31.12.99 £000	31.12.00 £000
Stock at cost to the group	50	1,000
Cash	900	
less Creditors due within one year		
Bank Overdraft		900
	950	100
Share Capital		
Ordinary Shares of £1 each	10	10
Revenue Reserves	940	90
	950	100

Circle's Profit and Loss Account becomes :

	£000	£000
Sales		4,000
Opening Stock	50	
Purchases	3,500	
	3,550	
less Closing Stock	1,000	2,550
		1,450
Administrative and selling costs		2,300
Trading Profit		(850)
Balance brought forward		940
		90

Consolidations

[A] <u>Goodwill</u> arising on Square's Purchase of 55% of Circle

	£000	£000
Cost of shares		100
Net Asset Backing at date of acquisition		
55% of (10 + 10)	11	<u>89</u>

[B] Balance Sheet <u>Minority Interests</u> at 31.12.99   £000
45% of 950   <u>427.5</u>

[C] <u>Profit and Loss Minority Interests</u> - Year to 31.12.00
45% of loss of 850   (<u>382.5</u>)

[D] Balance Sheet <u>Minority Interests</u> at 31.12.00   £000
45% of 100   <u>45</u>

[E] <u>Consolidated Revenue Reserves</u> at 31.12.99

Square	190	
Circle 55% of (940 - 10)	<u>511.5</u>	701.5
Goodwill write off [A]		<u>89</u>
		<u>612.5</u>

The consolidated Balance Sheet at 31st December 1999 will appear as follows :

	£000
Stock, at cost to the group (100 + 50)	150
Cash	<u>900</u>
	<u>1,050</u>
Share Capital	
Ordinary Shares of £1 each	10
Consolidated Revenue Reserves [E]	<u>612.5</u>
	622.5
Minority Interests [B]	<u>427.5</u>
	<u>1,050</u>

Modern Accounting 2

The Consolidated Profit and Loss Account for the year to 31 December 2000 will appear as follows :

	£000	£000
Sales outside the group		4,500
(4,000 + 4,000 - 3,500)		
Opening Stock	150	
Purchases (Square only)	1,000	
Other manufacturing costs	1,000	
	2,150	
less Closing Stock (100 + 1,000)	1,100	1,050
		3,450
Administrative and selling costs		4,100
Trading (Loss)		(650)
Minority Interests [C]		382.5
		(267.5)
Balance brought forward [E]		612.5
		345

The consolidated Balance Sheet at 31st December 2000 will appear as follows :

	£000
Stock, at cost to the group (100 + 1,000)	1,100
Cash	200
	1,300
less Creditors due within one year	
Bank Overdraft	900
	400
Share Capital	
Ordinary Shares of £1 each	10
Consolidated Revenue Reserves [P & L]	345
	355
Minority Interests [D]	45
	400

In this example the accounts of the *purchaser* were restated so that both the reserves and stock were reduced. Sometimes it is suggested that the profit should be eliminated from the reserves of the *vendor*. Superficially this may appear logical because it was the vendor that made the original inter-group profit.

However when the goods are eventually sold outside the group, it is the *current owner* that will make any profit or loss above or below the inter-group price. Also the Minority Interests in the purchaser will not be a correct proportion of the net assets included in the consolidated Balance Sheet if the profit is eliminated from the vendors reserves.

The most logical rule is to eliminate all inter-group profit from the company holding the goods at the Balance Sheet date.

Inter-Group Accounts

If one company within a group owes money to another company within the same group, then the liabilities of the first company should contain a creditor which can be cancelled against the debtor which should be in the assets of the other company. Debtors and creditors on a consolidated Balance Sheet should contain only sums owed by and owing to those *outside* the group.

Proposed Dividends From a Subsidiary

A Proposed Dividend in the current liabilities of a subsidiary should be cancelled against the Dividend Receivable in the current assets of the holding company. If no Dividend Receivable yet exists, then it must be created by debiting the current assets and crediting Profit and Loss. If the subsidiary is partly held, then the holding company's proportion of the dividend can be cancelled and the proportion to be paid to the minority interests should be left as a current liability.

Cash in Transit

Sometimes the Debtor inter-group account exceeds the Creditor inter-group account because a cheque is still in the post at the Balance Sheet date. In this case cancel as much as possible and then add the remaining difference to the Group Cash and Bank balances.

Goods in Transit

Sometimes the Debtor inter-group account exceeds the Creditor inter-group account because some goods are still in transit at the Balance Sheet date. In this case cancel as much as possible and then

Modern Accounting 2

add the remaining difference to the Stock of the purchaser company. Such stock will usually have some inter-group profit on it that will need to be eliminated before the consolidation can continue.

Try to answer the following questions before looking at the answers (which are at the end of this chapter).

Question 8.9 (Answer 8.9 is on page 298)

Glasgow Ltd is a manufacturer selling goods both to its subsidiary Fife Ltd and to outside customers. All of Glasgow's purchases are made from outside the group. Glasgow sets its selling prices so that each sale gives a mark-up on manufacturing costs of 200%. In Glasgow's accounts stock is valued at manufacturing cost with no element of administrative or selling overhead.

Fife Ltd makes all of its purchases from its holding company, Glasgow, and makes all of its sales to outside customers. Fife is not a manufacturer and, in Fife's accounts, stock is valued at the direct cost (to that company) of purchase. Glasgow bought its stake in Fife some years ago when the reserves of Fife were £20,000. Any goodwill was immediately written to group reserves.

The Balance Sheets of both companies at 31st December 1999 read as follows :

	Glasgow £000	Fife £000
6,000 Ordinary Shares in Fife at cost	200	
Stock, at cost to the company	1,000	600
	1,200	600
Share Capital		
Ordinary Shares of £1 each	10	10
Revenue Reserves	1,190	590
	1,200	600

The Profit and Loss Accounts of both companies for the year to 31 December 2000 read as follows :

Consolidations

	£000	Glasgow £000	£000	Fife £000
Sales		6,000		8,000
Opening Stock	1,000		600	
Purchases	2,000		5,000	
Other manufacturing costs	500		-	
	3,500		5,600	
less Closing Stock	1,500		3,000	
		2,000		2,600
Gross Profit		4,000		5,400
Administrative and selling costs		3,000		3,000
Trading Profit		1,000		2,400
Balance brought forward		1,190		590
		2,190		2,990

The Balance Sheets of both companies at 31st December 2000 read as follows :

	Glasgow £000	Fife £000
6,000 Ordinary Shares in Fife at cost	200	
Stock, at cost to the company	1,500	3,000
Cash	500	
	2,200	3,000
Share Capital		
Ordinary Shares of £1 each	10	10
Revenue Reserves	2,190	2,990
	2,200	3,000

REQUIRED : Consolidated Balance Sheets for Glasgow Ltd at 31 December 1999 and 2000 and a Consolidated Profit and Loss Account for the year to 31 December 2000.

Question 8.10 (Answer 8.10 is on page 300)

The Draft Balance Sheets of Lisbon plc and its subsidiary, Oporto Ltd, at 31st December 2000 read as follows :

	Lisbon		Oporto	
	£000	£000	£000	£000
Fixed Assets				
Plant at NBV		410		750
70,000 Ordinary Shares in Oporto at cost		306		
		716		
Current Assets				
Stock	250		405	
Trade Debtors	190		360	
Current Account - Oporto	500			
Bank	30		200	
	970		965	
less Creditors due within one year				
Trade Creditors	180		285	
Current Account - Lisbon			480	
Proposed Dividend	200		100	
	380		865	
Net Current Assets		590		100
		1,306		850
Share Capital				
Ordinary Shares of £1 each		600		100
Revenue Reserves		706		750
		1,306		850

Lisbon bought its stake in Oporto on 1st January 1998 when the Reserves of Oporto were £80,000. Goodwill on this purchase is to be depreciated over 6 years straight line. The draft Balance Sheet of Lisbon does not take account of the dividend proposed by Oporto. At 31 December 2000 Oporto had posted a cheque for £20,000 to Lisbon but this had not yet arrived at Lisbon's offices.

REQUIRED : The consolidated Balance Sheet of Lisbon at 31st December 2000.

Question 8.11 (No Answer to This Question has been Included in This Book)

The Draft Balance Sheets of Madrid plc and its subsidiary, Zaragoza Ltd, at 31st December 2000 read as follows :

	Madrid £000	Madrid £000	Zaragoza £000	Zaragoza £000
Fixed Assets				
Plant at NBV		350		610
80,000 Ordinary Shares in Zaragoza at cost		440		
		790		
Current Assets				
Stock	320		110	
Trade Debtors	210		400	
Current Account - Madrid			230	
Bank	40		80	
	570		820	
less Creditors due within one year				
Trade Creditors	120		90	
Current Account - Zaragoza	170			
Proposed Dividend	300		150	
	590		240	
Net Current Assets		(20)		580
		770		1,190
Share Capital				
Ordinary Shares of £1 each		200		100
Revenue Reserves		570		1,090
		770		1,190

Madrid bought its stake in Zaragoza on 1st January 1999 when the Reserves of Zaragoza were £200,000. Goodwill on this purchase is to be depreciated over 5 years straight line. The draft Balance Sheet of Madrid does not take account of the dividend proposed by Zaragoza. At 31 December 2000 Madrid had posted a cheque for £60,000 to Zaragoza but this had not yet arrived at Zaragoza's offices.

REQUIRED : The consolidated Balance Sheet of Madrid at 31st December 2000.

Modern Accounting 2

Question 8.12 (Answer 8.12 is on page 301)

Vienna plc bought its stake in Innsbruck Ltd some years ago when the reserves of Innsbruck were £50,000. Any goodwill was immediately written to group reserves. The draft Balance Sheets of both companies at 31st December 1999 read as follows :

	Vienna £000	Vienna £000	Innsbruck £000	Innsbruck £000
Fixed Assets				
Plant at NBV	800			1,050
9,000 Ordinary Shares in Innsbruck at cost	300	1,100		
Current Assets				
Stock, at cost to the company	2,000		1,900	
Debtor - Innsbruck	1,200			
Bank	100		200	
	3,300		2,100	
Creditors : Amounts Due Within One Year				
Creditor - Vienna			800	
Proposed Dividend	1,000		100	
	1,000	2,300	900	1,200
		3,400		2,250
Share Capital				
Ordinary Shares of £1 each		100		10
Revenue Reserves		3,300		2,240
		3,400		2,250

The draft Profit and Loss Accounts of both companies for the year to 31 December 2000 read as follows :

	Vienna £000	Vienna £000	Innsbruck £000	Innsbruck £000
Sales		10,000		7,650
Total Expenses		6,550		7,000
Trading Profit		3,450		650
Dividends Received		450		
Net Profit		3,900		650
Dividends : Paid	1,500		400	
Proposed	1,000	2,500	200	600
		1,400		50
Balance brought forward		3,300		2,240
		4,700		2,290

The draft Balance Sheets of both companies at 31st December 2000 read as follows :

Consolidations

		Vienna		Innsbruck
	£000	£000	£000	£000
Fixed Assets				
Plant at NBV	900			1,400
9,000 Ordinary Shares				
in Innsbruck at cost	300	1,200		
Current Assets				
Stock, at cost				
to the company	3,000		1,200	
Debtor - Innsbruck	1,400			
Bank	200		800	
	4,600		2,000	
Creditors : Amounts Due Within One Year				
Creditor - Vienna			900	
Proposed Dividend	1,000		200	
	1,000	3,600	1,100	900
		4,800		2,300
Share Capital				
Ordinary Shares of £1 each	100		10	
Revenue Reserves	4,700	4,800	2,290	2,300

Vienna sells goods both to its subsidiary Innsbruck and to outside customers. All of Vienna's purchases are made from outside the group. Vienna sets its selling prices so that each sale gives a mark-up on manufacturing costs of 100%. Innsbruck Ltd makes some of its purchases from its holding company, Vienna, and makes all of its sales to outside customers. In the year to 31st December 2000, in Innsbruck's records, the total of Innsbruck's purchases from Vienna was £400,000. In Innsbruck's accounts stock is valued at the direct cost (to that company) of purchase. The items in Innsbruck's stock (as shown on Innsbruck's Balance Sheets above) at (a) 31 December 1999 and (b) 31 December 2000 which had been purchased from Vienna had cost Innsbruck (a) £120,000 and (b) £200,000 respectively.

Vienna's Balance Sheets have not taken account of the dividends proposed by Innsbruck at either year end. The 'Dividends Received' on Vienna's Profit and Loss Account include the dividend proposed by Innsbruck at the end of 1999 and exclude the dividend proposed by Innsbruck at the end of 2000. At the end of each year the difference between (a) the Debtor for Innsbruck shown in Vienna's books and (b) the Creditor for Vienna shown in Innsbruck's books is solely due to goods in transit between the two companies.

REQUIRED : Consolidated Balance Sheets for Vienna plc at 31 December 1999 and 2000 and a Consolidated Profit and Loss Account for the year to 31 December 2000.

Modern Accounting 2

Question 8.13 (No Answer to This Question has Been Included in This Book)

Auckland plc bought its stake in Wellington Ltd some years ago when the reserves of Wellington were £50,000. Any goodwill was immediately written to group reserves. The draft Balance Sheets of both companies at 31st December 1999 read as follows :

	Auckland		Wellington	
	£000	£000	£000	£000
Fixed Assets				
Plant at NBV	900			2,100
7,000 Ordinary Shares				
in Wellington at cost	<u>500</u>	1,400		
Current Assets				
Stock, at cost				
to the company	1,000		2,400	
Debtor - Wellington	1,400			
Bank	<u>100</u>		<u>100</u>	
	<u>2,500</u>		<u>2,500</u>	
Creditors : Amounts Due Within One Year				
Creditor - Auckland			1,000	
Proposed Dividend	<u>2,000</u>		<u>1,100</u>	
	<u>2,000</u>	500	<u>2,100</u>	400
		<u>1,900</u>		<u>2,500</u>
Share Capital				
Ordinary Shares of £1 each		200		10
Revenue Reserves		<u>1,700</u>		<u>2,490</u>
		<u>1,900</u>		<u>2,500</u>

The draft Profit and Loss Accounts of both companies for the year to 31 December 2000 read as follows :

	Auckland		Wellington	
	£000	£000	£000	£000
Sales	13,170		10,000	
Total Expenses	<u>10,000</u>		<u>5,300</u>	
Trading Profit		3,170		4,700
Dividends Received		<u>1,330</u>		
Net Profit		4,500		4,700
Dividends : Paid	1,000		800	
Proposed	<u>2,000</u>	3,000	200	1,000
		1,500		3,700
Balance brought forward		<u>1,700</u>		<u>2,490</u>
		<u>3,200</u>		<u>6,190</u>

The draft Balance Sheets of both companies at 31st December 2000 read as follows :

Consolidations

	Auckland		Wellington	
	£000	£000	£000	£000
Fixed Assets				
Plant at NBV	800		3,000	
7,000 Ordinary Shares				
in Wellington at cost	500	1,300		
Current Assets				
Stock, at cost				
to the company	3,000		4,000	
Debtor - Wellington	1,000			
Bank	100		100	
	4,100		4,100	
Creditors : Amounts Due Within One Year				
Creditor - Auckland			700	
Proposed Dividend	2,000		200	
	2,000	2,100	900	3,200
		3,400		6,200
Share Capital				
Ordinary Shares of £1 each	200		10	
Revenue Reserves	3,200	3,400	6,190	6,200

Auckland sells goods both to its subsidiary Wellington and to outside customers. All of Auckland's purchases are made from outside the group. Auckland sets its selling prices so that each sale gives a mark-up on manufacturing costs of 100%. Wellington Ltd makes some of its purchases from its holding company, Auckland, and makes all of its sales to outside customers. In the year to 31st December 2000, in Wellington's records, the total of Wellington's purchases from Auckland was £1,100,000. In Wellington's accounts stock is valued at the direct cost (to that company) of purchase. The items in Wellington's stock (as shown on Wellington's Balance Sheets above) at (a) 31 December 1999 and (b) 31 December 2000 which had been purchased from Auckland had cost Wellington (a) £700,000 and (b) £500,000 respectively.

Auckland's Balance Sheets have not taken account of the dividends proposed by Wellington at either year end. The 'Dividends Received' on Auckland's Profit and Loss Account include the dividend proposed by Wellington at the end of 1999 and exclude the dividend proposed by Wellington at the end of 2000. At the end of each year the difference between (a) the Debtor for Wellington shown in Auckland's books and (b) the Creditor for Auckland shown in Wellington's books is solely due to goods in transit between the two companies.

REQUIRED : Consolidated Balance Sheets for Auckland plc at 31 December 1999 and 2000 and a Consolidated Profit and Loss Account for the year to 31 December 2000.

Modern Accounting 2

References :
[1] Section 736 of the Companies Act 1985
[2] Disappointing Marriage : a study of the gains from merger by G Meeks Univ Cambridge, Dept Applied Economics, Occasional Paper 51 (1977) CUP

Further Reading :
Consolidated Accounts by W G Martindale (Jurispublications)
Preparation of Consolidated Accounts by Neil D Stein (Financial Training)

Answer 8.1

Consolidated <u>Balance Sheet</u> at 31 December 2000

	£000
Fixed Asset : Land, at cost (100 + 500)	<u>600</u>
Share Capital (all Paris)	10
Consolidated Revenue Reserves (390 + 450 - 250)	<u>590</u>
	<u>600</u>

Consolidated <u>Profit and Loss</u> Account for the Year to 31 December 2000

	£000	£000
Sales (2,010 + 6,000)	8,010	
less Expenses (1,800 + 5,700)	<u>7,500</u>	
Trading Profit		510
Dividends Paid (all Paris)		<u>300</u>
		210
Balance brought forward (280 + 350 - 250)		<u>380</u>
		<u>590</u>

Answer 8.3

Consolidated <u>Balance Sheet</u> at 31 December 2000

	(a) £000	(b) £000
Fixed Asset : Land, at cost		
(80 + 600)	680	
(80 + 3/5 X 600)		440
Share Capital (all LA)	20	20
Consolidated Revenue Reserves		
(300 + 3/5 X (550 - 350))	420	420
	440	<u>440</u>
Minority Interests (2/5 X 600)	240	
	<u>680</u>	

Consolidations

Consolidated Profit and Loss Account for the Year to 31 December 2000

	£000	£000
Sales		
(110 + 2,000)	2,110	
(110 + 3/5 X 2,000)		1,310
less Expenses		
(90 + 1,750)	<u>1,840</u>	
(90 + 3/5 X 1,750)		<u>1,140</u>
Trading Profit	270	170
Minority Interests (2/5 X 250)	<u>100</u>	
	170	
Dividends Paid (all LA)	<u>20</u>	<u>20</u>
	150	150
Balance brought forward		
(240 + 3/5 X (400 - 350))	<u>270</u>	<u>270</u>
	<u>420</u>	<u>420</u>

Answer 8.5

	£000	£000
Workings [A] - Goodwill		
Cost of shares	2,000	
Net Asset Backing at date of acquisition :		
4/5 X (500 + 700)	960	<u>1,040</u>
Workings [B] - Minority Interests		
1/5 X 4,500		<u>900</u>
Workings [C] - Consolidated Revenue Reserves	(a)	(b)
Washington	7,500	7,500
Our share of NY post acquisition		
4/5 X (4,000 - 700)	<u>2,640</u>	<u>2,640</u>
	10,140	10,140
less immediate write off of all Goodwill	1,040	
less 5/10 dep'n of Goodwill		520
	<u>9,100</u>	<u>9,620</u>

Modern Accounting 2

Consolidated Balance Sheet at 30 June 2000

	(a) £000	(b) £000
Fixed Assets		
Freehold Property (2,500 + 1,100)	3,600	3,600
Plant at NBV (1,500 + 900)	2,400	2,400
Goodwill at NBV	520	
	6,520	6,000
Current Assets		
Stock (3,200 + 4,000)	7,200	7,200
Debtors (1,800 + 2,500)	4,300	4,300
Bank (500 + 0)	500	500
	12,000	12,000
less Creditors due within one year	6,000	6,000
Net Current Assets	6,000	6,000
	12,520	12,000
Share Capital (Washington only)	2,000	2,000
Consolidated Revenue Reserves [C]	9,620	9,100
	11,620	11,100
Minority Interests [B]	900	900
	12,520	12,000

Answer 8.7

	£000	£000
Workings [A] - Capital Reserve		
Net Asset Backing at date of acquisition :		
5/6 X (600 + 6,900)	6,250	
Cost of shares	200	6,050
Workings [B] - Minority Interests		
1/6 X 6,900		1,150
Workings [C] - Consolidated Revenue Reserves		
Cardiff	7,500	
Our share of Swansea post acquisition		
5/6 X (600)	(500)	1,400

Consolidated Balance Sheet at 31 December 2000

	£000
Fixed Assets	
Plant at NBV (1,700 + 3,900)	5,600
Working Capital (1,000 + 3,000)	4,000
	9,600
Share Capital	
Ordinary Shares of £1 each (all Cardiff)	1,000
Capital Reserve arising on consolidation [A]	6,050
Consolidated Revenue Reserve [C]	1,400
	8,450
Minority Interests [B]	1,150
	9,600

Consolidated Profit and Loss Account
for the year to 31 December 2000

	£000
Sales (36,000 + 5,000)	41,000
less Expenses (30,000 + 5,900)	35,900
Trading Profit	5,100
Taxation (2,300 - 300)	2,000
Group Profit after taxation	3,100
Minority Interests	100
	3,200
Dividends Paid	2,000
	1,200
Balance brought forward	200
	1,400

Answer 8.8

Workings [A] - Goodwill arising on London's purchase of 80% of Birmingham

	£000	£000
Cost of Shares		200
Net Asset Backing Behind Those Shares		
0.8 X (10 + 30)	32	168

Modern Accounting 2

Workings [B] - Net Asset Backing behind 70% of Ordinary shares in Manchester Ltd on 1.7.00 (date of acquisition)

		£000	£000
Net Assets per Balance Sheet 31.12.99			200
less Nominal Value of Preference Shares			180
			20
Loss for the first half of the year :			
Sales		1,002.7	
Expenses		1,500	
		497.3	
Half year - div on pref shares		2.7	500
			(480)
Fair Value Adjustment : Reorganisation Prov'n			300
			(780)
70% of Net Liabilities above :			
0.7 X 780		546	
Cost of shares		190	
Goodwill			736

Workings [C] - Consolidated Revenue Reserves at 31.12.99 (Manchester not yet part of group)

	£000	£000
Reserves of London Ltd	280	
80% of Post-Acquisition Loss of Birmingham		
0.8 X (10 - 30)	16	264
Goodwill on Birmingham Ltd written off - see [A]		168
		96

Workings [D] - Balance Sheet Minority Interests (in Birmingham) at 31.12.99

	£000
20% of Nominal Value plus reserves :	
0.2 X (10 + 10)	4

Workings [E] - Profit and Loss Minority Interests (in Birmingham and Manchester) for the Year to 31.12.00

Man'r Ltd	Trading Profit for year	£000	£000
	Trading Profit for year	505.4	
	First half loss	497.3	
		1,002.7	
	Second half year pref div	2.7	
		1,000	
	Reorganisation prov release	100	
	2nd half Profit Attrib Ord shrs	1,100	

	£000	£000
Workings [E] P & L MI continued		
Man'r Ord 30% - 0.3 X 1,100	330	
Man'r Pref Half year	2.7	
Bir'm Ltd 20% of 2,000	400	
		732.7

Workings [F] - Balance Sheet Minority Interests (in Birmingham and Manchester) at 31.12.00

		£000	£000
Bir'm Ltd	0.2 X 520		104
Man'r Ltd	Net Assets at 31.12.00 Restated :		
	Per Draft Balance Sheet	700	
	Unreleased Provision	200	
		500	
	Preference Shares	180	
	Attrib to all ord shares	320	
	30% Min in ord - 0.3 X 320	96	
	Preference Shares	180	
			276
			380

Consolidated Balance Sheet at 31 Dec 1999

	£000	£000
Fixed Assets :		
Plant at NBV (90 + 100)		190
less Creditors due after more than one year : Loan Stock		80
		110
Share Capital		
Ordinary Shares of £1 each (all London)	10	
Consolidated Revenue Reserves [C]	96	106
Minority Interests [D]		4
		110

Consolidated Profit and Loss Account

for the Year to 31st December 2000

	£000	£000
Sales (1,200 + 5,000 + 2,002.7)	8,202.7	
less Expenses(800 + 3,000 + 1,000 - 100)	4,700	
Group Trading Profit		3,502.7
less Minority Interests [E]		732.7
		2,770
Dividends Paid (all London)		900
		1,870

Modern Accounting 2

Note : Movements on Group Reserves
Balance brought forward	96	
Retained Profit per P & L	1,870	1,966
Goodwill on purchase of Manchester written off [B]		736
Group Reserves at 31.12.00		1,230

Consolidated Balance Sheet at 31 Dec 2000

	£000	£000
Fixed Assets :		
Land, at cost		700
Plant at NBV (140 + 200)		1,200
		1,900
less Creditors Due within One Year		
Provision / Accrual		200
		1,700
less Creditors Due After More than One Year		
20% Loan Stock Repayable 2500		80
		1,620
Share Capital		
Ordinary Shares of £1 each (all London)	10	
Consolidated Revenue Reserves [above]	1,230	
		1,240
Minority Interests [F]		380
		1,620

Answer 8.9

Fife's Balance Sheets can be restated as follows :

At	31.12.99	31.12.00
	£000	£000
Stock at cost to the group	200	1,000
	200	1,000
Share Capital		
Ordinary Shares of £1 each	10	10
Revenue Reserves	190	990
	200	1,000

Fife's Profit and Loss Account becomes :

Sales		8,000
Opening Stock	200	
Purchases	5,000	
	5,200	
less Closing Stock	1,000	4,200
Gross Profit to next page		3,800

Consolidations

Gross Profit from previous page	3,800
Administrative and selling costs	3,000
Trading Profit	800
Balance brought forward	190
	990

[A] Goodwill arising on Glasgow's Purchase of 60% of Fife

	£000	£000
Cost of shares	200	
Nat Asset Backing at date of acquisition		
60% of (10 + 20)	18	182

[B] Balance Sheet Minority Interests at 31.12.99   £000
40% of 200   80

[C] Profit and Loss Minority Interests - Year to 31.12.00
40% of profit of 800   320

[D] Balance Sheet Minority Interests at 31.12.00   £000
40% of 1,000   400

[E] Consolidated Revenue Reserves at 31.12.99

Glasgow	1,190	
Fife 60% of (190 - 20)	102	1,292
Goodwill write off [A]		182
		1,110

The *Consolidated Balance Sheet at 31st December 1999* will appear as follows :

	£000
Stock, at cost to the group (1,000 + 200)	1,200
Share Capital	
Ordinary Shares of £1 each	10
Consolidated Revenue Reserves [E]	1,110
	1,120
Minority Interests [B]	80
	1,200

The *Consolidated Profit and Loss Account* for the year to 31 December 2000 will appear as follows :

Modern Accounting 2

	£000	£000
Sales outside the group		9,000
(6,000 + 8,000 - 5,000)		
Opening Stock	1,200	
Purchases (Glasgow only)	2,000	
Other manufacturing costs	500	
	3,700	
less Closing Stock (1,500 + 1,000)	2,500	1,200
		7,800
Adminstrative and selling costs		6,000
Trading Profit		1,800
Minority Interests [C]		320
		1,480
Balance brought forward [E]		1,110
		2,590

The <u>Consolidated Balance Sheet at 31st December 2000</u> will appear as follows :

	£000
Stock, at cost to the group (1,500 + 1,000)	2,500
Cash	500
	3,000
Share Capital	
Ordinary Shares of £1 each	10
Consolidated Revenue Reserves [P & L]	2,590
	2,600
Minority Interests [D]	400
	3,000

Answer 8.10

[A] <u>Goodwill</u> arising on Lisbon's Purchase of 70% of Oporto

	£000	£000
Cost of shares	306	
Nat Asset Backing at date of acquisition		
70% of (100 + 80)	126	180
Depreciation over 6 years : £30,000 pa.		
NBV at 31.12.00 after 3 years : £90,000.		

[B] Balance Sheet <u>Minority Interests</u> at 31.12.00   £000
30% of 850   <u>255</u>

Consolidations

[E] Consolidated Revenue Reserves at 31.12.00
Lisbon :
Per draft Balance Sheet	706	
Dividend Receivable	<u>70</u>	
	776	
Oporto 70% of (750 - 80)	<u>449</u>	1,245
Goodwill write off [A]		<u>90</u>
		<u>1,155</u>

Consolidated Balance Sheet at 31st December 2000

	£000	£000
Fixed Assets		
Goodwill at NBV [A]	90	
Plant at NBV	<u>1,160</u>	1,250
Current Assets		
Stock (250 + 405)	655	
Trade Debtors (190 + 360)	550	
Bank (30 + 200 + 20)	<u>250</u>	
	<u>1,455</u>	
less Creditors due within One Year		
Trade Creditors (180 + 285)	465	
Proposed Dividend	200	
Dividend due to Minority Interests	<u>30</u>	
	<u>695</u>	
Net Current Assets		760
		<u>2,010</u>
Share Capital		
Ordinary Shares of £1 each		600
Consolidated Revenue Reserves [C]		<u>1,155</u>
		1,755
Minority Interests [B]		<u>255</u>
		<u>2,010</u>

Answer 8.12

	31.12.99	31.12.00
<u>Innsbruck's Stock</u> at		
Per Draft Balance Sheets	1,900	1,200
Goods in transit	<u>400</u>	<u>500</u>
	2,300	1,700
Unrealised Profit :		
0.5 X (120 + 400)	260	
0.5 X (200 + 500)		350
	<u>2,040</u>	<u>1,350</u>

Modern Accounting 2

Innsbruck's Balance Sheets can be restated as follows :

At		31.12.99		31.12.00
	£000	£000	£000	£000
Fixed Assets				
Plant at NBV		1,050		1,400
Current Assets				
Stock at cost to the group	2,040		1,350	
Bank	200		800	
	2,240		2,150	
Creditors Due Within One Year				
Creditor - Vienna	1,200		1,400	
Proposed Dividend	100		200	
	1,300		1,600	
		940		550
		1,990		1,950
Share Capital				
Ordinary Shares of £1 each		10		10
Revenue Reserves		1,980		1,940
		1,990		1,950

Innsbruck's Profit and Loss Account becomes :

	£000	£000	£000	£000
Sales			8,000	
Expenses per draft P & L	7,000			
less unrealised profit 1.1.00	260	9,740		
add unrealised profit 31.12.00		350	7,090	
Trading Profit			560	
less Dividends			600	(40)
Balance brought forward				1,980
				1,940

[A] <u>Goodwill</u> arising on Vienna's Purchase of 90% of Innsbruck

	£000	£000
Cost of shares	300	
Nat Asset Backing at date of acquisition		
90% of (10 + 50)	54	246

[B] Balance Sheet <u>Minority Interests</u> at 31.12.<u>99</u>   £000
10% of 1,990   <u>199</u>

[C] <u>Profit and Loss Minority Interests</u> - Year to 31.12.00
10% of profit of 560   <u>56</u>

Consolidations

[D] Balance Sheet <u>Minority Interests</u> at 31.12.<u>00</u> £000
10% of 1,950   <u>195</u>

[E] <u>Consolidated Revenue Reserves</u> at 31.12.<u>99</u>
Vienna per draft 3,300
90% of Div prop by I <u>90</u> 3,390
Innsbruck 90% of (1,980 - 50) <u>1,737</u> 5,127
Goodwill write off [A]   <u>246</u> <u>4,881</u>

The <u>Consolidated Balance Sheet at 31st December 1999</u> will appear as follows : £000 £000
Fixed Assets
 Plant (800 + 1,050)   1,850
Current Assets
 Stock (2,000 + 2,040) 4,040
 Bank (100 + 200) <u>300</u>
  <u>4,340</u>
Creditors Due Within One Year
 Proposed Dividend 1,000
 Dividend to Minority Interests <u>10</u>
  <u>1,010</u> <u>3,330</u>
    <u>5,180</u>

Share Capital
 Ordinary Shares of £1 each 100
Consolidated Revenue Reserves [E] <u>4,881</u> 4,981
Minority Interests [B]   <u>199</u>
    <u>5,180</u>

The <u>Consolidated Profit and Loss Account</u> for the year to 31 December 2000 will appear as follows : £000 £000
Sales outside the group   16,950
 (10,000 + 7,650 - 200 - 500)
less Expenses (6,550 + 7,090 - 200 - 500) <u>12,940</u>
Trading Profit   4,010
Minority Interests [C]   <u>56</u>
   3,954
Dividends :
 Paid 1,500
 Proposed <u>1,000</u> <u>2,500</u>
    1,454
Balance brought forward [E]   <u>4,881</u>
    <u>6,335</u>

Modern Accounting 2

The <u>Consolidated Balance Sheet at 31st December 2000</u> will appear as
follows :
	£000	£000
Fixed Assets		
Plant (900 + 1,400)		2,300
Current Assets		
Stock (3,000 + 1,350)	4,350	
Bank (200 + 800)	<u>1,000</u>	
	<u>5,350</u>	
Creditors Due Within One Year		
Proposed Dividend	1,000	
Dividend to Minority Interests	<u>20</u>	
	<u>1,020</u>	4,330
		<u>6,630</u>
Share Capital		
Ordinary Shares of £1 each	100	
Consolidated Revenue Reserves [P & L]	<u>6,335</u>	6,435
Minority Interests [D]		<u>195</u>
		<u>6,630</u>

304

Chapter Nine

Foreign Currencies

In theory, a UK company could conduct part of its business through a foreign branch but it would normally be unwise to do so. If a UK company holds Fixed Assets in a foreign country or has employees working overseas, then it will normally set up separate companies registered in each of the countries in which it operates. These separate companies act to distinguish the different parts of the business that will be subject to different codes of taxation and other forms of regulation by the officials of each country.

There are circumstances in which a US corporation *can* gain advantages by setting up overseas businesses as branches of the US corporation and only later establishing separate local companies. However this is outside the scope of this book and this Chapter concentrates on the position of UK holding companies.

If a UK company enters into one-off single transactions in foreign currencies, then there may be currency profits or losses if the exchange rate moves while the company holds monetary assets or liabilities denominated in foreign currencies. These currency profits and losses are similar to the monetary gains and losses of CPP (see Chapter 2). The purchase or sale is translated into sterling (a) at the date of the transaction and not (b) at the date that creditors or debtors were settled or (c) at the date that sterling was exchanged to or from the foreign currency.

The book-keeping for these one-off transactions is explained in the following example.

Modern Accounting 2

Example of a Single UK Company with One-off Foreign Currency Transactions

Cosmo plc was incorporated on 1st January 2000 and undertook the following transactions in the year to 31st December 2000 :

1. On 1.1.00 100,000 ordinary shares of £1 each were issued at par for cash.
2. On 1.2.00 Plant and Machinery (Fixed Assets) were purchased for A500,000 on credit when the rate of exchange was £1 = A20.
3. On 1.3.00 £40,000 was converted into B100,000.
4. On 1.4.00 £30,000 was converted into A700,000.
5. On 1.5.00 A500,000 was paid to the supplier of Plant and Machinery when the rate of exchange was £1 = A25.
6. On 1.6.00 Goods were purchased for B50,000 on credit when £1 = B2.
7. On 1.7.00 Goods were sold for C200,000 on credit at a time when £1 = C4.
8. On 1.8.00 B50,000 was paid to the supplier of Goods when the rate of exchange was £1 = B1.25
9. On 1.9.00 C200,000 was received from the Customer when the rate of exchange was £1 = C5.
10. On 1.10.00 Goods were purchased for B36,000 on credit when £1 = B1.2
11. On 1.11.00 Goods were sold for C420,000 on credit when £1 = C6.
12. On 1.12.00 C140,000 was converted into £20,000.

At 31.12.00 Stock on hand had cost B12,000 and had all come from the latest purchase on 1.10.00. The year end rates of exchange were £1 = A50 = B1 = C8. In the year to 31.12.00 plant is to be depreciated by 10% of cost.

Let us set up T accounts to record the above transactions.

Share Capital

£000		£000
	1.1.00 £ Cash Book	100

Foreign Currencies

£ Cash Book

	£000		£000
1.1.00 Share Capital	100	1.3.00 B Cash Book	40
1.12.00 C Cash Book	20	(converted into B100,000)	
(converted from C140,000)		1.4.00 A Cash Book	30
		(converted into A700,000)	
		31.12.00 Balance c/f	50
	120		120

A Cash Book

	A000	rate	£000		A000	rate	£000
1.4.00 £ Cash Book	700	-	30	1.5.00 Supplier Plant	500	25	20
				31.12.00 Currency Loss		-	6
				31.12.00 Balance c/f	200	50	4
	700		30		700		30

B Cash Book

	B000	rate	£000		B000	rate	£000
1.3.00 £ Cash Book	100	-	40	1.8.00 Supplier Goods	50	1.25	40
31.12.00 Currency Profit		-	50	31.12.00 Balance c/f	50	1	50
	100		90		100		90

C Cash Book

	C000	rate	£000		C000	rate	£000
1.9.00 Customer	200	5	40	1.12.00 £ Cash Book	140	-	20
				31.12.00 Currency Loss		-	12.5
				31.12.00 Balance c/f	60	8	7.5
	200		40		200		40

Fixed Asset - Plant at Cost

	£000		£000
1.2.00 Supplier (A500,000)	25		

Supplier of Plant

	A000	rate	£000		A000	rate	£000
1.5.00 A Cash Bk	500	25	20	1.2.00 Plant at cost	500	20	25
31.12.00 Currency Profit		-	5				
	500		25		500		25

Modern Accounting 2

Purchases

	£000		£000
1.6.00 Supplier (B50,000)	25		
1.10.00 Supplier (B36,000)	<u>30</u>	31.12.00 P & L	<u>55</u>

Supplier of Goods for Resale

	B000	rate	£000		B000	rate	£000
1.8.00 B Cash Book	50	1.25	40	1.6.00 Purchases	50	2	25
				1.10.00 Purchases	36	1.2	30
31.12.00 Bal c/f	36	1	36	31.12.00 Currency Loss	-		21
	<u>86</u>		<u>76</u>		<u>86</u>		<u>76</u>

Sales

	£000		£000
		1.7.00 Customer (C200,000)	50
31.12.00 P & L	<u>120</u>	1.11.00 Customer (C420,000)	<u>70</u>

Customer

	C000	rate	£000		C000	rate	£000
1.7.00 Sales	200	4	50	1.9.00 C Cash Book	200	5	40
1.11.00 Sales	420	6	70	31.12.00 Currency Loss	-	27.5	
				31.12.00 Balance c/f	420	8	52.5
	<u>620</u>		<u>120</u>		<u>620</u>		<u>120</u>

Currency Profits and Losses

	£000		£000
31.12.00		31.12.00	
Loss on B Liability to Supplier of Goods	21	Profit on A Liability to Supplier of Plant	5
Loss on holding A Currency	6	Profit on holding B Currency	50
Loss on holding C Debt from Customer	27.5	P & L	12
Loss on holding C Currency	12.5		
	<u>67</u>		<u>67</u>

The Final Accounts would appear as follows :

Profit and Loss Account for the Year to 31 December 2000

	£	£
Sales		120,000
Purchases	55,000	
less Closing Stock	10,000	45,000
Gross Profit		75,000
Depreciation	2,500	
Currency Loss	12,000	14,500
Net Profit		60,500

Balance Sheet as at 31st December 2000

	£	£
Fixed Asset		
Plant at cost	25,000	
less Depreciation	2,500	22,500
Current Assets		
Stock	10,000	
Debtor	52,500	
Cash in £	50,000	
Cash in As	4,000	
Cash in Bs	50,000	
Cash in Cs	7,500	
	174,000	
less Creditor due within one year	36,000	138,000
		160,500
Share Capital		100,000
Revenue Reserves		60,500
		160,500

Dangers in This 'Traditional' Approach

The T accounts shown in this example have had their main double entry restricted to £ sterling figures. If bank accounts, debtors or creditors have been in foreign currencies, then any movements on those accounts have had to be translated into sterling at the date of the movement. Taking the A Cash Book as an example, the true double entry has been the £000 column and the A000 column has been a 'memorandum' column included for information.

There are three problems with this approach. Firstly it is illogical that the £ sterling translation of transactions in another currency should be the 'true' double entry. Most book-keepers will be aware that a main purpose in keeping a cash book for a foreign currency bank account is to know how much of that foreign currency is held. The so-called 'memorandum' column is the vital information and the so-called 'true double entry' is like a tail wagging a dog.

Secondly it is inviting errors to mix different currencies in 'true double entry' and 'memorandum' columns. It is obvious that dollars will be confused with pounds and French Francs will be confused with Swiss Francs. We need a system where the individual currencies are kept as separate as possible.

Thirdly this 'traditional' system will delay the recording of foreign currency transactions until the exchange rate with the pound is known. A key feature of any good system should be that it enables transactions to be recorded as soon as possible. In this system one could know that a customer had paid 1,000 Swiss Francs but be unable to record that fact until one knew the rate of exchange between the Swiss Franc and the Pound on the day of the payment was made.

The 'Interface' System for Recording Foreign Currency Transactions

If there are likely to be several transactions in the same foreign currency, it may be worth setting up a separate double entry system in that currency. The is called the 'interface system' because there will have to be an interface account in the sterling records to handle money converted to and from the foreign currency. Equally there will have to be an interface account in the foreign currency records for the same purpose.

The disadvantage of the interface system is that no precise sterling records of each foreign currency transaction are kept. Instead groups of transactions are translated into sterling at average rates in order that final accounts can be prepared. Inevitably these average rates mean that there is some element of estimation in the computation of sales and expenses in the foreign currency. Any overestimate or underestimate will usually be compensated for by an equivalent over or underestimate in the foreign currency profit or loss and the overall profit or loss for a period should be almost correct.

Foreign Currencies

The overwhelming advantage of the interface system is that it is simple and it should reduce the errors where book-keepers confuse currencies. If the books are kept by hand, then some system of colour coding should distinguish the dollar records from the sterling records. If the books are kept on computer systems, then every attempt should be made to avoid any possible confusion between the different records. It may be worth restricting each screen to one currency or using an different computer program for the foreign currency in order that no data entry clerk - however tired - could make the confusion.

The Cosmo plc Example With Book-keeping Under the Interface System

The rates of exchange on every day in the year to 31 December 2000 have been averaged as : £1 = A40 = B1.5 = C6. The £ records would appear as follows :

Share Capital

	£000		£000
		1.1.00 £ Cash Book	100

£ Cash Book

	£000		£000
1.1.00 Share Capital	100	1.3.00 B Interface	40
1.12.00 C Interface	20	(converted into B100,000)	
(converted from C20,000)		1.4.00 A Interface	30
		(converted into A700,000)	
		31.12.00 Balance c/f	50
	<u>120</u>		<u>120</u>

A Interface

	£000		£000
1.4.00 £ Cash Book	30		

B Interface

	£000		£000
1.3.00 £ Cash Book	40		

C Interface

	£000		£000
		1.12.00 £ Cash Book	20

The A records would appear as follows :

A Cash Book

	A000		A000
1.4.00 £ Interface	700	1.5.00 Supplier of Plant	500
		31.12.00 Balance c/f	200
	<u>700</u>		<u>700</u>

£ Interface

	A000		A000
		1.4.00 A Cash Book	700

Fixed Asset - Plant at Cost

	A000		A000
1.2.00 Supplier	500		

Supplier of Plant

	A000		A000
1.5.00 A Cash Book	<u>500</u>	1.2.00 Plant at cost	<u>500</u>

The B records would appear as follows :

B Cash Book

	B000		B000
1.3.00 £ Interface	100	1.8.00 Supplier of Goods	50
		31.12.00 Balance c/f	50
	<u>100</u>		<u>100</u>

£ Interface

	B000		B000
		1.4.00 B Cash Book	100

Purchases

	B000		B000
1.6.00 Supplier	50		
1.10.00 Supplier	36		

Supplier of Goods for Resale

	B000		B000
1.8.00 B Cash Book	50	1.6.00 Purchases	50
		1.10.00 Purchases	36

The C records would appear as follows :

C Cash Book

	C000		C000
1.9.00 Customer	200	1.12.00 £ Interface	140
		31.12.00 Balance c/f	60
	200		200

£ Interface

	C000		C000
1.12.00	140		

Sales

	C000		C000
		1.7.00 Customer	200
		1.11.00 Customer	420

Customer

	C000		C000
1.7.00 Sales	200	1.9.00 C Cash Book	200
1.11.00 Sales	420		

Four Trial Balances can be extracted from each of the sets of books. The three foreign currency trial balances must be converted to pound equivalents. The rates of exchange will be (i) those at the end of the year for monetary items held at the end of year, (ii) those

Modern Accounting 2

at the date of the transactions for Fixed Asset purchases and sales and (iii) average rates for Sales and Purchases. The interface accounts will be set to the equivalents in the sterling trial balance. The Currency Profits and Losses are the differences on the converted foreign currency trial balances.

			Dr £000	Cr £000
£ Trial Balance				
Share Capital				100
£ Cash Book			50	
A Interface			30	
B Interface			40	
C Interface				20
			120	120

	Dr	Cr		Dr	Cr
A Trial Balance	A000	A000	Rate	£000	£000
A Cash Book	200	50		4	
£ Interface		700	-		30
Fixed Asset, Cost	500	20		25	
Currency Loss				1	
	700	700		30	30

	B000	B000	Rate	£000	£000
B Trial Balance					
B Cash Book	50	1		50	
£ Interface		100	-		40
Purchases	86	1.5		57.3	
Creditor to Supplier		36	1		36
Currency Profit					31.3
	136	136		107.3	107.3

	C000	C000	Rate	£000	£000
C Trial Balance					
C Cash Book	60	8		7.5	
£ Interface	140	-		20	
Sales		620	6		103.3
Debtor - Customer	420	8		52.5	
Currency Loss				23.3	
	620	620		103.3	103.3

Foreign Currencies

The Final Accounts would appear as follows :
Profit and Loss Account for the Year to 31 December 2000

	£	£
Sales		103,333
Purchases	57,333	
less Closing Stock	10,000	47,333
Gross Profit		56,000
Depreciation		2,500
		53,500
Currency Profit (31.3 - 23.3 - 1)		7,000
Net Profit		60,500

The Balance Sheet at the end of the year will be the same as that on page 319. The differences between this Profit and Loss Account and that on page 319 arise from translating Sales and Purchases at the average rates for the year rather that the actual rate at the date of each individual sale and purchase. These differences are counterbalanced by the currency loss/profit so the final profit remains the same.

Closing entries in each of the foreign currency records should write all accounts other than monetary assets and liabilities against the interface account. Equally all non-monetary assets that were held in the foreign currency records (in this case the Fixed Asset) are brought into the sterling records. Thus the opening trial balances on 1st January 2001 will be as follows :

	Dr	Cr
£ Trial Balance	£	£
Fixed Asset, cost	25,000	
Fixed Asset, depreciation		2,500
Stock at 1.1.01	10,000	
£ Cash Book	50,000	
A Interface	4,000	
B Interface	14,000	
C Interface	60,000	
Share Capital		100,000
Revenue Reserves		60,500
	163,000	163,000

Modern Accounting 2

	Dr	Cr
A Trial Balance	A000	A000
A Cash Book	200	
£ Interface		200
	200	200
B Trial Balance	B000	B000
B Cash Book	50	
Creditor to Supplier		36
£ Interface		14
	50	50
C Trial Balance	C000	C000
C Cash Book	60	
Debtor - Customer	420	
£ Interface		480
	480	480

The Journal Entries required at the end of year to produce these opening trial balances for the next year are as follows :

	Dr	Cr
£ Records - Journal Entries	£	£
Revenue Reserves (P & L)		60,500
C Interface (Sales)	103,333	
B Interface (Purchases)		57,333
Stock	10,000	
Accumulated Depreciation		2,500
A Interface (Currency Loss)		1,000
B Interface (Currency Profit)	31,333	
C Interface (Currency Loss)		23,333
	144,666	144,666

Entries to the Profit and Loss Account

	Dr	Cr
Fixed Asset at cost	25,000	
A Interface		25,000
	25,000	25,000

Bringing the Plant into the £ Records

                                              Foreign Currencies

	Dr	Cr
A Records - Journal Entries	A000	A000
£ Interface	500	
Fixed Asset		500
	<u>500</u>	<u>500</u>
B Records - Journal Entries	B000	B000
£ Interface	86	
Purchases		86
	<u>86</u>	<u>86</u>
C Records - Journal Entries	C000	C000
Sales	620	
£ Interface		620
	<u>620</u>	<u>620</u>

In this simple example there were only two sales and two purchases. It is almost as easy to convert each at the precise rate of exchange as it is to use the average rate of exchange. The interface method and average rates of exchange are more useful if there are many foreign currency sales, expenses and/or purchases in a year.

Try to answer the following questions before looking at the answers (which are at the end of this chapter).

Modern Accounting 2

Question 9.1 (Answer 9.1 is on page 346)

Politan plc was incorporated on 1st January 2000 and undertook the following transactions in the year to 31st December 2000 :

1. On 1.1.00 200,000 ordinary shares of £1 each were issued at par for cash.
2. On 1.2.00 £60,000 was converted into B120,000.
3. On 1.3.00 Goods were purchased for B150,000 on credit when £1 = B1.5.
4. On 1.4.00 £40,000 was converted into C200,000.
5. On 1.5.00 Plant and Machinery (Fixed Assets) were purchased for C100,000 on credit when the rate of exchange was £1 = C4.
6. On 1.6.00 Goods were sold for A800,000 on credit at a time when £1 = A4.
7. On 1.7.00 C100,000 was paid to the supplier of Plant and Machinery when the rate of exchange was £1 = C3.
8. On 1.8.00 A800,000 was received from the Customer when the rate of exchange was £1 = A5.
9. On 1.9.00 B100,000 was paid to the supplier of Goods when the rate of exchange was £1 = B2.5
10. On 1.10.00 Goods were purchased for B300,000 on credit when £1 = B1.5
11. On 1.11.00 A600,000 was converted into £110,000.
12. On 1.12.00 Goods were sold for A600,000 on credit when £1 = A6.

At 31.12.00 Stock on hand had cost B90,000 and had all come from the latest purchase on 1.10.00. The year end rates of exchange were £1 = A7 = B3 = C2. In the year to 31.12.00 plant is to be depreciated by 20% of cost. The average rates of exchange during the year to 31 December 2000 were : £1 = A5 = B2 = C3.

REQUIRED : Set up T accounts to record these transactions under (i) the Traditional Method and (ii) the Interface Method. Prepare final accounts for the year to 31 December 2000 from each set of T accounts.

Foreign Currencies

Question 9.2 (Answer 9.2 is on page 352)

Continuing question 9.1, produce end-of-year journal entries under the interface method and show the opening trial balances required (under that method) to start the new year, 2001.

A Single Company Compared to a Group with Foreign Subsidiaries

There is little dispute as to how to account for the foreign currency transactions of a UK based company with no foreign subsidiaries. Almost invariably the 'Historical-Temporal' system of foreign currency translation is used. The 'Historical-Temporal' system means that each purchase and sale is translated at the rate of exchange obtaining when the transaction took place. Equally almost invariably all exchange rate profits and losses will be treated as part of the standard profits shown on the Profit and Loss Account.

However the situation is not so clear-cut when a UK based company with a foreign subsidiary. Sometimes the Historical-Temporal method is used but more often the 'Closing Rate' (sometimes called the 'Net Investment') method is used. Usually foreign exchange profits and losses will be divided between those that are shown openly on the face of the Profit and Loss Account and those that are more discretely confined to a note to the accounts as a 'movement on reserves'. In the last Chapter write-offs of Goodwill through such notes was stated to be controversial. Similar controversy surrounds foreign exchange profits and losses.

The Division of Exchange Rate Profits and Losses

Usually those profits (or losses) arising within a company's own accounts as expressed in that company's own currency are treated as part of the standard P & L profits. This is true for both the holding company and the subsidiary. However those profits (or losses) arising on consolidation are treated as a movement on reserves.

An exception is made where a company has borrowed in the currency of its subsidiary to finance investment in that subsidiary. In this case the foreign currency profit (or loss) would be treated as a movement on reserves even though it must be taken in the holding company's own accounts. The logic behind this exception is that such borrowing is very close to borrowing made directly by the subsidiary.

The Historical-Temporal Method

This is the method that has been used so far in this chapter. Under this method the following rates of exchange are used:

	Item	Rate of Exchange
1	Non-Monetary Assets on the Balance Sheet	Date of Purchase of Asset
2	Accumulated Depreciation of Fixed Assets on the Balance Sheet	Date of Purchase of Asset
3	Monetary Assets and Liabilities on the Balance Sheet	Balance Sheet Date
4	Sales, Purchases and Expenses on the P & L	Average During Year (in theory Date of Transaction)
5	Opening Stock on the P & L	Date of Purchase (Likely to be close to start of year)
6	Closing Stock on the P & L	Date of Purchase (Likely to be close to end of year)
7	Depreciation of Fixed Assets on the P & L	Original Date of Purchase of the Asset

This method is logical and consistent and, if all the transactions occur within a UK based company with no foreign subsidiaries, it requires no additional effort.

However a foreign subsidiary usually prepares its accounts first in its own foreign currency. The translation into £ sterling is normally done as an afterthought. The Historical-Temporal method requires several different rates of exchange to be used in translating the Balance Sheet and several different rates of exchange to be used in translating the Profit and Loss Account. In particular, detailed analyses of Fixed Assets and Accumulated Depreciation have to be kept because each Fixed Asset and element of Depreciation has to be translated at the rate obtaining when that individual Fixed Asset was purchased.

The Closing Rate Method

Under this method the following rates of exchange are used:

	Item	Rate of Exchange
1	Non-Monetary Assets on the Balance Sheet	Balance Sheet Date
2	Accumulated Depreciation of Fixed Assets on the Balance Sheet	Balance Sheet Date
3	Monetary Assets and Liabilities on the Balance Sheet	Balance Sheet Date
4	Sales, Purchases and Expenses on the P & L	Average During Year
5	Opening Stock on the P & L	Average During Year
6	Closing Stock on the P & L	Average During Year
7	Depreciation of Fixed Assets on the P & L	Average During Year

As currently implemented, there is much less logic and consistency to the Closing Rate method. It appears slapdash but convenient. However there are some underlying reasons why it has found favour in the UK. Later in this Chapter we will examine its relationship to Current Cost Accounting (CCA) and also the impact of a loss of faith in one's own currency (in this case £ sterling) as a stable measure of value.

If the same long term Fixed Assets (such as land and buildings) are going to be translated each year at a different rate of exchange (the Balance Sheet rate), it is evident why some accountants believe that some foreign currency profits (or losses) are mere accounting adjustments and should not be shown on the face of the Profit and Loss Account.

An Example Comparing the Historical-Temporal Method to the Closing Rate Method

UK Hold Ltd has owned 100% of Foreign Sub SA since Foreign Sub was incorporated in 1990. Foreign Sub produces accounts in Mellow Dollars. Foreign Sub purchased its stocks close to each Balance Sheet date. Foreign Sub's most recent accounts read as follows :

Modern Accounting 2

Balance Sheet as at

	31.12.99		31.12.00	
	M$m	M$m	M$m	M$m
Fixed Assets				
Cost		500		500
Accumulated Depreciation		340		390
		160		110
Current Assets				
Stock	100		120	
Debtors	110		130	
Bank	10		100	
	220		350	
less Creditors due within one year	60	160	90	260
		320		370
less Creditors due after one year				
Loans denominated in M$		200		200
		120		170
Share Capital		50		50
Revenue Reserves		70		120
		120		170

The Fixed Assets of Foreign Sub SA are depreciated by 10% pa on cost with a full year's depreciation in the year of purchase. The same Fixed Assets are held on 31.12.99 as on 31.12.00 and are made up from two purchases : (i) M$200m spent in 1992 and (ii) M$300m spent in 1994.

Profit and Loss Account for the year to 31 December 2000

	M$m	M$m
Sales		250
Opening Stock	100	
Purchases	150	
	250	
less Closing Stock	120	130
		120
Sundry Expenses	20	
Depreciation	50	70
		50
Reserves brought forward		70
		120

There were no transactions in the records of UK Hold Ltd in the year to 31 December 2000. The Balance Sheets of UK Hold Ltd read as follows :

	31.12.99 £000	31.12.00 £000
Shares in wholly owned subsidiary (Foreign Sub SA), at cost	<u>10</u>	<u>10</u>
Share Capital	6	6
Revenue Reserves	<u>4</u>	<u>4</u>
	<u>10</u>	<u>10</u>

Rates of Exchange	Date	
in 1990 (when Foreign Sub was incorporated)		M$5,000 = £1
in 1992 (purchase of FA)		M$4,000 = £1
in 1994 (purchase of FA)		M$3,000 = £1
on 31.12.99		M$2,500 = £1
on average during 2000		M$2,400 = £1
on 31.12.00		M$2,300 = £1

The closing rate net assets of Foreign Sub in £000 can be produced by translating the 1999 Balance Sheet at an exchange rate of 2,500 and the 2000 Balance Sheet at 2,300 as follows :

	31.12.99		31.12.00	
	£000	£000	£000	£000
Fixed Assets				
Cost		200		217
Accumulated Depreciation		<u>136</u>		<u>169</u>
		64		48
Current Assets				
Stock	40		52	
Debtors	44		57	
Bank	<u>4</u>		<u>43</u>	
	88		152	
less Creditors due within one year	<u>24</u>	<u>64</u>	<u>39</u>	<u>113</u>
		128		161
less Creditors due after one year				
Loans denominated in M$		<u>80</u>		<u>87</u>
		<u>48</u>		<u>74</u>

Modern Accounting 2

Since Hold UK Ltd has no assets other than its 100% stake in Foreign Sub, the net assets on the previous page will also be the net assets for the Consolidated Balance Sheet. The shareholders' funds on the Closing Rate Consolidated Balance Sheet will appear as follows :

	31.12.99	31.12.00
	£000	£000
Share Capital (Hold UK alone)	6	6
Consolidated Revenue Reserves	<u>42</u>	<u>68</u>
	<u>48</u>	<u>74</u>

The <u>Historical-Temporal</u> translation requires an analysis of Fixed Assets :

Date of Purchase	Cost M$m	Exch Rate £000	Cost £000	Depn 99 M$m	Depn 99 £000	P & L £000	Depn 00 £000
1992	200	4000	50	160	40	5	45
1994	<u>300</u>	3000	<u>100</u>	<u>180</u>	<u>60</u>	<u>10</u>	<u>70</u>
	<u>500</u>		<u>150</u>	<u>340</u>	<u>100</u>	<u>15</u>	<u>115</u>

Consolidated Balance Sheet (HT) at 31.12.99 31.12.00

	£000	£000	£000	£000
Fixed Assets				
Cost		150		150
Accumulated Depreciation		<u>100</u>		<u>115</u>
		50		35
Current Assets				
Stock	40		52	
Debtors	44		57	
Bank	<u>4</u>		<u>43</u>	
	88		152	
less Creditors due within one year	<u>24</u>	<u>64</u>	<u>39</u>	<u>113</u>
		114		148
less Creditors due after one year				
Loans denominated in M$		<u>80</u>		<u>87</u>
		<u>34</u>		<u>61</u>
Share Capital (Hold UK alone)		6		6
Consolidated Revenue Reserves		<u>28</u>		<u>55</u>
		<u>34</u>		<u>61</u>

Foreign Currencies

On the <u>Closing Rate Profit and Loss Account</u> all translations will be at the average exchange rate of 2,400 :

	£000	£000
Sales		104
Cost of Sales		<u>54</u>
		50
Sundry Expenses	8	
Depreciation	<u>21</u>	<u>29</u>
Profit for the year		<u>21</u>

The <u>Historical-Temporal Profit and Loss Account</u> uses different exchange rates for stocks and depreciation :

	£000	£000
Sales		104
Opening Stock (at 2,500)	40	
Purchases	<u>63</u>	
	103	
less Closing Stock (at 2,300)	<u>52</u>	
		<u>51</u>
		53
Sundry Expenses	8	
Depreciation (analysis prev page)	<u>15</u>	<u>23</u>
Profit for the year		<u>30</u>

Thus the movements on the Consolidated Revenue Reserves must be as follows :

	Closing Rate £000	Hist-Temp £000
brought forward on 1.1.00 :		
Reserves of UK Hold Ltd per own BS	4	4
Retained post-acquisition profit of subsidiary		
- diff between Net Assets of FS at 31.12.99 and		
the original capital contributed of 10	<u>38</u>	<u>24</u>
	42	28
Profit for the year per P & L	21	30
Exchange Rate Profit (Loss) - Balancing figure	5	(3)
Reserves at 31.12.00	<u>68</u>	<u>55</u>

Foreign Currency Consistently Gaining Strength Against Home Currency

In this example the mellow dollar consistently rose against the pound. When that happens :
(a) the Closing Rate Balance Sheet will always show higher net assets than the Historical-Temporal Balance Sheet.
(b) the Historical-Temporal Profit and Loss Account will always show higher profits (or lower losses) than the Closing Rate Profit and Loss Account.
(c) The Closing Rate accounts will always show a Currency Profit arising on consolidation.
(d) The Historical-Temporal accounts may show a Currency Loss on consolidation (if monetary liabilities of the foreign subsidiary exceed its monetary assets). If the H-T accounts do show a Currency Profit, then it will be less than that shown under the Closing Rate Method.

Home Currency Consistently Gaining Strength Against Foreign Currency

When this happens :
(a) the Historical-Temporal Balance Sheet will always show higher net assets than the Closing Rate Balance Sheet.
(b) the Closing Rate Profit and Loss Account will always show higher profits (or lower losses) than the Historical-Temporal Profit and Loss Account.
(c) The Closing Rate accounts will always show a Currency Loss arising on consolidation.
(d) The Historical-Temporal accounts may show a Currency Profit on consolidation (if monetary liabilities of the foreign subsidiary exceed its monetary assets). If the H-T accounts do show a Currency Loss, then it will be less than that shown under the Closing Rate Method.

Inconsistent Fluctuations of Exchange Rates

If one currency has become stronger and then weaker compared with the other, no broad conclusions can be drawn as to the effect of changing between the two methods of currency translation.

The Price Parity Theory of Exchange Rates

According to this theory, exchange rates should move to equalise prices in different countries. Thus if a basket of goods costs £1,000 in the UK and 10,000 Fr Francs in France, then exchange rates should move towards £1 = 10 FrF.

If there are fewer Francs to the Pound, then exports from the UK to France should be encouraged and those exports will eventually result in purchases of Pounds and sales of Francs. Those businesses considering investing in either France or the UK should prefer the UK because they should find it easier to make a profit producing in the lower cost country. Such investment will encourage capital movements into the UK and, once again, this should have the effect of increasing demand for pounds.

Vice versa if there are more than 10 Francs to the pound, then exports from France to the UK should be encouraged and investment funds would be steered from the UK and towards France until price parity between the two countries was obtained.

Countries with high rates of inflation should have currencies which become weaker in exchange markets. Countries with low rates of inflation should have strong currencies.

Later in this Chapter is a consideration of whether empirical evidence supports this theory and whether other factors may prevent the theory being a full explanation of exchange rate movements. However at this stage let us assume that this theory is perfect.

(a) High Inflation at Home with (b) Stable Prices in the Country of the Foreign Subsidiary

If all prices remain absolutely stable in the country of the foreign subsidiary, then exchange rate changes should reflect solely inflation at home. The closing rate method would show foreign assets at cost in 'real' terms in the pounds at Balance Sheet dates. If there are no assets held at home and readers of accounts understand the definitions of the statistics they are being shown, then this may be preferable to providing H-T statistics. However if the foreign assets have to be added to home assets, then the result is not valid because the home assets are shown at historic currency cost whereas the foreign assets have the equivalent of an inflation adjustment. Previous years' Balance Sheets and Profit and Loss Accounts are not expressed in the same 'currency' as this year's Balance Sheet.

The Historical-Temporal Method follows all the principles of historic currency cost accounting and suffers from all the defects of this system that were discussed in the early chapters. If there are home assets and home profits, then the addition of the foreign figures to the home figures in a consolidation is a valid addition of statistics with the same definition.

(a) Stable Prices at Home with (b) High Inflation in the Country of the Foreign Subsidiary

If all prices remain absolutely stable at home, then exchange rate changes should reflect solely inflation in the country of the foreign subsidiary. The closing rate method will have all the problems of historic currency cost accounting in high inflation. The net assets of the subsidiary will be stated below cost and foreign profits will be overstated because of stock and depreciation. Successive Balance Sheets and Profit and Loss Accounts are not expressed in currency with the same command over goods and services. As before, the addition of (i) home assets and profit to (ii) the foreign closing rate figures is not a valid merging of comparable statistics.

The Historical-Temporal Method solves problems of inflation in the foreign country. If the home currency represents stability, then expressing all figures as they would have been had they been incurred in the home currency at the date they were incurred, should produce fully inflation adjusted figures in stable units of measurement.

CCA and the Closing Rate Method

Current Cost Accounting requires replacement costs. If a foreign subsidiary of ours owns a machine in Zedland, then it is the cost of replacing *in Zedland* (and not in the UK) that is the true current cost (assuming we can ignore realisable and economic values). Thus CCA for a multi-national group will involve specific price indexes in each country of operation.

First the local currency accounts should be expressed in CCA. Once this has been done, the Balance Sheets are in costs at the Balance Sheet date and the P & Ls are in costs at the average rate. Thus the only logical method of currency translation is the Closing Rate Method. If the home figures are also in CCA, then addition of home and foreign closing rate figures is fully valid.

Foreign Currencies

The Historical-Temporal Method and CPP

The last heading was *first* CCA and *then* Closing Rate whereas the heading above is first Historical-Temporal and then CPP. CPP uses a single consumer price index and that should reflect prices in the home currency.

First the historic currency cost accounts of the foreign subsidiary should be translated into pounds under the H-T method. Once this has been done, the historic pounds are converted to £CPP.

CCA, the Closing Rate Method and CPP

CCA in CPP is a variation on CCA. As with CCA, only the closing rate method is logical. In this case the three stages are : (i) CCA in the local currency, (ii) the closing rate method of translation into pounds and (iii) translation of the historic pounds into £CPP using a home-based consumer price index.

Invalid Combinations

It does not make sense for the Historical-Temporal method to be used with CCA (whichever comes first). It does not make sense for the closing rate method to be used with CPP unless the underlying accounts are already in CCA.

Should Currency Profits and Losses be Hidden Away from the Profit and Loss Account?

Unfortunately not all readers of accounts reconcile Balance Sheets with Income Statements. In a logical world it would hardly matter whether an item were shown on the Profit and Loss Account or in a note headed 'Movements on Reserves'. It would be up to the reader to decide whether each item was a true profit (or loss) or an artificial accounting adjustment that would reverse itself in the following year.

In the case of currency profits or losses readers would need to have the figure analysed between profits and losses in different currencies and they would need to know the net monetary assets (or liabilities) in each currency held at Balance Sheet dates and maximum movements in those net monetary assets throughout the year. If the closing rate method is being used, they would also need an analysis of the geographic location of Fixed Assets.

If the currency profit (or loss) arises from holding a constant net monetary asset (or liability) position while the exchange rate fluctuates above and below a constant mean position, then it is not unreasonable to view the currency profit (or loss) as a mere accounting adjustment. What has been gained this year will probably be lost next year (and vice versa). This analysis would ignore the Price Parity Theory.

On the other hand, if the exchange rate does follow the Price Parity Theory, then exchange rate profits and losses on holding net monetary items could be seen as part of the profit or loss made from trading in that way in that country.

Polly Peck

Polly Peck was a UK public company with subsidiaries in Northern Cyprus. It collapsed in a spectacular fashion after showing considerable profits on its Consolidated Profit and Loss Account partly balanced by Currency Losses deducted as a movement on reserves. Inflation in Northern Cyprus was very high and the Northern Cypriot Lire was a weak currency. Every year the Pound would buy more Lire than the year before.

The details of the Polly Peck collapse are unclear and may become clearer when an enquiry reports and litigation has run its course. However it has been claimed that Polly Peck subsidiaries paid farmers in lire for their citrus crops before those crops were ready for picking. The same subsidiaries sold the citrus fruit on credit terms at prices denominated in lire after the fruit had been harvested and packed. Thus it has been claimed that the subsidiaries held heavy monetary assets in lire which gave rise to losses as the value of the lire fell.

The following example is intended to illustrate a principle and there is no suggestion that it resembles any activities which may have been undertaken by any subsidiary of Polly Peck :

On 1.1.00 Citrus SA had a bank balance of L4m as its only asset. On that date it paid farmers L4m in advance for fruit yet to be picked. On 31.12.00 Citrus SA sold the fruit for L8m on credit terms with the money due on 1.4.01. Rates of exchange were :
at 1.1.00 L1,000 = £1; on average during the year 2000 : L2,000; at 31.12.00 L4,000 = £1 and 1.4.01 L5,000 = £1.

In this case the L4m bank balance on 1.1.00 had a sterling equivalent at that date of £4,000. In local currency the company has made a profit of L4m in the year which translated at the average rate of exchange is £2,000. The debt at the end of the year of L8m can be translated at the year-end rate of exchange as £2,000 but it will actually realise £1,600 if it is converted back to sterling when it is received. The currency losses on these transactions could be accounted for as £4,000 in 2000 and £400 in 2001 and they somewhat dwarf the apparent trading profit of £2,000.

The accounting standard in force when Polly Peck showed its currency losses as a movement on reserves required that losses due to a *permanent* change in exchange rates were shown on the Profit and Loss Account. Deciding whether an exchange rate movement is temporary or permanent might be better left to the judgement of individual readers of accounts rather than left in the hands of company directors.

Does the Price Parity Theory Explain All Exchange Rate Movements?

The Price Parity Theory does appear to explain most large exchange rate movements over the medium term - say of over 50% over a five year period. It is true that countries with high rates of inflation such as some South American countries have currencies whose values consistently decline in comparison with the currencies of countries, such as Germany and Japan, which have low rates of inflation.

However the theory is less satisfactory when considering smaller exchange rate movements in the short term - say of under 20% over a year. Exchange rates between the Pound and the US Dollar during some years of the 1980s are difficult to reconcile with the Price Parity Theory. The following are some of the reasons commonly believed to explain the deficiencies in the short term application of the theory :

1   In the short run capital flows can be so large that they overwhelm changes in demand for currencies to pay for current trade in goods and services. In the long run even these capital flows will be influenced indirectly by comparative prices but, in the short run, they may be more influenced by a search for political stability or higher interest rates.

2. Time lags and imperfect information will prevent businesses immediately recognising that prices in different countries are out of alignment and their formulating strategies to profit by this (and hence realign).
3. Certain price differences are caused by transport costs, cultural differences, the marketing strategies of a monopolist, different distribution networks, government regulation or indirect taxation. These differences cannot be corrected by individuals.
4. Governments intervene with (i) direct purchases and sales in currency markets, (ii) exchange controls and (iii) interest rate policies.

Try to answer the following questions before looking at the answers (which are at the end of this chapter).

Question 9.3 (Answer 9.3 is on page 353)

Alpha Ltd has owned 100% of Beta SA since Beta was incorporated in 1990. Beta produces accounts in Bean Pennies. Beta purchased its stocks close to each Balance Sheet date. Beta's most recent accounts read as follows:

Balance Sheet as at	31.12.99		31.12.00	
	BPm	BPm	BPm	BPm
Fixed Assets				
Cost		1,100		1,100
Accumulated Depreciation		740		850
		360		250
Current Assets				
Stock	200		500	
Debtors	300		600	
Bank	20		10	
	520		1,110	
less Creditors due within one year	50	470	40	1,070
		830		1,320
less Creditors due after one year				
Loans denominated in BP		100		100
		730		1,220
Share Capital		100		100
Revenue Reserves		630		1,120
		730		1,220

Foreign Currencies

The Fixed Assets of Beta SA are depreciated by 10% pa on cost with a full year's depreciation in the year of purchase. The same Fixed Assets are held on 31.12.99 as on 31.12.00 and are made up from two purchases : (i) BP400m spent in 1992 and (ii) BP700m spent in 1994.

Profit and Loss Account for the year to 31 December 2000

	BPm	BPm
Sales		10,000
Opening Stock	200	
Purchases	4,000	
	4,200	
less Closing Stock	500	3,700
		6,300
Sundry Expenses	5,600	
Depreciation	110	5,710
		590
Reserves brought forward		630
		1,220

There were no transactions in the records of Alpha Ltd in the year to 31 December 2000. The Balance Sheets of Alpha Ltd read as follows :

	31.12.99 £000	31.12.00 £000
Shares in wholly owned subsidiary (Beta SA), at cost	1,000	1,000
Share Capital	800	800
Revenue Reserves	200	200
	1,000	1,000

Rates of Exchange — Date

in 1990 (when Beta was incorporated)	BP100 = £1
in 1992 (purchase of FA)	BP200 = £1
in 1994 (purchase of FA)	BP400 = £1
on 31.12.99	BP800 = £1
on average during 2000	BP900 = £1
on 31.12.00	BP1,000 = £1

REQUIRED : Prepare Consolidated Balance Sheets and Profit & Loss Account for Alpha using (a) the Closing Rate Method of currency translation and then (b) the Historical Temporal Method.

Question 9.4 (Answer 9.4 is on page 355)

Gamma Ltd has owned 100% of Delta Inc since Delta was incorporated in Seldomia in 1980. Delta produces accounts in Seldomian Marks. Both Gamma and Delta purchased their stocks close to each Balance Sheet date. The most recent historic cost accounts of the companies read as follows :

	Gamma		Delta	
Balance Sheets as at	31.12.99	31.12.00	31.12.99	31.12.00
Fixed Assets	£000	£000	SMm	SMm
Plant at Cost	4,000	4,000	900	900
Accum Depn on Plant	2,200	3,000	425	470
	1,800	1,000	475	430
Shares in subsidiary	100	100	-	-
	1,900	1,100	475	430
Current Assets				
Stock	1,300	2,200	300	400
Debtors	1,500	2,300	200	300
Bank	1,100	1,000	10	200
	3,900	5,500	510	900
less Creditors	1,000	1,500	100	200
Net Current Assets	2,900	4,000	410	700
	4,800	5,100	885	1,130
Share Capital	500	500	100	100
Revenue Reserves	4,300	4,600	785	1,030
	4,800	5,100	885	1,130

Profit and Loss Accounts for the year to 31 December 2000

	£000	£000	SMm	SMm
Sales		11,800		6,890
Opening Stock	1,300		300	
Purchases	9,600		6,000	
	10,900		6,300	
less Closing Stock	2,200	8,700	400	5,900
		3,100		990
Sundry Expenses	2,000		700	
Depreciation	800	2,800	45	745
		300		245
Reserves brought forward		4,300		785
		4,600		1,030

Foreign Currencies

The Fixed Assets of Gamma are depreciated by 20% pa on cost with a full year's depreciation in the year of purchase. The Fixed Assets of Delta SA are depreciated by 5% pa on cost with a full year's depreciation in the year of purchase. In both companies the same Fixed Assets are held on 31.12.99 as on 31.12.00. In Gamma the Fixed Assets are made up from a purchase of £3m in 1997 and a purchase of £1m in 1998. In Delta the Fixed Assets are made up from a purchase of SM400m in 1985 and a purchase of SM500m in 1995.

Rates of Exchange	Date
in 1980 (when Delta was incorporated)	SM1,000 = £1
in 1985 (purchase of FA)	SM800 = £1
in 1995 (purchase of FA)	SM1,250 = £1
on 31.12.99	SM700 = £1
on average during 2000	SM800 = £1
on 31.12.00	SM900 = £1

REQUIRED : Prepare Historic Cost Consolidated Balance Sheets and Profit & Loss Account in raw currency for Gamma using (a) the Closing Rate Method of currency translation and then (b) the Historical Temporal Method.

Question 9.5 (Answer 9.5 is on page 357)

Continuing Question 9.4 above, the following price indexes have been calculated :

	UK Specific Plant	UK Specific Stock	UK General Consumer	Seldomia Specific Plant	Seldomia Specific Stock
1985	-	-	100	105	-
1995	-	-	120	140	-
1997	110	-	140	-	-
1998	120	-	160	-	-
31.12.99	130	102	170	160	120
Avg for yr to 31.12.00	135	120	175	165	130
31.12.00	140	138	180	170	140

REQUIRED : Prepare Consolidated Balance Sheets and Profit & Loss Account for Gamma using (a) CCA in raw currency, (b) CCA in CPP and (c) Historic Cost in CPP. (For CCA ignore MWCA and GA; assume that Current Cost Reserves on 1.1.00 arise solely from the Fixed Assets held at that date.)

Modern Accounting 2

Question 9.6 (No answer to this question has been included in this book.)

Omega Ltd has owned 100% of Iota Inc since Iota was incorporated in Raria in 1980. Iota produces accounts in Rarian Marks. Both Omega and Iota purchased their stocks close to each Balance Sheet date. The most recent historic cost accounts of the companies read as follows:

	Omega		Iota	
Balance Sheets as at	31.12.99	31.12.00	31.12.99	31.12.00
Fixed Assets	£000	£000	RMm	RMm
Plant at Cost	6,000	6,000	1,200	1,200
Accum Depn on Plant	3,000	3,600	440	560
	3,000	2,400	760	640
Shares in subsidiary	100	100	-	-
	3,100	2,500	760	640
Current Assets				
Stock	1,000	2,000	400	500
Debtors	1,000	2,500	300	400
Bank	1,000	2,000	50	200
	3,000	6,500	750	1,100
less Creditors	1,000	2,500	100	300
Net Current Assets	2,000	4,000	650	800
	5,100	6,500	1,410	1,440
Share Capital	500	500	100	100
Revenue Reserves	4,600	6,000	1,310	1,340
	5,100	6,500	1,410	1,440

Profit and Loss Accounts for the year to 31 December 2000

	£000	£000	RMm	RMm
Sales		11,000		10,000
Opening Stock	1,000		400	
Purchases	7,600		7,070	
	8,600		7,470	
less Closing Stock	2,000	6,600	500	6,970
		4,400		3,030
Sundry Expenses	2,400		2,880	
Depreciation	600	3,000	120	3,000
		1,400		30
Reserves brought forward		4,600		1,310
		6,000		1,340

Foreign Currencies

The Fixed Assets of both companies are depreciated by 10% pa on cost with a full year's depreciation in the year of purchase. In both companies the same Fixed Assets are held on 31.12.99 as on 31.12.00. In Omega the Fixed Assets are made up from a purchase of £6m in 1995. In Iota the Fixed Assets are made up from a purchase of RM500m in 1994 and a purchase of RM700m in 1998.

Rates of Exchange Date	
in 1980 (when Iota was incorporated)	RM1,000 = £1
in 1994 (purchase of FA)	RM1,100 = £1
in 1998 (purchase of FA)	RM1,200 = £1
on 31.12.99	RM1,100 = £1
on average during 2000	RM1,000 = £1
on 31.12.00	RM900 = £1

REQUIRED : Prepare Historic Cost Consolidated Balance Sheets and Profit & Loss Account in raw currency for Omega using (a) the Closing Rate Method of currency translation and then (b) the Historical Temporal Method.

Question 9.7 (No answer to this question has been included in this book.)

Continuing Question 9.6 above, the following price indexes have been calculated :

	UK Specific Plant	UK Specific Stock	UK General Consumer	Raria Specific Plant	Raria Specific Stock
1994	-	-	105	100	-
1995	110	-	110	-	-
1998	-	-	120	150	-
31.12.99	120	110	130	160	110
Avg for yr to 31.12.00	115	105	140	165	120
31.12.00	110	100	150	170	130

REQUIRED : Prepare Consolidated Balance Sheets and Profit & Loss Account for Omega using (a) CCA in raw currency, (b) CCA in CPP and (c) Historic Cost in CPP. (For CCA ignore MWCA and GA; assume that Current Cost Reserves on 1.1.00 arise solely from the Fixed Assets held at that date.)

Choosing the Currency in Which to Borrow or Deposit

The nominal cost of borrowing - or return from deposits - differs between currencies. Strong currencies tend to have low money rates of interest and weak currencies tend to have high money rates of interest. In Chapter 6 the difference between the stated rate of interest (the 'money' rate) and the 'real' rate of interest (the rate net of inflation and currency exchange rate depreciation) was explained.

Let us assume that the money rate of interest is 10.25%pa in Xland and the Xland rate of inflation is 5%pa. In Yland the money rate of interest is 15.5% and the rate of inflation is 10%pa. Using the formula for the real rate of interest from Chapter 6 (page 187) the real rate of interest in each country is 5%pa. If, over the long term, there is some validity to the Price Parity Theory of Exchange Rates, then it might appear that any company would be indifferent between borrowing or depositing in Xland or Yland.

It seems logical that companies depositing would be attracted to the currencies with the highest real rates of interest and companies borrowing would be attracted to currencies with the lowest real rates of interest. It also seems logical that all currency losses or profits on borrowing or deposits should be netted against the interest paid or received. Comparing a company with deposits in Xland with another company with deposits in Yland, it appears misleading to show the nominal rates of return as profits in the Profit and Loss Account separately from the currency losses of the second company.

Unfortunately most taxation systems (including that in the UK) discriminate against borrowings in strong currencies and deposits in weak currencies. Generally only the nominal interest paid or received is allowed or taxed as a 'revenue' item in the year and any currency loss or gain is treated as a 'capital' item. Such 'capital' items are normally subject to lower levels of allowance or tax (if allowed or taxed at all) and at some later date when the 'capital' sums are repaid.

Also weak currencies tend to be controlled by governments liable to impose sudden changes in the rules of taxation and exchange control. The real rate of interest can only be ascertained in arrears because the rate of inflation for the coming year can only be estimated. Weak currencies tend to have rates of inflation which are not only higher but also more difficult to measure and more subject to fluctuation.

Foreign Currencies

If the sole proprietor of a business believed that it was possible to forecast (a) real rates of interest net of taxation and (b) the price parity theory was perfect, then all the investments of such a proprietor would probably be financed from borrowings in the currency with the lowest real cost net of taxation. If this proprietor believed that it was possible to forecast the real returns from investments in all currencies, then such a proprietor would be likely to invest in the currency with the highest real return net of taxation.

However most managers have to take account of the way in which results are reported to shareholders. (Indeed above a certain level of gearing even sole proprietors would have to take account of the impact of accounting statements on the confidence of lenders.) And most managers do not have faith in their ability to forecast future exchange rates or rates of inflation.

Financing a Foreign Subsidiary and Accounting with the Closing Rate Method

The closing rate method encourages financing all investment in foreign subsidiaries by borrowing in the currency of investment. Fixed Assets of foreign subsidiaries on a Consolidated Balance Sheet will fluctuate depending on the rate of exchange at the end of each accounting year. Most managers will prefer to have those fluctuations counter-balanced by equivalent loans denominated in the same currency and thus fluctuating in sympathy.

It is sometimes suggested that earnings in one currency should be matched against interest payable in the same currency. This would be sensible if the foreign subsidiary's earnings (before interest) were expected to be stable in its own currency - or fluctuated in sympathy with interest rates in its own currency.

Example
Propinvest set up a subsidiary in Xland to buy land for X4m on 31.12.2000. Rates of exchange on 31st December were :

Year	2000	2001	2002
	X1 = £1	X1 = £2	X2 = £1

If the Propinvest group matches this investment with borrowing in Xs (and leaves the land at cost in its accounts) then its Consolidated Balance Sheets will now include the following figures :

at 31 December	2000	2001	2002
	£m	£m	£m
Land at cost	4	8	2
less Liability	4	8	2

If the Propinvest group matches this investment with borrowing in £s (and leaves the land at cost in its accounts) then its Consolidated Balance Sheets will now include the following figures :

at 31 December	2000	2001	2002
	£m	£m	£m
Land at cost	4	8	2
less Liability	4	4	4
	–	4	(2)

Financing a Foreign Subsidiary and Accounting with the Historical-Temporal Method

The Historical-Temporal method encourages financing investment in the Fixed Assets of foreign subsidiaries by borrowing in the home currency. Now the Fixed Assets of foreign subsidiaries on a Consolidated Balance Sheet will *not* be affected by the rate of exchange at the end of each financial year.

(However if the working capital requirements of the foreign business remain constant in the foreign currency, then these will fluctuate on Consolidated Balance Sheets. As with the Closing Rate Method this may encourage matching working capital investment with local finance.)

Example
Using the Propinvest example (see above), under the H-T method if the group matches this investment with borrowing in Xs (and leaves the land at cost in its accounts) then its Consolidated Balance Sheets will now include the following figures :

at 31 December	2000	2001	2002
	£m	£m	£m
Land at cost	4	4	4
less Liability	4	8	2
	–	(4)	2

If the group matches this investment with borrowing in £s (and leaves the land at cost in its accounts) then its Consolidated Balance Sheets will now include the following figures :

at 31 December	2000	2001	2002
	£m	£m	£m
Land at cost	4	4	4
less Liability	4	4	4

Currency Profits and Losses Netted Against Interest

On page 319 it was stated that (with one exception) exchange rate profits and losses *within* a company are usually treated as part of the standard profits on the P & L. In answering the following questions net such profits and losses against the related interest paid and received. You may need to refer to the last chapter (Chapter 8) because the following questions deal with consolidations where there are minority interests and pre-acquisition profits.

Further Reading

Accounting for Overseas Operations (Gower Publishing, 1986) C A Westwick

How to Account for Foreign Currencies (Macmillan, 1984) Jeff Pearcy

Currency Fluctuation (Woodhead-Faulkner, 2nd ed 1984) Wainman

SSAP20 Foreign Currency Translation (ASB)

Try to answer the following questions before looking at the answers (which are at the end of this chapter).

Modern Accounting 2

Question 9.8 (Answer 9.8 is on page 364)

The following draft Balance Sheets and Profit & Loss Accounts were extracted on 31st March 2000 for Thames plc and its overseas subsidiary Rhein GMBH :

	Thames £000		Rhein X000	
Fixed Assets				
Cost		9,000		8,000
Depreciation		3,000		2,000
		6,000		6,000
Shares in Rhein at cost - 90% interest acquired 1 April 1997		100		
Net Current Assets		7,900		14,000
		14,000		20,000
Creditors : amounts due after more than one year				
X Loans	1,000		1,000	
Y Loans	2,000	3,000	1,000	2,000
		11,000		18,000
Share Capital		3,000		4,000
Revenue Reserves		8,000		14,000
		11,000		18,000

Profit and Loss Accounts for the year to 31 March 2000

		Thames		Rhein
Trading profit		5,800		8,310
less interest :				
on loans denominated in X	200		250	
on loans denominated in Y	100	300	60	310
Profit before taxation		5,500		8,000
Taxation		1,500		2,000
		4,000		6,000
Dividend Paid		1,000		
		3,000		
brought forward		5,000		8,000
		8,000		14,000

The following information is relevant :

342

Foreign Currencies

1   Rhein's retained reserves at 1st April 1997 were 5,000 (in X000s)

2   The long term liabilities shown in the two draft Balance Sheets above (that are foreign currency liabilities to the company concerned) are not correctly stated. They have been left as the balances brought forward at the start of the year (translated into the respective currencies at the exchange rates ruling on 31.3.99). No new borrowing or repayment of nominal capital has been made during the year.

3   100 (in £000) of the X Long Term Liability shown on Thames' Balance Sheet was borrowed on 1 April 1997 to finance the purchase of shares in Rhein.

4   Rates of exchange have been :

	X to £	Y to £
1.4.97	5	20
1.4.99	5	19
Average for year to 31.3.00	6	18
1.4.00	7	17

5   The company uses the closing rate (net investment) method for consolidating foreign subsidiaries.

REQUIRED : Consolidated Accounts for Thames.

Modern Accounting 2

Question 9.9 (No answer to this question has been included in this book.)

The following draft Balance Sheets and Profit & Loss Accounts were extracted on 30th June 2000 for Mersey plc and its overseas subsidiary Elbe GMBH :

	Mersey £000		Elbe Z000	
Fixed Assets				
Cost		3,000		1,000
Depreciation		1,000		500
		2,000		500
Shares in Elbe at cost -				
60% interest acquired 1 July 1995		4,000		
Net Current Assets		5,000		2,000
		11,000		2,500
Creditors : amounts due after more than one year				
Z Loans	2,000		800	
L Loans	3,000	5,000	900	1,700
		6,000		800
Share Capital		1,000		100
Revenue Reserves		5,000		700
		6,000		800

Profit and Loss Accounts for the year to 30 June 2000

Trading profit		5,200		1,580
less interest :				
on loans denominated in Z	100		30	
on loans denominated in L	600	700	150	180
Profit before taxation		4,500		1,400
Taxation		1,500		800
		3,000		600
Dividend Paid		1,000		
		2,000		
brought forward		3,000		100
		5,000		700

Foreign Currencies

The following information is relevant :

1   Elbe's retained reserves at 1st July 1995 were 500 (in Z000s)

2   The long term liabilities shown in the two draft Balance Sheets above (that are foreign currency liabilities to the company concerned) are not correctly stated. They have been left as the balances brought forward at the start of the year (translated into the respective currencies at the exchange rates ruling on 30.6.99). No new borrowing or repayment of nominal capital has been made during the year.

3   All of the Z Long Term Liability shown on Mersey' Balance Sheet was borrowed on 1 July 1995 to finance the purchase of shares in Elbe.

4   Rates of exchange have been :

	Z to £	L to £
1.7.95	7	17
1.7.99	7	17
Average for year to 30.6.00	6	18
1.7.00	5	20

5   The company uses the closing rate (net investment) method for consolidating foreign subsidiaries.

6   Any Goodwill arising on the purchase of Elbe should be written against consolidated reserves.

REQUIRED : Consolidated Accounts for Mersey.

Modern Accounting 2

Answer 9.1

Share Capital

	£000		£000
		1.1.00 £ Cash Book	200

£ Cash Book

	£000		£000
1.1.00 Share Capital	200	1.2.00 B Cash Book	60
1.12.00 A Cash Book	110	(converted into B120,000)	
(converted from A600,000)		1.4.00 C Cash Book	40
		(converted into C200,000)	
		31.12.00 Balance c/f	210
	<u>310</u>		<u>310</u>

A Cash Book

	A000	£000		A000	£000
1.8.00 Customer	800	160	1.11.00 £ Cash Book	600	110
			31.12.00 Currency Loss		21
			31.12.00 Balance c/f	200	29
	<u>800</u>	<u>160</u>		<u>800</u>	<u>160</u>

B Cash Book

	B000	£000		B000	£000
1.2.00 £ Cash Book	120	60	1.9.00 Supplier of Goods	100	40
			31.12.00 Currency Loss		13
			31.12.00 Balance c/f	20	7
	<u>120</u>	<u>60</u>		<u>120</u>	<u>60</u>

C Cash Book

	C000	£000		C000	£000
1.4.00 £ Cash Book	200	40	1.7.00 Supplier of Plant	100	33
31.12.00 Currency Profit		43	31.12.00 Balance c/f	100	50
	<u>200</u>	<u>83</u>		<u>200</u>	<u>83</u>

Fixed Asset - Plant at Cost

	£000		£000
1.5.00 Supplier (C100,000)	25		

Supplier of Plant

	C000	£000		C000	£000
1.7.00 C Cash Book	100	33	1.5.00 Plant at cost	100	25
			31.12.00 Currency Loss		8
	<u>100</u>	<u>33</u>		<u>100</u>	<u>33</u>

Foreign Currencies

Purchases

	£000		£000
1.3.00 Supplier (B150,000)	100		
1.10.00 Supplier (B300,000)	<u>200</u>	31.12.00 P & L	<u>300</u>

Supplier of Goods for Resale

	B000	£000		B000	£000
1.9.00 B Cash Book	100	40	1.3.00 Purchases	150	100
31.12.00 Currency Profit		143	1.10.00 Purchases	300	200
31.12.00 Balance c/f	350	117			
	<u>450</u>	<u>300</u>		<u>450</u>	<u>300</u>

Sales

	£000		£000
		1.6.00 Customer (A800,000)	200
31.12.00 P & L	<u>300</u>	1.12.00 Customer (A600,000)	<u>100</u>

Customer

	A000	£000		A000	£000
1.6.00 Sales	800	200	1.8.00 A Cash Book	800	160
1.12.00 Sales	600	100	31.12.00 Currency Loss		54
			31.12.00 Balance c/f	600	86
	<u>1,400</u>	<u>300</u>		<u>1,400</u>	<u>300</u>

Currency Profits and Losses

	£000		£000
31.12.00		31.12.00	
Loss on C Liability to Supplier of Plant	8	Profit on B Liability to Supplier of Goods	143
Loss on holding A Currency	21	Profit on holding C Currency	43
Loss on holding A Debt from Customer	54		
Loss on holding B Currency	13		
P & L	90		
	<u>186</u>		<u>186</u>

The Final Accounts would appear as follows :

Modern Accounting 2

Profit and Loss Account for the Year to 31 December 2000

	£000	£000
Sales		300
Purchases	300	
less Closing Stock	60	240
Gross Profit		60
Depreciation		5
		55
Currency Profit		90
Net Profit		145

Balance Sheet as at 31st December 2000

	£000	£000
Fixed Asset		
Plant at cost	25	
less Depreciation	5	20
Current Assets		
Stock	60	
Debtor	86	
Cash in £	210	
Cash in As	29	
Cash in Bs	7	
Cash in Cs	50	
	442	
less Creditor due within one year	117	325
		345
Share Capital		200
Revenue Reserves		145
		345

(ii) the INTERFACE METHOD - £ RECORDS :

Share Capital

£000		£000
	1.1.00 £ Cash Book	200

£ Cash Book

	£000		£000
1.1.00 Share Capital	200	1.2.00 B Interface	60
1.12.00 A Interface	110	1.4.00 C Interface	40
		31.12.00 Balance c/f	210
	310		310

Foreign Currencies

A Interface

	£000		£000
		1.12.00 £ Cash Book	110

B Interface

	£000		£000
1.2.00 £ Cash Book	60		

C Interface

	£000		£000
1.4.00 £ Cash Book	40		

A RECORDS :

A Cash Book

	A000		A000
1.8.00 Customer	800	1.11.00 £ Interface	600
		31.12.00 Balance c/f	200
	<u>800</u>		<u>800</u>

£ Interface

	A000		A000
1.11.00 A Cash Book	600		

Sales

	A000		A000
		1.6.00 Customer	800
		1.12.00 Customer	600

Customer

	A000		A000
1.6.00 Sales	<u>800</u>	1.8.00 C Cash Book	<u>800</u>
1.12.00 Sales	600		

B RECORDS :

B Cash Book

	B000		B000
1.2.00 £ Interface	120	1.9.00 Supplier of Goods	100
		31.12.00 Balance c/f	20
	<u>120</u>		<u>120</u>

Modern Accounting 2

£ Interface

	B000		B000
		1.2.00 B Cash Book	120

Purchases

	B000		B000
1.3.00 Supplier	150		
1.10.00 Supplier	300		

Supplier of Goods for Resale

	B000		B000
1.9.00 B Cash Book	100	1.5.00 Purchases	150
31.12.00 Balance c/f	350	1.10.00 Purchases	300
	<u>450</u>		<u>450</u>

C RECORDS :

C Cash Book

	C000		C000
1.4.00 £ Interface	200	1.7.00 Supplier of Plant	100
		31.12.00 Balance c/f	100
	<u>200</u>		<u>200</u>

£ Interface

	C000		C000
		1.4.00	200

Fixed Asset - Plant at Cost

	C000		C000
1.5.00 Supplier	100		

Supplier of Plant

	C000		C000
1.7.00 C Cash Book	<u>100</u>	1.5.00 Plant at cost	<u>100</u>

Trial Balances for the T Accounts above

£ Trial Balance	£000	£000
Share Capital		200
£ Cash Book	210	
A Interface		110
B Interface	60	
C Interface	40	
	<u>310</u>	<u>310</u>

Foreign Currencies

	Dr	Cr		Dr	Cr
	A000	A000	Rate	£000	£000
A Trial Balance					
A Cash Book	200		7	29	
£ Interface	600		-	110	
Sales		1400	5		280
Customer	600		7	86	
Currency Loss				55	
	<u>1400</u>	<u>1400</u>		<u>280</u>	<u>280</u>
B Trial Balance	B000	B000	Rate	£000	£000
B Cash Book	20		3	7	
£ Interface		120	-		60
Purchases	450		2	225	
Supplier		350	3		117
Currency Profit					55
	<u>470</u>	<u>470</u>		<u>232</u>	<u>232</u>
C Trial Balance	C000	C000	Rate	C000	C000
C Cash Book	100		2	50	
£ Interface		200	-		40
Fixed Assets	100		4	25	
Currency Profit					35
	<u>200</u>	<u>200</u>		<u>75</u>	<u>75</u>

The Balance Sheet under the Interface Method will be the same as under the Traditional Method. The Profit and Loss Account is as follows :

Profit and Loss Account for the Year to 31 December 2000

	£000	£000
Sales		280
Purchases	225	
less Closing Stock	<u>60</u>	<u>165</u>
Gross Profit		115
Depreciation		<u>5</u>
		110
Currency Profit (55 - 55 + 35)		<u>35</u>
Net Profit		<u>145</u>

Modern Accounting 2

Answer 9.2

	Dr	Cr
£ Records - Journal Entries	£000	£000
Revenue Reserves		145
A Interface (Sales)	280	
B Interface (Purchases)		225
Stock	60	
Accumulated Depreciation		5
A Interface (Currency Loss)		55
B Interface (Currency Profit)	55	
C Interface (Currency Profit)	35	
	<u>430</u>	<u>430</u>
Fixed Asset	25	
C Interface	—	<u>25</u>
A Records - Journal Entries	A000	A000
Sales	1400	
£ Interface	—	<u>1400</u>
B Records - Journal Entries	B000	B000
£ Interface	450	
Purchases	—	<u>450</u>
C Records - Journal Entries	C000	C000
£ Interface	100	
Fixed Assets	—	<u>100</u>
Opening Trial Balances	Dr	Cr
	£000	£000
Fixed Asset at cost	25	
Fixed Asset - Depreciation		5
Stock	60	
£ Cash Book	210	
A Interface	115	
B Interface		110
C Interface	50	
Share Capital		200
Revenue Reserves		145
	<u>460</u>	<u>460</u>
	A000	A000
A Cash Book	200	
£ Interface		800
Customer	600	
	<u>800</u>	<u>800</u>

352

Foreign Currencies

	Dr	Cr
	B000	B000
B Cash Book	20	
£ Interface	330	
Supplier		350
	350	350

	C000	C000
C Cash Book	100	
£ Interface		100
	100	100

Answer 9.3

Closing Rate Consolidated Balance Sheets (at an exchange rate of 800 at 31.12.99 and 1,000 at 31.12.00)

	31.12.99 ₤000	31.12.99 ₤000	31.12.00 ₤000	31.12.00 ₤000
Fixed Assets				
Cost		1,375		1,100
Accumulated Depreciation		925		850
		450		250
Current Assets				
Stock	250		500	
Debtors	375		600	
Bank	25		10	
	650		1,110	
less Creditors due within one year	62	488	40	1,070
		938		1,320
less Creditors due after one year				
Loans denominated in BP		125		100
		813		1,220
Share Capital		800		800
Consolidated Revenue Reserves		13		420
		813		1,220

Historical-Temporal analysis of Fixed Assets :

Date of Purchase	Cost BPm	Exch Rate	Cost ₤000	Depn 99 BPm	Depn 99 ₤000	P & L ₤000	Depn 00 ₤000
1992	400	200	2,000	320	1,600	200	1,800
1994	700	400	1,750	420	1,050	175	1,225
	1,100		3,750	740	2,650	375	3,025

Modern Accounting 2

Consolidated Balance Sheet (HT) at

	31.12.99		31.12.00	
	£000	£000	£000	£000
Fixed Assets				
Cost		3,750		3,750
Accumulated Depreciation		2,650		3,025
		1,100		725
Current Assets				
Stock	250		500	
Debtors	375		600	
Bank	25		10	
	650		1,110	
less Creditors due within one year	62	488	40	1,070
		1,588		1,795
less Creditors due after one year				
Loans denominated in BP		125		100
		1,463		1,695
Share Capital		800		800
Consolidated Revenue Reserves		663		895
		1,463		1,695

Closing Rate Profit and Loss Account (av rate of 900)

	£000	£000
Sales		11,111
Cost of Sales		4,111
		7,000
Sundry Expenses	6,222	
Depreciation	122	6,344
Profit for the year		656

Historical-Temporal Profit and Loss Account

	£000	£000
Sales		11,111
Opening Stock	250	
Purchases	4,444	
	4,694	
less Closing Stock	500	
		4,194
		6,917
Sundry Expenses	6,222	
Depreciation	375	6,597
Profit for the year		320

Foreign Currencies

Movements on Consolidated Revenue Reserves

	Closing Rate £000	Hist-Temp £000
brought forward on 1.1.00 :		
Reserves of Alpha Ltd per own BS	200	200
Retained post-acquisition profit of subsidiary		
- diff between Net Assets of Beta at 31.12.99 and		
the original capital contributed of 1,000	(187)	463
	13	663
Profit for the year per P & L	656	320
	669	983
Exchange Rate Loss	249	88
Reserves at 31.12.00	420	895

Answer 9.4

Closing Rate Consolidated Balance Sheets (at an exchange rate of 700 at 31.12.99 and 900 at 31.12.00)

	31.12.99 £000	£000	31.12.00 £000	£000
Fixed Assets				
Cost		5,286		5,000
Accumulated Depreciation		2,807		3,522
		2,479		1,478
Current Assets				
Stock	1,728		2,645	
Debtors	1,786		2,633	
Bank	1,114		1,222	
	4,628		6,500	
less Creditors due within one year	1,143	3,485	1,722	4,778
		5,964		6,256
Share Capital		500		500
Consolidated Revenue Reserves		5,464		5,756
		5,964		6,256

Historical-Temporal analysis of Fixed Assets of Delta :

Date of Purchase	Cost SMm	Exch Rate	Cost £000	Depn 99 SMm	Depn 99 £000	P & L £000	Depn 00 £000
1985	400	800	500	300	375	25	400
1995	500	1,250	400	125	100	20	120
	900		900	425	475	45	520

355

Modern Accounting 2

<u>Consolidated Balance Sheet (HT)</u> at

	31.12.99		31.12.00	
	£000	£000	£000	£000
Fixed Assets				
Cost		4,900		4,900
Accumulated Depreciation		<u>2,675</u>		<u>3,520</u>
		2,225		1,380
Current Assets				
Stock	1,728		2,645	
Debtors	1,786		2,633	
Bank	<u>1,114</u>		<u>1,222</u>	
	4,628		6,500	
less Creditors due within one year	<u>1,143</u>	<u>3,485</u>	<u>1,722</u>	<u>4,778</u>
		<u>5,710</u>		<u>6,158</u>
Share Capital		500		500
Consolidated Revenue Reserves		<u>5,210</u>		<u>5,658</u>
		<u>5,710</u>		<u>6,158</u>

<u>Closing Rate Profit and Loss Account</u> (av rate of 800)

	£000	£000
Sales (11,800 + 6,890,000/800)		20,412
Cost of Sales (8,700 + 5,900,000/800)		<u>16,075</u>
		4,337
Sundry Expenses (2,000 + 700,000/800)	2,875	
Depreciation (800 + 45,000/800)	<u>856</u>	<u>3,731</u>
Profit for the year		<u>606</u>

<u>Historical-Temporal Profit and Loss Account</u>

	£000	£000
Sales		20,412
Opening Stock (1,300 + 300,000/700)	1,728	
Purchases (9,600 + 6,000,000/800)	<u>17,100</u>	
	18,828	
less Closing Stock (2,200 + 400,000/900)	<u>2,645</u>	
		16,183
		4,229
Sundry Expenses	2,875	
Depreciation (800 + 45)	<u>845</u>	<u>3,720</u>
Profit for the year		<u>509</u>

Foreign Currencies

<u>Movements on Consolidated Revenue Reserves</u>
	Closing Rate £000	Hist-Temp £000
brought forward on 1.1.00 :		
Reserves of Gamma Ltd per own BS	4,300	4,300
Retained post-acquisition profit of subsidiary		
- diff between Net Assets of Delta at 31.12.99 and		
the original capital contributed of 100	<u>1,164</u>	<u>910</u>
	5,464	5,210
Profit for the year per P & L	<u>606</u>	<u>509</u>
	6,070	5,719
Exchange Rate Loss	314	61
Reserves at 31.12.00	<u>**5,756**</u>	<u>**5,658**</u>

Answer 9.5 *(a) CCA in raw currency*

[A] Current Cost of <u>Plant</u> - Gamma

Date of Purchase	Historic Cost £000	Factor	Current Cost 31.12.99	Factor	Current Cost 31.12.00
1997	3,000	130/110	3,545	140/110	3,818
1998	<u>1,000</u>	130/120	<u>1,083</u>	140/120	<u>1,167</u>
	<u>**4,000**</u>		<u>**4,628**</u>		<u>**4,985**</u>

[B] Accumulated Depreciation/Replaciation - Gamma

Date of Purchase	Acc Dep 31.12.99	Factor	Acc Rep 31.12.99	Acc Dep 31.12.00	Factor	Acc Rep 31.12.00
1997	1,800	130/110	2,127	2,400	140/110	3,055
1998	<u>400</u>	130/120	<u>433</u>	<u>600</u>	140/120	<u>700</u>
	<u>**2,200**</u>		<u>**2,560**</u>	<u>**3,000**</u>		<u>**3,755**</u>

[C] Current Cost of Plant - <u>Delta</u>

Date of Purch	Hist Cost SMm	Factor	CC '99 SMm	CC '99 £000	Factor	CC '00 SMm	CC '00 £000
1985	400	160/105	610	871	170/105	648	720
1995	<u>500</u>	160/140	<u>571</u>	<u>816</u>	170/140	<u>607</u>	<u>675</u>
	<u>**900**</u>		<u>**1,181**</u>	<u>**1,687**</u>		<u>**1,255**</u>	<u>**1,395**</u>

[D] Accumulated Depreciation/Replaciation - Delta

Date of Purchase	Dep '99 SMm	Rep '99 SMm	Rep '99 £000	Dep '00 SMm	Rep '00 SMm	Rep '00 £000
1985	300	457	653	320	518	576
1995	<u>125</u>	<u>143</u>	<u>204</u>	<u>150</u>	<u>182</u>	<u>202</u>
	<u>**425**</u>	<u>**600**</u>	<u>**857**</u>	<u>**470**</u>	<u>**700**</u>	<u>**778**</u>

Modern Accounting 2

[E] Year to 31.12.00 - P & L Replaciation - Gamma

Date of Purchase	Hist Cost P & L Dep'n	Factor	Replaciation	Depreciation Adjustment
1997	600	135/110	736	
1998	200	135/120	225	
	800		961	161

[F] Year to 31.12.00 - P & L Replaciation - Delta

Date of Purchase	Dep'n SMm	Factor	Rep'n SMm	D A SMm	Exchange Rate	D A £000
1985	20	165/105	31			
1995	25	165/140	29			
	45		60	15	800	19

[G] COSA - Gamma (a)   (c)

	Hist Cost	Factor	CC Midpoint	diff (a) v (c)
Opening Stock	1,300	120/102	1,529	229
Closing Stock	2,200	120/138	1,913	287
				516

[H] COSA - Delta

	Hist Cost SMm	Factor	CC Mid SMm	diff SMm	Exchange Rate	COSA £000
Opening Stock	300	130/120	325	25		
Closing Stock	400	130/140	371	29		
				54	800	67

[I] Current Cost Reserve

			Gamma			Delta
	£000	£000	£000	SMm	SMm	SMm
CC Plant '99 [A] & [C]			4,628			1,181
Acc Rep'n '99 [B] & [D]			2,560			600
			2,068			581
Hist Cost NBV			1,800			475
Balance at 31.12.99			268			106
Year to 31.12.00 :						
COSA [G] & [H]			516			54
Increase in CC Plant [A] & [C] :						
CC 31.12.00		4,985			1,255	
CC 31.12.99		4,628			1,181	
			357			74
			1,141			234
less Backlog Replaciation :						
Acc 31.12.00 [B] & [D]	3,755				700	
Acc '99 [B]&[D] 2,560				600		
P & L [E]&[F] 961	3,521		234	60	660	40
Balance at 31.12.00			907			194

Foreign Currencies

CCA Balance Sheets		Gamma		Delta
	31.12.99	31.12.00	31.12.99	31.12.00
	£000	£000	SMm	SMm
CC of Plant [A/C]	4,628	4,985	1,181	1,255
Acc Rep'n [B/D]	2,560	3,755	600	700
	2,068	1,230	581	555
Shares in subsid	100	100		
Net Current Assets	2,900	4,000	410	700
	5,068	5,330	991	1,255
Share Capital	500	500	100	100
CC Reserve [I]	268	907	106	194
Revenue Reserves	4,300	3,923	785	961
	5,068	5,330	991	1,255

CCA P & L Year to 31.12.00	Gamma		Delta
	£000	SMm	SMm
HC Profit per Q	300		245
COSA [G] & [H]	516	54	
DA [E] & [F]	161	15	
	677		69
CC (Deficit) Surplus on trading	(377)		176
Revenue Reserves b/f per Q	4,300		785
Revenue Reserves c/f as above	3,923		961

CCA Consolidated Balance Sheets

		31.12.99		31.12.00
	£000	£000	£000	£000
Fixed Assets				
Replacement Cost [A] + [C]		6,315		6,380
Accumulated Replaciation [B] + [D]		3,417		4,533
		2,898		1,847
Current Assets [as Closing Rate Answer 9.4]				
Stock	1,728		2,645	
Debtors	1,786		2,633	
Bank	1,114		1,222	
	4,628		6,500	
less Creditors within 1 yr [Ans 9.4]	1,143	3,485	1,722	4,778
		6,383		6,625
Share Capital		500		500
Current Cost Reserve [I] (268 + 106 @ 700)	419		
(907 + 194 @ 900)			1,123
Consolidated Revenue Reserves		5,464		5,002
		6,383		6,625

CCA Consolidated Profit and Loss Account
Year to 31st December 2000

	£000	£000	£000
Sales [as Answer 9.4]			20,412
Historic Cost of Sales [as Closing Rate Ans 9.4]	16,075		
add Cost of Sales Adjustment [G] + [H]	_583_		
Replacement Cost of Sales		<u>16,658</u>	
		3,754	
Sundry Expenses [as Answer 9.4]		2,875	
Historic Cost Depreciation [as Closing Rate Ans 9.4]			
	856		
Depreciation Adjustment [E] + [F]	_180_		
Replaciation		<u>1,036</u>	3,911
Current Cost (Deficit) on Trading			<u>(157)</u>

Movements on Consolidated Revenue Reserves

	£000
brought forward on 1.1.00 [as Answer 9.4]	5,464
Current Cost Deficit on Trading	_157_
	5,307
Exchange Rate Loss	305
Reserves at 31.12.00	<u>5,002</u>

Answer 9.5 (b) CCA in £CPP

[J] Net Monetary Assets

		31.12.99	31.12.00
		£000	£000
Per Consolidated Balance Sheets earlier :			
Debtors		1,786	2,633
Bank		<u>1,114</u>	<u>1,222</u>
		2,900	3,855
less Creditors		<u>1,143</u>	<u>1,722</u>
		<u>1,757</u>	<u>2,133</u>

Movements in Net Monetary Assets :	£000	£000	£000
brought forward (as above)			1,757
Sales (as earlier Consol P & L)		20,412	
Purchases (as H-T Ans 9.4)	17,100		
Sundry Expenses (as earlier)	2,875		
Currency Loss on holding SMs			
(as H-T Answer 9.4)	_61_	20,036	_376_
carried forward (as above)			<u>2,133</u>

Foreign Currencies

Monetary Loss in £000CPP$_{31.12.00}$ on holding 1,757 for the whole year and 376 from the midpoint to the end of the year :

$$1{,}757 \times \frac{180 - 170}{170} + 376 \times \frac{180 - 175}{175} = 114$$

[K] <u>Historic Cost of Sales in £CPP</u>

	£000CPP$_{31.12.00}$
Opening Stock 1,729 X 180/170	1,830
Purchases 17,100 X 180/175	<u>17,589</u>
	19,419
less Closing Stock	<u>2,645</u>
	<u>16,774</u>
Replacement Cost of Sales (16,658 from part (a))	
16,658 X 180/175	<u>17,134</u>
Therefore Holding Gain on stock in £000CPP$_{31.12.00}$	
17,134 - 16,774	<u>360</u>

[L] <u>Plant</u>   £000CPP$_{31.12.00}$
CC NBV at 1.1.00 :
Per part (a) - £000 2,898
2,898 X 180/170   3,068

Replaciation in P & L per part (a) - £000 1,036
1,036 X 180/175   <u>1,066</u>
                                                2,002
CC NBV at 31.12.00 (Per part (a))   <u>1,847</u>
Holding Loss on plant   <u>155</u>

CCA Consolidated Balance Sheets in CPP

'00 Net Assets as per part (a); '99 Net Assets as per part (a) indexed to £CPP by multiplying by 180/170 :

	31.12.99		31.12.00	
	£000CPP$_{31.12.00}$		£000CPP$_{31.12.00}$	
Fixed Assets				
Replacement Cost		6,686		6,380
Accumulated Replaciation		<u>3,618</u>		<u>4,533</u>
		3,068		1,847
Current Assets				
Stock	1,830		2,645	
Debtors	1,891		2,633	
Bank	<u>1,180</u>		<u>1,222</u>	
	4,901		6,500	
less Creditors within 1 yr	<u>1,210</u>	3,691	<u>1,722</u>	4,778
		<u>6,759</u>		<u>6,625</u>

Modern Accounting 2

	£000CPP$_{31.12.00}$	£000CPP$_{31.12.00}$
Net Assets 1.1.00	6,759	6,759
CCA Deficit on trading		276
		6,483
Holding Gain on Stock [K]	360	
Holding Loss on Plant [L]	155	205
		6,688
Currency Loss (61 X 180/175)		63
		6,625

CCA Consolidated Profit and Loss Account in CPP
Year to 31st December 2000

		£000CPP$_{31.12.00}$
Sales 20,412 X 180/175		20,995
Replacement Cost of Sales 16,658 X 180/175		17,134
		3,861
Sundry Expenses 2,875 X 180/175	2,957	
Replaciation 1,036 X 180/175	1,066	
Monetary Loss [J]	114	4,137
Current Cost (Deficit) on Trading		(276)

Answer 9.5 (c) Historic Cost in £CPP

[M] Cost of Plant

Date of Purchase	Cost £000	Factor	Cost £000CPP$_{31.12.00}$
Gamma :			
1997	3,000	180/140	3,857
1998	1,000	180/160	1,125
	4,000		4,982
Delta (see H-T Answer 9.4 for £ Costs) :			
1985	500	180/100	900
1995	400	180/120	600
	900		1,500
Consolidated	4,900		6,482

[N] Depreciation on Plant

Date of Purchase	Accumulated 31.12.99 £000	Accumulated 31.12.99 £000CPP	P & L £000	P & L £000CPP	Accumulated 31.12.00 £000CPP
Gamma :					
1997	1,800	2,314	600	771	3,085
1998	400	450	200	225	675
	2,200	2,764	800	996	3,760

Foreign Currencies

Date of Purchase	Accumulated 31.12.99 £000	Accumulated 31.12.99 £000CPP	P & L £000	P & L £000CPP	Accumulated 31.12.00 £000CPP
Delta (see H-T Answer 9.4 for £ Dep'n) :					
1985	375	675	25	45	720
1995	100	150	20	30	180
	475	825	45	75	900
Consolidated	2,675	3,589	845	1,071	4,660

Historic Cost Consolidated Balance Sheets in CPP

	31.12.99 £000CPP$_{31.12.00}$	31.12.00 £000CPP$_{31.12.00}$
Fixed Assets		
Cost [M]	6,482	6,482
Accumulated Depreciation [N]	3,589	4,660
	2,893	1,822
Current Assets (as CCA in CPP)		
Stock	1,830	2,645
Debtors	1,891	2,633
Bank	1,180	1,222
	4,901	6,500
less Creditors within 1 yr	1,210 3,691	1,722 4,778
	6,584	6,600

	£000CPP$_{31.12.00}$	£000CPP$_{31.12.00}$
Net Assets 1.1.00	6,584	6,584
Trading Profit		79
		6,663
Currency Loss (as CCA in CPP)		63
		6,600

Historic Cost Consolidated Profit and Loss Account in CPP

Year to 31st December 2000   £000CPP$_{31.12.00}$

Sales (as CCA in CPP)		20,995
Opening Stock [K]	1,830	
Purchases [K]	17,589	
	19,419	
less Closing Stock	2,645	16,774
		4,221
Sundry Expenses (as CCA in CPP)	2,957	
Depreciation [N]	1,071	
Monetary Loss [J]	114	4,142
Profit on Trading		79

Answer 9.8

[A] <u>Rhein</u> at 31.3.<u>99</u> (last year's Balance Sheet)

	X000	£000
Net Assets :		
Share Capital	4,000	
Reserves (brought fwd on P & L)	8,000	
	12,000 @ 5X=£	2,400

[B] <u>Rhein</u> at 31.3.<u>00</u> :

	X000	£000
Fixed Assets - Cost	8,000 @ 7X=£	1,143
Acc Depreciation	2,000	286
	6,000	857
Net Current Assets	14,000	2,000
	20,000	2,857
Long Term Loans :		
Denominated in X	1,000	143
Denominated in Y 1,000 X 19/5 X 7/17 (see note 2)		
	1,565	224
	17,435	2,490
Share Capital	4,000	
Revenue Reserves (taking account of note 2)	13,435	
	17,435	

Shareholders' Equity last year (31.3.99) [A]		2,400
Profit this year to 31.3.00 :		
per draft accounts	6,000	
less currency loss on Y loan	565	
translated at average rate	5,435 @ 6X=£	906
		3,306
Net Assets above at year end rate		2,490
Therefore <u>currency loss on consolidation</u>		<u>816</u>

[C] <u>Minority</u> Interests (Balance Sheet) at 31.3.00
10%   0.1 X 2,490 [B]   249

[D] <u>Rhein</u> at 31.3.<u>97</u> (date of purchase)

	X000	£000
Net Assets :		
Share Capital	4,000	
Reserves (note 1)	5,000	
	9,000 @ 5X=£	1,800

Thames purchased 90% of Rhein at 31.3.97, therefore net asset backing behind the shares at the date of purchase :

0.9 X 1,800	1,620
Cost of Shares	100
<u>Capital Reserve</u> arising on consolidation	<u>1,520</u>

[E] Consolidated Revenue Reserves

	£000	£000
Thames :		
Per draft accounts in question		8,000
Currency Gains (losses) on Long Term Loans :		
(i) X loan to invest in Rhein (note 3)		
100 X (7 - 5)/7	29	
(ii) Remaining X loans		
900 X (7 - 5)/7	257	
(iii) Y Loan		
2,000 X (19 - 17)/17	(235)	51
		8,051
Rhein :		
Post Acquisition 1.4.97 to 1.4.99		
Net Assets 1.4.99 [A]	2,400	
Net Assets 1.4.97 [D]	1,800	
	600	
0.9 X 600	540	
This year's profit 906 (in £000) [B]		
Thames' share : 0.9 X 906	815	
Currency Loss on consolidation [B]		
0.9 X 816	(734)	621
		8,672

Consolidated Balance Sheet at 31 March 2000

	£000	£000
Fixed Assets		
Cost 9,000 + 1,143[B]	10,143	
Depreciation 3,000 + 286[B]	3,286	6,857
Net Current Assets 7,900 + 2,000[B]		9,900
		16,757
Creditors : amounts due after more than one year		
Denominated in X 1,000-29[E]-257[E]+143[B]	857	
Denominated in Y 2,000 + 235[E] + 224[B]	2,459	3,316
		13,441
Share Capital		3,000
Capital Reserve arising on consolidation [D]		1,520
Consolidated Revenue Reserves [E]		8,672
		13,192
Minority Interests [C]		249
		13,441

Profit and Loss Accounts in £000s
Year to 31 March 2000

	Thames	Rhein @ 6X=£	Consolidated
Trading Profits	5,800	1,385	7,185
Interest payable	(300)	(52)	
Currency Gains [E] 257-235	22		
Currency Losses [B]		(94)	
Net Cost of Finance			424
Profit before taxation	5,522	1,239	6,761
Taxation	1,500	333	1,833
Profit after taxation	4,022	906	4,928
Minority Interests			91
			4,837
Dividend Paid	1,000		1,000
	3,022	906	3,837

Note to the accounts :
Consolidated Revenue Reserves
brought forward (Thames 5,000 + Rhein[E] 540)		5,540
Currency Losses		
(on consol 734 less gain on X loan to fund inv 29)		705
		4,835
Retained Profit for the year (see above)		3,837
		8,672

Chapter Ten

Interdivisional Pricing

'Interdivisional Pricing' refers to prices set for transactions between two entities that are wholly owned by the same group. Sometimes these transactions are between two divisions of the same company. Sometimes these transactions are between two separate companies both of which have the same holding company.

If one company makes sales to its *partly-held* subsidiary (or associated company), then this does *not* involve interdivisional pricing because the two entities are not wholly owned and a part of the transactions can be considered to be made outside the group.

Definitions

For the purposes of the discussion in this chapter the 'intermediate' or 'intermediate product' is the good or service transferred from one part of the group to another part. The 'consuming division' is the part of the group that buys and pays for the intermediate. The 'producing division' is the part that sells the intermediate to the consuming division.

For example Pressed Steel Fisher is part of the Rover car group. It stamps out car body parts and sells them to the car assembly parts of the Rover group. In this case the assembly plants are the 'consuming divisions', the car body parts are the 'intermediate products' and Pressed Steel Fisher is the 'producing division'.

Reasons for Interdivisional Pricing

Sometimes managers of divisions within groups criticise the current interdivisional pricing policies without initially asking why the group has any policy at all. Why account for transactions between one part of a group and another part of the same group? Why have a price between wholly owned entities? The two main reasons are examined below :

1 Legal requirement for separate accounts

Every company has to produce its own separate set of statutory accounts. If one company has provided goods or services to another company in the same group, then a charge must be made in order to meet the statutory obligations of incorporation. If (i) both companies are (and always have been) profitable, (ii) both companies are incorporated and operate in the UK, (iii) the statutory accounting obligations are the only reasons for making the charge and (iv) no management decisions will be taken based on accounting figures influenced by the charge, then the precise price may not be important. Such a charge merely reallocates profit from one arm of the group to another.

2 Management Control and Decision Making

Managers may want to know the 'profit' made by different parts of the organisation. Since these 'profit' figures may be dependant on the interdivisional prices, they may need to be treated with caution and they may lead to irrational decision-making. Managers may also believe that separate profit statements for different parts of the group will change employee motivation. They may help to provide targets for profit and for cost reduction.

Other Factors Affecting Interdivisional Pricing

1 Separate Tax Regimes

If two companies in the same group operate in different countries, then the group may try to arrange for profit to be made wherever it suffers the least tax. Companies operating in high tax areas will be encouraged to make low charges for any services rendered to other group companies but may accept high charges from other group companies. Companies operating in low tax areas will be encouraged to make high charges for any services rendered to other group companies but will receive low charges from other group companies.

The authorities of high tax areas will be aware that this is likely and will look for evidence to challenge inter-group transfer prices. They may have the ability to conduct surprise searches of the company's hard copy and computer files. They are unlikely to accept that internal management accounting data can be produced using one set of charges and statutory accounts can be produced using different rates. The costs incurred and revenues made outside the high tax area can become highly sensitive data that is never revealed within the high tax area. Thus an attempt to minimise group taxation can result in the managers of individual companies taking management decisions on the basis of incomplete and/or misleading information.

3   Exchange Control

Some countries operate exchange control restrictions to restrict the export of capital and income. Such restrictions have the same effect as high tax regimes. They encourage companies in their territories to charge as little as possible when selling to other group companies outside the country and to pay as much as possible when buying from group companies outside the country.

Exchange controls are difficult to enforce and lead to black and 'grey' markets in the currency. The government itself may try to manage several different currency markets - ostensibly for different purposes - perhaps trying to separate an 'investment' currency market from a 'consumer product' currency market. Politicians will always be tempted to blame 'speculators', foreigners and racial minorities for the ill effects of exchange controls. Calls for patriotism to 'enable exchange controls to work' may lead to authorities taking ever more draconian powers to examine the transfers of international groups. This means that exchange controls are even more likely than high taxation to prevent local managers being given information on the true costs and revenues of other parts of the group.

4   Price Control and Price Negotiation

A group of companies may wish to arrange for the company selling the final product into a particularly visible market to appear

Modern Accounting 2

to make a low profit. Sometimes there are official price controls but more often this device is to aid negotiations and relations with important customers, consumer groups and those acting on behalf of consumers.

5   Employee Motivation and Demotivation.

Many employees wish to act in the best interests of their employer. If their local company appears to make a loss on certain activities, then it is difficult to motivate them to increase the volume of those activities. If they believe that certain costs incurred within the group could be reduced by sub-contracting outside the group, they may have little loyalty to the group (even though they are completely loyal to their local company).

Open discussion of divisional profits and losses can be a powerful motivator reminding the team of the profit objective. But a secretive attitude suggests dishonesty. There are few human activities where it is easy to motivate a team without letting them know the results of their previous actions. Sports coaches do not ask their charges to 'do their best' while refusing to let them know the score. Neither do such coaches tell them the score in ambiguous ways suggesting that the result depends on the method of measurement.

In many businesses junior staff take important decisions relating to price negotiation, customer service and the selling effort put behind different products. Sometimes the top managers are not aware of the importance of these decisions by juniors. Transfer prices will influence all these decisions. If the price to an external customer is £20 per unit and the price to another group company is £10 per unit, then it seems logical to most employees to satisfy the external customer first and let the group company wait.

Different Bases for Calculating Interdivisional Prices

1   Open Market Value

Tax gatherers and authorities policing exchange control normally argue that transfer prices should be on the basis of 'market value'. If there is an open market for the product where no individual purchasers or vendors dominate the market and every day hundreds of sales of identical product are sold at competitive prices in open view, then it is possible to determine 'market value'.

If intergroup transfers are made at market value, then it seems logical that the profits made in each part of the group should be an indication of which companies should be expanded, which contracted and how the managers of the different companies should be rewarded. One key assumption behind the concept of market value is that the purchasing company could obtain all its current requirements for the intermediate product with the same (or better) long-term reliability by buying outside the group at the market price. The same is true for the producer of the intermediate product. It is implied that the producer could sell all the units currently sold within the group (both now and in the future) to outside customers at the market price.

If transfers at market price make the producer of the intermediate make a loss while the consumer of the intermediate makes a handsome profit, then it seems logical to close down the producer. If transfers at market price make the consumer of the intermediate make a loss while the producer of the intermediate makes a handsome profit, then it seems logical to close down the consumer. This assumes that (a) the current market situation is expected to continue, (b) these losses are caused by relevant costs and not by sunk costs or allocated common costs (see Chapter 15 of Modern Accounting 1) and (c) there is no way of improving the efficiency of the loss making group company.

However many inter-group transfers are of unique services and components. Managers can spend a long time arguing what charge an external supplier would make were they to be offered the business but 'market value' can never be determined with any precision while the current internal supplier exists. It can be that such a value can be estimated with an upper estimate just 20% above the lower estimate but the upper estimate makes the producer very profitable while the lower estimate drives it into loss.

2   Cost Plus

Under a Cost Plus system of transfer prices the producers of the intermediate calculate their cost, add on a profit margin based on a percentage of cost and then charge that to the consumer company. Such a system actively discourages efficiency in the producing company because the higher their costs the greater their apparent profits.

This system is in surprisingly widespread use. Frequently the managers of such groups persuade themselves that this system is equivalent to market value pricing because 'every producer's costs must be roughly the same'. It is easier to make that assumption than to question the costs and efficiencies of colleague companies. Most managers are aware that transfer prices may influence decisions to close down certain parts of the group and it can appear more politic and kinder to adopt this system.

A few years of cost plus transfers will drive most groups into heavy overall losses. The accounts show that the losses are all made in the companies consuming intermediate products from other parts of the group but, before their consuming part of the group is closed down, even the most shy managers tend to argue that the transfer pricing system has allowed the costs of the intermediate producers to destroy their business. They are likely to claim that they would be profitable if they could buy the intermediate outside the group.

3   Market Minus

Several groups in the early 1990s are in the position described in the last paragraph. They are moving towards Market Minus transfer pricing. Under this system the transfer price of the intermediate is determined as the price charged for the final product outside the group less a percentage. Thus the profits of the consuming companies will be (a) a straight percentage of the total outside sales less (b) the costs incurred within the consuming companies. If the consuming companies are simple distribution and sales operations with Fixed Costs but no Variable Costs, then the consuming companies will maximise their own profits when they maximise total sales. This will mean that (assuming normal demand curves) the consuming companies will have an incentive to set selling prices lower than those required to maximise group profits.

Even where the consuming companies are not simple distribution channels but have variable costs of their own, they will not be influenced by the variable costs of the producers of the intermediate and thus they will not have an incentive to set selling prices so that Marginal Revenue equals Group Marginal Cost (see Chapter 15 of Modern Accounting 1).

4 Fixed Basis

Sometimes managers are unable to agree on any one of the three bases described above. Eventually a senior manager from the group head office may insist that transfers are made at an arbitrary price which is centrally determined and appears to have no relation to the costs of the producing company, the selling prices of the consuming company or to any market-price (if one exists) for the intermediate product.

Conflicts between Profit Maximisation for the Group and That for an Individual Company

If the companies making sales outside the group are able to control their own selling prices, they will have an incentive to set selling prices (i) higher than the optimal point (from the group's point of view) if transfer prices are set on a cost-plus or on a fixed basis and (ii) lower than the optimal point (from the group's point of view) if transfer prices are set on a market minus basis.

Example of Transfers on a Fixed Basis

Air Supplies Ltd and Filternational Ltd are part of the same group. Air Supplies Ltd. sell a part used by the aerospace industry called a 'cleanair unit'. Each cleanair unit requires one 'microfilter'. Air Supplies buy all microfilters from Filternational Ltd at a transfer price of £600 per filter. As usual no competitor produces a product which is precisely identical to those of Air Supplies or those of Filternational but there are several competitors producing products that are fairly similar. Whether the outside customers are fully aware of the competing products and their similarities is difficult to say.

Neither Air Supplies nor Filternational have any significant capacity constraints. At present Air Supplies sell each cleanair unit for £1,500 and they sell 200 such units each week. They believe that the market is price sensitive and, while their product is better than those produced by the competitors, their selling prices are 'uncompetitive'. They estimate that they could sell 400 units each week if the price were dropped to £1,400. At present each week Filternational sell 200 microfilters to Air Supplies for £600 and 300 microfilters to outside customers for £800 each.

Modern Accounting 2

Each cleanair unit has a variable cost to Air Supplies of £1,375 which is (a) £600 for the microfilter plus (b) £775 for other variable costs. Each microfilter has a variable cost to Filternational of £450. The fixed costs per week are £20,000 for Air Supplies and £130,000 for Filternational. The current profits per week of the two companies will be as follows :

	Air Supplies £000	Air Supplies £000	Filternational £000
Sales to Outside Customers :			
200 Cleanair Units @ £1,500		300	
300 Microfilters @ £800			240
Transfers of Microfilters within the group :			
200 Microfilters @ £600	120		120
			360
Outside variable costs :			
200 units @ £775	155	275	
500 units @ £450			225
Contribution		25	135
Fixed Costs		20	130
Profits		5	5

If the estimate of Cleanair units that could be sold at £1,400 each is correct (and lowering that price has no impact on any other factor) the profits per week of the two companies if Air Supplies drops its price to £1,400 will be as follows :

	Air Supplies £000	Air Supplies £000	Filternational £000
Sales to Outside Customers :			
400 Cleanair Units @ £1,400		560	
300 Microfilters @ £800			240
Transfers of Microfilters within the group :			
400 Microfilters @ £600	240		240
			480
Outside variable costs :			
400 units @ £775	310	550	
700 units @ £450			315
Contribution		10	165
Fixed Costs		20	130
(Loss) Profit		(10)	35

Thus group profits per week at current prices are (5 + 5) £10,000. If Air Supplies lowered its price, then group profits would rise to (-10 + 35) £25,000 per week. Air Supplies would show worse results but this would still benefit the group. So long as the current transfer price between the two companies obtains, it is unlikely that the managers of Air Supplies will wish to lower their prices.

The managers of Filternational are probably complaining that the current transfer price is too low in comparison with the price they can obtain from outside customers but, if it was raised, it would induce the managers of Air Supplies to increase the price of Cleanair units. The result depends on the impact that such a further price hike would have on sales volume but, if the demand curve for Cleanair units is linear, this would further reduce group profits.

This example implies that interdivisional transfer pricing above marginal cost to the group will lead to over-pricing of the final product. This is often true but it needs to be qualified in two respects. There is a later section in this Chapter on links between the outside demand for the intermediate and the price charged for the final product. There is also a section on how the costs of businesses are not outside the control of those businesses but are affected by the motivation of managers to reduce them and how that motivation may be affected by transfer pricing at marginal cost.

Example of Transfers on a Market Minus Basis

Chips Galore Ltd and Partstronic Ltd are part of the same group. Chips Galore sell an integrated circuit called a Powerdivider exclusively through Partstronic. Partstronic sell a variety of electronic products as well as the Powerdividers from Chips Galore.

Neither Chips Galore nor Partstronic have any significant capacity constraints. At present Partstronic sell 500 Powerdividers each week for £500 each. The managers of Partstronic estimate that they could sell 1,000 Powerdividers each week if the price were dropped to £400. The transfer price between Chips Galore and Partstronic is fixed at 80% of total sales value achieved outside the group.

Each Powerdivider has a variable cost to Chips Galore of £300. The variable cost of each Powerdivider to Partstronic is (a) the transfer price to Chips Galore plus (b) £10 for other variable costs. Partstronic makes sales of other products amounting to £100,000 per week on which it incurs variable costs of £80,000 per week. The fixed costs per week of Chips Galore are £40,000. The fixed costs per week of Partstronic are £60,000.

The current profits per week of the two companies will be as follows :

	Partstronic £000	Partstronic £000	Chips Galore £000
Sales to Outside Customers :			
Other Products		100	
500 Powerdividers @ £500		250	
		350	
Transfers of Powerdividers within the group :			
80% of outside sales value	200		200
Variable Costs on Powerdividers	5		150
Variable costs on other products	80	285	
Contribution		65	50
Fixed Costs		60	40
Profits		5	10

If the estimate of Powerdividers that could be sold at £400 each is correct (and lowering that price has no impact on any other factor) the profits per week of the two companies if Partstronics drops the price to £400 will be as follows :

	Partstronic £000	Partstronic £000	Chips Galore £000
Sales to Outside Customers :			
Other Products		100	
1,000 Powerdividers @ £400		400	
		500	
Transfers of Powerdividers within the group :			
80% of outside sales value	320		320
Variable Costs on Powerdividers	10		300
Variable costs on other products	80	410	
Contribution		90	20
Fixed Costs		60	40
Profit (Loss)		30	(20)

Thus group profits per week at current prices are (5 + 10) £15,000. If Partstronic lowered its price, then group profits would fall to (30 - 20) £10,000 per week. Partstronic would show better results but this would still harm the group. So long as the current transfer price arrangements between the two companies obtain, it is almost inevitable that the managers of Partstronic will wish to lower their prices below the point at which group profits are maximised.

The managers of Chips Galore are probably demanding that they (a) be allowed to set minimum selling prices for Partstronic or (b) be allowed to set up their own distribution business in competition with Partstronic or to sell to other distributors outside the group. The managers at the centre of the group may refuse these demands in the hope that Chips Galore will react to the current situation by reducing its costs.

Transfers at Marginal Cost

In Chapter 15 of Modern Accounting 1 there is a discussion on setting selling prices. This must involve estimating the reaction of customers to different prices - in other words, estimating the relationship between the volume demanded and the price charged. This relationship is normally referred to as the 'demand curve'. In that Chapter it was stated that profits are maximised when marginal revenue equals marginal cost.

Thus it appears logical to set transfer prices at marginal cost to the producing division because this will encourage the consuming division to set the selling price of the final product at the point where it will maximise group profits. Most businesses assume a simple cost model with Fixed Costs and Variable Costs and thus they assume that marginal cost per unit equals a constant Variable Cost per unit.

If transfer prices are set in this way, the Producing Division will always make a loss equal to its Fixed Costs. The Producing Division has no hope of making a profit and has no incentive to control its costs. The Consuming Division should initially make large apparent profits because it is not being charged with any of the Producing Division's Fixed Costs and neither is it being charged a profit margin by the Producing Division. Such easy large apparent profits in the

Consuming Division may well discourage the Consuming Division from actively controlling their costs.

Thus a system which appears wholly logical only works if the motivational impact on the control of costs can be ignored. Transfer Pricing on a marginal cost basis does encourage sensible setting of selling prices but its disadvantages are likely to prevent most groups from adopting it.

The Impact of the Price Charged for the Final Product on the Market for the Intermediate Product

An unstated but key assumption behind the analysis of the Air Products/Filternational example was that the price charged by Air Products for Cleanair units had no impact on the outside sales of Microfilters by Filternational. In practice it is normal to assume that the higher the price charged for the final product, the better the demand for the intermediate product. Some of the outside purchasers of the intermediate are likely to be competitors to the consuming division. The higher the volume of sales made by the consuming division, the more that competition will be squeezed.

Olivetti assemble personal computers (PCs) and they also own a manufacturer of microprocessors which sells both to other parts of Olivetti and to other assemblers. Each PC requires at least one microprocessor. If one could assume that Olivetti were a significant player in the PC market, they could have at least a temporary impact on the general market price of PCs which, in turn would have an impact on the pricing and profitability of their microprocessor operations.

Reasons for Separating Divisions

The discussion in this Chapter so far may appear to suggest that groups of companies are best managed from the centre. If one could ignore the human element, this must be true because all information can (in theory) be marshalled in the centre and the centre can be given the objective of maximising group profits (rather than the profits of individual divisions).

However one *cannot* ignore the human element. The workers, managers, customers and suppliers of businesses are all human beings with separate needs, wills and agendas. There is plenty of evidence that human beings ensure that organisations above a certain size grow inefficiencies.

Autonomy for Each Division versus Central Control

The more autonomy that is granted to each division, the more the managers of that division can be held responsible for their own results and the more that those working for a division can identify with the interests of *their* division.

However we have already seen that maximisation of a division's profits is not necessarily the same as maximisation of group profits. There are likely to be conflicts of interests between the heads of each division because each will recognise the others as competitors for the next promotion within the group. It may be in their personal interests *not* to co-operate and to do all they can to reduce the profits of the other divisions within the group.

Tied Vendors and Tied Purchasers

Much discussion within many groups of companies concerns whether one part of the group should be able to buy from outside the group even though similar goods or services are available from within the group. Equally some vendors may prefer not to supply internal group customers - especially if the vendor has capacity constraints or if the vendor believes that the internal customers make unreasonable demands or are poor payers.

Several large UK groups try to get different divisions to agree interdivisional transfer prices between themselves with no direction from the centre. They talk of 'internal markets' and 'arms length transactions'. However sometimes this market philosophy stops short of allowing consumers to buy externally or allowing producers to refuse to sell internally. 'Negotiations' can be somewhat of a sham if one side knows that the other side has to agree.

It is a common belief that internal suppliers are the worst suppliers to a consuming division and an equally common belief that internal customers are the worst customers of a producing division. A normal reason for these beliefs and attitudes is that the relationship between supplier and customer is not one that either side believes that it has freely entered into - or believes that it can freely exit from. Given the tied nature of the relationship it is not surprising that many of the supplies are provided in a bloody-minded fashion and that the consuming division reponds with like-minded behaviour.

Central Services

The numerical examples in this Chapter have concerned the transfer of intermediate *goods* between a producing division and a consuming division (mainly because it is easier to devise examples with clear unit costs and prices). However the same principles apply to the provision of services such as computing, accounting, office accomodation, maintenance, design, cleaning, light, heat and power.

Further Reading

Divisional Performance : Measurement and Control (Financial Executives Research Foundation Inc, New York, 1965) David Solomons

Strategies and Styles : the Role of the Centre in Managing Diversified Corporations (Basil Blackwell, 1987) Michael Goold & Andrew Campbell

Pricing Decisions : A Practical Guide to Interdivisional Pricing Policy (Business Books, 1979) Alexander Young

Transfer Pricing : Techniques and Uses (National Association of Accountants, US, 1980) Ralph L Benke Jr & James Don Edwards

Try to answer the following questions before looking at the answers (which are at the end of this chapter).

Interdivisional Pricing

Question 10.1 (Answer 10.1 is on page 383)

Howard Machinery Ltd and Pumpomatic Ltd are part of the same group. Howard Machinery Ltd. sell an industrial washing machine. Each washing machine requires one water pump. Howard Machinery buy all water pumps from Pumpomatic Ltd at a transfer price of £50 per pump. As usual no competitor produces a product which is precisely identical to those of Howard Machinery or those of Pumpomatic but there are several competitors producing products that are fairly similar. Whether the outside customers are fully aware of the competing products and their similarities is difficult to say.

Neither Howard Machinery nor Pumpomatic have any significant capacity constraints. At present Howard Machinery sell each washing machine for £1,000 and they sell 100 such units each week. They estimate that they would sell only 40 units each week if the price were raised to £1,100. At present each week Pumpomatic sell 100 water pumps to Howard Machinery and 300 water pumps to outside customers for the same price of £50 each.

Each washing machine has a variable cost to Howard Machinery of £960. This variable cost is (a) £50 for the water pump plus (b) £910 for other variable costs. Each water pump has a variable cost to Pumpomatic of £5. The fixed costs per week of Howard Machinery are £3,000. The fixed costs per week of Pumpomatic are £16,000.

REQUIRED :
(a) Calculate the profits per week made by each company (i) in the present situation and (ii) if the selling price of each washing machine was £1,100.
(b) Advise (i) the group and (ii) the management of Howard Machinery on whether it is worth raising the current selling price by £100 and the assumptions behind your calculations in (a) above.
(c) Assuming that the demand curve for Howard Machinery's product is linear, calculate the selling price for washing machines that will maximise group profits and show the profits per week for each company if this pricing policy is adopted.

Question 10.2 (Answer 10.2 is on page 385)

FM Industrie SA and Flow (UK) Ltd are part of the same group. FM Industrie SA sell a FlowMeter which is distributed in the UK exclusively by Flow (UK). Flow (UK) sell a variety of products as well as the FlowMeters from FM Industrie SA.

Neither FM Industrie SA nor Flow (UK) have any significant capacity constraints. At present Flow (UK) sell 100 FlowMeters each week for £100 each. The managers of Flow (UK) estimate that they could sell 150 FlowMeters each week if the price were dropped to £80. The transfer price between FM Industrie SA and Flow (UK) is fixed at 80% of total sales value achieved outside the group.

Each FlowMeter has a variable cost to FM Industrie SA of £60. The variable cost of each FlowMeter to Flow (UK) is (a) the transfer price to FM Industrie SA plus (b) £5 for other variable costs. Flow (UK) makes sales of other products amounting to £5,000 per week on which it incurs variable costs of £3,000 per week. The fixed costs per week of FM Industrie SA are very high but these are shared between its business in several world markets. The fixed costs per week of Flow (UK) are £2,500.

REQUIRED :

(a) Calculate the profits per week made by each company (i) in the present situation and (ii) if the selling price of each FlowMeter was £80.

(b) Advise (i) the group and (ii) the management of Flow (UK) on whether it is worth dropping the current selling price by £20 and the assumptions behind your calculations in (a) above.

(c) Assuming that the demand curve for FlowMeters is linear, calculate the selling price for FlowMeters that will maximise group profits and show the profits per week made by each company if this pricing policy is adopted.

Answer 10.1

Current profits per week :

	Howard Machinery £000	£000	Pumpomatic £000
Sales to Outside Customers :			
100 Washing Machines @ £1,000	100		
300 Pumps @ £50			15
Transfers of Pumps within the group :			
100 Pumps @ £50	5		5
			20
Outside variable costs :			
100 units @ £910	91	96	
400 units @ £5			2
Contribution		4	18
Fixed Costs		3	16
Profits		1	2

If the estimate of Washing Machines that could be sold at £1,100 each is correct (and raising that price has no impact on any other factor) the profits per week of the two companies if Howard Machinery raises its price to £1,100 will be as follows :

	Howard Machinery £	£	Pumpomatic £
Sales to Outside Customers :			
40 Washing Machines @ £1,100	44,000		
300 Pumps @ £50			15,000
Transfers of Pumps within the group :			
40 Pumps @ £50	2,000		2,000
			17,000
Outside variable costs :			
40 units @ £910	36,400	38,400	
340 units @ £5			1,700
Contribution		5,600	15,300
Fixed Costs		3,000	16,000
Profit (Loss)		2,600	(700)

Thus group profits per week at current prices are (1 + 2) £3,000. If Howard Machinery raised its price, then group profits would fall to (2.6 - 0.7) £1,900 per week but Howard Machinery's own profits would rise. The assumptions are as in the example on page 374. The general formula for a linear demand curve is $P = A - BQ$ (see Chapter 15 of Modern Accounting 1). In this example we have 2 price points and quantities :

Modern Accounting 2

£1,000 = A - 100 B and £1,100 = A - 40 B.

Therefore B = 5/3 and A = 1,167 and the demand curve must be
$$P = 1,167 - 5Q/3.$$

Multiply both sides by Q to get Total Revenue (PQ):
$$PQ = 1,167 Q - 5 Q^2 / 3$$

Differentiate to get Marginal Revenue (dPQ/dQ) :
$$dPQ/dQ = 1,167 - 10 Q / 3$$

Marginal Cost to the group is the sum of the external variable costs incurred within Pumpomatic (£5) and within Howard (£910). Therefore Group Marginal Cost is £915. At the optimal point Marginal Cost equals Marginal Revenue :
$$915 = 1,167 - 10 Q / 3$$
Therefore Q = 75.6 say 76 units. Fitting this Q into the demand curve :
$$P = £1,167 - (5 \times 76) / 3 = £1,040$$

Thus the optimal price for washing machines (from the group's point of view) is £1,040 at which point 76 machines per week would be sold. The profits per week of each company would be as follows :

	Howard Machinery		Pumpomatic
	£	£	£
Sales to Outside Customers :			
76 Washing Machines @ £1,040		79,040	
300 Pumps @ £50			15,000
Transfers of Pumps within the group :			
76 Pumps @ £50	3,800		3,800
			18,800
Outside variable costs :			
76 units @ £910	69,160	72,960	
376 units @ £5			1,880
Contribution		6,080	16,920
Fixed Costs		3,000	16,000
Profit		<u>3,080</u>	<u>920</u>

Interdivisional Pricing

Answer 10.2

Current profits per week :

		Flow (UK)	FM Industrie
	£	£	£
Sales to Outside Customers :			
Other Products		5,000	
100 FlowMeters @ £100		10,000	
		15,000	
Transfers of FlowMeters within the group :			
80% of outside sales value	8,000		8,000
Variable Costs on FlowMeters	500		6,000
Variable costs on other products	3,000	11,500	
Contribution		3,500	2,000
Fixed Costs		2,500	not known
Profits		1,000	

If the estimate of FlowMeters that could be sold at £80 each is correct (and lowering that price has no impact on any other factor) the profits per week of the two companies if Flow (UK) drops the price to £80 will be as follows :

		Flow (UK)	FM Industrie
	£	£	£
Sales to Outside Customers :			
Other Products		5,000	
150 FlowMeters @ £80		12,000	
		17,000	
Transfers of FlowMeters within the group :			
80% of outside sales value	9,600		9,600
Variable Costs on FlowMeters	750		9,000
Variable costs on other products	3,000	13,350	
Contribution		3,650	600
Fixed Costs		2,500	not known
Profit		1,150	

Although the question does not give us the Fixed Costs of FM, we can tell that lowering the selling price of FlowMeters must reduce group profits because it reduces the total contribution of both companies - although it raises the profits of Flow (UK). The assumptions are as stated in the example on page 376.

385

The general formula for a linear demand curve is P = A - B Q (see Chapter 15 of Modern Accounting 1). In this example we have 2 price points and quantities :
$$£100 = A - 100 B \text{ and } £80 = A - 150 B.$$

Therefore B = 0.4 and A = 140 and the demand curve must be
$$P = 140 - 0.4 Q.$$

Multiply both sides by Q to get Total Revenue (PQ):
$$PQ = 140 Q - 0.4 Q^2$$

Differentiate to get Marginal Revenue (dPQ/dQ) :
$$dPQ/dQ = 140 - 0.8 Q$$

Marginal Cost to the group is the sum of the external variable costs incurred within Flow (UK) (£5) and within FM (£60). Therefore Group Marginal Cost is £65. At the optimal point Marginal Cost equals Marginal Revenue :
$$65 = 140 - 0.8 Q$$
Therefore Q = approximately 94 units. Fitting this Q into the demand curve :
$$P = £140 - 0.4 \times 94 = £102.40$$

Thus the optimal price for FlowMeters (from the group's point of view) is £102.40 at which point 94 machines per week would be sold. The profits per week of each company would be as follows :

	Flow (UK) £	Flow (UK) £	FM Industrie £
Sales to Outside Customers :			
Other Products		5,000	
94 FlowMeters @ £102.40		9,626	
		14,626	
Transfers of FlowMeters within the group :			
80% of outside sales value	7,700		7,700
Variable Costs on FlowMeters	470		5,640
Variable costs on other products	3,000	11,170	
Contribution		3,456	2,060
Fixed Costs		2,500	not known
Profits		956	

This is such a small change from the present position that it is unlikely that it is worth implementing especially since it depends on assumptions such as a linear demand curve.

Chapter Eleven

Computer Accounting

Computer 'Accounting' almost always means Computer Book-keeping. An accounting program may produce printed Balance Sheets and Profit and Loss Accounts but these often need hand modification and they are not the main purpose of most systems. The main purpose is to handle large quantities of transaction data. Sometimes the term 'Executive Systems' is used to sell programs which provide summaries and analysis of the transaction data and these Executive Systems may be closer to accounting than book-keeping. In the following discussion Word Processing and Spreadsheets are not included in the definition of 'Computer Accounting' or 'Computer Systems'.

A Common Standard for Accounting Packages?

Most novices approach this area knowing that it is possible to describe the 'traditional' hand-written book-keeping records. Modern Accounting 1 contained Chapter 17 which illustrated all the main traditional books. Given this background it surprises most novices that it is not possible to describe a formula that everyone follows for computer accounting.

The Advantages of Computer Systems :

1   Set formats are provided for tasks with menus and prompts to help the user.

2   Information is held in Electronic Files. These are easy to sort and, if the certain details of each query have been

programmed in advance, they make it easy to retrieve information.

3. Calculations can be automated improving speed and accuracy.
4. If the task has those elements at which computer systems excel, then speed of transaction processing is improved. This can improve customer service - for example by giving faster and more reliable delivery times.
5. Over the long term computers may reduce the costs of data processing.

The Disadvantages of Computer Systems :

1. Set routines have to be devised for each sort of transaction. These should cover all possible transactions in a category and so may include time-wasting sub-routines not needed for many transactions of the same category.
2. The set routines may not cover some transactions. There will always be an odd circumstance not envisaged when the routines were established.
3. Electronic files are inherently less secure than hand-written media. They cannot be read directly by human eye and are not permanently embedded in their media. There is no 'fingerprint' similar to hand-writing to indicate the author of the data.
4. Most computer systems are (a) less dependant on the hardware and (b) more dependant of the training and documentation provided to those will use them than many business managers realise. This leads to the installation of systems which the staff are unable to operate.
5. Computer systems require specification in advance of (a) transaction types and numbers, (b) requirements for output and (c) methods of input. Since businesses alter over time, these specifications rarely reflect the current requirements.
6. Computer systems can be slower than alternatives if (a) the systems are poorly designed or (b) the tasks are not suitable for the designed system.

7   Computer systems can be frustrating when they fail. All computer systems have bugs. Most expensive custom-designed systems have serious bugs.
8   Businesses can become dependant on systems which their senior managers do not understand.
9   In the short run Computer Systems are more expensive than hand-written systems.

What Makes an Area Suitable for a Computer Application?

1   A large number of transactions with common elements.
2   The ability to forecast with reasonable accuracy the data that will be input and the information required as output.
3   A body of staff who will act as operators and actively want (or can be persuaded) to use a computer system.
4   A clearly identifiable business benefit from instituting a new computer system. Frequently these arise from integrating accounting systems with other business systems and they can result in improved customer service, job control, stock control or cash collection.
5   The availability of a generous budget for installation and documentation of the new system and staff training.

The above list should make it clear that, for many small businesses, full computer accounting systems are not suitable. They do not have large numbers of transactions with common elements, they are in a state of perpetual flux and are not able to forecast their input or output requirements, they employ people may be suspicious of any new system, they have not identified any clear business benefit from instituting a new computer system and they have insufficient funds to install the system or release staff for training. Such small businesses would be better advised to confine their computing requirements to word processing and spreadsheets. Much of their 'hand-written' records can be produced on spreadsheets.

Linking (Integrating) Accounting Systems With Other Systems

Traditional accounting records are expressed solely in currency; they do not attempt to trace physical movements of goods or to handle non-currency units of measure. The serious business benefits that most often arise from Computer Accounting come from links to systems for (i) order taking from customers, (ii) maintaining records of uncompleted orders (the 'order book'), (iii) customer records and customer service details, (iv) stock records and (v) stock ordering from suppliers.

Without these links it would be difficult to justify the cost of many business computer accounting systems. These links can make the benefits of maintaining electronic files outweigh the security (and other) disadvantages.

Technical Aspects :
Files, Records, Fields and Characters

The order of the above terms is deliberate. Computer Files contain several Records. Records contain several Fields and Fields contain Characters. The structure of a computer accounting system's files, records and fields may not follow a traditional system but it is easier to introduce these concepts with an illustration where each element has an easily recognised counterpart.

Many businesses store copies of their sales invoices in a binder. Within that binder documents are in Invoice Number order. The computer equivalent of the binder would be a 'file'. Each copy invoice would be a separate 'record' in the file.

Let us assume that each invoice follows a set format with just four pieces of information. (i) The invoice number appears at the top followed by (ii) the date, then (iii) the customer's name and finally (iv) the sum owed. Each of those separate pieces of information would be a 'field' within each record. If a computer system were to adopt a file and record structure which mirrored the paper binder, it would be essential to ensure that all sales invoices had all four fields in the same order and that no invoices had any more than these four fields. The first field is the invoice number field and normally the first field is the 'key field'. A key field is the field used for sorting records within a file.

There are several ways of expressing dates such as DDMMYY (12.03.99) or DDMMMYY (12 MAR 99). Which ever method is specified all field 2s must follow it within each record. If DDMMYY is chosen, then field 2 may be 6 characters long. It is unlikely that separators (full stops) between the day and month (and month and year) will be included. However an extra character may be added to the end of each field as an 'end of field marker'. Each one of the characters is coded as a number between 0 and 255 inclusive. Such numbers can be contained in a 'byte' of 8 binary digits. The best known coding system for the English alphabet is ASCII but other coding systems used to be common and can still be found in traditional mainframe environments.

File Sizing

Any computer system is designed with maximum file sizes. If these are exceeded the response time will become unacceptably slow and past a certain point the system itself will refuse to operate.

With hand-written records the capacity limits are easier to accept because they are visible. Once a binder is full, it is obvious that more binders are required. If the present system requires clerks to have immediate access to a whole hall full of binders, then it is evident that the current system must be broken down into more manageable units.

Unfortunately electronic storage is more difficult to envisage and businesses can exceed the capacity limits of their computer accounting systems.

File, Record and Field Specifications

These specifications are set when the system is designed and it is vital that they are understood by those who will oversee the operation of the system and by those who will attempt to amend the system in the future. Most systems will use files with fixed record and field lengths. In other words, field 3 of one record will have the same number of characters as field 3 of another record and each record will consist of the same number of fields.

The requirements of most businesses change over time. There must be a delay between designing a system and installing it and so most systems are already solutions for yesterday's problem by the time they are installed. This means that the File, Record and Field Specifications will be subject to many modifications and it becomes necessary to maintain records of different versions of the specifications.

For this reason a number of 'fourth generation' languages and database systems provide means of separating the programmer from the precise way in which a file will be maintained in order that a new field can be added to each record without wholesale amendments to every read or write operation in every program that uses that file.

The Systems Life Cycle

Older textbooks on Data Processing describe the 'Systems Life Cycle' in great detail. This breaks down the process of installing a new computer system into 5 or 6 stages with feasibility studies, the establishment of committees and system specifications all occurring well before any large expenditure is made. Essentially a contract is to be made between (a) those who will install the system, (b) user departments and (c) the top management authorising the expenditure and recognising the implications of this project on future IT projects. Several books admit that many real installations do not follow these 5 or 6 stages and they ascribe the failure of many large installations to the absence of one or other of the initial stages of the life cycle.

There are hidden assumptions behind the Systems Life Cycle. It is assumed that (a) the organisation is exceptionally stable and very large, (b) the new system will be very expensive, (c) that the process of installation will be long (probably more than one year) and (d) that, once installed, the 'solution' will remain in place for an even longer time. In practice even large and stable organisations are attracted by new hardware and software developments and any long installation will find that the 'contract' signed by user departments is difficult to enforce. The longer the managers of user departments wait, the more likely they are to demand changes in the specifications.

Today it is often recognised that it is preferable to break a large project down into smaller self-contained stages and to 'prototype'. If the users who provided the specifications are still doing the same jobs and if they are given some benefit as shortly as possible after they specified, there is more likely to be a constructive dialogue between user departments and analysts.

Open-Item and Balance-Forward Sales Ledger Systems

Traditional hand-written sales ledger accounts are 'balance-forward' systems. At the end of every month the balance is carried from one side of the account to be bought to the other side - but no attempt is made on the face of the account to analyse the balance into which particular invoices are still outstanding. An 'open-item' system distinguishes between those sales invoices which have been paid by the customer (the 'closed items') and those that are still outstanding (the 'open items'). This distinction can be a major benefit of a computerised sales ledger - especially if it is combined with programs for automatically generating statements and debt collection letters.

An Example of a Sales Ledger File

Each record in this file has 6 fields as follows :

1. Customer number (Primary Key Field)
2. Flag for Transaction Type - 1 = Invoice; 2 = Receipt. (Secondary Key Field)
3. Invoice reference number/Receipt reference number (Tertiary Key Field)
4. Date (DDMMYY)
5. Invoice total value in pennies/Receipt total value in pennies.
6. Flag for Open or Closed status - 1 = Closed; 2 = Open.

This is a simplification of what is normally required. No provision has been made for transactions which are not simple invoices or receipts. Note that fields 2 and 6 will be 'flags' which will contain numbers that indicate some fact about the record. Field 1 (the customer number) would point to a record in a master file of customer names and addresses; it is not good practice to repeat such data in the records of each transaction for that customer. The first 7 records of the file appear as follows :

Field :	1	2	3	4	5	6
Record :						
1	1011	1	158	110100	10000	1
2	1011	1	165	150100	25000	1
3	1011	2	298	270200	35000	1
4	1012	1	150	100100	11000	2
5	1012	1	162	150100	36500	2
6	1012	1	171	160100	10000	2
7	1012	2	292	260200	9000	2

Modern Accounting 2

These records can printed out in traditional format as follows :

Customer number 1011 : Bloggs Ltd

2000	£	2000	£
11 Jan Invoice 158	100.00		
15 Jan Invoice 165	250.00	27 Feb Receipt 298	350.00
	350.00		350.00

Customer number 1012 : Greens Ltd

2000	£	2000	£
10 Jan Invoice 150	110.00		
15 Jan Invoice 162	365.00	26 Feb Receipt 292	90.00
16 Jan Invoice 171	100.00	28 Feb Balance c/f	485.00
	575.00		575.00
01 Mar Balance b/f	485.00		

As the accounting year progresses, this sales ledger file will grow as more invoices and receipts are added to it. The calculation of balances on each account and summary statistics can be left to be done by programs on each printout or screen display. Often only at the ends of accounting years would fully closed items more than 6 months old at the year end be weeded from the file.

Bought In Packaged Computer Accounting Software

Packaged software obviously suffers from the disadvantage that it has not been designed for any specific business and it is unlikely to bring the advantages of integrating the book-keeping with other parts of the business. If the staff who will operate the system have not used this particular package before, they will need training courses and/or a long time experimenting and studying the manuals.

However the real advantages of packaged software arise when the same staff work for a number of businesses all of which use the same package. Then the initial costs of training and experimentation can be minimised.

Further reading

The Accountants' Guide to Computer Systems (John Wiley 1982) William E Perry

Chapter Twelve

Monthly Management Information Packs

'Executive computer systems' were mentioned in the last chapter. These systems allow managers to view accounting data on screens and to obtain printouts which each manager can tailor to show only the information which that manager requires and in the format required. These systems will become more popular but they may not replace the traditional monthly information packs (MIPs) that are common in large businesses because (a) not all managers wish to spend much time at computer terminals and (b) the MIP is a form of 'publishing'. In this context 'publishing' means that a manager will read the monthly pack not only to gain information but also because each managers knows that all the other managers will read the MIP.

Profit Data in MIPs

The front page of most MIPs resembles a detailed Profit and Loss Account for the whole business. One column shows the actual results for the month just ended, the next shows the budget for the month just ended and frequently there are two further columns showing the actual and budget figures for the year-to-date. Less often the actual results for the equivalent month last year are shown and equally infrequently moving annual totals - giving a full 12 months to the end of the month just ended - are included.

The variances are the differences between the actual figures and the budgeted figures. These variances may be shown with the other figures but usually there are too many columns already on the main P & L statement and, if variances are shown at all, there are relegated to a separate page. It can be very effective if the items with significant variances are printed in bold type while the items close to budget are printed in a less dramatic font.

Balance Sheets in MIPs

Balance Sheets are often less significant in the MIP. The pages containing the data tend to come after those dealing with the Profit and Loss Account and they are shown in less detail. This is partly because the Fixed Assets, Long Term Liabilities and Shareholders' Funds are outside the control of many of the recipients of the MIP and tend to be more stable over the year.

The parts of a Balance Sheet that will normally be highlighted will be those relating to working capital - especially those relating to stocks and debtors. Unfortunately some of the stock figures may well be inaccurate because full physical stock counts may not take place each month. This is particularly unfortunate because many UK businesses are trying to tighten control on stocks, to move further towards 'just in time' manufacturing and to push Return on Capital Employed as a measure on which managers should be judged.

Splitting the Results Between the Different Parts of a Business

The way in which a business is divided for reporting purposes in the MIP can be a sensitive issue causing argument between managers. The more divisions are made the easier it is to see which parts of the business are performing better than others. However, equally, the more divisions are made the worse are the problems over transfer pricing and dividing common overheads. The profits of one area may be dependant on the sales of another area. Typically the spare parts side of an engineering business is dependant on the sales of the complete product division. For example car manufacturers often make low percentage margins on their sales of completed cars but high percentage margins on their sales of spare parts.

If the parts division is separated from the main car assembly division, the parts division may appear much more successful. The sales of parts are not directly related to the sales of completed cars in the *same* year. However if the car assembly division were closed, the parts business might wither over the next eight years.

Data on Future Events

The page after the financial results of the immediate past month will often contain the budget for the current month and the month following. If possible, data on the outstanding order book should be on the same page in order that managers can compare it with the budget and see how much is yet to be sold. If the order book can be expressed in a way that makes the individual orders recognisable, this enables managers to make adjustments as orders are cancelled, increased and brought forward.

The data on how expenses have been incurred for the future is frequently less satisfactory in MIPs. It is surprising how many managers keep their own running records of how they have arranged future items in their expenditure budgets. Some of the reasons for not sharing the data with other managers are explored in the case study on Dysfunctional Budgeting in the next Chapter.

Non-Monetary Units

Many accountants automatically express data in monetary units. The first figure on their profit statements will be Total Sales in pounds. When asked, they may analyse those sales by product category but they are likely to keep the units in pounds. In a consumer electronics business they might say that the sales were £30,000 Televisions and £20,000 Hi-Fi Units.

Yet many non-accountants relate more easily to data in non-monetary units. If the sales and production figures are expressed in units of product, they may have greater impact with many managers. In the electronics business it may be better to say that 300 TVs and 400 Hi-Fi Units were sold. The money values should also be shown - but not just in total but also by average value per unit.

In retail chains the money values per store and per square metre of selling space should be shown. Data relating to numbers of employees joining, leaving and continuing in the period should be shown next to employment costs and production and sales per employee.

Common Costs, Sunk Costs and Relevant Costs - Relating Financial Accounts to Data for Decision-Making

In Chapter 15 of Modern Accounting 1 it was explained that, for certain management decisions, Common Costs and Sunk Costs should be ignored. (Common Costs are those which will be the same no matter which decision is taken and Sunk Costs are those which have already been incurred and cannot be avoided.) Some managers find it difficult to accept that management accounting data can be produced on a different basis from the financial accounting data. In particular they find it difficult to ignore costs which will affect the profits shown in financial accounts and they are suspicious of internal documents which appear to show 'only half the picture'.

If a schedule has been produced ignoring common and sunk costs in order that known decisions can be taken, it is wise not to use the word 'profit' but instead to refer to a 'Surplus before Common Costs'. Where possible, the internal management accounting figures should be reconciled with the financial accounting figures. Even where the reconciliation is complicated, it is better to include it in an appendix in order that no reader believes that something is being hidden from them.

Data on Stocks and Average Production Costs

Many businesses wish to persuade their production managers of the virtues of Just-in-Time manufacturing and the maintenance of minimum stock levels. The persuasion is likely to be ineffective if the MIPs (a) highlight average production costs per unit including overheads and (b) do *not* highlight stock levels in days of usage and sales.

Average production costs per unit are normally minimised by working a plant to capacity with large batch runs ignoring fluctuating market demand for individual products. Production managers exhibit rational behaviour when they build for stock if they believe that (a) they are judged on average production costs and (b) that the loudest complaints arise when demands for product cannot be met on time.

Discussion Topics

1. Consider the reports that should be included in the MIP of a car assembly plant such as the Dagenham plant of Ford or the Cowley plant at Rover.
2. Consider the reports that should be included in the MIP of a supermarket group such as the J Sainsbury or Tesco.
3. Consider the reports that should be included in the MIP of a professional practice such as a firm of consulting engineers with 200 employees.

Suggestions for further reading relating to this topic are on page 407.

Chapter Thirteen

Budgeting

'Budgeting' is a term which covers several connected activities with separate objectives :

1   Forecasting the Future

An objective forecast of what is most likely to happen in the coming accounting period should highlight limiting factors. There may be a shortage of capital, labour, materials or plant capacity if no avoiding action is taken. Logically one might hope for more than one forecast. In theory there must be a series of probability distributions but it would rarely be sensible to ask most practical business people for the mean or standard deviation of any of them. Asking for the (a) most likely, (b) worst and (c) best scenarios will obtain a better response.

2   Motivation of Principals and Staff

Some businesses tie the budgeting process to the setting of goals for individual members of staff and (by implication) for departments and groups of staff. This is almost always the case with sales and marketing staff but it can be applied to staff handling expenditure if the goals are expressed in terms of a given performance for a given sum of expenditure. There are different theories as to how best to motivate staff to give the best performance. It has been suggested that goals should be set just above those most likely to be achieved. It is also claimed that staff can be de-motivated if goals are rarely met and are better motivated if goals are almost always attained.

3   Allocation of Expenditure Limits

There are managers in large businesses who have spent no time in Sales Departments. They often think of budgets as being authorities to spend up to a certain limit. In large organisations where the culture is not profit-orientated the budgeting process can be largely concerned with squabbles as to whose expenditure budget is to be increased and whose expenditure budget is to be cut. There are circumstances in which it can be difficult to determine effective measures of the outputs from certain expenditure departments and hence to assess their cost-effectiveness or whether the business needs them to expand or contract.

4   Part of the Monitoring and Control Process

Some accountants see the budgeting process as a means to obtain agreed standards against which actual performance can be judged. This idea is reasonable if the original standards (or budgets) are logical.

5   Setting and Communicating Common Goals and Reinforcing Team Identities

In larger organisations the profit objective may not be clear to many staff in their day-to-day work. It is suggested that if staff are involved in setting budgets (or, at the least, provided with budget data) they will be reminded of the need for profit to ensure the organisation's survival. It is also suggested that some staff may be reminded that they are part of a sub-group within a team and that their actions will have an effect on other members of the team.

6   Two-Way Communication Between Junior Staff and Top Management

Writers on this subject frequently refer to the need for full *commitment* from all members of staff to the budget and how this can be obtained from a 'bottom up' approach. It is suggested that the alternative 'top down' approach - where top managers merely dictate their requirements - leads to stifling the ideas of the rest of the team, low morale and a lack of commitment.

It is normally accepted that even the most democratic bottom up approach will be 'iterative'. In other words the data will originate from lower level managers and then be refined, edited and added to before being returned the original lower level managers for their further comments or approval. The iterative nature of the process means that the proposed budget data should go up and down the levels of the organisation until each level has indicated full approval. Cynics wonder how often this approval is fully freely given (or, in practice, asked for from all low level managers).

7 Raising Fresh Finance and Communicating With Current Financiers

Publicly quoted companies are usually advised to give presentations on their prospects to investment analysts. Banks, other lenders and providers of new equity may ask for business plans and forecasts of future profits before committing fresh finance or agreeing to extend existing arrangements. If the financiers are wise they will ask to see the internal budget data circulating between managers to reconcile how this ties in with the business plans that they have been shown. In large organisations these requests are anticipated and this may influence acceptable budget data and the willingness to indulge in a wholly bottom up approach.

Conflicts in the Above Objectives.

The first objective (forecasting) requires an honest appraisal of the *range* of possible futures. In theory such an objective forecast would be best prepared by somebody with access to all company information but without any personal career to pursue within the business. In practice, however, the individuals preparing forecasts are likely to be part of the management team and immersed in the internal politics of the company.

All the other objectives require single-point forecasts (that is ignoring the full range of possibilities) set either just above or just below the most likely outcome (in other words, the mode of the probability distribution).

Concentrating on the third objective (Allocating Expenditure Limits) can destroy team-working and any motivational benefits. In many larger organisations it leads to managers deliberately 'padding' their forecasts - in other words, building in hidden 'slush funds' to cover contingencies. If managers believe that underspent budgets result in lower expenditure limits in the following year, it can lead to illogical expenditure close to the year-end.

The Budget Cycle

Most companies use their standard accounting year as their budget year and this can produce excessive work-loads in accounting departments just before and just after the year-end. There are a very few large publicly quoted groups which start their budget year half way through their financial accounting year. One hotel group has a 31st December financial accounting year-end and a 30th June budget year-end. This spreads the work more evenly for the accounting departments but (in other less tightly controlled groups) it might lead to confusion amongst the other managers.

The initial data for the preparation of the budget is normally collected at least 6 months before the start of the budget year. Different businesses have different approaches to how often the figures are sent back and forth between the different levels of managers, how much 'bottom up' input is sought and how much commitment and agreement is required from different levels. The final budget figures are normally signed off approximately a month before the start of the budget year.

While the preparation of next year's budget proceeds, the monthly management information packs analyse the differences between this year's actual outcome versus this year's budget. That analysis may well affect next year's budget.

The time taken by non-financial managers on the budgeting process differs between businesses. There are some (normally unsuccessful) businesses where the process is one seen as an accounting function requiring little time or commitment from non-financial managers. There are other businesses (often more successful) where the non-financial managers spend a surprisingly high proportion of their time on this process.

Budgets, Forecasts, Tactical Plans and Strategic Plans.

Different organisations use these words to convey slightly different concepts. Normally the budget is set before the start of the year and cannot be changed as conditions alter during the year. Some businesses require managers to update their forecasts for the remaining months of the budget year as the year progresses. Thus the budget was agreed before the start of the year and a forecast is the latest estimate for the next few months.

Budgeting

Tactical and strategic plans tend to be expressed only partly in numeric terms and mainly in words. Tactical plans tend to be for the next 12 months and strategic plans tend to be for a longer period or to have implications for a longer period. In some businesses managers can become cynical of strategic planning because a long term plan with few numbers invites grandiose schemes which are not profit orientated.

The Budget as a 'Contract'

Some groups of companies allow their individual businesses considerable autonomy but require monthly financial reports from each business in great detail. Such groups (especially those controlled from the US) can talk of the budget as a 'contract'. The idea is that each Chief Executive of a separate business has promised a certain profit performance to the centre. That performance must be provided or there will be career implications for the Chief Executive. If external conditions prevent profits being achieved in the manner planned, then some other plan must be implemented.

The danger in such an approach is that an individual year's budget may be achieved by damaging the future of the business. This might be by cutting marketing expenditure, training or new product development. This is less likely to happen if managers realise that they need to produce a good performance from the same business in future years which, in turn, has implications for personnel policies allowing job moves between divisions in the group.

Some of the rhetoric surrounding budget non-compliance in large organisations needs to be viewed in the light of actual experiences. Some company cultures appear at first to be somewhat harsh and yet the individual managers do not appear distressed. Presumably they know how the internal processes *actually* work. There are (usually unsuccessful) businesses where budget non-compliance appears to have no effect on those managers who are responsible. Sometimes (especially in 'matrix' structures) it is difficult to determine who is responsible.

Consider the following case study in order to discuss the question that follows it. (No answer to this question has been included in this book.)

Question 13.1

This year's Christmas functions at Amalgamated Conglomerated were not joyous. They took place in the Catering Block where the Works Canteen is on the ground floor and the Management Luncheon Hall and Senior Executive Dining Room are on the first floor. These three areas still had their old names - even though the catering staff for the Works Canteen and the Management Hall had been made redundant some four years back. In the Management Hall there were still some vending machines offering chocolate and glutinous soup but the machines that had been installed in the Works Canteen had long since been vandalised and removed.

In the Management Hall there was a particularly frosty atmosphere. This was partly caused by the cold because the heating had been turned down as an economy measure. And it was partly caused by the noise from the other two areas. There was the sound of drunken brawling rising from below and next door the main board directors were enjoying Karaoke.

"I think that is what is called 'close' harmony," muttered Alistair Wattie irritably to his new assistant, George. "Few notes are in tune but most are close."

"How are your budget negotiations going?" asked Harold Williams of Alistair joining him uninvited. Harold looked slightly unsteady on his feet and he was smiling at Alistair as if they were great friends. George had already learned that, while it was unlikely that Alistair had any great friends, it was certain that, even if he had, Harold would not be among them.

Alistair took a large intake of breath. After a significant pause he murmured "I'm sure they are under control."

"I hear on the grapevine that young George here has responded positively to the request to state which areas will be affected if we suffer a 20% cut in our budgets. You are so lucky to have him as your assistant, Alistair. He's given the centre a wealth of good ideas."

Alistair's face drained of colour, his eyes narrowed and his thin lips contorted into a humourless smile. "I am pleased to hear that, Harold. Perhaps you could leave us in order that I can congratulate George personally."

Budgeting

Once Harold had swayed off to join another group, Alistair turned on his assistant in fury. "Don't you realise that, our positions, status and salary are determined by the size of our department, the number employed and the amount we spend? When I started this department, it was only a grade 1 department employing me and two others. By dint of hard work I have built it up into what it is today - a grade 5 department employing 20 including - at this moment - a Deputy Head. Every year we are asked to state the consequences of a budget squeeze. And every year the better department Heads - those that can fight on behalf of their departments - recount blood-curdling stories of the dire consequences of any cuts. Harold himself always says that any cuts would sadly prevent his department from being able to process invoices to customers."

George tried to defend himself. "But I argued that expenditure in some categories had to be increased."

"You innocent fool! That's 'virement'. You don't think they will allow us virement."

"What is 'virement'?"

"Virement is where an underspend in one area is allowed to be offset against an overspend in another area." Alistair changed the focus of his attack on George. "Don't think I haven't noticed what you've been doing. You've been wasting your time improving the efficiency of the department. If I allowed you to continue, you'd prove that we can produce more with less money." Alistair's tone became slightly more conciliatory. "I don't mind you experimenting to find ways of improving our output. But you must only put your ideas into full scale once we have won an increased budget. Then I can explain that they are the result of additional expenditure."

"Sir, I am worried about the finances of the whole company. Even if you do win increased budget from the start of the next year, I think it may be cut back before the year is over."

"I agree. But I know how to cope with that. We must spend almost the whole year's budget in the first two months before the cutbacks arrive."

"Does every department do that?"

"Most but not all. Wimps like Simpson are so scared of running out of funds near the end of the year that they starve their operations in the early months to build up a reserve. A reserve

Modern Accounting 2

which the rest of us can make good use of." Alistair allowed himself a smile. "Do you think you can spend enough in the first two months?"

"No problem there," George replied. "You remember those supplies last month where we arranged that the invoices would arrive early next year with next year's date on them." A worried frown darkened George's face. "But I am still worried about this year. We have overspent. What will be the reaction when they find we have spent more than we had budget."

"There will be some shouting and table thumping," Alistair said casually. "But it is not a sufficient overspend to affect our careers. Remember that our long term futures are determined by the size of our department. An overspend this year strengthens our hand in arguing for increased resources next year. Any underspend automatically means less budget next year."

Harold staggered back into view. "Have you heard," he whispered in a conspiratorial slur. "Jenkins wants to introduce something called 'zero based' budgeting this year."

"And what is that?" asked Alistair.

A foolish grin spread over Harold's face. "Instead of budgets for next year being based on those for this year, every department is going to start with a zero budget and have to argue for each item of expenditure from scratch."

"That will take for ever," exclaimed George.

"Yes," Alistair agreed cautiously. "It will certainly benefit those who are good at internal politics and those who can write long reports arguing their case persuasively. It won't help those who waste their time on frivolous activities..."

"Like getting new customers and satisfying those we have," interrupted Harold.

"Surely there must be a better way of organising budgets," George mused. "Shouldn't they be a team-building process, helping us to work together. Setting targets and objectives, that sort of thing. Getting commitment, releasing new ideas."

The other two looked at George with mild contempt.

George continued "All costs should be tied to benefits. We should be profit orientated rather than empire builders."

Alistair gave a slight shudder. "George, you've been in my department for a year now. Perhaps it's time to broaden your experience. Perhaps Simpson has a vacancy?"

"That's another thing." George was oblivious to their reaction. "In this company, some of the high fliers are moved on before their mistakes can catch up with them. People fight for capital expenditure but it's then installed by others without the same commitment. Too often decisions are made by those who are too distant. All top-down decision making and no commitment to profit." Suddenly George realised that the other two were staring at him in horror. "That may be an unsophisticated way of looking at things," he ended lamely.

Determine which parts (if any) of the budgeting process within Amalgamated Conglomerated could be improved. Suggest how you would try to improve them.

Further Reading on Management Information Systems

Business Information Systems : Analysis Design & Practice (Addison-Wesley, 1989) Graham Curtis

The Information Centre : Managing the Growth of End-User Computing for Corporate Advantage (Quiller Press, 1989) Keith Patching

Practical Information Policies : How to Manage Information Flow in Organisations (Gower Press, 1990) Elizabeth Orna

Further Reading on Budgeting

The Basic Arts of Budgeting (Business Books, 1976) T S McAlpine

Modern Accounting 2

Index

Absorbtion Costing & DCF	178	Cost of Equity	193
Accounting for Rising Prices	11	Cost of Equity & Taxation	194
Acc Statements and Inflation	1-10	Cost of Sales : CCA	73
Accumulated Dep'n : CPP	13	Cost Plus Pricing	371
Annuity Factors	202	CPP	3,11-50
Associated Companies	278	- Accumulated Depreciation	13
Autonomy for Divisions	379	- Balance Sheet	15-17
Average Index Numbers	22-23	- Depreciation	24
Budget Cycle	402	- Dividends	24
Budgeting	399-407	- Profit & Loss	21-33
Budgets - Publication of	240	- Stock	24
Capital Rationing	216,217	- Tax	24,125
Capital Reserve	265	Cumulative Discount Factors	202
Cash in Transit	283	Currency Profits & Losses	319,329
CCA	3,51-102	- & Interest	341
- Cost of Sales	73	Currency to Borrow	338
- Depreciating Fixed Assets	62	Currency to Lend	338
- Depreciation	70	Current Cost	57
- Double Entry	57	Current Cost Reserve	61,79-80
- Formats	80	Current Purchasing Power	11
- in CPP	51,133-168	DCF	169-219
- Leasehold Premises	81	- Yield	198
- Monetary Assets	68	- & Absorbtion Costing	178
- Ratios	123	- & Depreciation	174
- Replaciation	70	- & Inflation	186
- Stocks	66	- & Interest Paid	181
- & Closing Rate	328	- & Specific Price Increases	189
- Closing Rate & CPP	329	- & Taxation	192
Central Control	379	- & Working Capital	174
Central Services	380	Depreciating Fixed Assets : CCA	62
Characters	390	Depreciating Fixed Assets : CPP	13
Closing Rate	320-321	Depreciation Adjustment	73
- & Financing	339	Depreciation & DCF	174
Comparative Figures CCA	120	Depreciation : CCA P & L	70
Computer Accounting	387-394	Depreciation : CPP P & L	24
Computer Systems		Deprival Value	52-57
- Advantages	387-388	Discounted Payback	218
- Disadvantages	388-389	Dividends and Replaciation	106
Connected Financing	181	Dividends : CPP	24
Consolidated Accounts	243-304	Economic Income	231-242
- T Accounts	270	Economic Value	52,204
- Definitions	272	Equivalent Service Potential	120
Constant Purchasing Power	11	Ex Ante Income	234
Consuming Division	367	Ex Post Income	235
COSA	73	Executive Systems	385,387
- Debtors & Creditors	105	Expenditure Limits	400
- & Seasonality	105	Fair Value	263-264
Cost of Loan Interest	200	Fields	390
Cost of Capital & Risk	195	File Sizing	391
Cost of Control	256-262	Files	390

Index

Financial Capital Maintenance Concept	90
Fixed Basis Pricing	373
Forecasting Future	215,399
Foreign Branch	305
Foreign Currency	305-366
- Book-keeping	306
- One Off Transactions	306
Formats : CCA	80
Gearing Adjustment	90
Goods In Transit	283
Goodwill	256-262
Gordon Growth Model	194
Grand Metropolitan	126
Group Accounts	243-304
Historical-Temporal	320
- & CPP	329
- & Financing	340
Holding Gains	103
Hyper-Inflation	127
Ideal Income	231
Incremental Figures	182
Index of Retail Prices	4,16,128
Inflation	
- Accounting	11
- & Accounting Statements	1-10
- & Balance Sheets	1
- & Comparative Figures	1,2,6,9,18-21
- & Cost of Sales	2,7
- & Depreciation	2,6
- & Fixed Assets	1,3-4,11-13
- & Gross Profit	2,7
- & Liabilities	1,5
- & Profit & Loss A/Cs	2
- & DCF	186
Insurance Liabilities	5
Integrating Accounting Systems	389-390
Interdivisional Pricing	367-386
- & Exchange Control	369
- & Final Pricing	369
- & Open Market	370
- & Motivation	370
- & Tax	368
Interest Paid & DCF	181
Interest & Time Periods	206
Interface System	310
Intermediate	367
Internal Markets	379
Internal Rate of Return	198
International Group	319
Inter-Group Accounts	283
Inter-Group Profits	278
IRR	198

IRR v NPV	215
IRRs Multiple	199
Leasehold Premises : CCA	81
Loan Stock	269
Management Information	395-398
Marginal Cost Transfers	377
Market Minus Pricing	372
Merger Accounting	278
Miller	108,196
Minority Interests	251
MIP	395-398
MIP & Stocks	398
Modigliani	108,196
Monetary	
- Assets	8-9,14
- Assets : CCA	68
- Gains	8-9,24-29,126
- Liabilities	8-9,14
- Losses	8-9,24-29,126
- Working Capital Adjustment	90
Monitoring	399
Motivation	370,399
Multiple IRRs	199
Net Present Value	172
NPV	172
NPV v IRR	215
Open Item	392
Operating Capacity	61,104
Packaged Software	394
Payback	218
Pension Funds	108
Perpetuities	182
PINCCA	60,118
Polly Peck	330
Post Acquisition Reserves	244
Pre Acquisition Reserves	247
Predictive Ability	109
Preference Shares	269
Present Value	5,172
Price Index Nos for CCA	60,118
Price Indexes	4,11
Price Parity Theory	327
Producing Division	367
Profit Maximisation Company	373
Profit Maximisation Group	373
Proposed Dividend	283
Purchase & Replacement	211
Rappaport	241
Real Cost of Capital	186
Real Terms Fall	115
Real Terms Rise	114
Realisable Value	4-5,52,123
Realised Holding Gains	61
Records	390

Reinsurance	5
Related Companies	278
Replacement Cost	4-5,52,123
Replacement Cost of Sales	73
Replacement Philosophy	119
Replaciation : CCA	70
Revaluation	4-5
Risk & Cost of Capital	195
Robert Maxwell	130
RPI	4,16,128
Sandilands	112
Selling Prices	103,114
Sensitivity Analysis	214
Shareholder Value	241
Soft Loans	181
Specific Price Increases & DCF	189
Spreadsheets & NPV & IRR	214
Stock : CPP	24
Stocks & MIP	398
Stocks : CCA	66
Strategic Value	241
Subjectivity CCA	120
Subsidiary	243
Systems Life Cycle	392
Tax : CPP	24
Taxation & Cost of Equity	194
Taxation & DCF	192
Terminal Value	211
Tied Purchasers	379
Tied Vendors	379
Time Periods & Interest	206
Unrealised Holding Gains	61
Valuation	4-5
Value	4-5
Value to the Business	57
Variances	395
WACC	196
Weighted Average Cost of Capital	196
Windfall	110
Working Capital & DCF	174